Supernatural Cities

Supernatural Cities

Enchantment, Anxiety and Spectrality

Edited by Karl Bell

THE BOYDELL PRESS

First published 2019
The Boydell Press, Woodbridge

ISBN 978-1-78327-441-3

The Boydell Press is an imprint of Boydell & Brewer Ltd
PO Box 9, Woodbridge, Suffolk IP12 3DF, UK
and of Boydell & Brewer Inc.
668 Mt Hope Avenue, Rochester, NY 14620–2731, USA
website: www.boydellandbrewer.com

A catalogue record of this publication is available
from the British Library

The publisher has no responsibility for the continued existence or accuracy of URLs for
external or third-party internet websites referred to in this book, and does not guarantee
that any content on such websites is, or will remain, accurate or appropriate

This publication is printed on acid-free paper

MIX
Paper from
responsible sources
FSC
www.fsc.org   FSC® C013056

Printed and bound in Great Britain by TJ International Ltd, Padstow, Cornwall

For Jo.

Contents

—◁◇◇▷—

Urban Spectrality

Illustrations

The editor, contributors and publisher are grateful to all the institutions and persons listed for permission to reproduce the materials in which they hold copyright. Every effort has been made to trace the copyright holders; apologies are offered for any omission, and the publisher will be pleased to add any necessary acknowledgement in subsequent editions.

Contributors

Karl Bell is a Reader in Cultural History at the University of Portsmouth and director of the Supernatural Cities project (supernaturalcities.co.uk/). He is the author of *The Magical Imagination: Magic and Modernity in Urban England, 1780–1914* (2012), and the award-winning *The Legend of Spring-Heeled Jack: Victorian Urban Folklore and Popular Culture* (2012). His research explores various aspects of the fantastical imagination, often focusing on its relationship with landscape and environment.

Oliver Betts is the Research Lead at the National Railway Museum. He completed his PhD at the University of York in 2014, focusing on the perceptions and realities of working-class life in three slum communities in late Victorian Britain. His current research interests cover the relationship between technologies, the city and day-to-day life in turn-of-the-century Britain and the wider world.

Alex Bevan is an Associate Lecturer at the University of Lincoln, UK, where she is completing a doctoral research project entitled 'Gothic: Literary Travel and Tourism'. Her research interests include the Gothic, spatial philosophy, tourism studies, the long nineteenth century and twenty-first century literature.

María del Pilar Blanco is Associate Professor of Spanish American Literature and Fellow in Spanish at Trinity College, University of Oxford. She is the author of *Ghost-Watching American Modernity: Haunting, Landscape, and the Hemispheric Imagination* (2012) and co-editor, with Esther Peeren, of *Popular Ghosts: The Haunted Spaces of Everyday Culture* (2012) and *The Spectralities Reader: Ghosts and Haunting in Contemporary Critical Theory* (2013). She is currently completing a second monograph entitled *Modernist Laboratories: Science and the Poetics of Progress in Spanish America, 1870–1930*.

Tracy Fahey is Head of Department in Fine Art and Head of Centre of Postgraduate Studies in Limerick School of Art and Design (LSAD), LIT. In 2013 she established the LSAD research centre *ACADEMY* where she also acts as principal investigator. Her main area of research is Irish Gothic and the Gothic nature of domestic space. She has chapters on this subject in *Living Gothic: Histories, Practices and Legacies*, ed Lorna Piatti-Farnell and Maria Beville (2014), *The Gothic Compass: New Directions in Scholarship and Inquiry*, ed. Lorna Piatti-Farnell and Donna Lee Brien (2015), *International Gothic in the Neo-Liberal Age*, ed. Linnie Blake and Agnieszka Soltysik Monnet (2017), *Imagining Irish Suburbiain Literature and Culture*, ed. Eoghan Smith and Simon Workman (2018) and *Landscapes of Liminality: Between Place and Space*, ed. Dara Downey, Ian Kinane and Elizabeth Parker (2018). She has also published in the areas of medical Gothic, transgressive art, contemporary Gothic art, pedagogy and contemporary design practice. She also writes short fiction that focuses on folklore and the uncanny and is published in thirteen UK and US anthologies.

Deirdre Flynn is Assistant Professor of Irish Studies in the School of English, Drama, Creative Writing and Film in University College Dublin. She worked professionally as a journalist for a number of years and is currently managing editor of the journal *Sibeal*. Her academic publications include articles and book chapters relating to Irish and contemporary literatures.

William Pooley is a Lecturer in Modern European History at the University of Bristol. His research focuses on the interactions between folk cultures and 'modernity' in nineteenth-century France. He has published articles on oral storytellers, family history, masculinity, witchcraft and anthropological history. Recent publications include 'The Singing Postman: the Mobility of Traditional Culture in Nineteenth-Century France', *Cultural and Social History* 13 (2016), 'Native to the Past: History, Anthropology, and Folklore in *Past and Present*', *Past & Present* 239 (2015), 'Man to Man: Placing Masculinity in a Legend Performed for Jean-François Bladé', in *Unsettling Assumptions: Tradition, Gender, Drag*, ed. Diane Tye and Pauline Greenhill (2014) and 'Can the "Peasant" Speak? Witchcraft and Silence in Guillaume Cazaux's "The Mass of Saint Sécaire" ', *Western Folklore* 71 (2012). His forthcoming monograph is entitled *The Bloodstained Sand: Body and Landscape in Nineteenth-Century France*.

Elena Pryamikova is the Head of the Chair of Social and Political Studies, Ural State Pedagogical University (USPU). Her major fields of academic interest include studies of urban daily life and social studies of education.

David J. Puglia is Assistant Professor of English at The Bronx Community College of the City University of New York, where he teaches courses in folklore and writing. He received his PhD in American Studies from Penn State University, and is the author of *South Central Pennsylvania Legends and Lore* (2012) and co-author with Trevor Blank of *Maryland Legends: Folklore from the Old Line State* (2014). He is the editor of the journal *New Directions in Folklore*, past president of the Middle Atlantic Folklife Association and a member of the Executive Council of the International Society for Contemporary Legend Research. In 2011, he won the International Society for Contemporary Legend Research's David Buchan Prize for his research on Goatman. He is currently at work on his third book, *Welcome to Baltimore, Hon: Vernacular Wars and Local Identity*.

William Redwood completed a PhD on modern magic at University College London. He teaches, researches and writes in the city.

Morag Rose is a Lecturer in Geography at the University of Liverpool. Her research focuses on gender, psychogeographies and public space. In 2006 she founded the LRM (Loiterers Resistance Movement), a Manchester-based psychogeographical collective interested in exploring, enchanting and critically engaging with the city. They celebrated ten years of creative mischief and finding magick in the Mancunian rain with an exhibition at People's History Museum called *Loitering with Intent: The Art and Politics of Walking*. She contributed 'Confessions of an Anarcho-Flaneuse, or, Psychogeography The Mancunian Way' to *Walking Inside Out: Contemporary British Psychogeography*, ed. Tina Richardson (2015).

Alevtina Solovyova is currently completing her PhD. She is a Lecturer in the Institute of Oriental and Classical Studies and the Centre for Typological and Semiotic Folklore Studies at the Russian State University for the Humanities.

Tom Sykes is Senior Lecturer in Creative Writing at the University of Portsmouth. His research interests include political psychogeography, eco-dystopian imagery in New Wave science fiction novels and Orientalist literary constructions of Manila as an urban space. He is the author of *The Punisher's Paradise: Journeys in Duterte's Philippines* (2018). His academic publications have appeared in the journals *Social Identities*, *Children's Literature Review* and *Foundation: The International Review of Science Fiction*. His travelogues and feature articles have appeared in the *The Telegraph*, *The Times*, *The Scotsman*, *Private Eye*, *New Statesman* and *New Internationalist*.

Natalya Veselkova is an Associate Professor in the Department of Applied Social Studies, Ural Federal University (UrFU). Her major fields of academic interest are urban studies, methods of social studies and social studies of time.

Mikhail Vandyshev is an Associate Professor in the Department of Applied Social Studies, Ural Federal University (UrFU). His major fields of academic interest include studies of industrial cities, migration processes and social risks.

David Waldron is a Lecturer in History and Anthropology at Federation University Australia and a member of the Collaborative Research Centre in Australian History (CRCAH), with a research focus on folklore and community identity. He is the author of *Sign of the Witch: Modernity and the Pagan Revival* (2008), *Shock! The Black Dog of Bungay: A Case Study in Local Folklore* (2010), *Snarls from the Tea-Tree: Victoria's Big Cat Folklore* (2013) and *Goldfields and the Gothic: A Hidden Heritage and Folklore* (2016).

Sharn Waldron is a Jungian analyst and a member of the British Jungian Analytical Association and the International Association of Analytical Psychologists. She has been a psychotherapist for the past twenty years and during that time has worked in government agencies, community health, industry and in private practice.

Felicity Wood is a Professor in the Department of English at the University of Fort Hare, South Africa. Her particular area of research interest is the way in which contemporary Western and westernised societies partake in aspects of mystery, ritual and magic, especially in economic and socio-political contexts and the present-day workplace. She is the author of *Universities and the Occult Rituals of the Corporate World: Higher Education and Metaphorical Parallels with Myth and Magic* (2018) and *The Extraordinary Khotso: Millionaire Medicine Man of Lusikisiki* (2007).

Acknowledgements

—◆◆◆—

Firstly, I would like to thank the contributors to this collection. This book has been several years in the making and I very much appreciate everyone's hard work, sustained interest, and unflagging enthusiasm over that time. I hope all involved enjoy the final result of our collective efforts.

This book grew from the Supernatural Cities project, an individual research project that subsequently morphed into a collaborative, multi-disciplinary project at the University of Portsmouth. I would like to acknowledge the Humanities Faculty's generous financial support over the last four years, and I especially want to thank Professor Matthew Weait, Professor Dave Andress, and Professor Francis Pakes. Without their willingness to support this rather unusual research project we would not have been able to achieve all that we have. I would also like to thank all my colleagues in the History department for their encouragement and camaraderie. It is very much appreciated.

Many thanks to all the Supernatural Cities project members, past and present: Alison Habens, Tom Sykes, Eilis Phillips, Beatrice Ashton-Lelliot, Amanda Garrie, Karen Fielder, Alex Pavey, Mark Eyles, Maggie Bowers, and Belinda Mitchell. It is a genuine pleasure working with such a diverse, stimulating, and engaged group of scholars and practitioners from Architecture, English Literature, Creative Writing, Games Development, and History. The Supernatural Cities project frequently operates at the intersection between academic research and creative practices and I would also like to thank the following talented individuals for their creative input and involvement: William Sutton, Roy Hanney, Christine Lawrence, Charlotte Comely, Matt Wingett, Tessa Ditner, and John Sackett.

In helping to develop the ideas that underpin this collection, I would like to thank all those who have given papers at or attended our annual conferences. In particular, I want to thank my co-hosts. It was great to work with Tracy Fahey, Deirdre Flynn and Maria Beville on the 'Gothic Cities' conference at the Limerick School of Art and Design in 2017, and equally with Sam George, Kaja Franck and Bill Hughes on the 'Urban Wyrd' conference at the University of Hertfordshire in 2018.

I would like to thank everyone at Boydell who has been involved in the commissioning and publication of this book. Special thanks go to Megan Milan, Nick Bingham, and Sean Andersson for the smooth and professional way they have helped steer this collection through that process. In addition, I would like to thank the anonymous reviewers for their comments and suggestions, and Francis Eaves for some sharp copyediting. Thanks also to Stefan Dickers and the Bishopsgate Institute for allowing me to use one of Harold Burdekin's evocative images of nocturnal London for the book's cover.

Finally, I would like to thank my wife, Jo, for patiently tolerating the havoc that research and writing necessarily inflicts on our work-life balance.

Introduction

Mapping the Urban Mindscape: The City and the Supernatural

—◈—

KARL BELL

Cities are one of our most potent symbols of modernity. By contrast, supernatural beliefs and practices are commonly positioned as traditional, unmodern, even anti-modern. This simplistic dichotomy is largely an inheritance from post-Enlightenment advocates of modernity who consciously sought to position the supernatural as representative of an age of ignorance and 'superstition' that they claimed to have either abandoned or escaped. Their repeated assertions that supernatural beliefs would fade under the dual impact of urbanisation and industrialisation have proved almost as difficult to eradicate as those beliefs themselves. Despite what has been termed a 'spectral turn' in recent scholarship, one that has resulted in an innovative expansion of cultural geography and literary studies into the realms of affective and supernatural landscapes, the scholarly exploration of urban supernatural cultures remains diffuse and the subject woefully understudied.[1] Given our current historical moment and anticipated near future – that of a predominantly urban

[1] See, for example, Tim Edensor, 'The Ghosts of Industrial Ruins: Ordering and Disordering Memory in Excessive Space', *Environment and Planning D: Society and Space* 23 (2005), 829–49; Steve Pile, *Real Cities* (London, 2005); Julian Holloway, 'Enchanted Spaces: The Séance, Affect, and Geographies of Religion', *Annals of the Association of American Geographers* 96 (2006), 182–7; *Cultural Geographies* 15 (2008) (special issue on 'spectro-geographies'); Andrew Smith and William Hughes (eds), *Ecogothic* (Manchester, 2013); Christine Berberich, Neil Campbell and Robert Hudson (eds), *Affective Landscapes in Literature, Art and Everyday Life*

global society struggling with environmental anxieties while groping for enchantment (currently best reflected in the mass media's near-saturation with magical and supernatural tropes and narratives) – it seems both appropriate and timely that this book should take steps to rectify that.

In *Cities – Reimagining the Urban*, Ash Amin and Nigel Thrift propose that fantasy may offer escape from the urban experience but that it can only ever provide fleeting relief.[2] This collection seeks to advance more complex and nuanced claims for the social and cultural functions of the supernatural imaginary beyond escapism, arguing that it enables a richer (but largely hidden) relationship with the urban environment, and in doing so often articulates real-world urban social and political issues. In differing ways around the globe and over centuries, supernatural ideas and entities have enabled urban dwellers to articulate and manage anxieties ranging from exterior concerns about socio-economic pressures and cultural or political tensions to interior concerns linked to a sense of spatial unease, environmental and historical guilt, communal breakdown and reconstruction, and perceived boundaries between the self and the other. Yet it also suggests more positive and empowering aspects of the supernatural, considering its function in acts of cultural appropriation and spatial enrichment, the ongoing adaptation of an inherited cultural imaginary, its role in urban community formation and identity politics, and an attempt to satisfy the urge to (re-)enchant the urban environment. This collection thus encourages us to recognise the prevalence, importance, and vitality of the supernatural as an intrinsic element of urban cultures in the modern world, intimately and endlessly interwoven into the fabric and experiences of everyday urban existence.

With contributions from historians, anthropologists, ethnographers, folklorists, Gothic and literary scholars, and (psycho)geographers, this collection undertakes a multidisciplinary and international exploration of urban supernatural ideas, beliefs, practices, and narratives on five continents, from the late eighteenth to the early twenty-first century, the period that witnessed the rise of the world's modern cities. In doing so, it seeks to enhance our understanding of occult (in both meanings of the word) histories of urban sociability and communal formation, the collective imaginary, urban cultural functions, the influence of affective urban environments, and the expression and adaptability of supernatural beliefs across historical periods and global locations.

(Farnham, 2015); Shane McCorristine, *The Spectral Arctic: A History of Dreams and Ghosts in Polar Exploration* (London, 2018).

[2]   Ash Amin and Nigel Thrift, *Cities: Reimagining the Urban* (Cambridge, 2002), pp. 122–3.

It contributes to our understanding of both modern cities and the modern supernatural in a number of ways.

Firstly, it provides glimpses into hidden geographies within the known city, not necessarily unseen physical places so much as their affective typographies of emotion, memory, and influence. Jo Frances Maddern and Peter Adey have noted how '[f]ear, anxiety and terror, or indeed awe, excitement and wonder are experienced and felt sometimes beneath any conscious registering', and, to date, the urban histories of these emotions have remained largely unexplored.[3] Echoing the teeming visibility and bustling stimuli of urban life, the supernatural life of the city, while often muted or invisible, shows how a city's hidden histories equally teem with energy, powers, entities, and its stories. This collection thus engages with and furthers 'a vitalized understanding of space' and the mental lives of those who dwell within it.[4] In doing so, it expands the range of what geographer Steve Pile (by way of Walter Benjamin) has termed urban 'phantasmagorias'. Pile suggests that different cities have different phantasmagorias, some emphasising magic or ghosts, others vampires, others giants. These 'reveal the desires and fears of cities, and they do so differently in different places'.[5] By exploring the specific phantasmagorias of historical and geographically diverse cities, we can appreciate the distinctive 'structures of feeling' that their particular supernatural entities and elements foster, enabling us to engage not just with the physical environment, but with the emotional and imaginative topologies enfolded within them. Underlying this study, then, is the notion that spatial practices are discursive, that the urban environment has an affective influence and that, in turn, its inhabitants read, charge, and change its spaces.

Secondly, the collection seeks to broaden our understanding of how the supernatural has diverse application and meaning as a body of cultural beliefs and practices. As the contributions show, the supernatural has cultural, psychological, sociological, political, economic, and environmental meanings. In the embodiment of urban anxieties in ghosts and bogeymen, in the expression of desires and fears through magic, and in forming many of these elements into supernatural narratives, one sees attempts to assert influence and meaning, to construct fluid and amorphous communities bound by the stories they exchange. Urging an appreciation of the complexities of the supernatural's manifestations and functions, this collection reads the supernatural as variously disruptive or reaffirming, threatening or enriching, binding or

---

[3]   Jo Frances Maddern and Peter Adey, 'Editorial: Spectro-geographies', *Cultural Geographies* 15 (2008), 291–5 at 293.
[4]   Holloway, 'Enchanted Spaces', p. 182.
[5]   Pile, *Real Cities*, p. 22. See pp.19–24.

separating, imbued with the potential for resistance and alterity, yet also for conformity and conservatism.

Thirdly, in taking a global perspective, this book expands its scope beyond the European (and, more broadly, Western) focus of many histories of modern supernatural beliefs, most of which approach such things as national rather than specifically urban experiences, and as (safely remote) historical rather than contemporary ones. While London, Paris, and New York are necessarily examined in this collection as cities of modern world significance, they are set in a broader context of other great cities of the world, encouraging an awareness of how our over-familiar (in Western analysis) focus on these particular urban centres needs to be readjusted in order to appreciate the diverse supernatural cultures of those on other continents and in the other hemispheres. In making this adjustment, we need to appreciate that while the urban supernatural should be examined within its local context, contemporary cities are not isolated from supernatural narrative influences from elsewhere. While the circumstances out of which narratives are fashioned are usually local, their tropes or motifs, especially those relating to ghosts, often have connections to broader influences, be these transnational folklore, globally popular horror films and videogames, or, more recently, technologically-facilitated practices of supernatural storytelling – perhaps the best example of which is the cyber-generated pseudo-folklore of Slender Man. A transnational focus enables us to identify cross-cultural supernatural resonances and connections, the nature of which informs the three broadly thematic sections that structure this collection. These are not presented as reductive or totalising interpretations; not as underlying structures, so much as ways of recognising connections between the local and the global, the micro and the macro. Each study differs in its own historical, geographical, and cultural dynamic, and shared themes do not suggest mono-narratives of modern urban development. It is not that similar cultural processes occurred in different cities at different times; each is located in its culturally specific time and space. Yet each is more than a localised curiosity: the contributions to this volume demonstrate the ways in which, in different forms and contexts, an engagement with supernatural beliefs and practices is a common element in the urban experience of the last three centuries.

This book covers continents and centuries and, as with any initial map of vast terrains, can be little more than a preliminary sketch: its studies form landmarks, and its themes trails, that others may opt to visit in more depth or break from and move beyond. It is hoped that, in so doing, they might add accruals, greater sophistication, and hitherto unrecognised routes forward. Given its scope, this collection adopts a deliberately broad but diverse interpretation of the 'urban' and 'supernatural'. The following chapters explore a range of conurbations, encompassing provincial Irish and English cities, some of the great historical metropolises of Europe, the Americas, and Asia, nineteenth- and twentieth-century industrial frontier towns of Australia and the Soviet-era Urals, the rapidly growing cities of contemporary South Africa, and the mega-cities of Tokyo and Beijing. This enables us to consider how the operation and application of the supernatural in urban centres is influenced by their variation in size, density, age, and influence. The various studies indicate that whether there are abundant and fertile depths of urban history in which to seed ghosts, or the first tentative shoots of culture from which to grow something new, the presence of the supernatural is to be found in all. The urban supernatural thus appears to respond to a sense of cultural lack (a desire to enrich the functionality of one's environment) as much as of cultural excess (a way of articulating the psychological experience of the urban). Importantly, the contributors show that the supernatural, far from being a static cultural inheritance from the past, has continually been transplanted, appropriated, adapted, and updated to accommodate and express the socio-cultural anxieties and needs of the particular urban environment in which it has manifested. This vitality and ubiquity disrupt any sweeping assumptions about (Western) cultural opposition to and (Eastern) acceptance of the supernatural. Such notions come to seem rooted in crude rationalist-modern occidental/exotic-traditional oriental divides: tired cultural standpoints encrusted with the rust of old imperialist attitudes.

The temporal and geographical scope of this collection requires scholars to move with the shifts and changes that occur as part of the ongoing updating of the cultural lexicon of 'the supernatural', which is for these purposes understood in a broad sense, as that which lies beyond the limits of 'accepted' knowledge and understanding: those elements that challenge the boundaries of hegemonic, rational epistemologies. The category encompasses 'traditional' magical practices, but also engages with the secular enchantment of the psychogeographic dérive, with ghosts and other folkloric entities, as well as with cryptozoology – creatures of uncertain ontology – and with folkloric, uncanny, and hauntological experiences. An engagement with modern magic requires an appreciation of the eclectic nature of its appropriated influences. As T. M. Luhrmann noted, modern ritual magic is often an assemblage of ideas and practices, drawing freely from 'paganism, astrology, mysticism … [and] kabbalism', but also incorporating literary influences, including early works of anthropology, compilations of legend, and mythography.[6] In particular cases, when studying the Ural towns of the Soviet era, we move beyond the supernatural per se to consider the near-superhuman heroics of industrial and environmental engineering, and allusions to the unsettling, almost sentient power of the natural environment itself. By remaining attentive to the semantic shifts from supernatural to preternatural and paranormal, we can appreciate the multifaceted, culturally specific aspects that operate beneath broad and malleable terms like 'haunting', 'magic', and 'the supernatural'.

In adopting a multidisciplinary approach, this collection fits with a long tradition of exploring the mental life of the modern city from a range of perspectives. The late nineteenth-century study of what Anthony Vidler terms 'the pathology of the city' was conducted 'by the emerging new disciplines of sociology, psychology, political geography and psychoanalysis'.[7] In the twentieth century those disciplines were augmented by the works of (psycho) geographers, historians, philosophers, and literary scholars.[8] A multidisciplinary approach reveals the ways in which we frequently address similar issues and related ideas from different disciplinary perspectives, often with very little sense of cross-disciplinary interaction. As demonstrated by this collection, our understanding of the urban supernatural depends as much on how and when we are looking as where we are looking. Themes, images, and ideas find repeated connections and resonances across chapters that are distinguished by disciplinary perspective, approach, and source material as much as by the experiences of different centuries or continents. By demonstrating the diverse ways in which such topics have, can, and might be explored, this collection hopes to foster future dialogue across disciplinary boundaries. In doing so, it offers a first step towards sketching out a field ripe with interdisciplinary

---

[6] T. M. Luhrmann, *Persuasions of the Witch's Craft: Ritual Magic in Contemporary England* (London, 1994), p. 6. This appropriation and melding of various magical elements and histories is also seen in the twentieth-century development of Wicca. See Ronald Hutton, *The Triumph of the Moon: A History of Modern Pagan Witchcraft* (Oxford, 2001).

[7] Anthony Vidler, *Warped Space: Art, Architecture, and Anxiety in Modern Culture* (Cambridge, MA, 2001), p. 25.

[8] Key works include: Georg Simmel, 'The Metropolis and Mental Life', in *Simmel on Culture*, ed. David Frisby and Mike Featherstone (London, 1997), pp. 174–85; Walter Benjamin, *The Arcades Project*, trans. Howard Eiland and Kevin McLaughlin (Cambridge, MA, 2002); Guy Debord, *Theory of the Dérive* (London, 1997); Michel Foucault, 'Of Other Spaces', *Diacritics* 16 (1986), 22–7; Michel de Certeau, *The Practice of Everyday Life* (Berkeley, CA, 1984); Henri Lefebvre, *The Production of Space* (Oxford, 1991).

potential and international relevance, one that attempts to connect the local and the global, the real and the imaginary, social sciences and the humanities.

Navigating the spectro-spatial turn

The spatial turn emphasised the way space and place are never simply background scenery to the unfolding of historical events, but active in their cultural construction. As Russell West-Pavlov puts it, 'Space is the agency of configurement, and the fabric of configurations is from the outset spatial. It is in those spatial processes of configuration and reconfiguration that human life takes place and unfolds its unceasing dynamic.'[9] While engaging with space as an agent in shaping the cultures that operate within it, a focus on the supernatural connects to an existing body of urban spatial theory, while also challenging some of its structuring assumptions and understandings.

In exploring this concealed life of the city, the following chapters suggest there are no new urban spaces; glutted with history, already and always supersaturated with cultural meaning, city space is a continual appropriation by different groups and individuals. The studies in this collection thus explore what Henri Lefebvre termed 'representational spaces': spaces that are known and appropriated through their cultural symbols, in these cases mutable supernatural signifiers.[10] In most accounts, this involves transforming spaces into places via ritualistic acts, sometimes magical or religious practices, but perhaps most frequently through the act of storytelling. Narratives distinguish certain places, giving them presence and meaning in the communal imagination.[11] For all their conservative nature, their assistance in aiding a sense of community formation and as a repository of collective (mis)remembering, supernatural stories also destabilise by granting heterogeneous meanings to places. Post-Enlightenment discourses that seek to marginalise the supernatural inadvertently imbue such stories with power to foster heterotopian potential, generating 'places of epistemological and representational disorder' that subvert or disrupt conventional spatial orders through possessing their own spatial logic and often their own distinct rules of behaviour.[12] Yet heterotopias are not necessarily fixed; everyday locations can also be temporarily

---

[9]   Russell West-Pavlov, *Space in Theory: Kristeva, Foucault, Deleuze* (Amsterdam, 2009), p. 25. For a concise introduction to spatial theories and approaches, see Robert T. Tally Jr, *Spatiality* (Abingdon, 2013).

[10]   See Lefebvre, *Production of Space*, p. 39.

[11]   See Karl Bell, *The Magical Imagination – Magic and Modernity in Urban England, 1780–1914* (Cambridge, 2012), pp. 227–59; Yi-Fu Tuan, *Space and Place: The Perspective of Experience* (Minneapolis, 1977), pp. 161–2.

[12]   West-Pavlov, *Space in Theory*, p. 137.

translated through cultural activities such as carnivals or fairs.[13] While recognising alterity as a part of spatial understanding and practice, and arguing that such spaces can be linked to challenges to dominant 'norms', Foucault's notion of the heterotopia was spatially oriented in (and restricted to) actual, empirical counter-sites. The supernatural introduces a less easily located notion of heterotopia. Ghosts and hauntings lace a diffused, potential geography into the physical landscape of the city; anywhere may become subject to supernatural manifestation, but not everywhere does. Thus they urge to us move beyond thinking in terms of static locations in the manner of the ancient notion of *genius loci*, or spirit of place, to engage with disordering eruptions, intersections, or infusions of supernatural possibility into the mundane environment.

The fusion of the spatial and spectral can usefully build upon the developing body of literature that examines the affective relationship between the environment and psychology, between the exterior and interior, between the city and emotions; a relationship that Deborah Stevenson claims is 'complex and little understood within urban studies'.[14] David Crouch has recently blurred these boundaries by suggesting that landscapes are not external objectivities, but the alchemical production of environment, emotions, and imagination: 'Landscape occurs in a co-production … in which we are participants; landscape is … felt, imagined; it can be affected and can affect'.[15] Such a view encourages a reassessment of our relationship with the urban environment. Both the remnants of intermingled, fragmented temporalities of urban histories and their modern spatial expanse seem to speak to a sense that while cities are human constructs, they possess a gestalt quality that renders them unknowable. As Julian Wolfreys observes, 'The city resists ontology, and thus affirms its alterity, its multiplicities, its excesses, its heterogeneities … .'[16] Since the city can never be understood or conceptualised as a whole it always possesses an uncertain, spectral quality of its own.

Building upon this, Jessica Tiffin has drawn attention to the estranging nature of the urban experience, in terms both of the limited perception of the physical city and of one's sense of belonging. This encourages cities to be experienced largely as imaginary constructs based on 'the need to extrapolate

[13]   Fran Tonkiss, *Space, the City and Social Theory* (Cambridge, 2005), pp. 133–4.
[14]   Deborah Stevenson, *The City* (Cambridge, 2013), p. 96. For some key works on affective landscapes, see the texts listed in note 1 above. See also James Donald, *Imagining the Modern City* (Minneapolis, 1999).
[15]   David Crouch, 'Afterword: From Affect to Landscape and Back', in *Affective Landscapes*, ed. Berberich et al., pp. 243–4.
[16]   Julian Wolfreys, *Writing London, Volume 2: Materiality, Memory, Spectrality* (Basingstoke, 2004), p. 4.

beyond their reality to account for their hidden, exclusive spaces'.[17] It is in the interstices and possibilities of this occluded and excluded experience that the supernatural can find purchase. One could suggest that the supernatural serves as a way of filling the gaps in the fragmented, subjective urban experience, but that does not quite explain why ideas of it are often collectively formed and reinforced through drawing upon a shared cultural lexicon of the monstrous, the magical, the haunted. Such an instinct does not appear to derive from a desire to create a wholeness from the city's fragmentary elements, but rather from a way of appropriating and re-reading the fragments beyond their mundane meaning. As will be outlined in the themes introduced below and variously demonstrated in the chapters that follow, we need to reflect upon what factors determine the transition from the fragmented known to the enriched understanding provided by the supernatural imaginary and the symbolic power of the fantastical. Such a process is not necessarily based on a search for enhanced knowledge as a way of augmenting the unknown and articulating the hidden.

Yet the multiplicity of the unknown (and unknowable) city is not completely disempowering, for it grants imaginative spaces and enclaves for play, worship, enactment, and agency. Despite the fantastical dimension to magical practices and supernatural narratives, these can be understood, in this context, as variants of what Michel de Certeau identified as practices of everyday life. His rather romanticised ideal of pedestrians enacting forms of heroic but largely unconscious resistance to urban planning, remaking urban spaces according to their own random, personalised perambulations, meant the implementation of their agency was typically undirected and lacked clear purpose. Supernatural narratives enact a more conscious (re-)creation of urban spaces, by creating ulterior ways of knowing and experiencing them, ways that disrupt and enrich their 'normal' understandings.[18] As will be demonstrated in the chapters that follow, magic, monsters, and ghosts enable urban dwellers to talk about social and environmental anxieties, spatialised communal politics and power relations, providing them with both an alternative viewpoint on social realities and a subversive means of articulating political critique. That said, such articulations are often indirect and expressed through diffuse and amorphous narrative communities, making it difficult to identify or channel them as weapons of the weak or cultural tools of resistance. Ghosts do not speak directly, with a single voice, or to a single purpose. Accepting this, however, should not detract from the fact that populating urban space with entities

---

[17] Jessica Tiffin, 'Outside/Inside Fantastic London', *English Academy Review* 25 (2008), 32–41 at 34.

[18] De Certeau, *Practice of Everyday Life*, p. 31.

and powers that are deemed to dwell beyond the 'real' speaks to a search for agency, an urge to affect our affective urban environments. The melding of the mundane and the magical creates a potent hybrid that is at once located in the familiar yet imbued with a destabilising sense of 'otherness'. Such actions can be understood as expressions of spatial inscription – an overwriting of existing spatial narratives to enrich them and claim them for the initiated. Yet the fostering of communities is necessarily based as much upon exclusion as inclusion. To this extent, such spatial practices involve too an element of spatial encryption – concealed readings that feed into the hidden, exclusory nature of the urban experience. These two broad ideas underpin the themes that structure this book.

Themes: enchantment, anxiety, and spectrality

The following chapters are structured into three themed sections, although contributions within each of these conform to a broadly chronological order. The individual studies encourage us to consider the way in which these thematic connections operate across different cultural, geographical, and historical circumstances, and in so doing create a dialogue between the local and the general. While placed in their most apposite sections, many chapters also speak to one another across these structuring arrangements. For example, William Pooley's and Alevtina Solovyova's chapters appear at opposite ends of the collection, but show how magical practices and supernatural beliefs are embroiled in perceptions of urban modernisation and problematised narratives of tradition and progress, be these in nineteenth-century Paris or twenty-first century Beijing.

The first section explores urban enchantment: the way magical beliefs and practices have served to enhance or articulate cultural, communal, and personal perceptions of self, otherness, and urban space. When engaging with urban enchantment across the chapters included here, one might usefully bear in mind William Whyte's observation that moves towards re-enchantment have happened before, and therefore tend to be cyclical.[19] Neither disenchantment nor enchantment remain constant, nor are they singular or

---

[19]   Whyte demonstrates this through the example of a re-enchanted view of architecture in the nineteenth century, one that opposed eighteenth-century notions of functional sacred spaces. See William Whyte, 'Buildings, Landscapes, and Regimes of Materiality', *Transactions of the Royal Historical Society*, sixth series, 28 (2018), 135–48 at 142–5. See also Jane Bennett, *The Enchantment of Modern Life: Attachments, Crossings, and Ethics* (Princeton, NJ, 2011).

mono-directional, but are apt to change, overlap, and interact.[20] Since the late 1990s, an increasing body of scholarly work has challenged the idea of modernity as an age of disenchantment, and in doing so has come to advance a more heterodox understanding of modernity itself.[21] Indeed, it is the dialectic between enchantment and disenchantment that empowers the urban supernatural. As our first section suggests, this process can take several forms.

Although edged with anxieties about both magical powers and modern urban living, the first two chapters in this section demonstrate the role of magical adaptation and divergences in the cultural presentation of occult powers. William Pooley analyses the way the nineteenth- and early twentieth-century Parisian press simultaneously attacked and stimulated witchcraft belief, which was itself adapting to the French capital's modern consumerist culture. Keen to present magic as the backward 'other' to Paris's modern self-identity, attempts at distancing it through association with rural and lower-class beliefs were compromised by the Parisian elite's own interest in (re-)enchantment and their dabbling in supernatural practices. Felicity Wood explores, by contrast, urban enrichment of a different kind, considering the dangers of enchantment through the allure of both the supernatural *mamlambo*, a spirit that provides wealth and power, and blessers, wealthy men who provide young women with money or gifts in exchange for sex, in South Africa's contemporary cities. Fulfilling a desire for occult access to power and wealth, the *mamlambo* serves as a warning of the dangerous enchantment offered by modern, urban aspirational living and a critique of capitalist consumer culture, one in which the spirit's owner becomes enslaved by their own greed, and where there is a

---

[20] Similarly, Blanco and Peeren remind us that the current spectral turn is but the latest of several in the modern period. See María del Pilar Blanco and Esther Peeren (eds), *Popular Ghosts: The Haunted Spaces of Everyday Culture* (New York, 2010), p. xi. See also Terry Castle, *The Female Thermometer: Eighteenth-Century Culture and the Invention of the Uncanny* (Oxford, 1995) and Marina Warner, *Phantasmagorias: Spirit Visions, Metaphors, and Media into the Twenty-first Century* (Oxford, 2006).

[21] See, for example: Owen Davies, *Witchcraft, Magic and Culture 1736–1951* (Manchester, 1999) and his *America Bewitched: The Story of Witchcraft after Salem* (Oxford, 2013); Willem de Blécourt and Owen Davies (eds), *Witchcraft Continued: Popular Magic in Modern Europe* (Manchester, 2004); Alex Owen, *The Place of Enchantment: British Occultism and the Culture of the Modern* (Chicago, 2004); Corinna Trietel, *A Science for the Soul: Occultism and the Genesis of the German Modern* (Baltimore, 2004); Simon During, *Modern Enchantments: The Cultural Power of Secular Magic* (Cambridge, MA, 2002); Michael Saler, *As If: Modern Enchantment and the Literary Prehistory of Virtual Reality* (Oxford, 2012); Chris Goto-Jones, *Conjuring Asia: Magic, Orientalism and the Making of the Modern World* (Cambridge, 2016).

price to be paid for succumbing to such desires. Indicative of the resonances between urban supernatural practices around the world, it is interesting to note that despite their historical and geographical differences, these chapters both appear to reflect and build upon Peter Geschiere's anthropological work on the occult in postcolonial Cameroon. Geschiere's study presents witchcraft and sorcery as intimately bound up with processes of modernisation, especially attempts to gain influence over political and economic changes, and to accumulate wealth and power.[22] Echoing Pooley's (self-)contradictory Parisians and Wood's aspirational but entrapped urban dwellers, Geschiere reads magic as 'both a resource for the powerful and also a weapon for the weak against new inequalities', a practice and belief in which the masses and the elite variously invest in its 'levelling and accumulative tendencies'.[23]

Secondly, this section considers magic's contribution to urban spatial enrichment, the construction of imagined topographies and occult connections. This is seen in Tracy Fahey's use of ethnographically based art practices to explore the folkloric enrichment of urban space in Limerick. Serving as memorates, boundary markers, and cautionary tales, stories of traditional Irish folkloric entities are enfolded into a storyscape that integrates with imaginative ease into the contemporary city. The use of communal art practices as a way to both preserve and disseminate local folklore also reveals a remarkable consistency in storytelling over generations, a cultural practice that speaks to the strength of local storytelling traditions and the spatialised urban identity in which it is located (and which it helps maintain). In contrast to Fahey's emphasis on the communal, William Redwood provides an anthropological consideration of occult powers and energies in contemporary London, indicating how ritual magic and personal re-enchantment enables creative recoding of and occult connections between urban spaces. In doing so, he not only alters and enchants our understanding of London's known geographies, but encourages an appreciation of urban magic as an assemblage, or bricolage; an approach and practice that attunes to the complex, heterodox cultures that exist in our modern cities.

Given centuries of attack, defamation, and dismissal by orthodox religion and modern secularists alike, we tend 'naturally' to posit magic and the supernatural in negative terms. However, its more active and assertive applications are also its more positive functions; re-reading and re-enchanting mundane

---

[22]   Peter Geschiere, *The Modernity of Witchcraft: Politics and the Occult in* Postcolonial Africa (Charlottesville, VA, 1997), pp. 2–3. See also Jean Comaroff and John Comaroff, *Modernity and Its Malcontents: Ritual and Power in Postcolonial Africa* (Chicago, 1993).

[23]   Geschiere, *Modernity of Witchcraft*, p. 16.

spaces and places, maintaining and reinforcing communal identities (albeit with a necessary 'othering' of the excluded), serving as a protective warning against urban dangers, or empowering individual practitioners with a sense of knowledge and agency. Both Fahey's banshee and Wood's *mamlambo* teach lessons, although it is only by hearing tales of those who have ignored those lessons that we can (vicariously) move beyond the boundaries of normality and enter a supernatural terrain, one that is enfolded within the mundane in such a way that to simply cross the street or loiter too long in a particular place is to venture into an altered realm, one that was there all along, mapped only by the stories we tell about it.

Developing Deborah Stevenson's observation that 'fear … can be a powerful motivator shaping how space is both used and regarded', the second themed section of this book explores urban anxieties.[24] Those examined in this section can be divided into two types. The first is social: a perception of encroaching urban threats which leads to the fearing and demonising of others. As the earlier chapters in this section show, there is no better way to scapegoat undesirable others, to exclude and distance them, than to make monsters of them. Oliver Betts examines how H. P. Lovecraft's short story *The Horror at Red Hook* encapsulated the author's racial and urban anxieties in 1920s New York, and explores the othering fostered by the city's occult cultures in that period. Moving forward fifty years, David Puglia uses the cryptoid Goatman of Washington DC to investigate how fears of urban encroachment (with attendant fears about crime and racial intermixing) and suburban anxiety at the rural fringes were projected in the 1970s on to this semi-folkloric character, a personified (and almost literal) scapegoat. This tendency towards demonisation finds more overt hellish conceptualisations in Tom Sykes's reflections on Western imaginings of Manila. As Sykes suggests, a persistent 'othering' of the Philippine capital as hell may shore up belief in the modern, Western self, but it is also embroiled in an inescapable sense of colonial guilt and cultural biases that westerners would rather leave unspoken. Thus, while a politics of the supernatural can be seen at work in urban enchantment, it perhaps becomes more explicit when articulating urban anxiety.

The second type of anxiety draws upon the supernatural, the Gothic, and the monstrous to express environmental anxieties, fears, and dangers. Natalya Veselkova, Mikhail Vandyshev, and Elena Pryamikova focus on the new industrial towns in the Urals in the mid-twentieth century Soviet Union. Here, engineering feats that attempted to re-shape nature led to nature itself becoming threatening and uncanny, while more recent stories express concerns,

---

[24] Stevenson, *The City*, p. 99.

sometimes veiled by humour, about the legacy of industrialisation, pollution, and radiation. Alex Bevan then considers the London Underground as a heterotopian Gothic space that reflected socio-cultural anxieties about increasing modernity and an attendant counter-narrative about tragedy, hauntings, and the affective influence of such spaces. Moving from collective unease to individual anxieties about the fragmented self in late twentieth-century Tokyo, Deirdre Flynn's exploration of Hakuri Murakami's novel *Hard Boiled Wonderland and the End of the World* examines the personal struggle and uncanny doubling that accompany the protagonist's attempt to escape the hyper-real postmodern Japanese city for a fantasy town of his subconscious.

These urban anxieties and psychological responses to the environment can perhaps best be approached and understood through the prism of the urban Gothic.[25] Sara Wasson has highlighted the Gothic's key characteristics as a claustrophobic, often incarcerating sense of space, and an interest in heightened emotions such as horror, terror, anguish, or paranoia.[26] Gothicised space is fearful, anxiety-ridden, often rooted in a lack of agency, a loss of control, and a sense of the environment's dominance over its inhabitants. This stylised, imaginative engagement with the environment, one frequently associated with the supernatural or the uncanny, took a particular urban form in the nineteenth century. Fred Botting has indicated how earlier Gothic fiction's interest in the wilderness as a reflection of mental turmoil was relocated to the urban environment in the early to mid–nineteenth century, enacting a metaphorical translation in which 'the dark alleyways of cities were the gloomy forests and subterranean labyrinths'.[27]

The Gothic's link between exterior environment and interior unease echoes late nineteenth-century concerns about the modern city as a phobic space in which particular mental anxieties and topophobic disorders – especially neurasthesia, agoraphobia, and claustrophobia – were endemic.[28] The pace of change and the physical expansion of the nineteenth-century European city left its inhabitants estranged from both their built environment and most

---

[25] While usefully advancing our appreciation of the unsettling and affective qualities of the environment, EcoGothic studies such as those found in Smith and Hughes's *Ecogothic* and 'The EcoGothic in the Long Nineteenth Century' special issue of *Gothic Studies* (16:1 [2014]) have not yet explored the urban in a sustained manner. This should be redressed by Holly-Gale Millette and Ruth Heholt (eds), *New Urban Gothic: The Global Gothic in the Age of the Anthropocene* (Basingstoke, forthcoming).

[26] Sara Wasson, *Urban Gothic of the Second World War: Dark London* (Basingstoke, 2010), p. 2.

[27] Fred Botting, *Gothic* (London, 1996), p. 123.

[28] See Vidler, *Warped Space*, pp. 25–49.

of their fellow city-dwellers. This suggests that the urban Gothic was not simply a transference of older environmental tropes to a new, urban context. Instead it evoked a different set of spatial and social concerns, both modern and urban, and to this extent the late nineteenth century became the period in which 'a distinctively urban Gothic was crystallized'.[29] This is best seen in Victorian London, a city that has been repeatedly reflected through the urban Gothic's dark lens. Roger Luckhurst suggests it was the unprecedented scale of late nineteenth-century London, 'the first megalopolis of the modern era', that caused it to become 'a sublime object that evokes awe and evades rational capture'.[30]

Responsive to the 'spatial turn', Gothic criticism has attempted to move away from an overemphasis on psychological interiority to develop an appreciation of the spatialised and historicised specifics in which an urban Gothic milieu manifested. Particularly pertinent to the transnational interests of this study, Luckhurst's emphasis on the importance of locality leads him to propose that 'the ghosts of London are different from those of Paris, or those of California'.[31] Wasson, similarly, emphasises the way in which 'Gothic modes are inflected for particular times and places', and hence there is a need to ensure the Gothic is 'not only ... historicised but *localised*'.[32] Therefore the urban Gothic becomes an important way of linking the local and the general, enabling us to appreciate the nuances of its geographical, historical, and cultural particularities through the lens of the Gothic's broadly familiar conventions. While inflected by such differences, however, the urban Gothic's rich register of fears – its ability to speak to anxieties about both the environment and its threatening inhabitants, to 'other' spaces and social groups and yet also articulate concerns about the fragility of the individual's identity in the modern city – ensures its haunting presence throughout this collection.

---

[29] Roger Luckhurst, 'The Contemporary London Gothic and the Limits of the "Spectral Turn" ', *Textual Practice* 16 (2002), 527–46 at 530.

[30] Ibid., p. 531.

[31] Ibid., p. 542. Luckhurst's approach has been followed by historically specific studies of Gothic London. See Jamieson Ridenhour's *In Darkest London: The Gothic Landscape in Victorian Literature* (Lanham, MD, 2013), Wasson, *Urban Gothic*, and also Lawrence Phillips and Anne Witchard (eds), *London Gothic: Space, Place, and the Gothic Imagination* (London, 2010).

[32] Wasson, *Urban Gothic*, pp. 3–4. The transnational focus of this collection encourages questions about the extent to which the urban Gothic remains a largely Western perception. While it has figured as part of a Western imperial gaze, this perception needs to be offset by more recent representations of a postcolonial Gothic. See, for example, Andrew Smith and William Hughes (eds), *Empire and the Gothic: The Politics of Genre* (Basingstoke, 2003).

The third thematic section of this book focuses on spectrality, on ghosts, haunted topographies, their links to communal memory and the urban past – its loss, recall, re-imagining – and a related destabilising or problematising of urban spatial meanings. While scholarly interest in haunting has become sufficiently widespread to generate reference to a 'spectral turn', that ready application has in itself become rather problematic. The idea of spectrality has shown itself capable of being applied to almost anything and everything, especially a hauntological sense of those things that are often most significant to scholarly research: theorisation, conceptualisation, hermeneutics. While Jacques Derrida's *Spectre of Marx* was instrumental in stimulating this interest in the spectral, his spectro-politics tends to lack actual ghosts.[33] Instead, the ghosts and hauntings were metaphors for memory, nostalgia, guilt, past trauma. Such an approach is not totally without its uses in the context of this study. For example, Tim Edensor has skilfully evoked the language of ghosts, haunting, and the spectral when considering the place of industrial ruins in the post-industrial city, and in so doing has advanced our appreciation of the affective environment. However, his ghosts are affective spaces, sensory strangeness, haunting traces, not the ghosts of local lore or ethnographic investigation.[34] Concerned by Derrida's drift into ahistorical abstractions, other scholars have subsequently stressed the need for greater emphasis on the ghost's generative loci, on its spatial, as much as temporal, existence and meaning.[35] Through engaging with specific places and historical periods, our third section explores the importance of considering the city as located in time and space. The spectral entangles with the spatial and temporal aspects of the urban experience more overtly than in the other sections. As Vidler argues, haunted by the past and by uncertainty about its future, urban space evokes 'a psychology of anxiety, whether nostalgically melancholic or progressively anticipatory'.[36]

For most urban centres examined in this section, haunting serves as a way of engaging with exploitative colonial or industrial pasts. David and Sharn

---

[33] Jacques Derrida, *Spectres of Marx: The State of the Debt, the Work of Mourning, and the New International* (New York, 1994). Seemingly inspired by Derrida's spectro-politics, the spectral turn has given rise to the study of spectro-aesthetics and spectro-geographies. See Julian Wolfreys, *Victorian Hauntings: Spectrality, Gothic, the Uncanny and Literature* (Basingstoke, 2002), p. 12; Maddern and Adey, 'Editorial: Spectro-geographies'.

[34] Edensor, 'Ghosts of Industrial Ruins'.

[35] See: Luckhurst, 'Contemporary London Gothic'; Blanco and Peeren, *Popular Ghosts*, pp. xvi–xvii; Karl Bell, 'Civic Spirits? Ghost lore and Civic Narratives in Nineteenth-Century Portsmouth', *Cultural and Social History* 11 (2014), 51–68.

[36] Vidler, *Warped Space*, p. 3.

Waldron consider the supernatural folklore of the nineteenth-century Ballarat goldfields as a means of understanding the suppressed, haunted history of Australia's industrial settlements and the poverty, loss, and violence that helped forge the region's fortunes. Although she adopts a very different approach, the exploitative past also forms an element of Morag Rose's psychogeographic exploration of the waterways of post-industrial Manchester. In this, she teases out contemporary spatial apprehensions, fears about the submerged entities – ghostlike in their absent presence – that may dwell in or near the water, and memories of an abandoned industrial heritage that lie close to the surface of the present. Taking a different perspective, but one still oriented towards the haunting traces of a problematic past, María del Pilar Blanco introduces us to a spectral cartography of past political events in Mexico City, the absence-presence of the emperor Maximillian, and places where time is out of joint because the past clings tightly to the present. Her exploration reiterates Derek McCormack's observation that '[t]he spectral is … a constitutive element of geographical experience, taking place as a persistent and unsettling capacity of place to enchant and haunt … The spectral is sensed persistence without the fullness of presence … '.[37] As in many of the chapters in this section, time (and the sense of modernity built upon it) is shown to be not linear, but prone to looping into endless returns, traces, and echoes.

Just as enchantment and anxiety include something of each in the other, so haunting and the spectral are not purely about guilt, trauma, or fear of the past. As various contributors demonstrate, the urban dweller's relationship to the past can also be a source of reassuring tradition, even comfort; one that serves to assist in the formation of more amorphous urban communities. Alevtina Solovyova's ethnographic study of contemporary urban ghostlore in Beijing reveals how traditional religious rituals and spirit beliefs are being adapted, updated, and at least tacitly challenging the powerful forces of state disenchantment and modern urban influences. These findings add to and resonate with a body of scholarship that is exploring the sacred and the supernatural in modern China. Perhaps most pertinently to this section, Keping Wu has argued that the pace of urbanisation is a generative factor in creating ghost stories in contemporary Chinese cities. Wu sees ghosts as being newly created, rather than simply the lingering remnants of older beliefs: 'caused by uncertainties brought by urban commercialisation and industrialisation … the

---

[37] Derek McCormack, 'Remotely Sensing Affective Afterlives: The Spectral Geographies of Material Remains', *Annals of the Association of American Geographers* 100 (2010), 640–54 at 642.

unfamiliar interactions conditioned by urban spaces'.[38] Here the supernatural is a contemporary response to the contemporary experience of urbanisation. One of the very processes historically touted to snuff out supernatural beliefs has become an intrinsic generator of their ongoing existence. Solovyova suggests that Beijing's ghosts, much like modern magic, are an assemblage of influences, old and new. These chapters suggest that, far from having laid our ghosts to rest beneath the concrete and glass of the modern urban environment, we continue to catch them reflected darkly in its mirrored surfaces.

Despite these functions, there is something rather impotent about the spectral. Ghosts are weakened not just by their lack of coherent meaning or purpose among those who tell the stories, but also inherently. Present but absent, spectral agency (or its use as a voice of others seeking agency) is never sufficiently strong, focused, or consistent. As Luckhurst notes, ghosts may serve 'as the emblem of resistance to the tyranny of planned space, but this resistance is necessarily occluded and interstitial, passed on only between initiates'.[39] If they serve as a muted form of resistance, that resistance is usually tacit, for while a community's potential to manifest ghost stories may innately destabilise and 'other' particular urban spaces, that destabilising goes largely unrecognised by those beyond the initiated.

Our three themes thus represent not just different functions but also differing levels of agency within the urban supernatural. Magical enchantment, be it in the form of powers, energies, or supernatural beings, serves as the most assertive gesture towards urban agency and a desire for, if not control, then at least supernaturally enriched comprehension of the urban environment. While magic may be no more tangible than ghosts, its purpose and functioning is certainly imbued with a more coherent and directed sense of agency.[40] By contrast, urban unease, expressed via folkloric monstrosities, the urban Gothic, or uncanny doubling, frequently signifies a sense of disempowerment in the face of environmental anxieties. Hovering suitably between enchantment and anxiety, the spectral makes assertions of spatial alterity, but often

---

[38] Keping Wu, ' "Ghost city": Religion, Urbanization and Spatial Anxieties in Contemporary China', *Geoforum* 65 (2015), 243–5 at 245. See also Joseph Bosco, 'Young People's Ghost Stories in Hong Kong', *Journal of Popular Culture* 40 (2007), 785–807; Mayfair Mei-Hui Yang, 'Spatial Struggles: Postcolonial Complex, State Disenchantment, and Popular Reappropriation of Space in Rural Southeast China', *The Journal of Asian Studies* 63 (2004), 719–55 at 751.

[39] Luckhurst, 'Contemporary London Gothic', p. 532.

[40] For more on this, see Christopher Lehrich, *The Occult Mind: Magic in Theory and Practice* (New Delhi, 2007), pp. 160–4. See also Marcel Mauss, *A General Theory of Magic* (London, 2001).

remains too diffuse to articulate coherently the latent guilt, trauma, or protest that ghosts bring with them as they trail the past back into the modern city.

Regardless of whether the urban supernatural finds active, impotent, or somewhat indeterminate expression in between, the multidisciplinary contributions collected in this study demonstrate how all three themes can enhance our understanding of urban cultures, past and present, and the operation of ever shifting, frequently contradictory urban identities around the world. The supernatural enables complex but amorphous communities to locate themselves within their urban environment, whilst serving to voice and manage anxieties associated with those localities, their inhabitants, and their histories. Frequently alluded to through contributors' repeated references to the subterranean and the submerged, the muted cultural politics of the urban supernatural, its positive and negative elements of imaginative enrichment and critique, empowerment and anxiety, speaks to an exuberance of the urban invisible. It is these hidden histories and cultures, and the largely unseen or unrecognised cities in which they are located, that this collection seeks to unveil. In doing so, the cultural imaginary of magic, monsters, and ghosts serves to reveal crooked and oblique pathways into the modern urban mindscape, advancing our understanding of affective urban environments and the cultural experiences and identities formed within them.

Bibliography

Amin, Ash, and Nigel Thrift, *Cities: Reimagining the Urban* (Cambridge, 2002)

Bell, Karl, *The Magical Imagination: Magic and Modernity in Urban England, 1780–1914* (Cambridge, 2012)

——, 'Civic Spirits? Ghost lore and Civic Narratives in Nineteenth-Century Portsmouth', *Cultural and Social History* 11 (2014), 51–68

Benjamin, Walter *The Arcades Project*, trans. Howard Eiland and Kevin McLaughlin (Cambridge, MA, 2002)

Bennett, Jane, *The Enchantment of Modern Life: Attachments, Crossings, and Ethics* (Princeton, NJ, 2011)

Berberich, Christine, Neil Campbell and Robert Hudson (eds), *Affective Landscapes in Literature, Art and Everyday Life*, (Farnham, 2015)

Blanco, María del Pilar and Esther Peeren (eds), *Popular Ghosts: The Haunted Spaces of Everyday Culture* (New York, 2010)

Blécourt, Willem de and Owen Davies (eds), *Witchcraft Continued: Popular Magic in Modern Europe* (Manchester, 2004)

Bosco, Joseph, 'Young People's Ghost Stories in Hong Kong', *Journal of Popular Culture* 40 (2007), 785–807

Botting, Fred, *Gothic* (London, 1995)

Castle, Terry, *The Female Thermometer: Eighteenth-Century Culture and the Invention of the Uncanny* (Oxford, 1995)

Comaroff, Jean and John Comaroff, *Modernity and Its Malcontents: Ritual and Power in Postcolonial Africa* (Chicago, 1993)

Crouch, David, 'Afterword: From Affect to Landscape and Back', in Berberich et al. (eds), *Affective Landscapes*, pp. 230–7

Davies, Owen, *Witchcraft, Magic and Culture 1736–1951* (Manchester, 1999)

——, *America Bewitched: The Story of Witchcraft after Salem* (Oxford, 2013)

Debord, Guy, *Theory of the Dérive* (London, 1997)

De Certeau, Michel, *The Practice of Everyday Life* (Berkeley, CA, 1984)

Derrida, Jacques, *Specters of Marx: The State of the Debt, the Work of Mourning, and the New International* (New York, 1994)

During, Simon, *Modern Enchantments: The Cultural Power of Secular Magic* (Cambridge, MA, 2002)

'The EcoGothic in the Long Nineteenth Century', special issue, *Gothic Studies* 16:1 (2014)

Edensor, Tim, 'The Ghosts of Industrial Ruins: Ordering and Disordering Memory in Excessive Space', *Environment and Planning D: Society and Space* 23 (2005), 829–49

Elmarsafy, Ziad, Anna Bernard and David Atwell (eds), *Debating Orientalism* (New York, 2013)

Foucault, Michel, 'Of Other Spaces', *Diacritics* 16 (1986), 22–7

Geschiere, Peter, *The Modernity of Witchcraft: Politics and the Occult in Postcolonial Africa* (Charlottesville, VA, 1997)

Goto-Jones, Chris, *Conjuring Asia: Magic, Orientalism and the Making of the Modern World* (Cambridge, 2016)

Holloway, Julian, 'Enchanted Spaces: The Séance, Affect, and Geographies of Religion', *Annals of the Association of American Geographers* 96 (2006), 182–7

Hutton, Ronald, *The Triumph of the Moon: A History of Modern Pagan Witchcraft* (Oxford, 2001)

Kroger, Lisa, 'Panic, Paranoia and Pathos: Ecocriticism in the Eighteenth-century Gothic Novel', in Smith and Hughes (eds), *Ecogothic*, pp.15–27

Lefebvre, Henri, *The Production of Space* (Oxford, 1991)

Lehrich, Christopher, *The Occult Mind: Magic in Theory and Practice* (New Delhi, 2007)

Luckhurst, Roger, 'The Contemporary London Gothic and the Limits of the "Spectral Turn" ', *Textual Practice* 16 (2002), 527–46

Luhrmann, T. M., *Persuasions of the Witch's Craft: Ritual Magic in Contemporary England* (London, 1994)

Maddern, Jo Frances and Peter Adey, 'Editorial: Spectro-geographies', *Cultural Geographies* 15 (2008), 291–5

Mauss, Marcel, *A General Theory of Magic* (London, 2001)

McCormack, Derek P., 'Remotely Sensing Affective Afterlives: The Spectral Geographies of Material Remains', *Annals of the Association of American Geographers* 100 (2010), 640–54

McCorristine, Shane, *The Spectral Arctic: A History of Dreams and Ghosts in Polar Exploration* (London, 2018)

Millette, Holly-Gale and Ruth Heholt (eds), *New Urban Gothic: The Global Gothic in the Age of the Anthropocene* (Basingstoke, forthcoming).

Owen, Alex, *The Place of Enchantment: British Occultism and the Culture of the Modern* (Chicago, 2004)

Phillips, Lawrence and Anne Witchard (eds), *London Gothic: Space, Place and the Gothic Imagination* (London, 2010)

Pile, Steve, *Real Cities* (London, 2005)

Ridenhour, Jamieson, *In Darkest London: The Gothic Landscape in Victorian Literature* (Lanham, MD, 2013)

Said, Edward, *Orientalism* (London, 1978).

Saler, Michael, *As If: Modern Enchantment and the Literary Prehistory of Virtual Reality* (Oxford, 2012)

Simmel, Georg, 'The Metropolis and Mental Life', in *Simmel on Culture*, ed. David Frisby and Mike Featherstone (London, 1997), pp. 174–85

Smith, Andrew and William Hughes (eds), *Ecogothic* (Manchester, 2013)

—— and ——(eds), *Empire and the Gothic: The Politics of Genre* (Basingstoke, 2003)

Stevenson, Deborah, *The City* (Cambridge, 2013)

Tally, Robert T., Jr, *Spatiality* (Abingdon, 2013)

Tiffin, Jessica 'Outside/Inside Fantastic London', *English Academy Review* 25 (2008), 32–41

Tonkiss, Fran, *Space, the City and Social Theory* (Cambridge, 2005)

Trietel, Corinna, *A Science for the Soul: Occultism and the Genesis of the German Modern* (Baltimore, 2004)

Tuan, Yi-Fu, *Space and Place: The Perspective of Experience* (Minneapolis, 1977)

Vidler, Anthony, *Warped Space: Art, Architecture, and Anxiety in Modern Culture* (Cambridge, MA, 2001)

Warner, Marina, *Phantasmagorias: Spirit Visions, Metaphors, and Media into the Twenty-first Century* (Oxford, 2006)

Wasson, Sara *Urban Gothic of the Second World War: Dark London* (Basingstoke, 2010)

West-Pavlov, Russell, *Space in Theory: Kristeva, Foucault, Deleuze* (Amsterdam, 2009)

Whyte, William, 'Buildings, Landscapes, and Regimes of Materiality', *Transactions of the Royal Historical Society*, sixth series, 28 (2018), 135–48

Wolfreys, Julian, *Writing London, Volume 2: Materiality, Memory, Spectrality* (Basingstoke, 2004)

——, *Victorian Hauntings: Spectrality, Gothic, the Uncanny and Literature* (Basingstoke, 2002)

Wu, Keping, ' "Ghost city": Religion, Urbanization and Spatial Anxieties in Contemporary China', *Geoforum* 65 (2015), 243–5

Yang, Mayfair Mei-Hui, 'Spatial Struggles: Postcolonial Complex, State Disenchantment, and Popular Reappropriation of Space in Rural Southeast China', *The Journal of Asian Studies* 63 (2004), 719–55

Urban Enchantment

1

Magical Capital: Witchcraft and the Press in Paris, c. 1789–1939

———◇◇◇———

WILLIAM POOLEY

ON 5 OCTOBER 1841, the Tribunal de Police in Paris judged a minor case of assault involving a navvy named Pestiaux, who had attacked one of his co-workers, named Gossin, with a shovel. Pestiaux showed no remorse, telling the judge that Gossin was not to be trusted: 'Those injuries should have affected him for longer … but he's a mischief-maker.' The judge wanted the court to be absolutely clear about what Pestiaux was suggesting:

> *The Judge*: What do you mean a 'mischief-maker'?
>
> *The Accused*: Dammit, he had it in for me and was always casting spells on me.
>
> *The Judge*: What you're saying defies common sense … What do you mean by 'spells'?

Pestiaux explained that Gossin had caused his tools to magically disappear, so that he could not work. When the judge asked why Gossin would do such a thing, Pestiaux said, 'Because he wanted to cause mischief … Mischief-makers, don't you see, they can't help themselves.' A medical expert testified that Pestiaux was not suffering from any mental disturbance, but the judge decided all the same that this was a case of 'monomania'. After sentencing him to a fine of 30 francs and another 120 francs to be paid to Gossin, the judge told Pestiaux that 'the court has been lenient towards you, but don't think you'll get away with this again: you could be sentenced to life'.

In reply, Pestiaux grumbled, 'I'm going back to the country ... there are no mischief-makers at home.'[1]

Contemporary newspapers expressed a strong sense of shock that such beliefs could exist in Paris itself: 'Good God, who would believe it! Witches capable of finding dupes in Paris! Paris the heartland of civilisation and enlightened thought!'[2] Historians have been similarly unwilling to recognise that witchcraft was an enduring presence in the life of the French capital from the Revolution to the Second World War. Long after sorcery had been decriminalised in France (1682), and even after the revolutionary criminal justice reforms of 1791 and 1810, the Parisian court system continued to host a series of conflicts over maleficent magic. In fact, the road-mender Pestiaux's parting shot to the court in 1831 turns the standard expectations historians often have of witchcraft as a rural 'survival' upside-down: Paris was plagued by witches, and the provinces would be a refuge from their mischief.[3]

What does this tell historians about the city that Walter Benjamin characterised as 'the capital of the nineteenth century', the place that newspapers believed was the 'heartland of civilisation and enlightened thought'? Pestiaux's belief in the magical powers of his colleague sits uncomfortably with the widely accepted image of Paris as the embodiment of urban 'modernity' in this period, a city characterised above all by 'frenetic circulation' and a self-conscious rejection of 'tradition'.[4] This rejection is clear in the incredulous comments journalists continued to make whenever cases of sorcery were reported in the capital, yet this hyper-modern culture never eradicated these scorned traditions. Thomas Cragin has argued that, if anything, the nineteenth century was the apogee of the traditional genre of sensationalised true crime, the *canard*, which preserved a set of attitudes towards crime and the criminal that historians more readily associate with the early modern period. Crime, from the point of view of the *canards*, was caused by sin, rather than the hereditary or environmental factors that the emerging sciences of criminology

---

[1] See *Gazette des tribunaux*, 6 October 1841, p. 1,324.

[2] The quotation appears in *Gazette des tribunaux*, 9 March 1828, p. 488.

[3] For a more careful exploration of the continuing importance of witchcraft, which nonetheless emphasises the importance of rural identity, see Owen Davies, 'Witchcraft Accusations in France, 1850–1990', in *Witchcraft Continued: Popular Magic in Modern Europe*, ed. Willem de Blécourt and Owen Davies (Manchester, 2004), pp. 107–32. For accounts, dated, emphasising rural 'survivals', see Judith Devlin, *The Superstitious Mind: French Peasants and the Supernatural in the Nineteenth Century* (New Haven, CT, 1987), pp. 100–19; Eugen Weber, *Peasants into Frenchmen: The Modernization of Rural France, 1870–1914* (Stanford, CA, 1976), pp. 23–9.

[4] See, for example: Christopher Prendergast, *Paris and the Nineteenth Century* (Oxford, 1992), pp. 1–30. The quotation from Benjamin is at 5.

debated.[5] If nineteenth-century Paris was defined by its crime, as Louis Chevalier first argued in the 1950s, why have historians had so little to say about Parisian crimes involving witchcraft?[6]

Partly, this can be put down to the tendency Cragin criticises for historians to over-emphasise novelty, at the expense the elements of Parisian popular culture that remained relatively unchanged. But there has also been a tendency to subsume witchcraft into other, more 'modern' topics, such as the *fin-de-siècle* 'flight from reason', when a range of artists, writers, and mystics, but also philosophers, scientists, and psychologists reasserted the value of irrational forces, and explored the power and meanings of the unconscious, hypnosis, and unexplained forces.[7] Similarly, the informal popular tradition of witchcraft surfaces in research into the influence of spiritualism and its French offshoot, spiritism, from the 1850s onwards, or into Mesmerism in France across the whole of the nineteenth century.[8] But many of the historians involved in such research have been more interested in the innovations of elite authors associated with the esoteric movements grouped under the term 'occultism' than in the continuing practices of sorcery that the outraged newspapers discussed.[9]

'Witchcraft' is easily confused with these other phenomena, both by historians and by contemporaries. While this confusion is part of the story of its continuing relevance to Parisians during the period considered, witch beliefs have a coherence interdependent with other supernatural beliefs. In a cross-cultural survey, Ronald Hutton has pointed out five defining characteristics of witchcraft. A witch, Hutton summarised, is 'a person who uses non-physical means to cause misfortune or injury to other humans'. The second key characteristic is that the witch 'works to harm neighbours or kin

---

[5]   Thomas Cragin, *Murder in Parisian Streets: Manufacturing Crime and Justice in the Popular Press, 1830–1900* (Lewisburg, PA, 2006), especially pp. 145–68; Michelle Perrot agrees about the endurance of the genre, but not about the conservatism of its message: see Michelle Perrot, 'Fait divers et histoire au XIXᶜ siècle', *Annales. Histoire, Sciences Sociales* 38 (1983), 911–19 at 911.

[6]   Louis Chevalier, *Labouring Classes and Dangerous Classes in Paris during the First Half of the Nineteenth Century* (London, 1973).

[7]   The literature is extensive. For instance: Ruth Harris, *Murders and Madness: Medicine, Law, and Society in the Fin de Siècle* (Oxford, 1989); Thomas Laqueur, 'Why the Margins Matter: Occultism and the Making of Modernity', *Modern Intellectual History* 3 (April 2006), 111–35; Alex Owen, *The Place of Enchantment: British Occultism and the Culture of the Modern* (Chicago, 2004).

[8]   Robert Darnton, *Mesmerism and the End of the Enlightenment in France* (Cambridge, MA, 1968); John Warne Monroe, *Laboratories of Faith: Mesmerism, Spiritism, and Occultism in Modern France* (Ithaca, NY, 2008).

[9]   For a recent collection of essays on a range of figures in the Occult movement, see Christopher Partridge (ed.), *The Occult World* (London, 2015).

rather than strangers'. Third, 'she or he earns general social disapproval, usually of a very strong kind', chiefly because the witch works surreptitiously and not for gain but, according to their victims, 'from motives of malice and spite'.[10] The fourth characteristic is 'the belief that the appearance of a witch figure is not an isolated and unique event. Witches are expected to work within a tradition, and generally use techniques, or are possessed of or by powers, that have been handed down within the society concerned from time immemorial or introduced into it from outside.' Finally, witches 'can be resisted by their fellow humans'.[11] While many of these characteristics may overlap with other supernatural beliefs, the fundamental idea of a tradition of humans maliciously working against their own communities using magical powers that can be resisted marks witchcraft off as a distinct historical phenomenon, with deeper popular roots than many of the occult beliefs that proliferated in the long nineteenth century. The confusion that contemporaries expressed is not simply terminological: it goes to the heart of the historiographical significance of modern witchcraft.

In the first section of this chapter, I explore the newspaper sources, showing how the very publications that thundered against witchcraft also stimulated and produced it. The second section explores how and why 'witchcraft' was distanced from the everyday life of modern Paris, and artificially separated from occult phenomena such as Mesmerism. The final section explores the syncretic phenomenon of modern witchcraft in Paris. Never entirely subsumed within other occult movements, witchcraft remained a practice primarily transmitted through informal conduits, both oral and manuscript, and primarily among the poorer, worse-educated, and socially marginalised sections of the population. But the cultural work that occultists and others performed to distance witchcraft was never enough: urban witchcraft remained a vital practice, which adapted to the changing social contexts of consumerism and an increasingly tightly regulated medical profession. Whatever elite writers claimed, the depressing recurrence of dramatic and tragic cases is a reminder that witchcraft was a part of the story that Parisians told themselves about themselves.

---

[10]   The distinction first suggested by Evans-Pritchard between conscious sorcery and involuntary witchcraft remains to be empirically explored for nineteenth-century France. For similar concerns, see Mary Douglas, 'Witch Beliefs in Central Africa', *Africa: Journal of the International African Institute* 37 (1967), 72–80; E. E. Evans-Pritchard, *Witchcraft, Oracles and Magic among the Azande*, new edn (Oxford, 1976).

[11]   Ronald Hutton, 'Anthropological and Historical Approaches to Witchcraft: Potential for a New Collaboration?', *The Historical Journal* 47 (June 2004), 421–3.

Producing witchcraft

There were many spaces where this conversation took place, including medical and psychological research, and within the criminal justice system itself. But it is in print culture that Parisian witchcraft was most dramatically exposed, described, constructed, and actively stimulated. The *Gazette des tribunaux*, which first appeared in 1825, stands at the centre of this developing print culture of crime and witchcraft. The *Gazette* was a serious publication covering notable legal developments and trials, but it rapidly developed a readership far beyond legal professionals. With its detailed coverage of the most dramatic and important cases, it played an important role in communicating legal knowledge to a wider public, just as the *canards* Cragin studied often reproduced court judgments and pleas. But it was above all the brief reports on unusual or dramatic cases that appeared in the *Gazette* that struck contemporaries, including novelists such as Honoré de Balzac and Eugène Sue.[12] Sue's *Mysteries of Paris* (1842–43) was so obviously crafted from these blood-curdling and unsettling snippets that one reviewer could write, 'So this is what you call the Mysteries of Paris! All you have done is to unearth the *Gazette des tribunaux* – which has had 12,000 subscribers these twenty years past. Could you find nothing more mysterious in Paris?'[13]

And witchcraft was an early staple of the *Gazette*'s coverage of unusual cases. Since the introduction of the new penal code in 1791, there had been no sense in which witchcraft itself was a crime. Certain specific practices of fortune-telling were mentioned in the legislation, but *maleficium* on its own could not in any sense be considered illegal.[14] Instead, the edges of witchcraft came into contact with laws against illegal medical practice, fraud, and crimes against the person. In 1826 alone, the *Gazette* mentioned four different legal cases involving sorcery, from frauds to violent assaults.[15] It is true that these were all provincial cases, but it did not take long for the editors to realise there were plenty of 'witches' operating in Paris itself. In 1828, they covered three cases of magic in the Parisian law courts and similar cases, including Pestiaux's violent attack on Gossin, popped up periodically for the rest of the period.[16]

---

[12]   Clive Emsley, *Crime, Police, and Penal Policy: European Experiences, 1750–1940* (Oxford, 2013), pp. 150–1.

[13]   Cited in Chevalier, *Labouring Classes and Dangerous Classes*, p. 6.

[14]   David Allen Harvey, 'Fortune-Tellers in the French Courts: Antidivination Prosecutions in France in the Nineteenth and Twentieth Centuries', *French Historical Studies* 28 (2005), 131–57.

[15]   *Gazette des tribunaux*, 27 October, 22 November, 3 December, and 4 December 1826.

[16]   *Gazette des tribunaux*, 9 March, 18 April, and 19 July 1828.

Although the *Gazette* habitually prefaced these stories with comments about how out of place witchcraft beliefs were in the nineteenth century, the accounts they carried reveal, if anything, a normalisation of witchcraft in the courts, and a series of accommodations, as the legal system attempted to draw distinctions between fortune-telling, healing, and witchcraft, and reluctantly recognised the slanderous power of the terminology of sorcery. Similar stories appeared in other newspapers, such as the *Gazette*'s rival *Le Courrier des tribunaux*, but also in mainstream publications, such as *Le Journal des débats politiques et littéraires*. Yet it was not until 1863 and the appearance of *Le Petit Journal* that another paper would display such a fascination with witchcraft.

Where the *Gazette* had largely appealed to a fairly elite audience of legal professionals and Parisian intellectuals, this new paper ushered in the era of mass journalism. Historians have often pointed to the radical innovations of *Le Petit Journal*, whose dramatic success was built on a combination of unashamedly populist stories of horrific murders, such as the 1869 Troppmann case, and a much lower price than any of its competitors.[17] By deliberately avoiding 'political' reporting, the editors paid a much lower tax on each copy sold, allowing them to sell each issue for five centimes, rather than fifteen, and hugely increasing their market.[18] By 1895, each daily issue had a print run of two million copies; and magic, Mesmerism, and modern witchcraft had a particular fascination for *Le Petit Journal*'s flamboyant founding editor, Timothée Trimm.[19] For almost eighty years up until the Second World War, *Le Petit Journal* and its imitators continued to carry dramatic, amusing, and gruesome stories of sorcery, largely divorced from any explicit political or social message.

From 1877 onwards, such sensationalist papers had competition from another type of newspaper, with a smaller readership and a special interest in sorcery: the radical left-wing press, who sought to reinforce the association between 'superstition' and the Church. There was an increasingly hostile relationship between these secularists and the Church in the late nineteenth century, culminating in the crises around the Dreyfus affair and the 1905 law regarding the separation of the churches and the state. Among the newspapers, *La Lanterne* led the secularist charge, and one of the ways it criticised the Church was by regularly reporting incredible stories of supernatural deceptions and their dupes. An editorial about one case of fraudulent

---

[17]   Véronique Gramfort, 'Les Crimes de Panti: quand Troppmann défrayait la chronique', *Romantisme* 27 (1997), 17–30.

[18]   On the paper more generally, see, for instance, Perrot, 'Fait divers et histoire au XIXe siècle'; Cragin, *Murder in Parisian Streets*.

[19]   See, for example, his editorial in *Le Petit Journal*, 12 January 1865.

healing from 1885 was typical in the way the paper linked magical beliefs to the Catholic Church:

> This is superstition pure and simple. The poor fool who spent two months rubbing himself with [an ointment made from] red worms and puppy [fat] – for the price of 1,640 francs – bluntly declared that he "did it out of faith". And why wouldn't he have faith? If he received his first communion when he was little, and if he went to church every now and then since, if he reads the right newspapers and is a good Christian, he learned to believe and even to venerate things that are much more extraordinary than the efficacy of red-worm-and-puppy-fat ointment.[20]

There is an irony to the vehemence that *La Lanterne* displayed towards the fraudulence of sorcery: the stories of modern 'superstition' that it and other newspapers reproduced do not always convey a strong sense of authenticity. If the nineteenth century was, as Scott Carpenter has argued, a period 'when issues about falseness were particularly sensitive', the newspapers did little to combat this.[21] Imprecision about dates, locations, and names means that many of the stories are near impossible to verify. Some were probably made up. There is at least one example, from 1882, which presents the story of 'Father Bloodsucker' as a news item, even though the story first appeared at the Beaumarchais Theatre in Paris twenty-five years before.[22]

In fact, the very newspapers that railed against superstitions also published self-conscious fictions about modern witchcraft. A story called 'The Bewitching' in *La Lanterne* explicitly cast modern-day Parisian occultists as the heirs of early modern witchcraft.[23] Other papers, such as *Le Petit Parisien* and *Le Matin*, ran similar material, either as short stories or as serialised novels, feeding the popular imagination with stories of witchcraft both historical and contemporary, illustrated with comical depictions of witches with their *grimoires* open in front of them. The lines were easily crossed, as newspapers ran factually dubious news features, or remarked as early as 1828 that the real-life protagonists of magical intrigues were like the witches 'from a Walter Scott novel'.[24] And fictions were taken on and lived by real people: 'the red witch' was a serialised novel by Delphi Fabrice in the 1870s long

[20] *La Lanterne*, 3 March 1885.
[21] Scott Carpenter, *Aesthetics of Fraudulence in Nineteenth-Century France: Frauds, Hoaxes and Counterfeits* (Farnham, 2009), p. 1.
[22] See *La Lanterne*, 8 April 1882.
[23] See *La Lanterne*, 27 March 1900.
[24] *Le Courrier des tribunaux*, March 1828.

Un sorcier, un vrai

Fig. 1. 'A witch, a real witch', illustration from a short story in *Le Matin*, 17 January 1926. Reproduced courtesy of the Bibliothèque nationale de France.

before it was the name of one of the most successful commercial witches of the early twentieth century.[25]

If the editors of left-wing newspapers like *La Lanterne* were sincere in their aims, they would have been disappointed to realise the actual effects of their stories, both fictional and 'real'. Their fascination with sorcery encouraged, rather than destroyed, belief in maleficent magic. First, as they themselves sometimes recognised, in drawing attention to witchcraft panics, they actively encouraged the fears they were condemning.[26] As Owen Davies has pointed out for witchcraft in England during the same period, literacy was a stimulus rather than a brake on sorcery, as many believers and practitioners learned

[25] 'Professor' Jean Talazac, the 'red witch', 'Moorys', was in trouble with the law several times in 1908, 1909, and 1916. See for instance his adverts in *Le Rire*, 3 June 1911, and, for his final trial, 7 January 1916.

[26] *Le Petit Journal*, 3 May 1872 noted this in its own coverage of a case from Marseille.

about magic from cheap print, including the newspapers.[27] I have yet to find a case in which participants claimed to have learned their beliefs from newspaper reports, but it is at the very least interesting to note that one of the groups discussed in the next section who were most often involved in magical conflicts – *concierges* – were also the stereotype of *Le Petit Journal*'s readership.[28] It was no accident, then, that the same newspapers also carried back-page advertisements for 'witches' whose criminal convictions they celebrated on their front pages.[29] *Le Matin*, for instance, ran an advert in February 1909 for

> ADDO, THE KING OF WITCHES who possesses mysterious secrets to guarantee success in life and revenge on your enemies, good luck, riches, a happy life. Appointments every day. For a free short book, write to The Witch Addo, 251, rue Saint-Denis.[30]

The same year, *Le Matin* sarcastically covered Addo's trial for fraud, remarking that 'times are hard for the fantasy merchants'.[31] And this hypocrisy was typical of the newspapers from the very beginning of their fascination with witchcraft. At the height of the mid-century craze for spirits and Mesmerism, the *Gazette des tribunaux* had no qualms about advertising a book called *The Salon Witch* or an occult work entitled *On Spirits* in the same years as it reported on the 'superstitions' of the population.[32] These adverts themselves entered into confusing performances of authenticity: one Madame Léonora who advertised in the deeply anti-religious *La Lanterne*, for instance, warned readers against falling prey to one of her impersonators, especially in the provinces.[33] This Parisian witch, her customers were told, was far superior to the rural sorcerers.

Distancing witchcraft

If witchcraft was being peddled by the very publications that argued it did not belong in the capital of modernity, why have historians failed to notice? The answer lies in the vigorous efforts elite cultures put into distancing witchcraft from modern life. This begins with the representatives of the new spiritual

---

[27]   Owen Davies, *Witchcraft, Magic and Culture, 1736–1951* (Manchester, 1999), pp. 120–66, esp. 162.

[28]   Perrot, 'Fait divers et histoire au XIXe siècle', p. 913.

[29]   Owen Davies has pointed out the same dynamic in England and Wales. See Owen Davies, 'Cunning-Folk in England and Wales during the Eighteenth and Nineteenth Centuries', *Rural History* 8 (April 1997), 97–107 at 100.

[30]   *Le Matin*, 25 February 1902.

[31]   *Le Matin*, 9 July 1909.

[32]   *Gazette des tribunaux*, 1 July 1853, for example.

[33]   *La Lanterne*, 22 December 1894.

movements. Hippolyte Léon Denizard Rivail, known as 'Allan Kardec', the founder of the French spiritist movement, was keen to emphasise that spiritism was not to be confused with charlatanism and fortune-telling.[34] Similarly, when Jules Favre, lawyer, critic of Napoleon III, and future Republican statesman, was called to defend a group of Mesmerists from the Imperial justice system in 1852, he argued that Mesmerism was a phenomenon quite different from the

> sorcerer with his star-studded hat, long robe, decorated with Kabbalistic symbols, [and] his wand in his hand … No, this is no witch, hiding in an attic, burning mysterious herbs, and drinking mysterious liquids from a glass; this is a man with a natural talent, who is particularly lucid when he is sleepwalking, and that is all.[35]

And Favre was at pains to point out that his clients were not just anyone: they came from what he called 'honourable families'. The newspapers were clear that something could only really be called witchcraft if it was not urban, but rural; not French or Parisian, but 'gypsy', colonial, or 'exotic'; not elite, but working class; not male, but female.

It was easiest for the newspapers to identify witchcraft when it was connected to the countryside. Pestiaux, as a rural immigrant, could well believe in witches in 1841. Similarly, Joseph Fouché, Napoleon's Minister of Police, reported several rural cases in his daily bulletins to the Emperor, but the only Parisian case he mentioned concerned a rural Alsatian woman who had travelled to the capital to bring a complaint against the witches who were plaguing her at home.[36] A case from La Lanterne in 1904 dramatised this relationship acutely. A woman who had put her baby out to wet-nurse in the Sarthe *département* was shocked to discover that when the baby had fallen ill, the wet nurse had resorted to the treatments of a local 'witch'. The mother called the police to alert them to this criminal negligence, rooted in rural superstition.[37] And in cases where evidence of witchcraft in the capital itself was incontrovertible, the newspapers resorted to stock formulas, based on stereotypes of the most 'superstitious' regions of France: 'This did not take place in deepest Brittany. It happened right here in Paris, in Ménilmontant'.[38]

[34] Monroe, *Laboratories of Faith*, p. 131.
[35] *Gazette des tribunaux*, 28 August 1852, pp. 829–30.
[36] Joseph Fouché, *La police secrète du premier empire; bulletins quotidiens adressés par Fouché à l'empereur*, ed. Ernest d'Hauterive (Paris, 1908), p. 364.
[37] *La Lanterne*, 24 September 1904.
[38] *La Lanterne*, 3 March 1885.

If witchcraft could exist at the heart of the city, it had to be the product of outsiders. From the 1820s through to the twentieth century, the newspapers referred to 'Bohemian' and 'Egyptian' fortune-tellers and magicians, although it is not always clear if they meant to refer specifically to the Romani people these terms signified, or just itinerants more generally.[39] Over time, however, the newspapers focused on new categories of ethnic and racial difference.[40] In 1906, a Mauritian fortune-teller known as 'the witch of the Allée des Veuves' was prosecuted for fraud, and in 1925 *Le Journal* reported the case of a suicidal 'negro' who believed he was being pursued by the shadow of a witch.[41] The connections these stories had to French colonialism are most obvious in the case of Hégésippe Légitimus, a socialist politician from Guadaloupe who was the first black man elected to the French National Assembly since 1793. Busy contesting a rigged criminal justice system that had arrested his political allies in Guadaloupe, Légitimus had nothing but scorn for the stories of his powers of witchcraft that the French press had reproduced.[42] The commercial magicians who found themselves prosecuted for fraud chose a different set of exotic cultural references, devoid of connotations of French colonialism. They preferred, instead, more esoteric connections, claiming 'Hindu' authority, or the power of the Manitou of the Algonquin peoples of North America.[43]

It was also easier for the newspapers to identify phenomena as 'witchcraft' if they only involved women. The papers reported on cases of jealousies and conflicts between women that resulted in attempted murders, or where a victim of witchcraft had killed herself out of fear of the supernatural powers of a former friend.[44] The newspapers easily recognised love magic as witchcraft, warning the 'young girls' who read about the sentencing of magicians and the misfortunes of their clients: 'Do not consult the tarot; listen to your heart and your reason, and above all beware of necromancers!'[45] The newspapers drew on and inflated concerns about the natural credulity of women, and

[39]   *Le Courrier des tribunaux*, October 1827; *Le Journal des débats politiques et littéraires*, 9 November 1826 ; *Le Matin*, 21 December 1902 and 15 December 1911.
[40]   As in Britain. See Thomas Waters, 'Maleficent Witchcraft in Britain since 1900', *History Workshop Journal* 80 (2015), 99–122 at 108.
[41]   *Le Matin*, 18 February 1906; *Le Journal*, 4 October 1925.
[42]   *Le Journal*, 27 February 1909.
[43]   For 'Hindu' magicians, see *La Lanterne*, 13 March 1922, and the 'Fakir' in Georges Simenon, *Les trois crimes de mes amis* (Paris, 2000 [1938]), p. 43. A healer known as Germaine de Rouen claimed a connection to the 'Great Manitou', among other sources of her power. See *La Croix*, 4–5 November 1928.
[44]   *Le Matin*, 27 April and 30 August 1904 (the suicide on the rue Chabrol); *La Lanterne*, 29 August 1906.
[45]   *Gazette des tribunaux*, 9 March 1828.

their susceptibility to superstition and mysticism, which were so prevalent during the period.[46]

These gendered stereotypes were overlaid with assumptions about social class, as the purveyors of love potions were assumed to come from the 'lowest strata of society'.[47] The stereotype of the witch's victim was the domestic servant, the maid, the cook, or the slightly more independent *concierge*, or a nurse.[48] Even better if the servant was one of the many young Breton women working in Paris, as Brittany with its Celtic language and traditions was associated with mysticism and 'superstition' by contemporaries, for reasons connected both to the association of the region with the Catholic uprisings against the Revolution in the 1790s, and with assumptions about a specifically 'Celtic' predisposition to supernatural belief.[49] Was there really a spate of duped servant-girls in the 1890s and early twentieth century, as the newspaper evidence suggests? Historians might suspect that *La Lanterne*, in particular, was guilty of over-inflating the scale of the problem, and using real cases to draw attention to problems that suited its editorial agenda. The papers took self-satisfied delight in ridiculing the insecure position of the young female servant, such as 'Mademoiselle Juliette B ...' who lost her self-fashioned 'dowry', on which she counted in order to marry a young man in a similar situation' to a fraudulent magician.[50] In these stories, presented with little verifiable detail, belief in witchcraft was the folly of the precarious.

Modern witchcraft

The work that newspapers did to distance sorcery from contemporary ideas and modern self-perceptions was doomed to failure.[51] The law, for a start, did not have the terminological subtlety accurately to separate occultism,

---

[46]   On Catholicism, 'superstition' and gender see, for instance: Harris, *Lourdes: Body and Spirit in the Secular Age* (New York, 1999); Ralph Gibson, 'Why Republicans and Catholics could not Stand each other in the Nineteenth Century', in *Religion, Society and Politics in France since 1789*, ed. Frank Tallett and Nicholas Atkin (London, 1991); Caroline Ford, *Divided Houses: Religion and Gender in Modern France* (Ithaca, NY, 2005).

[47]   *Gazette des tribunaux*, 29 December 1841.

[48]   A *concierge*: *Le Journal*, 15 February 1911; a nurse: *La Lanterne*, 2 December 1910; servants: *La Lanterne*, 4 January 1896, 9 March 1897, 7 February 1898 and *Le Matin*, 12 October 1903.

[49]   See the contemporary work of Anatole le Braz, which consolidated the image of the mystical Breton peasantry: *La légende de la mort chez les Bretons armoricains* (Paris, 1902).

[50]   *La Lanterne*, 28 October 1897.

[51]   For similar points about England and Britain, see Davies, *Witchcraft, Magic and Culture*; Ronald Hutton, *The Triumph of the Moon: A History of Modern Pagan*

fortune-telling, healing, charms, mediumship, and maleficent witchcraft from one another.[52] But the occultists themselves were also fascinated by older traditions of witchcraft. Occultists like Charles Lancelin carefully followed reports of rural witchcraft cases in search of the occult truths these beliefs might reveal.[53] The crime-fiction writer Georges Simenon wrote an autobiographical account of the dark underside to middle-class urban life after the First World War, where prostitution, paedophilia, and blackmail were entwined with dabbling in hypnotism and satanic rituals. Drunk and high on cocaine, he and his friends invoked Vishnu, Christ, Dante, and Schopenhauer in a dark room decorated with skulls and occult symbols. His companions went on to become 'doctors, lawyers, judges', but their curiosity concerning witchcraft did not necessarily get captured by the newspapers, even though it was an interest that led to several deaths, including the triple murder committed by Hyacinthe Danse in 1933.[54]

It is clear from the newspaper reports that many 'fortune-tellers' were also in the business of bewitchment to order. One told a court in 1913 that the real reason her client was disgruntled was that she had refused to cast the murderous spell over her client's illegitimate child that would allow her to remarry.[55] A professional magician like the 'red witch' Talazac, also known as Moorys, not only told fortunes, but also sold bottles of 'fatal magnetic water' capable of bringing ruin on a house, or causing arguments between spouses.[56] When a journalist visited his consulting room, he noted that the 'Professor of hypnotism' had decorated his chambers with Chinese and Persian artefacts and a statue of the Buddha. At one point, he claimed to be a Hindu 'Fakir', and his rituals appealed to Allah, Jesus, and Buddhism.[57] Hyacinthe Danse, the triple murderer Georges Simenon had known in the 1920s, also claimed to be able to cast harmful spells on his enemies.[58] In their sardonic coverage of 'the witch of the rue de Meaux', the journalists at *Le Matin* wrote that she knew 'how to call up, one by one, and sometimes at the same time, the Holy Spirit, the soul of the Queen of Sheba, or Napoleon'.[59] In the same year the newspaper reported

Witchcraft, new edn (Oxford, 1995), pp. 84–111; Waters, 'Maleficent Witchcraft in Britain since 1900', pp. 116–18.

[52] See Harvey, 'Fortune-Tellers in the French Courts'.

[53] Charles Lancelin, *La sorcellerie des campagnes*, new edn (Paris, 2008 [*c.* 1920]).

[54] Simenon, *Les trois crimes*, 59. The other death was a young man who killed himself after being 'hypnotised' by the 'Fakir'.

[55] *La Lanterne*, 3 May 1913.

[56] *La Lanterne*, 21 October 1908.

[57] *La Lanterne*, 3 July 1909.

[58] Simenon, *Les trois crimes*, pp. 159–60.

[59] *Le Matin*, 30 August 1904.

on another 'witch' who both practised 'spiritual Mesmerism' and claimed to be the daughter of Christ.[60]

These syncretisms are well known in the historiography of occultism and esotericism. The specific idea of 'witchcraft' played an important part in this world of Parisian spiritual bricolage, with practitioners often laying claim to the title 'witch'. This matters, because it was exactly the kind of language that a man like Pestiaux the road-worker would use to describe supernatural misfortune. Paying attention to 'witchcraft' is a way to rediscover the popular practices that sustained elite occultism from below, without necessarily becoming completely confused with it. It is important to avoid two easy mistakes here: the first is to argue that 'rural' witchcraft simply lingered longer in the city than historians realised, while the second is to see the influence of witchcraft on these new ideas as somehow superficial.

Parisian witchcraft was very different from the model of rural French witchcraft that anthropologists comprehensively described in the later twentieth century. For a start, the existence of actual maleficent witches is doubtful in the countryside, with anthropologists and historians generally assuming that no individual consciously chooses to identify as a witch.[61] By contrast, many of the problems around Parisian witchcraft stem from the wide availability of specialists who unashamedly claimed evil powers, even advertising them in print. Another major difference concerns religion. The priest, such an important figure in rural witchcraft, is essentially nowhere to be seen in the Parisian cases, which took place in contexts far removed from the rural parishes.[62] And, unsurprisingly, Parisian witchcraft has little to do with the male peasant's identification with his land, his animals, and his family, the symbolic whole that was threatened in rural witchcraft.[63] Instead, the image of Parisian witchcraft that emerges from the newspapers is more consumerist, individualist, and racially charged, a witchcraft that suits the capital of the nineteenth century, with its tensions and crises.

It is meanwhile problematic, moreover, to regard the influence of ideas about witchcraft on the contemporary spiritual climate as superficial. It is striking just how important 'witchcraft' specifically, rather than spiritual powers

---

[60]   *Le Matin*, 13 March 1904.

[61]   Jeanne Favret-Saada, *Les Mots, la mort, les sorts* (Paris, 1985), p. 43; Devlin, *The Superstitious Mind*, p. 105.

[62]   This is a point made in almost every book on rural witchcraft. For instance, Patrick Gaboriau, *La pensée ensorcelée: la sorcellerie actuelle en Anjou et en Vendée* (Les Sables-d'Olonne, 1987), pp. 55–66.

[63]   Although the 'red witch' Talazac mentioned above did advertise his powers to bring misfortune on a 'household': Favret-Saada, *Les Mots, la mort, les sorts*, pp. 333–4; Gaboriau, *La Pensée ensorcelée*, p. 34.

more generally, was to the humble Parisians who were most often caught up in trials involving supernatural powers. As *La Lanterne* put it in an 1882 article on 'Fourteen Witches in Paris',

> Make no mistake: by 'witches' we do not simply mean Tarot readers or fortune-tellers. There are thousands of those, and as they cause no harm, the authorities leave them alone. What we are calling witches are selling potions and spells, even in 1882 in the heart of the capital of France … '[64]

Parisians frequently put pragmatic trust in specialists claiming to be sorcerers. The word *sorcier* itself, and the specific practice of casting spells, maintained a certain integrity for this popular market. When they were disappointed with witches, ordinary people took them to court. In 1827, a witch called Saulnier showed the face of the thief who had stolen a plate to two servants from the household, and promised the return of the missing crockery. When it failed to materialise they took him to court.[65] Eighty years later, a woman who used a witch to try to get her husband back took the magician to court when the spell was unsuccessful.[66] Two years later a chambermaid consulted a different magician about her illicit passion for her married neighbour. The witch told her it was reciprocal, and when this turned out not to be the case the chambermaid took her to court, and had her sentenced to two months' imprisonment.[67]

While humble individuals played an important role as mediums in the development of Mesmerism in France, the historiography of the occult more broadly marginalises the kinds of people who found themselves briefly entangled in magical crises, but who left no diaries, novels, or spiritual treatises.[68] These humble individuals, historians have recently emphasised, were surprisingly willing to take their grievances to the police and to court.[69] Since this was true for crimes involving witchcraft just as it was for other crimes, historians are afforded a very different view of a whole current of the occult revival, and with it a different view of the capital of modernity: one in which the less educated parts of the population also played a role in a culture of mystery and magic that was characteristic of Paris during the whole period. Of course, it is easier

[64]   *La Lanterne*, 28 October 1882.
[65]   *Le Spectateur*, 1827 (no greater precision is given).
[66]   *Le Matin*, 24 February 1907.
[67]   *La Lanterne*, 15 April 1909. For other cases of litigious former clients in Paris, see *Gazette des tribunaux*, 9 March 1828, 18 November 1835; *Le Journal*, 15 February 1911.
[68]   The focus, instead, is often on interesting but well-known figures. See, for example, Thomas Williams, *Eliphas Lévi: Master of Occultism* (Tuscaloosa, AL, 1975); Christopher McIntosh, *Eliphas Lévi and the French Occult Revival* (Albany, NY, 1975).
[69]   Cragin, *Murder in Parisian Streets*, pp. 169–98; Clive Emsley, 'Policing the Streets of Early Nineteenth-Century Paris', *French History* 1 (1987), 257–82.

to find evidence that practitioners of magic were absorbing ideas from the occult revival than to prove that ideas flowed both ways, between elite writers and more practical magicians and their clients. But it is at least significant how much interest a range of figures in elite occultist circles took in contemporary popular witchcraft. The lawyer Maurice Garçon (1889–1967) published several historical studies of witchcraft, as well as legal defences of magical specialists he had conducted. Discussing 'modern black magic' in 1929, he wrote that it was a mistake to see 'witchcraft' as the preserve of the countryside. He himself had received an apparently deadly serious inquiry from a man from the 'liberal professions' about how to cast a fatal spell. For Garçon, black magic was both a hereditary rural tradition and a modern, urban practice, and the two belonged together.[70] In a similar way, occultists such as Charles Lancelin (1852–1942) and Jules de Mirville (1802–72) both recorded and passed judgement on rural witchcraft cases, seeking to incorporate the practices of the countryside into their own knowledge of ritual magic.[71]

Conclusion

In Paris on 19 April 1906, Julie Grenèche went to see a woman named Mademoiselle Lheriteau, who lived on the rue Marbeau, just next to the Bois de Boulogne. The two had been friends, but had recently fallen out, and ever since Julie Grenèche had been convinced that her bad luck and recurring headaches were the result of witchcraft. Mademoiselle Lheriteau did nothing to allay her fears: 'You are under the power of my candles! You'll kick the bucket before three days are out!' So Julie Grenèche arrived at her former friend's home, shot her with a revolver, and then went to hand herself in to the police.[72] Mademoiselle Lheriteau was fortunate enough to survive the attack, but plenty of others in similar situations were not.

Witchcraft remained a life-and-death matter in Paris throughout this period, but it could also simply be a quotidian bother. Notwithstanding their editorial amazement, the newspapers would sometimes comment upon just how much of it there was around; but it is harder to get to those cases that did

---

[70]   Maurice Garçon, 'La magie noire de nos jours', *Revue Métaphysique* 4 (1929), 260–9 at 265. For the long tradition of urban witchcraft in Paris, see Ulrike Krampl, *Les secrets des faux sorciers: police, magie et escroquerie à Paris au XVIIIe siècle* (Paris, 2011).

[71]   On Mirville and his interest in the Cidéville case, see Davies, 'Witchcraft Accusations in France, 1850–1990', p. 114; Lancelin is a clear-cut case of an occultist who specifically investigated rural sorcery: Lancelin, *La sorcellerie des campagnes*.

[72]   *Le Matin*, 27 April 1906

not result in dramatic police interventions.[73] *La Lanterne* reported a rare case in 1877, of a couple of greengrocers convinced their cupboard was bewitched, but for the most part these everyday cases passed virtually unnoticed. The dramatic criminal cases that made it to court constitute a poor guide to what most Parisians must have thought about sorcery. The willingness of clients to take magicians to court confirms that possible abstract belief was often paired with pragmatic scepticism. Yet the continuing incidents of violence against suspected witches, and the continuing importance of the term 'witch' itself are reminders that sorcery did mean something specific to Parisians during this period.

What can this teach historians about Paris in the long nineteenth century? Thomas Laqueur has criticised historians of the occult for over-inflating the influence of esoteric beliefs on modernist science, arguing that 'just being there' does not count.[74] I am not trying to claim that traditions of witchcraft influenced contemporary intellectual culture in as direct a way as, according to Mark Morrison, the alchemical revival paved the way for modern atomic science.[75] But there remains something to be said about how Paris understood itself through newspaper stories of modern witchcraft, and this amounts to more than 'just being there'.

For a start, the stories fit into an older tradition of the barbarism at the heart of the modern city: the existence of tribes of savages more like the characters from James Fenimore Cooper's novels than the citizens of a modern republic.[76] The flippant tone of some newspaper articles might suggest that fear of this primitive culture within the metropolis was receding, but the ease with which newspapers found examples gave the lie to their assumption that magic was disappearing. For many people, witchcraft remained a pragmatic solution, and if it failed then Parisians could turn to other powers, such as the police or courts, or take matters into their own hands. In this, Paris was no different from many other French and European cities of the time: Lille, Lyon, and Bordeaux all acted in a similar way as hubs for popular magic during this period.[77] Witchcraft never went away. And it does not capture the significance of this endurance to explain it through the influence of other forces, from Mesmerism at the mid-century, through spiritism and the 'flight from reason',

---

[73]   See, for instance, *Le Courrier des tribunaux*, March 1828.

[74]   Laqueur, 'Why the Margins Matter'.

[75]   Mark Morrisson, *Modern Alchemy: Occultism and the Emergence of Atomic Theory* (New York, 2007).

[76]   Chevalier, *Labouring Classes and Dangerous Classes*, pp. 39–40.

[77]   Jules Bois told a journalist in 1898 that Lyon, above all, was the hub of modern witchcraft. See *La Justice*, 15 April 1898.

to the effects of the First World War, which Georges Simenon believed gave his generation a taste for mystery.[78] While it could become bound up with these other movements and cultural moments, believers and practitioners of witchcraft also asserted its independence.

How was this tradition changing? In a book dealing with eighteenth-century 'false witches', Ulrike Krampl has argued that the key transition for popular magical practices was from the religious sphere to the economic. Where witchcraft was once subversive because of its relationship to Catholic beliefs, it was increasingly treated as economically problematic in a consumer society. Along with this came a shift in thinking about the 'witch' which came close to 'professionalising' magic.[79] This transition was complete by the twentieth century, with one Catholic newspaper sourly noting that in 1911 there were 34,607 'professional' magicians, fortune-tellers, and 'witches' in Paris.[80] Krampl also suggests three further directions for research into what happened to magic in the nineteenth century: the role of visual materials in substantiating and undermining belief, the role of an increasingly theatrical public science, and the importance of exchanges between popular fiction and magical practices.[81] To this could be added another three ways on which not only elite ideas about witches, but popular magical practices themselves were changing: the increasing exoticisation and racialisation of witchcraft, the psychologisation of sorcery and *envoûtement*, and new syncretisms that blended occult, Mesmerist, or spiritualist ideas with traditional witchcraft practices. Where the historiography of France's rural witch beliefs has tended to emphasise their conservatism and irrationality, the witchcraft of the capital was modern, practical, individualist, and consumerist, and touched upon problems of race that were alien to the world of the rural witches.[82] Perhaps Pestiaux was right after all: at least he knew where he was in the countryside.

---

[78]   Simenon, *Les trois crimes*, p. 113.
[79]   Krampl, *Les Secrets des faux sorciers*, pp. 71, 93, 127–56, 157–80.
[80]   *La Semaine religieuse du Diocèse de Lyon*, 26 May 1911, p. 497.
[81]   Krampl, *Les Secrets des faux sorciers*, p. 246.
[82]   Especially Devlin, *The Superstitious Mind*, pp. 100–19.

Bibliography

Printed primary sources

Fouché, Joseph, *La police secrète du premier empire; bulletins quotidiens adressés par Fouché à l'empereur*, ed. Ernest d'Hauterive (Paris, 1908)

Garçon, Maurice, 'La magie noire de nos jours', *Revue Métaphysique* 4 (1929), 260–9

Lancelin, Charles, *La sorcellerie des campagnes*, new edn (Paris, 2008 [*c.* 1920])

Le Braz, Anatole, *La légende de la mort chez les Bretons armoricains* (Paris, 1902)

Simenon, Georges, *Les trois crimes de mes amis* (Paris, 2000 [1938])

Newspapers

La Croix (Paris, 1880–1968)

Le Courrier des tribunaux (Paris, 1827–30)

Gazette des tribunaux: journal de jurisprudence et des débats judiciaires (Paris, 1825–1955)

Le Journal des débats politiques et littéraires (Paris, 1814–1944)

La Justice (Paris, 1880–1976)

La Lanterne: Journal politique quotidien (Paris, 1877–1938)

Le Matin (Paris, 1884–1944)

Le Petit Journal (Paris, 1863–1944)

La Semaine religieuse du Diocèse de Lyon (Lyon, 1893–1967)

Le Spectateur (Paris, 1884–)

Secondary sources

Carpenter, Scott, *Aesthetics of Fraudulence in Nineteenth-Century France: Frauds, Hoaxes and Counterfeits* (Farnham, 2009)

Chevalier, Louis, *Labouring Classes and Dangerous Classes in Paris during the First Half of the Nineteenth Century* (London, 1973)

Cragin, Thomas, *Murder in Parisian Streets: Manufacturing Crime and Justice in the Popular Press, 1830–1900* (Lewisburg, PA, 2006)

Darnton, Robert, *Mesmerism and the End of the Enlightenment in France* (Cambridge, MA, 1968)

Davies, Owen, 'Cunning-Folk in England and Wales during the Eighteenth and Nineteenth Centuries', *Rural History* 8 (April 1997), 91–107

——, *Witchcraft, Magic and Culture, 1736-1951* (Manchester, 1999)

——, 'Witchcraft Accusations in France, 1850–1990', in *Witchcraft Continued: Popular Magic in Modern Europe*, ed. Willem de Blécourt and Owen Davies (Manchester, 2004), pp. 107–32

Devlin, Judith, *The Superstitious Mind: French Peasants and the Supernatural in the Nineteenth Century* (New Haven, CT, 1987)

Douglas, Mary, 'Witch Beliefs in Central Africa', *Africa: Journal of the International African Institute* 37 (1967), 72–80

Emsley, Clive, 'Policing the Streets of Early Nineteenth-Century Paris', *French History* 1 (1987), 257–82

——, *Crime, Police, and Penal Policy: European Experiences, 1750–1940* (Oxford, 2013)

Evans-Pritchard, E. E., *Witchcraft, Oracles and Magic among the Azande*, new edn (Oxford, 1976)

Favret-Saada, Jeanne, *Les Mots, la mort, les sorts* (Paris, 1985)

Ford, Caroline, *Divided Houses: Religion and Gender in Modern France* (Ithaca, NY, 2005)

Gaboriau, Patrick, *La pensée ensorcelée: la sorcellerie actuelle en Anjou et en Vendée* (Les Sables-d'Olonne, 1987)

Gibson, Ralph, 'Why Republicans and Catholics could not Stand Each Other in the Nineteenth Century', in *Religion, Society and Politics in France Since 1789*, ed. Frank Tallett and Nicholas Atkin (London, 1991), pp. 107–20

Gramfort, Véronique, 'Les Crimes de Panti: quand Troppmann défrayait la chronique', *Romantisme* 27 (1997), 17–30

Harris, Ruth, *Murders and Madness: Medicine, Law, and Society in the Fin de Siècle* (Oxford, 1989)

——, 'Possession on the Borders: The "Mal de Morzine" in Nineteenth-Century France', *The Journal of Modern History* 69 (September 1997), 451–78

——, *Lourdes: Body and Spirit in the Secular Age* (New York, 1999)

Harvey, David Allen, 'Fortune-Tellers in the French Courts: Antidivination Prosecutions in France in the Nineteenth and Twentieth Centuries', *French Historical Studies* 28 (2005), 131–57

Hutton, Ronald, *The Triumph of the Moon: A History of Modern Pagan Witchcraft*, new edn (Oxford, 1995)

——, 'Anthropological and Historical Approaches to Witchcraft: Potential for a New Collaboration?', *The Historical Journal* 47 (June 2004), 421–3

Krampl, Ulrike, *Les secrets des faux sorciers: police, magie et escroquerie à Paris au XVIIIᵉ siècle* (Paris, 2011)

Laqueur, Thomas, 'Why the Margins Matter: Occultism and the Making of Modernity', *Modern Intellectual History* 3 (April 2006), 111–35

McIntosh, Christopher, *Eliphas Lévi and the French Occult Revival* (Albany, NY, 1975)

Monroe, John Warne, *Laboratories of Faith: Mesmerism, Spiritism, and Occultism in Modern France* (Ithaca, NY, 2008)

Morrisson, Mark, *Modern Alchemy: Occultism and the Emergence of Atomic Theory* (New York, 2007)

Owen, Alex, *The Place of Enchantment: British Occultism and the Culture of the Modern* (Chicago, 2004)

Partridge, Christopher (ed.), *The Occult World* (London, 2015)

Perrot, Michelle, 'Fait divers et histoire au XIXᵉ siècle', *Annales. Histoire, Sciences Sociales* 38 (1983), 911–19

Prendergast, Christopher, *Paris and the Nineteenth Century* (Oxford, 1992)

Waters, Thomas, 'Maleficent Witchcraft in Britain since 1900', *History Workshop Journal* 80 (2015), 99–122

Weber, Eugen, *Peasants into Frenchmen: The Modernization of Rural France, 1870–1914* (Stanford, CA, 1976)

Williams, Thomas, *Eliphas Lévi: Master of Occultism* (Tuscaloosa, AL, 1975)

2

Fatal Seductions, False Promises and Urban Enchantments: The *Mamlambo*, the Blesser and the Consumer in South African Cities

FELICITY WOOD

Two denizens of contemporary South African cities, one supernatural and the other human, form the focus of this chapter. The points of comparison between two present-day workers of magic, the *mamlambo* and the so-called blesser, are explored.[1] The mamlambo is a South African wealth-giving spirit, and the blesser tends to be a wealthy or relatively prosperous man who bestows money and material 'blessings' on young women, termed 'blessees', usually in exchange for sex. Both these figures are associated with the affluent aspects of city life. They draw on the deceptive enchantments of consumerism and the counterfeit glamour of prestigious commodities to bedazzle and manipulate those they encounter. Two types of magic are described: supernatural forms of enchantment and the metaphorically magical, when worldly possessions, such as money and prestigious commodities, may seem imbued with an almost otherworldly allure. Symbolically speaking, magic forms part of consumer capitalism, as this chapter will show.

---

[1] Italics are used for the first citation of terms from other languages. Thereafter, the words are not italicised. Many of these terms have become part of South African English and there are no concise, appropriate English equivalents for them.

Misty L. Bastian comments on the development of new forms of urban 'modern magic' in diverse parts of Africa, describing how longstanding occult presences are adapted or reinvented, 'the better to snare their old prey, human beings'.[2] The city mamlambo is one example of this tendency and, symbolically, so is the blesser. Liaisons with these figures are fuelled by the illusions, dreams and fantasies fostered by consumer capitalism and characterised by the forms of enslavement and deprivation it brings about. These toxic enchantments of the consumerist urban milieu are all-pervasive, infecting rural areas, villages and small towns.

South Africa is particularly vulnerable to temptations and deceptions of this kind. The country is riven by an unequal distribution of wealth, with dramatic distinctions between the affluent and the economically deprived. Unemployment is currently estimated to be at approximately 40 per cent.[3] Despite the country's economic predicaments, and the fact that the majority of its people are economically embattled, South African society is steeped in consumerism. Ever-expanding shopping malls tend to form one of the principal features of the country's urban landscapes: South Africa has the sixth highest number of shopping malls in the world.[4] There are various reason for this consumerist bent. For instance, South Africa is often perceived as a half-way house between rich nations and the developing world. There is widespread poverty, yet also much wealth, as the proliferation of shopping malls bears witness. These malls tend to be viewed as relatively safe investments (in contrast to potentially precarious options, such as industries and mining).[5] Their ever-increasing presence embodies and entrenches the Western-style consumerism that pervades South Africa. This predilection for Western consumer capitalist models is fostered by the country's Western-oriented neoliberal economic policies.

---

[2]   Misty L. Bastian, 'Vulture Men, Campus Cultists and Teenaged Witches: Modern Magics in Nigerian Popular Media' in *Magical Interpretations, Material Realities: Modernity, Witchcraft and the Occult in Postcolonial Africa*, ed. Henrietta Moore and Todd Sanders (London, 2001), pp. 75–6.

[3]   See Statistics South Africa, 2017, 'Poverty Trends in South Africa: an Examination of Absolute Poverty between 2006 and 2015', http://www.statssa.gov.za/?p=10341 (accessed 12 June 2019); 'Extreme Inequality in South Africa is Constraining Growth and Investment', https://www.engineeringnews.co.za/article/extreme-inequality-is-constraining-south-african-investment-and-growth-2018-04-10 (accessed 12 June 2019).

[4]   'SA has 6th Most Shopping Centres in the World and Building More', https://www.fin24.com/Companies/Retail/sa-has-6th-most-shopping-centres-in-the-world-and-building-more-20171224 (accessed 12 June 2019).

[5]   In this section and elsewhere, many of the points about South African economic dynamics were suggested in conversations with Mathew Blatchford.

The constantly expanding culture of consumerism fuels the commodity fetishism that has also become a distinctive feature of South African society. The preoccupation with high-priced items and luxury brands stems in part from the significance ascribed to prestigious commodities as objects bestowing a sense of self-worth and as symbols of status and achievement.[6] After its political transition in 1994, South Africa began to be viewed as a land of possibilities, where socio-political transformation would be linked to economic upliftment. However, such perceptions proved illusory. Consequently, many South Africans have resorted to consumerism, viewing it as a means of symbolic empowerment. The country's urban environments have been shaped by these factors, and so have perceptions of magic, whether supernatural or symbolic. The mamlambo and the blesser illuminate one another, and also cast light upon the seductive and destructive aspects of consumerism and commodity fetishism that have become driving forces in South Africa, as in many other societies, today.

Methods

The mamlambo originated among the Xhosa-speaking peoples in the Eastern Cape province in South Africa.[7] This chapter draws especially on oral accounts of mamlambos in Eastern Cape cities and towns, including East London and Mdantsane, an adjacent urban area, Queenstown, Alice (the university town where I work) and towns in the Transkei region of the Eastern Cape, one of the most poverty-stricken parts of the country. The narrators of the stories concerning the mamlambo were a diverse grouping, including students, elderly people, working-class individuals, urban professionals and the unemployed. The Eastern Cape's economy is primarily agricultural and many inhabitants of this province come from economically deprived backgrounds. As in other parts of South Africa, urban areas tend to be characterised by contrasts between pockets of affluence and ever-expanding zones inhabited by the financially desperate and the destitute. Consequently, even if they do not believe in the mamlambo, oral narratives concerning this being and the swift, seemingly effortless access to wealth it proffers tend to fascinate many in the province.

---

6 See for example Ton Otto, 'Work, Wealth and Knowledge: Enigmas of Cargoist Identifications', in *Cargo, Cult and Culture Critique,* ed. Holger Jebens (Honolulu, 2004), pp. 209–26 at 210–11.

7 Most of the information concerning the mamlambo derives from a series of interviews conducted in the Eastern Cape by Wendy Muswaka and Abbey Alao between 2008 and 2010; and in the Eastern Cape, KwaZulu-Natal and Lesotho by Felicity Wood, Sylvia Tloti and Michael Lewis between 1997 and 2008.

Interviews concerning the blesser, conducted with female students at the University of Fort Hare, Alice, are also discussed.[8] Such young women often tend to be cash-strapped, generally on account of their families' financially straitened circumstances. Yet as students they are subjected to intense pressure from their peers, the society around them and social media to accumulate high-status material possessions, thus conforming to the consumerist nature of their social milieu. Some respondents were blessees, while others knew blessees, or indicated that they would like to be 'blessed'.

Although Alice and various Transkei towns may seem far removed from major urban centres, this tends to render many of those who inhabit them, particularly young people, all the more susceptible to that which is associated with the allure of city life, including the money and commodities proffered by the mamlambo and the blesser. Urban environments may also seem to lend themselves to the extravagant indulgence in the luxuries of life that the blesser and the mamlambo may provide. Indeed, many of the liaisons with blessers mentioned in this chapter took place in East London, the city closest to Alice.

Occult economies

Alliances with the mamlambo and the blesser can be viewed as facets of what Jean and John Comaroff describe as 'occult economies': strange, shadowy practices and enterprises believed to generate money by magical (or metaphorically magical) means. Many occult economies are now thriving in Africa and the West, fuelled by the hope that affluence might be attainable through the agency of the supernatural or by exceptional, often mysterious methods. These wealth-making enchantments include the ownership of zombies, involvement in dubious ventures that promise to generate money as if by magic (such as pyramid schemes), chain letters, national lotteries and the *muti* trade in human body parts. As the Comaroffs indicate, occult economies and the 'almost preternatural profits' they offer appeal to numerous people, whether prosperous or economically deprived.[9] Making specific reference to the Cameroon, Peter Geschiere describes this form of money-making magic as 'the new witchcraft of wealth', linking it to the presence of Westerners on

---

[8]   Much of the discussion concerning the blesser draws on Tandiwe Sogoni's research findings. Her interviews with University of Fort Hare students in 2017 have proved especially significant. Sei Tiffany Mudariki also carried out important research into the blesser in 2017, providing ideas and insights.

[9]   Jean Comaroff and John L. Comaroff, 'Occult Economies and the Violence of Abstraction: Notes from the South African Postcolony', *American Ethnologist* 26 (1999), 279–303 at 284, 286, 279–81.

the African continent and the importation of luxury goods.[10] More broadly, the growth of occult economies in both Africa and the West stems from the expansion of consumer capitalism, the desires it has aroused and the disparities it has fostered.

This interconnectedness of sorcery and consumerism is sometimes manifested in the light-skinned appearance of the mamlambo and the costly clothes and accessories it favours. The blesser, similarly, is closely associated with money, an extravagant lifestyle and opulent possessions. The term 'blesser', with its mystical quality, is suggestive of the way in which this individual may seem a near-magical source of largesse, bestowing what is deeply desired. George Ritzer describes the aura of enchantment surrounding consumerism.[11] In a sense this is suggestive of how, in a consumer capitalist context, money and expensive commodities may seem to possess a near-magical potency, as might those who bestow them. First, let us consider the mamlambo.

The mamlambo

The mamlambo's full name derives from the Xhosa *u-Ma-Mlambo*, 'the mother of the river'. Many supernatural beings are believed to reside in water, and the word *mamlambo* is often used as a generic term for various water spirits. However the wealth-giving mamlambo is a relatively new supernatural presence, generated by socio-economic inequalities, Western economic pressures and the lure of consumerism. Belief in this being spread through southern Africa as a result of mass migrations from rural to urban areas. Unable to sustain themselves through traditional, communal means, people sought work in cities and towns, becoming drawn into the capitalist cash economy.[12]

An individual purchases medicine for *ukuthwala*, the Xhosa term for a dangerous, powerful procedure for long-term wealth, widely believed to involve the ownership of a wealth-giving spirit, from an occult practitioner. Ukuthwala is a mysterious process which may sometimes involve ritual ordeals and immersion in water, after which the mamlambo is said to manifest itself,

---

[10] Peter Geschiere, *The Modernity of Witchcraft: Politics and the Occult in Postcolonial Africa* (Charlottesville, VA, 1997), pp. 158, 119.

[11] George Ritzer, *Enchanting a Disenchanted World: Revolutionising the Means of Consumption* (London and New Delhi, 1999), p. x.

[12] See Felicity Wood, 'Wealth-Giving Mermaid Women and the Malign Magic of the Market: Contemporary Oral Accounts of the South African *Mamlambo*', in *Vernacular Worlds, Cosmopolitan Imagination*, ed. Stephanos Stephanides and Stavros Karayanni (Amsterdam, 2014), pp. 59–85 at 64–5; Isak Niehaus, *Witchcraft, Power and Politics: Exploring the Occult in the South African Lowveld* (Cape Town, 2001), pp. 45, 56, 61.

bestowing wealth on its owner.[13] The mamlambo is viewed as a malevolent spirit and ukuthwala is regarded as a form of sorcery, resembling a Faustian pact. It is said that sorrow, suffering and death await those who undergo ukuthwala, and also their loved ones. Even those who spend the money that appears after a chance encounter with a mamlambo are destined for disaster.

The mamlambo is a shape-shifter, although it is often said to adopt the form of a snake or an alluring woman or a handsome man. Originally, mamlambos were depicted as female. Traditionally men were the breadwinners, and they also tended to be the narrators of stories featuring this being. However, accounts of male mamlambos are increasing, indicative of socio-economic changes and shifting gender dynamics. For instance, many women occupy leadership positions in present-day South African society, and numerous women are the principal family breadwinners.[14]

It is rumoured that a mamlambo's owner is drawn into a sexual relationship with the being. Mamlambos are also said to lure those they meet into sexual encounters, after which money materialises. For instance, it is sometimes said that someone who has had sex with a mamlambo may awake to find heaps of banknotes strewn around them, or the money in their bank account may increase dramatically.[15] This is characteristic of certain manifestations of the occult in Africa, in which sexual and supernatural potency are interconnected, lending force to each other. For example, various South African witchcraft familiars, such as the dwarf-like *tokoloshe*, are characterised by their licentious behaviour.[16] In both its male and female forms, the mamlambo is an enticing, predatory figure, as is evident in the following account from the Alice area:

> During weekends, villagers come together. I am told that, sometime in 2006, there was a handsome man who would come, driving his posh car, and supply everyone with beer. Some even wondered where such a young man could be getting his money from, but no one ever got the courage to question him. It was said that each time he would come, he would take a young lady with him. It is said that the girls that he went with were never seen in the village.[17]

---

[13] For more information on the ukuthwala procedure, see Felicity Wood with Michael Lewis, *The Extraordinary Khotso: Millionaire Medicine Man of Lusikisiki* (Johannesburg, 2007), pp. 103–130.

[14] Wood, 'Wealth-Giving Mermaid Women', p. 63.

[15] See, for example, Wendy Muswaka, interview with Thembisa Dingane (2009), and interview with Malemane Liphoto (2009).

[16] Niehaus, *Witchcraft, Power and Politics*, p. 46.

[17] Muswaka, interview with Xolani Sithole (2009).

In small towns and villages, as the above account suggests, the mamlambo may often seem like a wealthy emissary from a city, surrounded as it is by commodities and status symbols that may seem emblematic of urban affluence. Just as many of those who disseminate stories of the mamlambo have moved to the cities, the mamlambo has made itself at home in urban environments, particularly on account of its association with wealth. An inhabitant of the Queenstown area remarked, 'My mother told me that mamlambos are found in the city where there is a fast lifestyle and people do not question who they date as long as they get money, since that is all that they are after.'[18]

There are numerous accounts of city mamlambos, generally in places where money is spent: it is rumoured that mamlambos have been sighted in shopping malls in East London and other towns, and in bars, nightclubs and even sex shops. For instance, someone described how a young man was seduced by a mamlambo in Adult World, East London.[19] A mamlambo was also said to frequent a bar in Alice.[20] Another person described how a bartender at a night club in Mdantsane noticed a beautiful woman who often came to the club and lured many men to her. She seduced him, and his penis became deformed and he discovered that she was a mamlambo. He eventually died.[21] A respondent from Soweto relates a similar story.[22] Furthermore, Seán Morrow and Nwabisa Vokwana were told that a wealthy businessman in Mdantsane kept a serpentine mamlambo in his swimming pool;[23] and it is worth noting that the previous South African president Jacob Zuma was rumoured to keep a mamlambo in his swimming pool in his luxury home in Nkandla. The city mamlambo has taken hold of the popular imagination to such an extent that it featured in a film entitled *Mamlambo*.[24] The movie, set in a modern-day South African city, features a mamlambo-type figure, a mysteriously enchanting young woman periodically alluded to as a mamlambo, who eventually brings about the death of the youth who becomes besotted with her.

Originally, mamlambos were believed to provide money and ensure that their owners' businesses or farming operations prospered. However, since the mass migrations to urban areas, mamlambos have also become increasingly

---

[18] Muswaka, interview with Thandile Nxaba (2010).
[19] See Muswaka, interview with Luxolo Lunxaba (2009); Wood, 'Wealth-Giving Mermaid Women', p. 68.
[20] Muswaka, interview with Sphamla Mhlobe (2010).
[21] Muswaka, interview with Nuvyo Maxanda (2009).
[22] Muswaka, interview with Noma (2009).
[23] Seán Morrow and Nwabisa Vokwana, ' "Oh Hurry to the River": The Meaning of *uMamlambo* Models in the Tyumie Valley, Eastern Cape', *Kronos* 30 (2004), 184–99 at 193.
[24] *Mamlambo*, directed by Palesa ka Letlaka Nkosi and Jeremy Nathan (1997).

closely associated with the trappings of Western consumerism, and ownership of a mamlambo often seems to have become bound up with acquiring prestigious material possessions. 'You know what, not everyone you see driving these latest posh cars have gained them through the fruits of their own labour', an interviewee from the East London area remarked.[25]

Present-day mamlambos like to adorn themselves in fashionable, costly clothes and tend to favour high-status commodities to draw attention to themselves and show off the wealth that they can provide.[26] Male mamlambos drive high-priced cars and lure women to them with money and gifts. A male mamlambo seen near Alice, for instance, was described as 'a very handsome young man who dressed in nice Western formal clothing and drove a posh car'.[27] Another person described how a male mamlambo 'driving an expensive car and wearing a very expensive outfit' frequented the area where she lived.[28] In a further account, a male mamlambo was said to have been glimpsed in Queenstown driving a Mahindra.[29] Nowadays, Alice mamlambos might possess an Apple iPhone – a much sought-after item in the Fort Hare student community. As this suggests, consumer capitalism has become so far-reaching, pervasive and influential that it has infiltrated the sphere of the occult, acquiring a mystical and magical as well as a monetary force.[30]

The blesser

Student researcher Abbey Alao observes, 'Male mamlambos look for greedy and dissatisfied females who are searching for wealthy men who would shower gifts and money on them.'[31] The blesser often adopts similar techniques. In 2015, a new form of wealth-giving magic seemed to be coming to the fore. Women, some of them unemployed or very young, began posting pictures

[25]   Muswaka, interview with Diko Manxeba (2009).
[26]   Abbey Alao, interview with Thandokazi Dyup (2009).
[27]   Muswaka, interview with anonymous respondent (2009).
[28]   Alao, interview with Nokuyulo Filtane (2008).
[29]   Muswaka, interview with anonymous respondent (2010).
[30]   Felicity Wood, 'Spirits in the Marketplace: The Market as a Site of the Occult in the South and West African Supernatural and Contemporary Capitalist Cosmologies', *Folklore* 126 (2015), 283–300 at 286, and *Universities and the Occult Rituals of the Corporate World: Higher Education and Metaphorical Parallels with Myth and Magic* (London, 2018), p. 30. As Derrida, in *Specters of Marx* (New York, 1994), and others note, Marx discussed the occult aspects of capitalism in the earlier part of the twentieth century in *Grundrisse* (Harmondsworth, 1973), *Capital* (Harmondsworth, 1976) and other works. Nowadays however, the links between the occult and aspects of capitalism have become more overt, in both Africa and the West.
[31]   Abbey Alao, research notes (2009).

of themselves on social media platforms such as Facebook, Twitter and Instagram, lounging on tropical beaches or adorned in designer outfits, with costly accessories from prestigious brands like Gucci, Versace and Chanel.[32] Most of them had expensive weaves – long dark straight tresses, often Asian – woven into their own hair. Transformed into embodiments of Western-style affluence, flaunting the glamorous lifestyle and an extravagant indulgence in luxury items that had been bestowed upon them by seemingly magical means, they aroused widespread fascination and envy. They posted messages claiming they had been 'blessed', and their blessers tended to be well-off, generally older men. Like the mamlambo, the blesser can be either male or female, and heterosexual or gay. However, since blessers often tend to be older men who target younger women, the male pronoun is used here to denote the blesser, and the female pronoun is used for the blessee.

There are various levels of blesser. A Level 1 blesser, for instance, might buy a blessee airtime, data and chocolates and take her out for inexpensive meals. A Level 2 blesser might buy a blessee an expensive weave and give her handbags, shoes and accessories from brands such as Prada, Gucci and Louis Vuitton. A Level 3 blesser might take a blessee on trips to local cities, buy her an iPhone and give her an allowance; while a Level 4 blesser might pay a blessee's rent and take her to beach resorts in Thailand or the Caribbean, for example, or to cities like London, New York, Miami and Dubai. A Level 5 blesser might provide a car, a house or an apartment (often remaining in his name), along with a lavish allowance.[33] Claire, a University of Fort Hare student, remarked, 'So basically as a blessee, you're selling your body for Gucci and Mac.'[34]

Initially it may not always be possible to tell the city mamlambo and the blesser apart, yet distinctions between them eventually emerge. Strange and supernatural phenomena are said to characterise encounters with the mamlambo. For example, it may change its form, and piles of money may suddenly appear. Its otherworldly nature is also evident in its inexplicable, irresistible allure. In contrast, many blessers may be physically unappealing (they may be ageing, overweight or impotent, for instance). Thus, they often tend to be hemmed in by physical limitations which the mamlambo appears to transcend.

---

[32] See, for example, Sei Tiffany Mudariki, research notes (2017).

[33] Tandiwe Sogoni, Group Interviews 1 and 2 (2017); Ntombizodwa Makhoba, 1 June 2016, 'Blessee: "I will never, ever date a man who is broke"', https://city-press.news24.com/Trending/blessee-i-will-never-ever-date-a-man-who-is-broke-20160601 (accessed 12 June 2019).

[34] Sogoni, Group Interview 3 (2017). Respondent's real name not used. In all the interviews concerning the blesser, the respondents' real names have been changed or withheld.

The blesser is especially a city presence, often frequenting affluent urban areas. Blessers tend to favour exclusive bars, clubs, restaurants and fashionable shops where they can flaunt their money and material possessions and indulge in displays of conspicuous consumption. 'In the city there are a lot more opportunities for blessers to show off what they can offer materially', student researcher Tandiwe Sogoni observes.[35] High-level blessers offer blessees the opportunity to indulge in the illusion that they are part of the urban elite. They provide access to those aspects of city life enjoyed by the wealthy and the privileged, including dinners at upmarket restaurants and weekends in fashionable hotels and resorts. Blessers offer blessees many shopping opportunities, often in large cities where high-status commodities are readily available. Blessees may be taken to major South African shopping malls, such as the Mall of Africa in Johannesburg and Canal Walk in Cape Town. Internationally, Dubai – a city perceived as characterised by its array of costly emporia – is a favoured destination.[36] As Tamara, a Fort Hare student maintained, 'Our parents force us to be content with peanuts while these blessers teach us to shoot for the stars; they show us that we deserve the highlife.'[37]

In South Africa, high-level blessers tend to frequent the largest, most expensive cities such as Cape Town and Johannesburg, periodically travelling to prominent international destinations such as Paris, London and New York, where they often visit exclusive bars and clubs, and shop for luxury items. East London blessers favour high-priced bars, restaurants and clubs, one of which was described as a place 'where the big boys play because the prices there are over the moon'.[38] The word 'blesser' has spiritual associations, suggestive of the extent to which consumerism has become a contemporary religion of a kind. For instance, Ritzer describes how many places in consumer capitalist societies, from shopping malls and restaurants to universities and national parks, have become 'cathedrals of consumption': sites of enchantment and contemporary places of worship.[39]

Associated as they are with urban affluence, with the capacity to bestow money and material possessions on their consorts by magic or by seemingly magical means, the blesser and the mamlambo are metaphorically akin. In various respects, these habitués of contemporary South African cities embody the deceptive enchantments of consumer capitalism and the perils awaiting

[35] Tandiwe Sogoni, research notes (2017).
[36] See Mudariki, research notes; Sogoni, research notes.
[37] Sogoni, Group Interview 5 (2017).
[38] Sogoni, Group Interview 2 (2017).
[39] Ritzer, *Enchanting a Disenchanted World*, pp. ix–x.

those who fall prey to them. The points of comparison between the blesser and the mamlambo illuminate this.

Need, greed and temptation

As a result of dramatic socio-economic changes, an ever-widening gap between rich and poor and the struggle for economic survival in rapidly expanding urban areas, the mamlambo has been increasingly turned to, as has the blesser. However, many different people, prosperous and economically embattled alike, are fascinated by the idea that money may be swiftly and effortlessly generated by mysterious, near-magical means. The *inyanga* (medicine man) Khotso Sethuntsa (1898–1972), a near-legendary seller of ukuthwala in South Africa, became exceptionally wealthy for this reason. People flocked to Khotso, as he was commonly known, viewing him as an avenue to affluence. 'The person who really wants wealth, he will contact Khotso', it was remarked.[40] The tantalising stories spread that riches lay within the grasp of any ordinary individual if they underwent ukuthwala.

Occult economies, Edmund L. Andrews observes, arouse widespread fascination, since they possess 'the magical allure of making money from nothing', offering a seemingly effortless short-cut to wealth.[41] 'People who need instant money look for blessers', Felicia Mbetha, a Fort Hare student, contended.[42] Comparably, stories concerning the mamlambo often tend to focus on the extent to which this being can suddenly transform poverty to prosperity, as is evident in the following tale:

> Long back, around the 90s, in a town known as Burgersdorp in the Eastern Cape, there was a man who was said to have transformed from rags to riches within a short space of time. This man, to begin with, survived through begging for food handouts from people. What surprised many people was that, more often than not, he was seen in a car with a beautiful woman. …
> It is said that within a short space of time, the man was in possession of a bottle store, supermarket, cars and even a farm.[43]

Many stories depicting contemporary owners of mamlambos describe how they indulge their cravings for extravagant, opulent material possessions, irrespective of other, more fundamental economic needs. For instance, a Zimbabwean man described how someone he knew went to South Africa in 2005

---

[40] Wood with Lewis, *Khotso*, p.108.
[41] Cited in Comaroffs, 'Occult Economies', p. 281.
[42] Sogoni, interview with Felicia Mbetha (2017).
[43] Muswaka, interview with Xolani Mawu (2009).

and returned to Harare 'driving the latest BMW. I was even surprised to see this man driving this posh car since I knew him to be a nobody who had depended on handouts.'[44]

Many become blessees out of financial need. Numerous messages posted on Blesserfinder and similar websites offering blessers and blessees the opportunity to make contact with one another seem to exude desperation, envisaging the blesser as a source of near-miraculous financial salvation. One person writes, 'i thought ill be able to cope but i cant … pls help me out any blesser willing to bless me everymonth … willing to do what pleases him'.[45] However, greed, not need, seems to be the predominant reason why individuals become blessees. The 'short-cuts to the good life' provided by the blesser tend to be more important than financial quick-fixes.[46] For instance, Faith, a student blessee, insisted, 'I also need that blesser money. We need that life they are giving us.'[47] A student who knew many blessees remarked that those who seek out blessers are motivated by a yearning for 'that luxury lifestyle. Those things are not things you need, but things you desire.'[48] Similarly, Felicia Mbetha maintained that blessees were attracted by 'the luxury benefits', such as designer clothes and accessories and vacations in fashionable hotels and resorts. A blesser, for instance, would be more likely to offer a R60,000 [rand] trip to Mauritius than subsidise a blessee's university fees.[49]

The mamlambo is manipulative, luring humans to it by flaunting Western-style status symbols and showering money on those it encounters. As Abbey Alao remarks,

> The mamlambo knows that the only way to attract victims is to lure them with expensive objects such as wealth, expensive attire and accessories. Most victims get carried away by these worldly possessions that are appealing to their eyes. The mamlambo's victims are usually intrigued by what they see and are thirsty to accumulate wealth. In some cases, some of the victims are from poverty-stricken homes and hopeless, while others are just people who are carried away by beauty at first sight.[50]

[44] Muswaka, interview with Charlemagne Matango (2009).
[45] Blesserfinder: home page: www.blesserfinder.com, https://web.facebook.com/Blesserfind/ (accessed 29 June 2017).
[46] Anneke Scheepers, 'Blesser–Blessee Relationships: The New Sugar Daddies or a Short Cut to the Good Life?', https://www.w24.co.za/Wellness/Mind/blesser-blessee-relationships-the-new-sugar-daddies-or-a-short-cut-to-the-good-life-20160509 (accessed 9 May 2016).
[47] Sogoni, interview with Faith (2017).
[48] Sogoni, Participant#5: Group Interview 2.
[49] Sogoni, interview with Mbetha.
[50] Alao, research notes.

Blessers entrap young women by similar means. Indeed, it is as if the prestigious commodities surrounding both the mamlambo and the blesser are imbued with a special magic that can bring about the prosperity they evoke. Just as well-dressed male mamlambos cruise in expensive cars through small towns in economically deprived areas, top-level blessers may spend extravagant amounts of money, drive luxury cars and prefer clothes and accessories from high-status international brands. Serge Cabonge, for instance, one of South Africa's best-known blessers, drives Ferraris and Porsches, and favours international labels such as Versace, Louis Vuitton, Billionaire and Burberry.[51] As Tandiwe Sogoni remarks, the blesser offers that for which so many yearn: a luxurious lifestyle, prestigious commodities and extravagant shopping opportunities.[52] Felicia Mbetha corroborates this: 'You are twenty-two, you have everything in the world that even a thirty-year-old that works, that has a degree, does not have. Who does not want that?'[53] Various posts on the Blesserfinder website are symptomatic of the temptation surrounding the blesser. For instance, one displayed a photograph of a young woman in a tropical beach resort, along with the following message: 'You are beautiful, why should you struggle. Get in touch with us, we link you up with a blesser.'[54] All that is offered by the mamlambo and the blesser may appear enticing, offering a means – whether supernatural or actual – to the same end. However, it comes at a cost.

Sacrifices and control

'This blesser thing, in as much as it can be nice, it is also dangerous', Zanele, one young woman from Alice, said.[55] Comparably, the allure of the mamlambo is intertwined with menace. This being embodies some of the sinister enchantments of Western consumer capitalism, to which Geschiere and the Comaroffs allude. The appeal it exerts appears comparable to the workings of witchcraft in its force and deadly consequences. According to the Comaroffs, witches 'embody all the contradictions of the experience of modernity itself, of

---

[51] Sogoni, interview with Thabo (2017). Sogoni, research notes; 'Serge Cabonge Shows Us What He Owns', https://youtube/Q9QJli8GGOM (accessed 1 May 2017).

[52] Sogoni, research notes.

[53] Sogoni, interview with Mbetha.

[54] 'Blesserfinder: Matching You with a Sugar Daddy Near You', http://www.702.co.za/articles/12596/blesserfinder-matching-you-with-a-sugar-daddy (accessed 10 February 2017).

[55] Sogoni, Group Interview 3.

its inescapable enticements, its self-consuming passions'.[56] These are evident in the accounts depicting the nature of the relationships between the mamlambo and its consort, and the blesser and the blessee; and in the descriptions of the price these wealth-givers exact in exchange for all they provide.

It is said that the mamlambo is possessive, demanding that its owner satisfy its needs and desires above all else. It demands sacrifices that come at a great personal and moral cost. Its owners are required to sacrifice those that they hold dear, such as family members and, as will become evident, their own well-being.[57] It is also said that the mamlambo will eventually control its owner, just as the craving for money and material possessions will come to govern peoples' lives, at the cost of their personal relationships. Whether literally or symbolically, then, a mamlambo's consort has to sacrifice those closest to her or him. Indeed, this sometimes seemed to have been the case with Khotso Sethuntsa, the renowned ukuthwala practitioner. His life appeared dominated by his adoration of money, and all too often his personal relationships seemed to take second place.[58]

Just as a mamlambo's owner comes to be controlled by this being, a blessee is subjugated to the whims of the blesser. She is generally required to put her blesser first, and be available at all times, irrespective of her own needs and commitments. As Zoleka, a young woman from East London, put it, 'As a blessee you lose your life. You have no say in whatever goes on in your life because the blesser will be calling all the shots. You do whatever he wants, whenever he wants.'[59] The blesser requires other, related sacrifices, some of which may encompass a blessee's sexuality, her personal relationships and her self-esteem. For instance, Faith confessed, 'It is not easy being a blessee. You have to swallow your pride and your morals.'[60] Similarly, Nosipho, another blessee, said, 'Even when I told him that I was uncomfortable he told me to relax and that things will get better once we do the deed. I did not like that shame.'[61]

As this suggests, hunger for money and material possessions can be disempowering, rendering those who harbour such yearnings more vulnerable to the manipulations of those that bestow them, be they the mamlambo or the blesser. A desire for the trappings of affluence may come to rule a blessee's life

---

[56]   Jean Comaroff and John Comaroff, 'Introduction', in *Modernity and Its Malcontents: Ritual and Power in Postcolonial Africa*, ed. eidem (Chicago, 1993), pp xi–xxvii at xxix.

[57]   Wood, 'Spirits in the Marketplace', 4–5; 'Wealth-Giving Mermaid Women', p. 74.

[58]   Wood with Lewis, *Khotso*, p. 66; Wood, 'Wealth-Giving Mermaid Women', p. 74.

[59]   Sogoni, Zoleka: Group Interview 5.

[60]   Sogoni, interview with Faith.

[61]   Sogoni, Nosipho: Group Interview 4.

or that of a mamlambo's owner, irrespective of the costs involved. A comment made by one of Khotso's wives is suggestive of this: 'Money had to flow in, one way or another. He loved the smell of it, coins and notes. There was no getting out of it.'[62] Comparably, as one young woman indicated, many blessees become ensnared by the addictive nature of the glamorous life and costly gifts offered by the blesser: 'Once you enter into the blesser lifestyle, there is no going back. How can you go back to your previous lifestyle when you have become used to a life of luxury?'[63] Similarly, Sindiswa, another young woman from East London, said that although her cousin's blesser abandoned her when she fell pregnant, she remained bound to all that he had represented: 'She would definitely be a blessee again', Sindiswa stated. 'She's all about that high life, and she does not see anything else for herself.'[64] Indeed, all that the blesser and the mamlambo provide feeds an ongoing addiction that cannot be fulfilled. The Comaroffs' depiction of Hausa soul-eaters in rural Niger, said to devour the soul-essence of those around them, is pertinent here. Soul-eaters are depicted as 'the personification of capricious commodities, the sirens of selfish desire'.[65] This description calls to mind the desires that have helped bring the mamlambo and the blesser into being, the craving for affluence and expensive items that they foster and their damaging consequences.

The various meanings of the term *ukuthwala* are worth considering. On one level, it denotes the procedure by means of which an individual acquires ownership of a mamlambo. However, it can also mean 'to abduct'. Arguably, then, those who undergo ukuthwala become carried away by their desire for wealth to the exclusion of much else. Moreover, the term *ukuthwala* may mean 'to bear a large burden on one's head' – in other words, to carry a load so heavy that it cannot be carried by hand. This suggests that those who take on the ownership of a mamlambo will be burdened by all that an alliance with the spirit entails, including the yearning for money and material possessions that binds them to this being.[66]

This may also be applicable equally to the blessee, who may find that the luxuries bestowed on her have become burdens, rather than blessings. They may feed an incessant desire for more, encumbering her with unfulfilled

---

[62] See Wood with Lewis, *Khotso*, p. 66; Wood, 'Wealth-Giving Mermaid Women', pp. 74–5.

[63] Sogoni, Participant#1: Group Interview 1.

[64] Sogoni, interview with Sindiswa (2017).

[65] Comaroffs, 'Introduction', p. xxv. The Comaroffs here reflect on Pamela Schmoll's study of soul-eating among the Hausa: see Pamela G. Schmoll, 'Black Stomachs, Beautiful Stones: Soul-Eating among Hausa in Niger', in *Modernity and Its Malcontents*, ed. Comaroff and Comaroff, pp.193–220.

[66] See Wood with Lewis, *Khotso*, p. 66.

yearnings. The following comment, made by someone who knew many bless-ees, depicts a state of this kind:

> Once you get used to your sixteen-inch weave or your R2,500 weave, you want a twenty-inch and by the time you get that twenty-inch, your J7 is not so cool anymore, you want an iPhone. Every day the standards you are trying to maintain as a blessee go up, they change.[67]

Rather than satisfying a hunger for money and commodities, both the mamlambo and the blesser leave their consorts with an insatiable craving, driven by desires that cannot be satiated. Consequently, many South African urban environments, both supernatural and actual, are haunted by disillusion and despair. Lamont Lindstrom contends that an unquenchable yearning (for wealth, power, fame, love or security, among much else) is a persistent form of desire in the West.[68] A longing of this kind is incessant, for aspirations of such a nature cannot readily be fulfilled. Marshall Sahlins describes how modern Western culture has fostered this state of greedy, dissatisfied wanting. In part, this inclination has been generated by the expansion of consumer capitalism, and helps sustain it. Thus desires of this kind have been celebrated, rather than interrogated.[69]

Disillusion and deprivation

It is said that the wealth attained from the mamlambo is not lasting, and that ultimately suffering and deprivation are visited upon its owner. Khotso's eventual fate is often viewed as an instance of this. He was beset by suffering and pain near the end of his life, and his wealth seemed to vanish after his death, leaving most of his family cash-strapped or destitute.[70] Just as the mamlambo will suddenly and capriciously turn against its owner, blessers are liable to discard blessees when they no longer have a use for them, depriving them of their glamorous lifestyle and often leaving them with little of lasting worth. For instance, after Sindiswa's cousin fell pregnant and her blesser abandoned her, she was left with nothing except costly items that were of little value to her and her child: 'She became a mother, she owns expensive shoes and a weave ... So she gained a baby and shoes because she does not have money.'[71] Thus, like

---

[67] Sogoni, interview with Mbetha.

[68] Lamont Lindstrom, 'Cargo Cult at the Third Millenium', in *Cargo, Cult and Culture Critique*, ed. Jebens, pp. 15–35 at 18, 31–3.

[69] Cited in Lindstrom, 'Cargo Cult', p. 34. See also Wood, *Universities and the Occult Rituals*, p. 163.

[70] Wood with Lewis, *Khotso*, pp. 263–96, 300–10.

[71] Sogoni, interview with Sindiswa.

an alliance with a mamlambo, a relationship with a blesser offers no long-term security. Faith's relationship with her first blesser, for example, only lasted a few weeks.[72]

The yearnings that give rise to liaisons with the mamlambo and the blesser, and their damaging consequences, suggest that the apparent desirability of the Western capitalist system, with its promises of individual affluence and easy access to covetable commodities, is a dangerous seductiveness. Niehaus indicates that the mamlambo, with its specific nature and associations, embodies a form of cultural critique.[73] Descriptions of the blesser can be viewed in a similar light. The mamlambo's owner, possessed by a hunger for money and material possessions, becomes owned by the being; while the blessee, craving high-status commodities, becomes a commodity purchased by the blesser. Thus, the consumer becomes the consumed, devoured by the desire for more. Accordingly, the consequences of liaisons with blessers and mamlambos are symptomatic of the costs of consumer capitalism.

The Comaroffs contend that various hazardous features of the African occult 'embody all the contradictions of the experience of [Western] modernity, its inescapable enticements, its self-consuming passions, its discriminatory tactics, its devastating social costs'.[74] These tensions, perilous desires and their deadly consequences are depicted in descriptions of liaisons with the blesser and the mamlambo, and the price they exact in exchange for all they provide. The mamlambo's tantalising promises of good fortune prove hollow; and the belief that a blesser can fulfil a blessee's needs and desires is equally illusory. Instead, the mamlambo's owner and the blessee may become so caught up in the pursuit of that which Lindstrom terms 'the bounty of modernity' – all that Western consumer capitalism is believed to provide – that they may not realise they have invested their hopes in dreams that will result in disillusion.[75]

As a result of their association with Western status symbols, the deceptive enchantment of consumer capitalism and the treacherous allure of money, the mamlambo and the blesser form part of what the Comaroffs term the dark 'magicalities of modernity'.[76] South Africa has fallen prey to these hazardous enchantments for various reasons, some of which have been explored above. However, another significant factor is the failure of political organisations to bring about a more equitable dispensation and create viable alternatives to

---

[72] Sogoni, interview with Faith.
[73] See Niehaus, *Witchcraft, Power and Politics,* p. 62.
[74] Comaroffs, 'Introduction', pp. xxix–xxx.
[75] Lindstrom, 'Cargo Cult', p. 24. See also Wood, *Universities and the Occult Rituals,* p. 172.
[76] Comaroffs, 'Introduction', p. xxx.

consumer-capitalist models. When promises and ideals prove hollow, magic may flow in to fill the void. Consequently, the dangerous enticements of consumerism have taken hold, fostered by the extent to which consumer capitalism has been perceived as an engine of progress when other ways forward seem to have stalled. On account of their bedazzling yet potentially perilous aspects, and the dreams and illusions they harbour, affluent urban environments in South Africa and elsewhere may appear to be imbued with aspects of the occult, and therefore seem appropriate sites for these literal and metaphorical workers of magic.

Acknowledgements

I am grateful to Tandiwe Sogoni, a student researcher who conducted valuable research into the blesser phenomenon, upon which this study draws; and to student researcher Sei Tiffany Mudariki for providing information and insights that have also informed this paper. I owe much to Wendy Muswaka and Abbey Alao, student researchers who assisted me in my research into the mamlambo from 2008 to 2010. My thanks to Mathew Blatchford for providing insights into South African economic issues. The National Research Foundation and the University of Fort Hare provided funding for part of this research.

Bibliography

Primary sources

Alao, Abbey, interview with Thandokazi Dyup (2009)
——, interview with Nokuyulo Filtane (2009)
——, research notes (2009)
Mudariki, Sei Tiffany, research notes (2007)
Muswaka, Wendy, - interview with anonymous respondent (2008)
——, interview with Thembisa Dingane (2009)
——, interview with Malemane Liphoto (2009)
——, interview with Luxolo Lunxaba (2009)
——, interview with Diko Manxeba (2009)
——, interview with Charlemagne Matango (2009)
——,interview with Xolani Mawu (2009)
——, interview with Nuvuyo Maxanda (2009)
——, interview with Noma (2009)
——, interview with Xolani Sithole (2009)
——, interview with anonymous respondent, Queenstown (2010)
——, interview with Sphamla Mhlobe (2010)
——, interview with Thandile Nxaba (2010)
Sogoni, Tandiwe, Group Interview 1, Alice (2017)

——, Group Interview 2, Alice (2017)
——, Group Interview 3, Alice (2017)
——, Group Interview 4, Alice (2017)
——, Group Interview 5, Alice (2017)
——, interview with Faith (2017)
——, interview with Felicia Mbetha (2017)
——, interview with Sindiswa (2017)
——, interview with Thabo (2017)
——, research notes (2017)

Secondary sources

Bastian, Misty L., 'Vulture Men, Campus Cultists and Teenaged Witches: Modern Magics in Nigerian Popular Media', in *Magical Interpretations, Material Realities: Modernity, Witchcraft and the Occult in Postcolonial Africa*, ed. Henrietta Moore and Todd Sanders (London, 2001), pp. 71–96

Blesserfinder: home page (2017) www.blesserfinder.com, https://web.facebook.com/Blesserfind/

'Blesserfinder: Matching You with a Sugar Daddy Near You', http://www.702.co.za/articles/12596/blesserfinder-matching-you-with-a-sugar-daddy

Comaroff, Jean and John Comaroff, 'Introduction', in eidem (eds), *Modernity and Its Malcontents*, pp. xi–xxvii

—— and —— (eds), *Modernity and Its Malcontents: Ritual and Power in Postcolonial Africa* (Chicago, 1993)

—— and John L. Comaroff, 'Occult Economies and the Violence of Abstraction: Notes from the South African Postcolony', *American Ethnologist* 26 (1999), 279–303

Derrida, Jacques, *Specters of Marx* (New York, 1994)

'Extreme Inequality in South Africa is Constraining Growth and Investment', http://www.engineeringnews.co.za/article/extreme-inequality-is-constraining-south-african-investment-and-growth-2018-04-10

Geschiere, Peter, *The Modernity of Witchcraft: Politics and the Occult in Postcolonial Africa* (Charlottesville, VA, 1997)

Lindstrom, Lamont, 'Cargo Cult at the Third Millennium', in *Cargo, Cult and Culture Critique*, ed. Holger Jebens (Honolulu, 2004), pp. 15–35

Makhoba, Ntombizodwa, 'Blessee: "I will never, ever date a man who is broke" ' https://city-press.news24.com/Trending/blessee-i-will-never-ever-date-a-man-who-is-broke-20160601

Mamlambo [film], directed by Palesa ka Letlaka Nkosi and Jeremy Nathan (1997)

Morrow, Seán and Nwabisa Vokwana, ' "Oh Hurry to the River": The Meaning of *uMamlambo* Models in the Tyumie Valley, Eastern Cape', *Kronos* 30 (2004), 184–99

Niehaus, Isak, *Witchcraft, Power and Politics: Exploring the Occult in the South African Lowveld* (Cape Town, 2001)

Otto, Ton, 'Work, Wealth and Knowledge: Enigmas of Cargoist Identifications', in *Cargo, Cult and Culture Critique*, ed. Holger Jebens (Honolulu, 2004), pp. 209–26.

Ritzer, George, *Enchanting a Disenchanted World: Revolutionising the Means of Consumption* (London and New Delhi, 1999)

'SA has 6th Most Shopping Centres in the World and Building More', https://www.fin24.com/Companies/Retail/sa-has-6th-most-shopping-centres-in-the-world-and-building-more-20171224

Scheepers, Anneke, 'Blesser–Blessee Relationships: The New Sugar Daddies or a Short Cut to the Good Life?', https://www.w24.co.za/Wellness/Mind/blesser-blessee-relationships-the-new-sugar-daddies-or-a-short-cut-to-the-good-life-20160509

Schmoll, Pamela G., 'Black Stomachs, Beautiful Stones: Soul-Eating among Hausa in Niger', in *Modernity and Its Malcontents: Ritual and Power in Postcolonial Africa*, ed. Jean Comaroff and John Comaroff (Chicago, 1993), pp.193–220

'Serge Cabonge Shows Us What He Owns' (2017), https//youtube/Q9QJli8GGOM

Statistics South Africa, 2017, 'Poverty Trends in South Africa: an Examination of Absolute Poverty between 2006 and 2015', http://www.statssa.gov.za/?p=10341

Wood, Felicity, *Universities and the Occult Rituals of the Corporate World: Higher Education and Metaphorical Parallels with Myth and Magic* (London, 2018)

——, 'Spirits in the Marketplace: The Market as a Site of the Occult in the South and West African Supernatural and Contemporary Capitalist Cosmologies', *Folklore* 126 (2015), 283–300

——, 'Wealth-Giving Mermaid Women and the Malign Magic of the Market: Contemporary Oral Accounts of the South African *Mamlambo*', in *Vernacular Worlds, Cosmopolitan Imagination*, ed. Stephanos Stephanides and Stavros Karayanni (Amsterdam, 2014), pp. 59–85

Wood, Felicity with Michael Lewis, *The Extraordinary Khotso: Millionaire Medicine Man of Lusikisiki* (Johannesburg, 2007)

3

The Banshee Lives in the Handball Alley: Limerick City as a Folk Gothic Site

——◇◇◇——

TRACY FAHEY

This chapter focuses on a substantial ethnographic collection recorded in the city of Limerick in the south-west of Ireland by Irish artists Michael Fortune and Aileen Lambert in 2004 and 2005, which later became two film pieces known collectively as *The Banshee Lives in the Handball Alley*.[1] These films were produced and shown in Limerick city as part of both the Cuisle Poetry Festival in 2004 and the Eva International biennial of fine art in 2005. The resulting films are works of fine art, but also form a contemporary archival collection of urban folktales that probe at the heart of the identity of the city as a folkloric, supernatural and Gothic site. In the work of these ethnographic artists the line between fine art practice and folklore almost disappears; this case study of *The Banshee Lives in the Handball Alley* powerfully illustrates the continuing relevance and use of folklore by communities within contemporary urban spaces. This chapter examines the stories at the core of this collection. It analyses these tales as legends in terms of their links to the past, but also in light of their continuing function in the present as memorates, as boundary markers and as cautionary tales. It also considers the way in which these tales were recorded, and reflects on the use of socially-engaged art practice and ethnographic art practice as ways of both preserving and disseminating folklore.

---

[1]   Michael Fortune and Aileen Lambert, *The Banshee Lives in the Handball Alley*, vol. 1, (Limerick, 2005).

The Banshee Lives in the Handball Alley was created in Limerick city. Limerick is the oldest city in Ireland, founded by Vikings as Hlymrekr in AD 812. Throughout its history, it has been a medieval walled town, a garrison city of military importance and the site of the Treaty of Limerick which concluded the Williamite wars of the seventeenth century in 1690.[2] This colourful history has given birth to a succession of legends relating to the identity of the city. According to different tales, Limerick was cursed by its own patron saint, St Munchin, first bishop of Limerick, the nearby river Shannon hosts its own sea monster, Cata, first recorded in the Book of Lismore, and the city and its environs boast a long tradition of storytelling and poetry.[3] Folktales include stories of the Devil appearing at Ballingarde House, of the prematurely buried Countess of Desmond and of the vengeful ghost of the Bishop's Lady and her struggles with Drunken Thady.[4] The city itself has rather a paradoxical identity. Since 1977 it has hosted Ireland's only fine art biennial, Eva International, and in 2014 it became Ireland's national city of culture, but it also has a contemporary reputation as a centre for criminality, drug-running and gangland feuds. It is an odd heterotopia characterised by vivid legends and a strong tradition of storytelling.

The Banshee Lives in the Handball Alley consists of an edited series of recordings of children's folktales which were made during two residencies, one a Storytelling Residency in 2004 co-ordinated by Limerick City Council as part of the Cuisle Poetry Festival, and the other in 2005, as part of the Eva International biennial. The children interviewed by Fortune and Lambert were from local schools, St Munchin's Boys School, and St Mary's Boys and Girls National Schools. These schools stand on a site called King's Island, the site of the original Viking city of Limerick. This is an area of great natural beauty by the river Shannon, beside the medieval quarter, and is also a working-class area of the city which has been disrupted by contemporary antisocial behaviour.

The two films in *The Banshee Lives in the Handball Alley* collection tell a total of one hundred and sixteen stories. A quantitative analysis is interesting, as it shows the preoccupations of the children recounting the tales. Thirty-four of the stories feature the titular banshee; thirteen of these reference her comb, four reference her cloak and another four tell of her rock. Seventeen stories are concerned with curfews and the supernatural manifestations that occur if

---

[2]   See, for example, Sean Spellissy, *The History of Limerick City* (Limerick, 1998), pp. 291–2.

[3]   Ibid., p. 152.

[4]   For further details of these folktales, see Tarquin Blake, *Haunted Ireland* (Dublin, 2014), pp. 102–7; Michael Hogan, *Drunken Thady & The Bishop's Lady by Michael Hogan – the Bard of Thomond* (Limerick, 2014).

curfew is broken. Twelve tales tell of the water-based Green Lady, and thirteen are devoted to stories of the handball alley and the manifestations therein. Eight stories describe the headless horseman, and four tell of the Death Coach. Another eight stories retell the tale of Drunken Thady and the Bishop's Lady. This repetition tells us of the value these tales still hold in contemporary culture, and of the way the supernatural characters in these stories continue to operate as warnings, as markers of perimeters and as reminders of the safety of home juxtaposed against the danger of the outside world. As Fortune said in an interview of 2017,

> I am keen to explore the threshold between current culture and traditional customs … between fact and fiction, and most especially how these elements shift and change so readily between each retelling, depending on the environment and the audience. Many of the stories will have the same repeated lines, the same meter, rising and falling, the same warnings and consequences, but are otherwise fluid and dependent on the personality and mood of the teller.[5]

Other accounts featured in the films tell of the fairy tree of Latoon, disappearing nuns, a ghost train that runs through Limerick, Halloween stories of sinister apparitions and a vengeful and murderous character known as The Milkman, whose visits to city dwellers bring death upon them. However, even analysing just one of these stories offers a great deal of information about the influence of folklore on contemporary Limerick society, and the continuing function of folklore in shaping identity.

The first story in the 2004 film, told by two boys from St Munchin's School, concerns a tale of the banshee:

> There was a banshee rock in Kelly's field but it's gone now because banshees, well there used to be banshees in Kelly's field, mainly one banshee, but the builders are after building soccer pitches, soccer pitches in Kelly's field, so the banshees are now gone down to Dally's field in Moyross …

Even the opening of this story incorporates multiple references to local landmarks like Dally's Field, Kelly's Field and the local council estate of Moyross. The local or vernacular roots of this Gothic tale are firmly linked with the notion of *genius loci*, that spirit of place that gathers around it a very specific sense of memory, community meaning and a kind of otherness that derives from dark passages in folklore. The banshee is the most popular icon in these

---

5   Manchán Magan, 'Away with the fairies: Irish folklore is alive and weird', *The Irish Times*, 28 February 2017. e-text at https://www.irishtimes.com/culture/books/away-with-the-fairies-irish-folklore-is-alive-and-weird-1.2986702 (accessed 6 June 2018).

stories; many of the variants tell of her combing her hair, and warn of the danger of picking up her comb or a torn piece of her cloak. Picking up these artefacts and – even worse – taking them indoors, can lead to repeated visitations or even death. Folklorists Patricia Lysaght and Dáithí Ó'hÓgáin explain that the banshee or fairy woman represents the connection between folklore and social cohesion and identity: the idea that there is a mystical connection between fairy folk and special clans.[6] The banshee is a very old archetype in Irish folklore, which nonetheless survives strongly in these urban vernacular folktales. The origin of the banshee is aligned with ancient Gaelic names – as Ó'hÓgáin puts it, 'the banshee laments only those who have O or Mac in their surname' – and acts as a narrative that protests against Norman colonisation of Ireland in the twelfth century.[7] In a similar vein, stories of the banshee that link to old Irish aristocratic families continued to be popular during the plantations of Leinster in the sixteenth and seventeenth centuries.

The contemporary survival of this legend in a solidly working-class area of urban Munster is of interest. As an archetype, the banshee is also connected with stories of war; local tales in County Clare recounted by *seanchai*, or traditional storyteller, Eddie Lenihan tell of sightings of the banshee washing bloody clothing by the site of battles.[8] Limerick, whose motto is *Urbs antiqua fuit studisque asperrima belli* ('Ancient city well versed in the arts of war'), has a long military history of battles and sieges that might offer a reason for the popular proliferation of local tales of the banshee in the city. However, the linkage of the figure of the banshee with local landmarks, and the mnemonic association between the two, could also point to possible reasons for the survival of these stories in the city of Limerick.

As well as the figure of the banshee this tale also references the entity of the headless horseman: 'There's the headless coachman and the headless horseman. The headless horseman was probably fighting with a banshee and he died or he just got his head chopped off.'[9] The range of folk references illustrated in this story is impressive. An analysis of this particular recording is fruitful, leading to several observations. Firstly, the recording does not present new stories, although by the boys' demeanour and some hesitancy in the recital, there's clearly some contemporary embellishment and improvisation that occurs in the piece. The stories told by these boys echo much older folktales.

---

[6]   See ibid., and Dáithí Ó'hÓgáin, *Myth, Legend and Romance: An Encyclopaedia of the Irish Folk Tradition* (London, 1991), p. 45.

[7]   Ó'hÓgáin, *Myth, Legend and Romance*, p. 46.

[8]   Eddie Lenihan and Carolyn Eve Green, *Meeting the Other Crowd* (Dublin, 2003), p. 198.

[9]   Fortune and Lambert, *The Banshee*.

In the 1930s, more than sixty years earlier, the Irish Folklore Commission Schools Collection was assembled. During this large project, more than a hundred thousand Irish children took part, in twenty-six counties, and, facilitated by their teachers, wrote neat pages about place-names, customs, crafts, feast-days, games they played and, of course, folktales they had heard.[10] Several of these stories reference the headless horseman, including an account from Gorteennaglogh, County Cavan, collected by Mary J. McGovern. This tells a local tale of an unfortunate man who was accidentally beheaded by a splinter after falling from his horse: 'Every night for a year after [the decapitation] the headless horseman was seen riding up and down the road. It is said that the devil and he had a fight one night and that the devil beat him.'[11]

There is also a clear link between the stories told in *The Banshee Lives in the Handball Alley* and the stories collected in Limerick as part of the Schools Folklore Collection. One of the tales collected by Fortune and Lambert, told by girls from St Mary's National School, references the Death Coach, known variously as 'the headless coach' and 'the Death':

> And my mother told me there there's such a thing that it's on some season … And at twelve o'clock you're not supposed … I think it's on Halloween. Twelve o'clock you're not supposed to walk the footpaths because it's the Death's time and they'll knock you off it. Yeah, that's true. That's true.[12]

A story recorded in 1937 was a tale told to a young student of Coonagh in Limerick city by a sixty year-old lady, a Mrs McInerney. The written version is remarkable in that it echoes both the themes and the narrative style of the piece recorded by Fortune and Lambert. It cites a man of Coonagh (a suburban area of Limerick city) who saw the Death Coach, the *Cóiste Bodhar*, anglicised in the recording as 'the Coachbow.'

> All of a sudden he heard a terrible noise and he ran and what do you think was coming after him but the Coachbow. They stopped him at once and took him up on the coach. They said that they were going to cut off his head but they gave him one chance. They said that if they caught him out late again they would kill him and that his spirit would drive the Coachbow … .[13]

The Death Coach in both the 1937 version and the 2004 version is known as *Cóiste Bodhar*, meaning death coach or deaf coach; the sight of it signifies

---

[10] For more information, see e-text on the Duchas.ie website: https://www.ucd.ie/folklore/en/collections/schoolscollectionduchas/ (accessed 7 June 2018).

[11] The Schools' Collection, volume 0969, p. 093.

[12] Fortune and Lambert, *The Banshee*.

[13] The Schools' Collection, volume 0597, p. 206.

that the spectator or a close relative will die, for once the coach travels in the living world it cannot return to the netherworld empty. The same Death Coach also appears in various accounts in the Schools Collection, including this one recorded in Rathfarnham, Dublin, by Proinnsias Ó Dubhthaigh:

> Many tales are told in the lonely houses of Rathfarnham to this day of the 'Death Coach' which noiselessly moved about on secret errands. No one seemed to know whence it came or where it went, but all agreed that a dead body was its load and headless its horseman and sack-muffled feet on the steeds of death.[14]

The headless horseman that drives the coach is known in Irish folklore as the Dullahan. The Dullahan's name in Irish is *Gan Ceann* (which literally translates as 'without head'). According to folk tales, his head looks and smells like rotten cheese, and he carries a whip made from the spinal column of a corpse; the whole coach décor is composed of dismembered human remains. The banshee sometimes accompanies the death coach, flying alongside wailing and screeching out a warning to certain families that one of their members is about to die.[15]

These very tangible links between the stories of the Schools' Collection and the stories gathered by Michael Fortune in *The Banshee Lives in the Handball Alley* all point to a remarkable consistency in the history of oral storytelling in the city of Limerick. The story of the Death Coach told by the girls from St Mary's National School is tellingly prefaced by the words 'And my mother told me … '. Many of the stories in this collection offer a family provenance of telling, with parents and grandparents cited as sources for the tales. It is useful to note that the community in which Fortune's collection was made is based on King's Island, the oldest part of the city, which has had a community presence since AD 812, so many of these stories may have been handed down for generations within the same families.

The fairy tree on the Ennis Road, referred to by the boys who told the first story of *The Banshee Lives in the Handball Alley*, is the famous Latoon whitethorn, known locally as a place for trooping fairies to congregate before going into battle. Seanchaí Eddie Lenihan, who wrote about the significance of this whitethorn in *Meeting the Other Crowd*, protested against the destruction of the bush in 1999 when it, and a portion of the locality, was scheduled for demolition for an imminent road scheme.[16] The story of Lenihan's passionate

---

[14] The Schools' Collection, volume 0998, p. 024.

[15] For more on this, see Patricia Lysaght, *The Banshee: The Irish Death-Messenger* (New York, 1997).

[16] See Lenihan and Green, *Meeting the Other Crowd*, pp. 12–14.

defence of the bush spread, featuring in *The New York Times* and on CNN, and the pressure of the campaign resulted in the road-builders changing the route of the road to save the bush. It is also of note that the boys refer to the curse falling on builders; a great many twenty-first century folklore dating from the crash of the 'Celtic Tiger' economy in Ireland in 2008 focuses on the fate of greedy developers who built on sacred sites like fairy forts.

So how do we define these stories recorded in *The Banshee Lives in the Handball Alley*? In Ireland, folklore developed as a set of narratives, traditions, rites and rituals, growing and evolving as a discourse of otherness within a colonial context. As O'Giollain states, '[T]he notion of folklore was predicated on the recognition of cultural difference: folklore belonged to the "others." '[17] Stacey McDowell, in *The Encyclopedia of the Gothic*, agrees that there is 'a sense of the "folk" as culturally other'.[18] Folklore and the Gothic are related through a myriad of connections concerning narrative, otherness and function. William Patrick Day correlates the Gothic with folklore, especially in terms of the characters who inhabit both types of narrative: 'Another convention of the Gothic atmosphere is the presence of the supernatural or monstrous; we know we have entered the Gothic world when we begin to encounter vampires and demons.'[19]

Fortune and Lambert's work can be described as a specific variant of Gothic: as 'Irish Vernacular Gothic', a term I have previously used to describe the specific sense of otherness that derives from shared Irish cultural and folk memories that enshrine rites, stories and rituals which hold a special and specific meaning for peoples of their community of origin.[20] It is a culturally produced and locally recognised form of 'living Gothic', preserved through collective memory.[21] It is bound up in rites, observances, re-enactments and retellings, all of which represent ways in which social memories are retained and transmitted.

The stories of *The Banshee Lives in the Handball Alley* are certainly Gothic stories. They are situated at liminal times; dusk, midnight and especially at Halloween, a time when the dead traditionally mingled with and walked among the living. The stories feature monsters and supernatural accounts, and

[17] Diarmuid Ó'Giolláin, *Locating Irish Folklore; Tradition, Modernity, Identity* (Cork, 2000), p. 164.
[18] Stacey McDowell, 'Folklore', in *The Encyclopedia of the Gothic*, ed. William Hughes, David Punter and Andrew Smith (Chichester, 2012), pp. 252–4 at 253.
[19] William Patrick Day. *In the Circles of Fear and Desire* (Chicago, 1985), p. 34.
[20] Tracy Fahey, 'A Dark Domesticity: Echoes of Folklore in Irish Contemporary Gothic', in *Living Gothic: Histories, Practices and Legacies*, ed. Maria Beville and Lorna Piatti-Farnell (London, 2014), pp. 152–69 at 153.
[21] See Beville and Piatti-Farnell (eds), *Living Gothic*.

the narrators are frequently unreliable. On further examination of these tales it could be argued that these stories are also *memorates*; they are accounts that bear witness to the veracity of the particular story. In *The Banshee Lives in the Handball Alley*, there are many references to family members who have witnessed these supernatural occurrences – brothers, sisters, aunts, uncles, fathers, mothers and grandparents. In terms of what type of folklore they represent, they can also be categorised as legends:

> Legend, typically, is a traditional, (mono) episodic, highly ecotypified, localized and historicised narrative of past events told as believable in a conversational mode. Psychologically, legend is a symbolic representation of folk beliefs and reflects the collective experiences and values of the group to whose tradition it belongs.[22]

Michael Fortune, in an interview in 2015, said of these stories, '[T]hese are stories that are passed on and told, values and belief structures that are passed on and told within families, within communities, and they're held dear.'[23] The stories, at their roots, offer warnings to children, they extol the virtues of abiding by curfews, avoiding supernatural manifestations and the sites associated with them. The route of transmission is made explicit in many of these stories; they are tales passed from grandparents to parents to children. Folklore is a key element in the formation of national, regional and local identity. It signifies belonging and a deep connection with tradition: 'The way you see me now is the way I really am, and it is the way of my forefathers.'[24] Alan Dundes agrees, remarking on the value of folklore to community identity:

> Not only does folklore serve as a kind of autobiographical ethnography, a mirror made by the people themselves, which reflects a group's identity, but it also represents valuable data which is relatively free from the outside observers' bias ... Folklore gives a view of a people from the inside-out rather than from the outside-in ... It is important to recognise that folklore is not simply a way of obtaining available data about identity for social scientists. It is actually one of the principal means by which an individual and a group discovers or establishes his or its identity.[25]

Collective memory as theorised by Durkheim and Halbwachs, and social memory discussed by Connerton and Fentress and Wickham, may be used as

---

[22] Timothy Tangherlini, *Interpreting Legend. Danish Storytellers and their Repertoires* (New York, 1994), p. 2.
[23] Tracy Fahey, recorded interview with Michael Fortune (Limerick, 2015).
[24] Erik Erikson, *Childhood and Society*, 2nd edn (New York, 1963), p. 129.
[25] Alan Dundes, *Folklore Matters* (Knoxville, TN, 1989.) pp. 34–5.

lenses through which to view the survival, transformation and interpretation of these folk stories and practices and their manifestation through contemporary fine art practice.[26] In many ways the function of these contemporary urban legends is as old as the function of folklore itself. It is no accident that most of these stories are based on perceived threats to the family unit or the home that appear in the immediate neighbourhood, often in the guise of supernatural beings. These stories not only tell us about issues of identity and social cohesion, but also operate as cautionary tales. In these films, legends are shown to have a cautionary function. As Linda Dégh comments, '[T]he legend tells us we can never be safe because extranormal powers may interfere with our lives at any time. The earth we know as our home is not entirely ours … .'[27] This sense of palpable danger is illustrated in many of the stories in *The Banshee Lives in the Handball Alley*. The seventeen stories concerned with the value of curfews act as warning stories. These tales feature strange happenings sited in the handball alley, and also multiple apparitions of the banshee, the Death Coach, the Headless Coachman and disappearing nuns. All are accompanied by warnings not to venture outside the home at night.

Analysing one of these stories, told by a girl from St Mary's National School, illustrates this function:

> My aunt was telling me on Halloween night. She lives across from the bank just, there's the bank and there's her house. And she was telling me that the headless coach would come out, so she was frightening me so I wouldn't go out and play no more. And she was telling me that he'd come out and take me away.[28]

Many of the tales such as this one focus on the idea of the world outside the home as a dangerous space. This is most probably because home is where people traditionally go in order to be safe. In pre-Christian Ireland, houses were built for shelter not only from the elements, but also from supernatural forces. Folklore acts to map and define local boundaries in the home and without. In Irish folklore, the most important of boundaries that appear in legends and folktales are those that divide the inside from the outside of the home.

---

[26]   See: Émile Durkheim, *The Elementary Forms of Religious Life* (1912), online version. e-text available at http://www.gutenberg.org/files/41360/41360-h/41360-h.htm (accessed 21 April 2018); Maurice Halbwachs, *On Collective Memory* (Chicago, 1992); Paul Connerton, *How Societies Remember* (Cambridge, 1989); James Fentress and Christopher Wickham, *Social Memory* (London, 1992).

[27]   Linda Dégh, *Narratives in Society: A Performer-Centered Study of Narration* (Bloomington, IN, 1995), p. 124.

[28]   Fortune and Lambert, *The Banshee*.

The home forms the first experience of boundaries; of a perimeter, that creates within it a space of safety. It demarcates inside from outside, the known from the unknown. If, as Freud claims, the womb is the first place where we experience the *Heimlich* and the *Unheimlich*, it follows that the home is the place where we first start to draw boundaries and map spaces between home and the outside world, and within the house itself. [29] From earliest times, houses have been linked through legends with fairy-lore, and the dead and with rites and rituals enacted in order to keep dangerous influences out. Many of the thirty-four tales of the banshee recorded by Fortune and Lambert are concerned with protecting the house against the banshee, who is frequently depicted as knocking on the door, or scratching her fingernails against the windows.

In the case of the banshee, the headless horseman and the Death Coach it can be seen that many of these dangerous influences were supernatural in origin. The Green Lady who appears as a common character in these children's stories is a classic example of such an apparition. According to the tales collected by Fortune and Lambert, the Green Lady is a malignant apparition who is found by the river banks around King's Island, where the children live:

> I was walking down the bank before and I was with my uncle. And it was on Halloween night because I asked him to. And everyone says if you pass the Green Lady on Halloween night she'll try to come up when someone's looking away and she'll try to take you.[30]

Jason Marc Harris explains that the 'traditional legend presents to its audience a sense of pervasive and perennial threats'.[31] These threats from supernatural beings could only be countered by use of protective rites, based on the accumulation of superstitious beliefs, and the transformation of these beliefs into rituals designed to protect. This is borne out by Dégh's assertion of the necessity to protect against the threats of legends: '[S]peaking the language of concern, fear and pain, legends reveal the desperate attempts people make to escape – to survive on the planet Earth or beyond – by finding irrational solutions, or by rationalising the irrational.'[32]

However, the figure of the Green Lady not only represents a threat, but serves a cautionary purpose. In Limerick, the presence of the Green Lady beside the water was a myth perpetrated by parents and grandparents in

---

[29] Sigmund Freud, 'The "Uncanny" ', in *The Complete Psychological Works of Sigmund Freud*, ed. and trans. James Strachey et al., vol. 17 (London, 1999 [repr.]), p. 144.

[30] Fortune and Lambert, *The Banshee*.

[31] Jason Marc Harris, *Folklore and the Fantastic in Nineteenth-Century British Fiction* (Aldershot, 2008), p. 5.

[32] Dégh, *Narratives in Society*, p. 442.

Fig. 2. The handball alley, Limerick. Image courtesy of Paul Tarpey, photographer.

order to signal to children to stay away from the deep waters of the Shannon river. Both legends and Gothic stories evidence a desire to map boundaries and frontiers, as observed by Harris in mapping the overlap between folklore and the Gothic: 'These topographical tensions [found in Gothic literature] are reminiscent of folk legends where supernatural beings also police the borders between wild and civilized locales.'[33] These legends are fluid, adaptable tales that focus on forbidden, transgressed space and liminal areas, all of which feature strongly in portrayals of the domestic in Irish art practice.

The handball alley in King's Island, Limerick is the focus of many of these tales. The most common legend associated with this site, and faithfully recounted by the children, is that this is a place of malignant apparitions conjured up by entering the place and following certain rituals:

Yeah I was in the handball alley last time, you know, playing the handball with him. And then it was getting dark, so now he tipped the four walls, you know the four walls in the handball alley? He said the Hail May and something came out. The Hail Mary backwards.[34]

However, in contemporary Limerick culture, this abandoned handball alley was a site of antisocial activity in 2004–05, when these tales were collected: a

---

[33] Harris, *Folklore and the Fantastic*, p. 18.
[34] Fortune and Lambert, *The Banshee*.

site of drug-taking and excessive drinking. Here again we have the pervasive influence of folklore continuing into the present through these vernacular Gothic stories. McDowell specifically links folklore to the Gothic tradition; the Gothic, she says, deploys folklore as 'a narrative framework upon which a range of modern fears can be expressed'.[35] It seems that the presence of the banshee was deliberately perpetrated as a myth by parents to keep the children away from the place. This, more than any scholarly analysis of the stories, offers a clear and vibrant testimony to the abiding power of the supernatural cautionary tale in contemporary culture.

During Eva International 2005, the two films, of together approximately one hour in duration, were screened in the handball alley itself. As Michael Fortune put it, 'We actually cleared out the banshees for the night and all the kids and their families turned out in droves.'[36] Later, the DVD recordings of the stories were distributed to the local audience: a fitting end to a project that had established a close connection with its community of practice. The recordings that were made are respectful of the stories, the artists are conspicuous by their absence and the resulting collection is held in a variety of locales: in galleries, in folklore collections and also – very importantly – within the community of origin in Limerick. As Magan puts it, '[T]he urban environment in which these children live is negotiated and charted by a mixture of ancient folkloric stories which have been intertwined with personal accounts and contemporary urban myths.'[37]

This project can be seen as the product of a mode of art referred to as *social practice*, the evolution of which has offered new ways for artists to engage outside the traditional venues of galleries and art schools. Social practice is an approach to art that involves engaging with communities of interest – like the schools in King's Island, Limerick – and documenting the result. This mode of art is collaborative, democratic and involves a sharing of knowledge between experts in art and experts in the subject of investigation. Commentators such as Claire Doherty in her *From Studio to Situations* manifesto consider social practice as revolving around the drawing together of communities, using space as a physical means of establishing a common locus.[38] An understanding of socially-engaged art is pivotal to a full understanding of how folklore, the Gothic and visual practice can come together in an animated and egalitarian way through projects like *The Banshee Lives in the Handball Alley*. The art of

---

[35] McDowell, 'Folklore', p. 253.
[36] Tracy Fahey, recorded interview with Michael Fortune (Limerick, 2015).
[37] Magan, 'Away with the fairies'.
[38] Claire Doherty, *From Studio to Situations: Contemporary Art and the Question of Context* (London, 2004).

social practice seeks to involve the public in mutual collaboration; it has been related to other engaged forms of fine art: 'other terms that share some kinship with social practice: activist art, social work, protest performance, performance, ethnography, community art, relational aesthetics, conversation pieces, action research.[39] Of all of these methods, it is *ethnographic art practice* that is the most relevant form when we discuss *The Banshee Lives in the Handball Alley*, for the film functions as an exemplar of the way that folklore engages with contemporary Gothic art. Ethnography, the research of peoples and cultures, is the main mode of studying folklore. Through the practice of ethnographic art, collective memories of folklore, as outlined by Durkheim and Halbwachs, are preserved, but also *transformed*, added to, changed, adapted for modern society and preserved as vernacular, living Gothic.[40]

This vernacular Gothic art also works to disseminate these dark tales and their variants in contemporary society through site-specific work based in domestic settings, using democratic media such as film, and propagating these tales, motifs and characters in local and community spaces. It highlights a mode of Gothic that is directly descended from Irish folklore, and which uses legends, rituals and superstitions to animate creative practice such as art. Folk Gothic art encompasses work that offers an interdisciplinary study of the marginal, the liminal, the dispossessed and the unspoken as influenced by Irish folklore. Fortune and Lambert's work can be seen as part of this vernacular folk Gothic tradition; working with living traditions that stitch themselves through history and culture to emerge in the present day, their elements changed, but their roots evident. This is a kind of site-specific Gothic that bubbles from the ground in the hidden springs of holy wells and from the strange superstitions that cling like cloth scraps round sacred rag-trees. The stories in *The Banshee Lives in the Handball Alley* possess a darkness of otherness found in shared stories – stories of pure terror which are distinct, regional and set in a specific locale. These are stories about forbidden places, behavioural codes transgressed and rites not followed. They appear as fireside tales, and reappear as urban legends. These Gothic works are infused with Irish folklore: in their subject matter derived from legends and superstitions, in their use of the folkloric notion of 'little-narratives' and in their attempts to map impossible stories on to real and tangible sites.[41] Fortune and Lambert focus on working with specific sites and communities in order to collect stories and rituals that

[39] Shannon Jackson, 'What is the "Social" in Social Practice?: Comparing Experiments in Performance', in *The Cambridge Companion to Performance Studies*, ed. Tracy C. Davis (Cambridge, 2008), pp. 136–50 at 136.
[40] See Durkheim, *Elementary Forms*; Halbwachs, *On Collective Memory*.
[41] Jean-Francois Lyotard, *The Postmodern Condition* (Manchester, 1984), p. 60.

inform their communal identity. This is one of the most fascinating intersections of all, when histories, stories and memories converge to create the kind of vernacular folk Gothic discussed above; a shared community counter-narrative with a clear and direct link to the folklore it draws from.

However, ethnographic art considers folklore in the sense of a living entity. This connects with Dundes and Pagter's notions of folklore as eternally new, continually evolving and instinctively responding to new circumstances.[42] This is an exciting way to consider folklore as a contemporary practice, existing side by side with evolving fine art practice. Ó'Giolláin also claims that folklore has been reinvented by new translations and transmutations: 'The point is that the continuity of traditional cultural elements is not necessarily compromised by embracing, rather than resisting, modernity ... part and parcel of the unavoidable and necessary engagement that every living tradition makes with change ... .'[43] The ethnographic artwork of Aileen Lambert and Michael Fortune, including *The Banshee Lives in the Handball Alley*, is based around notions of collecting, preserving and disseminating folklore in a way that is democratic and accessible. Fortune in particular has spoken about the importance of using social media platforms in the dissemination of his collections:

> The art world had no interest in my type of work. They couldn't bracket it; couldn't sell it. For many it upset their notion of what art was, and so I turned my back on them. The conventional art world bores me: the same people, making work in a bubble, preaching to the converted. I deliberately went local from day one. Last year I shifted my focus towards Facebook, bypassing the white-wall galleries to connect with people directly through their phones and tablets. It is about communicating with everyone, as opposed to an elite few.[44]

Many of Fortune and Lambert's other works are carried out as projects through public art schemes and local art commissions. Some of these projects include working with young people in schools and homes, some with older people in their homes, in social situations or residential care; the resulting work, most often in the form of DVDs, is often housed in a mixture of community archives, galleries and folklore collections.[45]

[42] See Alan Dundes and Carl R. Pagter, *Work Hard and You Shall be Rewarded: Urban Folklore from the Paperwork Empire* (Detroit, 1976), p. v.

[43] Ó'Giolláin, *Locating Irish Folklore*, p. 2.

[44] Magan, 'Away with the fairies'.

[45] Specific examples of these projects are: *Spoken Treasure* (2006); *That's What We Were Told, Anyway ...* (2006); *That's True, You Know* (2005); *A Walk In The May Dew* (2007); *Eggs in the Drills* (2008); *Half for You, Half for Me* (2010); *Following the*

Fortune and Lambert's use of social media such as Facebook and online video platforms such as Vimeo and YouTube to show film pieces have also brought their work to new and diverse online audiences. Aesthetically, their films seem naïve in technique; they often use handheld cameras to signify veracity, the presentation style is plain, and they use a still focus to signify a detachment from the aesthetics of fine-art film. These film narratives may appear as art with the artists missing, but an authorial presence, though invisible, can be seen through the editing and selection of stories for the finished films. The method of filming sets up an immediate relationship between the speaker and the viewer that mimics the traditional dynamic of speaker and listener in the act of tale-telling. Sweeney comments, regarding this process of transmission, 'The storyteller and the listener established the dynamic between performer and audience in Irish homes around the country. Stories were passed on and elaborated as they were transmitted by word of mouth (*bealoideas*).'[46]

Gothic may be about otherness, Fortune and Lambert seem to say, but it is a *shared* otherness, within a community, forming part of local, regional and national identity. Within the urban setting of *The Banshee Lives in the Handball Alley*, the survival of folk stories appears as a natural thing; the small community locally have passed on these stories from generation to generation. They are a testament to individual memory recalled by the subjects, based on the larger collective memory of the community and a social memory of repetition. Fortune and Lambert's work is endlessly curious about these tales that constitute social memory as well as folklore, yet the artists' gaze is detached, appraising and ethnographic. As Sarah Tuck writes of Fortune, 'His art practice continuously works to document social memories of folklore and map its evolution … Fortune's work neither eulogises progress nor sentimentalises the past … . His work provides a document of the carnivalesque of the everyday, of hybrid fictions in which memory is both partial and repetitive.'[47]

In the work of Fortune and Lambert, we find boundaries of fine art practice and folklore beginning to blur. Their ethnographic art practice presents exciting possibilities for both folklore and fine art practice in terms of participation and audience, as it is made in collaboration with community participants and screened in the communities of production as well as in galleries. It acts to revive and foreground pockets of culture that might otherwise lie undiscovered.

Whitethorn (2010); *Never Pick a Go-Go off the Ground* (2010); *The Fall of the Leaf* (2010).

[46] Bernadette Sweeney, 'Performing Tradition', in *Crossroads: Performance Studies and Irish Culture*, ed. Sara Brady and Fintan Walsh (London, 2009), pp. 21–33 at 25.

[47] Sarah Tuck, 'Introduction', in *Looking Room* catalogue (Cork, 2007), p. 1.

Fortune and Lambert's ethnographic art practice offers us a retelling of legends within the frame of their lens-based work and it captures a *communitas* linked by common narratives. Although the chief function of these stories may seem negative – that of the cautionary tale – they also have a cohesive function. In fact, in a lovely postscript to this project, in 2014 Fortune carried out a project called *Meet – The Mobile Irish Pub*. This project, which was originally devised by Lambert and Fortune in 2002, was commissioned as part of 'Limerick City of Culture 2014'. Fortune created a mobile pub with a Men's Shed Group in working-class Southill in Limerick city, where local men met to exchange stories of their community as an antidote to the contemporary cultural isolation experienced in the city. Fortune and Lambert's ethnographic practice of collecting contemporary versions of these legends within homes not only links the modern hearth with the ancient hub of tale-telling, but creatively blurs the lines between fine art and folklore itself. These vernacular Gothic tales, recorded as part of *The Banshee Lives in the Handball Alley*, survive in Ireland as part of a living Gothic tradition; despite the competition offered by television, internet and other sources, there is still a healthy tradition of storytelling and oral culture in Ireland. In Limerick city, therefore, folklore continues to evolve and to serve its original function in marking out dangerous spaces, offering cautionary tales and promoting community bonding through shared stories which shape a unique folkloric identity.

Bibliography

Beville, Maria, and Lorna Piatti-Farnell (eds), *Living Gothic: Histories, Practices and Legacies* (London, 2014)

Blake, Tarquin, *Haunted Ireland* (Dublin, 2014)

Connerton, Paul, *How Societies Remember* (Cambridge, 1989)

Day, William Patrick, *In the Circles of Fear and Desire* (Chicago, 1985)

Dégh, Linda, *Narratives in Society: A Performer-Centered Study of Narration* (Bloomington, IN, 1995)

Doherty, Claire, *From Studio to Situations: Contemporary Art and the Question of Context* (London, 2004)

Dundes, Alan, *Folklore Matters* (Knoxville, TN, 1989)

—— and Carl R. Pagter, *Work Hard and You Shall be Rewarded: Urban Folklore from the Paperwork Empire* (Detroit, 1976)

Durkheim, Émile, *The Elementary Forms of Religious Life* (1912), online version. e-text available at http://www.gutenberg.org/files/41360/41360-h/41360-h.htm

Duchas.ie website: https://www.duchas.ie/en/cbes/5177647/5176254/5200382

Erikson, Erik, *Childhood and Society* (2nd edn, New York, 1963)

Fahey, Tracy, 'A Dark Domesticity: Echoes of Folklore in Irish Contemporary Gothic', in Beville and Piatti-Farnell (eds), *Living Gothic*, pp. 152–69

Fentress, James and Christopher Wickham, *Social Memory* (New Perspectives on the Past), (London, 1992)

Freud, Sigmund, 'The "Uncanny" ', in The Standard Edition of the Complete Psychological Works of Sigmund Freud, ed. and trans. James Strachey et al., vol. 17 (London, 1999 [repr.])

Halbwachs, Maurice, *On Collective Memory* (Chicago, 1992)

Harris, Jason Marc, *Folklore and the Fantastic in Nineteenth-Century British Fiction* (Aldershot, 2008)

Hogan, Michael, *Drunken Thady & The Bishop's Lady by Michael Hogan – the Bard of Thomond* (Limerick, 2014)

Jackson, Shannon, 'What is the "Social" in Social Practice?: Comparing Experiments in Performance', in *The Cambridge Companion to Performance Studies*, ed. Tracy C. Davis (Cambridge, 2008), pp. 136–50

Lenihan, Eddie and Carolyn Eve Green, *Meeting the Other Crowd* (Dublin, 2003)

Lyotard, Jean-Francois, *The Postmodern Condition* (Manchester, 1984)

Lysaght, Patricia, *The Banshee: The Irish Death-Messenger* (New York, 1997)

Magan, Manchán, 'Away with the fairies: Irish folklore is alive and weird', *The Irish Times*, 28 February 2017; e-text at https://www.irishtimes.com/culture/books/away-with-the-fairies-irish-folklore-is-alive-and-weird-1.2986702

McDowell, Stacey, 'Folklore', in *The Encyclopedia of the Gothic*, ed. William Hughes, David Punter and Andrew Smith (Chichester, 2012), pp. 252–4

Ó'Giolláin, Diarmuid, *Locating Irish Folklore; Tradition, Modernity, Identity* (Cork, 2000)

Ó'hÓgáin, Dáithi, *Myth, Legend and Romance: An Encyclopaedia of the Irish Folk Tradition* (London, 1991)

Spellissy, Sean, *The History of Limerick City* (Limerick, 1998)

Sweeney, Bernadette, 'Performing Tradition', in *Crossroads: Performance Studies and Irish Culture*, ed. Sara Brady and Fintan Walsh (London, 2009), pp. 21–33

Tangherlini, Timothy, *Interpreting Legend. Danish Storytellers and their Repertoires* (New York, 1994)

Tuck, Sarah, 'Introduction', in *Looking Room* catalogue (Cork, 2007)

4

Urban Energy:
Cartographies of the Esoteric City

—◼◀◇▶◼—

WILLIAM REDWOOD

Where is significant, special or sacred to a magically-minded city-dweller? This chapter attempts to explain via a focus on the construction and experience of London within contemporary esoteric magic. Initially, in a section entitled 'Supernatural Subculture', the nature of esoteric magic is defined. Like so much late-modern spirituality, esoteric magic is an individualistic, apparently anarchic phenomenon with many and various manifestations, yet certain fundamental principles can and will be enumerated. The second section, 'Magical Maps', examines some sites of urban magical practice, ritual and significance, and explores what makes such places meaningful. The theory on which the paper draws in order to explain this is familiar in human geography, positing a model of 'place-with-meaning' – meaning shared by others. In the third and final section, 'Chaotic Cartographies', the focus of the chapter shifts to a somewhat different phenomenon: esoteric urban walks which are undertaken without a firm pre-existing notion of what meanings places may hold. These are *dérives* undertaken in a spirit of exploration, and they do not necessarily rely on preconceived understandings of place shared by others. This distinction is important analytically, because it requires us to draw upon different theory: rather less routine to human geography than the idea of meaningful places, the notion of the assemblage allows for the sort of unpredictability and inconsistency encountered in urban esoteric explorations. The second and third sections of this chapter then reflect a twin distinction in data and theory. These different approaches allow us to conclude that esoteric ideas of the city range from those which are clear-cut consensuses, to those which are contested, through to those which are idiosyncratic. The magical metaphor of 'energy' can be shown to be conducive not only to the wide range of multiplicity within urban esotericism but also, on a more scholarly level, to a model of the magical city which properly takes into account its dynamic and unstable nature. Ultimately, contemporary city magic calls us to take into account the 'fluid' condition of late modernity on the levels of both data and theory.

Supernatural subculture

Esoteric magic has been with us since at least the Renaissance; as with anything *re*-naissance, it draws on older ideas, or at least claims to. The most general idea is the discovery of 'inner' or 'hidden' knowledge. More specifically, several principles can be identified. Initially outlined will be an 'essential four', following Faivra.[1] First, correspondences exist between the visible world and an invisible realm: microcosm mirrors macrocosm and vice versa. More simply put, this entails that empirical events hold spiritual meanings because they are reflections of broader cosmic currents. Second, nature is viewed as alive. This ancient animism has found recent expression in Lovelock's 'Gaia Hypothesis', an influential idea within modern ecology.[2] It is also found in the notion that a mysterious energy is everywhere, in the earth, in the air and in all creatures and things. Third, the imagination is seen as vital, in the senses both of 'important' and of 'alive'; this means that 'dreams' are in some way 'real' and that 'fiction' can be a form of 'fact'. Fourth, there is self-transformation: the esotericist is less interested in performing miracles (for they are not deluded) than in seeking to transform themselves through the knowledge they acquire in the course of their spiritual experiences. Ideally such transmutation should be for the better, but the esoteric path is not held to be a straightforward one, and negative forces are said to pose a danger to the unwise or unready. Finally, one more facet of the esoteric worldview will be added, following Greenwood: there is an 'otherworld', and this other dimension (or dimensions) intersects with the material realm at certain times or places.[3] Within the framework provided by these guiding principles, esoteric magic is an individualistic, even anarchic phenomenon, with many and various manifestations. Roy Wallis used the term 'epistemological individualists' to characterise the attitudes of

---

[1]   Antoine Faivra, 'Introduction I', in *Modern Esoteric Spirituality*, ed. idem and Jacob Needleman (London, 1993), p. xv.

[2]   James Lovelock, *The Ages of Gaia: A Biography of our Living Earth* (London, 1995).

[3]   Susan Greenwood, *Magic, Witchcraft and the Otherworld: An Anthropology* (Oxford, 2000).

the persons involved.[4] T. M. Luhrmann noted their 'surprising spiritual diversity' and rhetorical claims that the only dogma was that 'there is no dogma'.[5] The individual is seen as the final arbiter of their own truth, and we shall see that this aspect of esotericism has important consequences for the esoteric city.

The word 'esoteric' may not be a familiar one beyond religious studies; indeed, when it occurs in popular usage, 'esoteric' can be a synonym for 'obscure and hard to grasp' ideas. However, as W. J. Hanegraaf has shown, much of that which is commonly referred to as 'New Age' thought owes a great debt to esotericism.[6] Whether or not they hold it in high esteem, many Westerners are likely to have encountered someone or something influenced by 'New Age' thought. Since the turn of the millennium, the term has fallen from favour amongst both scholars and spiritual seekers (a preferred label being 'alternative spirituality') but the generalising (and perhaps slightly disparaging) phrase 'New Age' is still widely recognised within popular Anglophone discourse.[7] The term will be avoided in this chapter, which will instead use the more specific phrase 'urban esoteric magic' – and for the sake of brevity, 'city magic', or simply 'magic' – to denote any magical belief or practice which is part of the Western esoteric tradition and encountered within an urban context. The examples provided later in this chapter make particular use of the idea of mysterious 'energies' and thin walls between this world and 'other' dimensions in certain parts of a city.

The research behind this chapter was ethnographic fieldwork undertaken as part of a PhD in social anthropology and subsequently expanded. This kind of research entails 'participant observation', whereby a social scientist lives amongst and interacts socially with the people they are studying, thus observing them in their 'natural habitat' and to some extent grasping what it must be like to belong to that group. A traditional anthropologist doing a study of a tribal group might well rely solely on such a method, but Western esotericists are a bookish group of people and use the internet, so written sources of information are also available to the researcher. These three methods of enquiry – face-to-face, bibliographic and online – were triangulated to produce research data, and it is upon a small subsection of these data that this chapter is

---

[4]   Roy Wallis, *The Elementary Forms of the New Religious Life* (London, 1984), p. 100.

[5]   T. M. Luhrmann, *Persuasions of the Witch's Craft: Ritual Magic in Contemporary England* (Cambridge, MA, 1989), p. 7.

[6]   W. J. Hanegraaf, *New Age Religion and Western Culture: Esotericism in the Mirror of Secular Thought* (New York, 1988).

[7]   Steven J. Sutcliffe and Marion Bowman (eds), *Beyond New Age: Exploring Alternative Spirituality* (Edinburgh, 2000); Steven Sutcliffe, *Children of the New Age: A History of Spiritual Practices* (London, 2003).

based. The locality was London, though the demographic included individuals from the USA and Australia: people were generally from Anglophone countries. While the examples of specific places provided in this chapter are all in London, urban esotericism can be found in any Euro-American city (although it lies beyond the scope of this research to elaborate local differences).

The question of how many esotericists are out there is one which has yet to be answered with certainty. Numerical estimates vary markedly, due to a plethora of problems both practical and theoretical. Personal privacy is one; not everyone is open about their religion or spirituality. Surveys may be shunned by many. The exact questions and categories featured in any survey will obviously circumscribe any answers returned and any conclusions which may be extrapolated therefrom. There is a range of labels for practices which might or might not be connected to, or influenced by, Western esoteric magic; scholars of religion will not necessarily use the same categories as do polling organisations or government departments compiling census forms (and the National Census periodically carried out across England and Wales has never yet made it compulsory to declare one's religion). Details of members of certain organisations, customers of certain retail outlets or even visitors to certain websites might be available, but any single individual can be a 'regular', a 'dabbler' or a 'one-timer'. As Luhrmann noted, a person's degree of involvement may be strong or weak, and vacillate over time.[8] Luhrmann settled on a judgement that 'in England several thousand people' were practising magic as a 'serious activity'.[9] Evans calculated that across Britain as a whole those involved in magic number 'perhaps at most some tens of thousands'.[10] These estimates keep numbers below 1 per cent of the population. Heelas and Woodhead produced a somewhat higher figure of 1.6 per cent, but this was based on their definition of social involvement in what they term the 'holistic milieu', a rather broader notion than esoteric magic. Having more in common with the terms 'New Age' and 'alternative spirituality', it includes such phenomena as alternative and complementary medicine.[11] While exact numbers are hard to produce, estimates do not suggest that magic in Britain is any bigger than for other 'minority religions'.

---

[8]   Luhrmann, *Persuasions of the Witch's Craft*, p. 4.
[9]   Ibid.
[10]   Dave Evans, *The History of British Magic after Crowley: Kenneth Grant, Amado Crowley, Chaos Magic, Satanism, Lovecraft, the Left Hand Path, Blasphemy and Magical Morality* (Harpenden, 2007).
[11]   Paul Heelas and Linda Woodhead with Benjamin Steel, Bronislaw Szerszynski and Karin Tusting, *The Spiritual Revolution: Why Religion is Giving Way to Spirituality* (Oxford, 2005).

However, if approached qualitatively, esoteric magic can at least be said to constitute some sort of cultural option. Might it be viewed as a subculture? The term 'subculture' has never been straightforward, and recently there has been a move towards 'post-subcultures' with regard to some youth movements.[12] Yet scholars such as Hodkinson argue that – so long as those being studied demonstrate certain characteristics which attest to a 'solidity' of subcultural identity and activity – the concept retains utility.[13] It was clear from fieldwork that esotericism constitutes a subculture in such a sense. However, as Paul Heelas and Michael York have both observed, the problem is that however 'solid' the 'centre' is, there will always be 'blurred edges', due to the differing levels of involvement already noted above.[14] A final and important characteristic of the esoteric subculture is that it tends to be loosely organised and polycentric. C. B. Campbell, Luhrmann and York have all noted that, lacking any overarching organisation, the subculture comprises individuals and small groups of individuals 'getting on with their own things' and not acting on orders from any sort of central authority.[15] The fieldwork which comprises the basis of this chapter confirmed this finding. However, free-spirited as esoteric magic may be, it cannot be assumed to be unproblematically subversive or resistant to the 'mainstream'; there are ways in which it is so, but there are also ways in which it is not, as will be shown in examples provided below. The ambiguity is heightened by the fact that 'wider society' is now extremely diverse and therefore, as Kevin Hetherington comments, 'it is just as difficult to locate the mainstream as it is the alternative to it'.[16] Perhaps it was ever thus; any imagined binary between 'establishment' and 'anti-establishment' has a simplistic quality to it. The word 'subculture', then, is preferable to the word 'counterculture' with regard to esoteric magic, and for the same reasons, this chapter will not conceptualise esotericism as (in itself) comprising any sort of 'social movement'.[17]

---

[12]   David Muggleton and Rupert Weinzierl (eds), *The Post-Subcultures Reader* (Oxford, 2003).

[13]   Paul Hodkinson, *Goth: Identity, Style and Subculture* (Oxford, 2002).

[14]   Paul Heelas, *The New Age Movement* (Oxford, 1996), p. 117; Michael York, *The Emerging Network: A Sociology of the New Age and Neo-Pagan Movements* (London, 1996), p. 26.

[15]   Luhrmann, *Persuasions of the Witch's Craft*, p. 32; York, *The Emerging Network*; C. B. Campbell, 'The Cult, the Cultic Milieu and Secularization', in *A Sociological Yearbook of Religion in Britain 5*, ed. Michael Hill (London, 1972), pp. 119–36.

[16]   Kevin Hetherington, *Expressions of Identity: Space, Performance, Politics* (London, 1998), p. 5.

[17]   Muggleton and Weinzierl, *The Post-Subcultures Reader*, p. 15.

Magical maps

The idea of the magical *city* is a relatively new one within esoteric thought. It was and can still be the case that the idea of urban magic is tricky to accept, even for people with esoteric practice high amongst their interests. Wilcock's *A Guide to Occult Britain*, written during the 1970s, has a section on London which is both quantitatively small (relative to other parts of the book) and qualitatively rather apologetic about cities in general, noting they are 'not the easiest places to discover magic'.[18] Wilcock is more inspired outside the urban realm, and most of his magical guidebook focuses on 'ancient sites along with innumerable burial mounds, hill forts, fairy circles, green men and dragon carvings'.[19] Some urban esotericists, consciously or otherwise, confine their esoteric experiences in the city to pockets of 'nature' within it, even if these are actually human-made pockets such as parks.

However, such a stance has not gone unchallenged, probably because it does not actually conform to the 'logic' of esoteric thought. Such thought runs as follows: cities have in many cases been sites of human habitation for centuries, so they may be ancient sites too, or at least have extensive history; beneath city pavements lies the land, the planet, and the planet is itself esoterically significant; and the majority of cities will contain esoteric 'energies' because such energies are ubiquitous. Thus, by the turn of the millennium, an esotericist from the United States could make the following counter-suggestion:

> You don't have to go to your gods. They are always with you, hiding in the building, the machines, the vermin. The spirit world hides in plain sight. It adapts. Its spirits are living and breathing in everything around you. They have always been there, waiting for you to find them again.[20]

This section will examine the part played by place spirits and 'earth energies' in urban esoteric practice. It will then survey the role of history in urban esoteric practice.

Magic is animistic and so natural phenomena are deemed to be alive. Often they are personified as a place spirit or *genius loci*. Such beings, fieldwork revealed, were not believed to be destroyed by urban development; their relationship to urbanisation may be ambivalent, but they stay. The idea of linkage between spiritual beings and a specific locality is one which is historically

---

[18] John Wilcock, *A Guide to Occult Britain: The Quest for Magic in Pagan Britain* (London, 1976), p. 40.
[19] Ibid., quotation inside front cover.
[20] Chris Penczak, *City Magick: Urban Rituals, Spells, and Shamanism* (York Beach, ME, 2001), p. 45.

ancient and culturally widespread. Rather more recent is the idea of earth *energies*. Patterns of mysterious force known variously as ley lines, earth lines, dragon lines, lines of force or just energy lines (the terms are usually used synonymously) are said to run through the land across the planet. The precise location of these lines, and shapes of any patterns which they may form viewed from above, varies according to whom one is speaking or whose work one is consulting. The notion can be traced back to the English antiquarian Alfred Watkins, writing during the 1920s.[21] It was developed (and made more mystical) by John Michell.[22] Later, and focusing specifically on London, came a number of works by Iain Sinclair, *Lud Heat* being a key text, in which churches created by the architect Nicholas Hawksmoor form points on a series of geometrical symbols which hold esoteric meaning and (in this case) malign magical energy.[23] Sinclair's influence on esoteric London has been marked, and his ideas find fame of sorts in *From Hell*, a graphic novel by Alan Moore and Eddie Campbell which became a Hollywood movie.[24] This is a dark vision of both London and magic, in which (amongst others) the Jack the Ripper murders take on an evil esoteric significance.

Added to these Anglocentric ideas are certain interpretations of aspects of ancient Chinese thought. As J. J. Clarke has noted, the practice of *feng-shui* has been stretched far from its original concern with the location of graves, to be combined with earth energy lines in both Europe and America.[25] This addition, an example of the 'affirmative orientalism' to which Fox drew attention, may add a certain respectability to the Western esoteric canon in the eyes of some.[26] However, it does so mainly at a stylistic level. Fundamentally, the guiding metaphor for this energy is what Erik Davis has termed the 'electromagnetic imaginary', his label for the *cultural* impact electricity has had on Western humanity. 'Our language', Davis writes, 'drips with electromagnetic metaphors, of magnetic personalities and live wires, of bad vibes and tuning

---

[21] Alfred Watkins, *The Old Straight Track: Its Mounds, Beacons, Moats, Sites and Mark Stones* (London, 1984 [1925]).

[22] John Michell, *The View over Atlantis* (London, 1973).

[23] Iain Sinclair, *Lud Heat and Suicide Bridge* (London, 1975).

[24] Alan Moore and Eddie Campbell, *From Hell* (London, 2000; series from 1989); *From Hell* [film], directed by Allen Hughes and Albert Hughes (20th-Century Fox, 2001).

[25] J. J. Clarke, *The Tao of the West: Western Transformations of Taoist Thought* (London, 2000), p. 83.

[26] R. G. Fox, 'East of Said', in *Edward Said: A Critical Reader*, ed. Michael Sprinkler (Oxford, 1992), pp. 144–56 at 152.

out, of getting grounded and recharging batteries'.[27] The same is true of magic, and this presents a paradox: an idea which would appear to stand against rationalism takes a surprisingly scientist form. Even though it can be inimical to effects of science and technology (such as damage to the environment), esotericism sees itself as a scientific endeavour.[28]

Fieldwork quickly revealed that there are multiple 'maps' of ley lines, depending on which books one reads and to whom one talks. There is debate within esotericism as to whether they retain their 'natural' patterns or are diverted or disrupted by modern developments.[29] Whoever is right (and esotericism stresses personal experience over positivism), the uncertainty implies a city which is relatively crowded with energy flows, and this point will be a recurring one here. The system can be imagined as a 'circuit-diagram' with 'electricity' buzzing along the various 'channels' or 'wires' and so the 'map' of the esoteric city thus becomes dynamic. Energy moves, sometimes by itself, and sometimes human agency can intervene and redirect it or alter its type. An example will serve to illustrate exactly this.

The Richard Budd Memorial is situated at the junction of Brixton Hill and Effra Road in Brixton, London. (It happens to be just metres away from the first street ever to be lit by electric lighting, Electric Avenue.). Almost ten metres in height, it is carved from stone which marks it out from its backdrop of the old, red London brick. (That brick is lightened by a ghost sign which once advertised Bovril, a beef extract which takes part of its name from *Vril*, a term given by Edward Bulwer-Lytton in one of his novels to a mysterious energy force.[30]) This 'memorial' is actually a mausoleum, erected in 1825 by Henry Budd in memory of his father Richard Budd (1746–1821), and it subsequently became the final resting place of various members of that family. According to some esoteric schemata, this site sits on a significant line of earth energy.[31] The memorial's Greek-style ornamentation includes a winged globe

---

[27] Erik Davis, *TechGnosis: Myth, Magic and Mysticism in the Age of Information* (London, 1998), p. 57.
[28] David J. Hess, *Science and the New Age: The Paranormal, Its Defenders and Debunkers, and American Culture* (Madison, WI, 1993).
[29] Penczak, *City Magick*, p. 83.
[30] Edward Bulwer-Lytton, *The Coming Race* (Edinburgh, 1871).
[31] I was told this more than once during fieldwork, and I take it to be related to the project of Christopher Street. This has been outlined in various books including *Earthstars: The Geometric Groundplan underlying London's Ancient Sacred Sites and its Significance for the New Age* (London, 1990), *London's Ley Lines: Pathways of Enlightenment* (London, 2011) and *London: City of Revelation* (London, 2011). The memorial is close to the main north–south axis in Street's schema. It is also above an underground river (the river Effra, after which Effra Road is named), and the

Fig. 3. Richard Budd Memorial. Photograph by William Redwood.

and an *ourobouros* (a snake eating its own tail), which are both laden with eso-teric meaning. During fieldwork, as part of a discussion of the carved magical symbols in this particular part of the city, one individual commented,

> Hmm, this merely confirms some of my theories about the Masonic Lodge that meets at Lambeth Town Hall. The apex of the capstone [of the memo-rial] would align with some of the cellars that extend out from the Town Hall. It is quite possible that they're using some form of occult ritual to capture and magnify the 'edgy' urban vibe of Brixton. It is entirely plausible that the first Brixton riot was caused by an accidental release of some of this energy![32]

Tim Cresswell has suggested that 'place' can be explained on three levels: it must have 'location', meaning it must be somewhere which can be expressed fairly objectively (via longitude and latitude, for example); it must have 'locale', by which he means it must have a material basis, be that geological or archi-tectural; and it must hold a 'sense of place': it must be meaningful (in one or more ways) in the minds of a group (or groups) of human beings.[33] Focus-ing on this third aspect of place, an explanatory model can be applied to this discussion of the Richard Budd Memorial, whereby a relatively regular urban artefact has been imbued with an irregular meaning. Some might find such meaning far-fetched, including as it does secret societies conducting some sort of social manipulation through secret rituals. However, there is clear suspicion of 'the establishment' and a clear link to local politics, both past and present. There is heteroglossia here: an imposition of inverted meanings which disrupt and subvert more hegemonic ones. An edifice commemorating a pillar of the establishment opposite a town hall represents – at least to some esotericists – a threatening convergence of architecture, political hegemony and alienation.

Such a view is by no means unique. Fieldwork revealed that Buckingham Palace, the Canary Wharf tower, the Millennium Dome and the Shard build-ing were all the subject of fear and concern. Rituals sometimes focused on

---

relatively complex traffic intersection constitutes a crossroads; one or both of these were often said to hold magical significance too, though they are not details which feature in the short example provided here.

[32] Anonymous informant, electronic discussion, March 2008. This comment, while I take it to have been intended seriously, was made during a discussion in which not all participants were esotericists, and as such, it attracted some incredulity and a little derision. There is no evidence to suggest that any of the Budds were involved in Freemasonry, though such an idea is of course difficult to disprove.

[33] Tim Cresswell, *Place: A Short Introduction* (Oxford, 2004), p. 7. Here Cresswell is drawing on the ideas of John A. Agnew, *Place and Politics in Modern Italy* (Chicago, 2002), p. 16.

disrupting energies concentrated or directed by these grand edifices of the establishment. Roger Luckhurst has surveyed the subgenre of 'dark occult' London fiction, fiction avidly read and drawn upon by esotericists, and linked it to very real problems with regard to 'top-down' planning and *laissez-faire* governance.[34] However, that is not to say that a binary model wherein dubious developments are resisted by creative and subversive esoteric ideas is entirely valid. Luckhurst seems to be unconvinced that these ideas constitute resistance in any real sense, and this reservation is one of the reasons why this chapter is careful not to class esotericism as 'counter-cultural'. Moreover, such a binary model risks essentialising esoteric thought as more anti-hegemonic than it may in fact be. Ethnographic method does not produce statistics; fieldwork showed, however, that at least some esotericists are socially conservative.[35] Gary Lachman has claimed that 'some, perhaps even most, occultists who dabbled in politics, or politicians who dipped into the occult, had right-wing, reactionary, and even fascist leanings', although this takes an historical rather than a contemporary view, and not one for which Lachman provides statistical support. However, it is fair to note that ideas of shadowy groups lurking at the heart of an evil establishment would not make sense to all urban magicians.[36] Meanings of place vary politically for esotericists (just as they do for anyone else, and so Westminster might be seen either the seat of a grand and good government or the centre of a conspiracy comprising Freemasons carrying out ritual pedocide, depending on political point of view. Furthermore, urban magical strife can sometimes seem far more personal than political. The American writer William Burroughs once claimed responsibility for putting a curse on (and thus closing down) a London coffee bar simply because its staff had been rude to him and the cheesecake had made him sick.[37]

This section has proceeded, as it were, from the ground up, and commenced with the rock on which the city stands, the spirits connected to it and the energy running through it. Another important facet of the esoteric city is history. One esotericist explains,

> As lovely as a trip to the open space of England is, I am a product of London. I never feel comfortable until I am hemmed in by the higgledy-piggledy buildings, until I sense, beneath my feet, the forgotten rivers forcing their way through the earth beneath the tarmac roads, until I walk with the ghosts

[34]   Roger Luckhurst, 'The Contemporary London Gothic and the Limits of the "Spectural Turn"', *Textual Practice* 16 (2002), 527–46.

[35]   See also Greenwood, *Magic, Witchcraft and the Otherworld*.

[36]   Gary Lachman, *Politics and the Occult: The Left, the Right and the Radically Unseen* (Wheaton, IL, 2008), p. xv.

[37]   Daniel Odier, *The Job: Interviews with William Burroughs* (London, 1989), pp. 18–19.

and murderers and kings and whores and marauders, until I am surrounded
by the stench of sex and the racket of anarchy, until I feel the dank beneath
this necropolis on my neck, until the noise of millions of narratives reaching
back centuries clogs my brain.[38]

In magic, the synchronic and the diachronic are not strictly separate. What (in
a rather different context) has been termed an 'archaeological uncanny' is very
much present.[39] Esotericism has a broad, encompassing conception of history.
There is that history which may be termed general, shared or mainstream –
the history of the school curriculum, the tourist guide and the mainstream
museums. Then there is a slightly less well-known kind of history, which might
variously fall into categories such as folklore, Forteana and urban legend.
Esoteric knowledge includes the locations where ghosts walk, whence UFOs
have been sighted and where there are interdimensional doorways waiting to
be opened.

One example of a site significant within this lesser-known history of
London is the Crossbones Graveyard. Overlooked by the Shard building and
some of the other newer arrivals on the city's ever-changing skyline, this location is close to, but crucially not in, central London. The only obvious sign
of anything unusual happening here is an outburst of colour and textures –
ribbons, feathers, flowers, toys, photographs, handwritten messages – attached
to an ordinary set of metal gates in Redcross Way, in the London borough
of Southwark. Within the ground just behind these gates lies the Crossbones
Graveyard (often known just as 'Crossbones'). It is no ordinary burial ground;
a council-funded plaque declares it to be a shrine to 'The Outcast Dead'. The
belief amongst esotericist visitors is that this was an unconsecrated location for
the burial of 'single women' (the current term would be sex workers) who had
been allowed to operate in the 'stews' (brothels) under special dispensation
dating back to the twelfth century. The trade was tolerated here because it was
outside what was considered to be London proper. However, its practitioners
were denied burial in conventional consecrated ground. Local esotericist John
Constable puts it nicely when he observes, 'With the City just over London
Bridge, being where all the wealth was, this was in every sense in its shadow.'[40]
Although the site of the graveyard itself is not easily accessible, by coincidence a public garden is located nearby. The hope is that, although future

[38] Anonymous esotericist, electronic communication, 6 March 2016.
[39] Michael Shanks, *The Archaeological Imagination* (Walnut Creek, CA, 2012).
[40] http://www.bbc.co.uk/news/uk-england-london-20489273 (accessed July 2018);
    Constable is author of *The Southwark Mysteries* (London, 1999), a cycle of plays and
    poems centred on Crossbones and said to be inspired by the raising of the spirit of
    one of those buried at the site.

redevelopment of the Crossbones site is likely, the garden at least will remain as a focus for remembrance. Esotericists can visit at any time, but monthly gatherings are held with processions, poetry and ritual. The most significant of these is that which coincides with All Hallows' Eve at the end of October, a night when the veil between the spirit world and that of the living is believed to be particularly thin.

In order to analyse Crossbones, we must engage with notions of marginality. This concept derives from the idea of a place having meaning, but relies on a particular kind of meaning: a marginal place is one at a literal or metaphorical 'edge' of a social world. In Western culture, any graveyard is a marginal space, and because Crossbones is an outcasts' graveyard, a double distancing would seem to be operative. A marginal place has become central to (at least some) esotericists' understanding of London, in a way reminiscent of Hetherington's observation that to certain social groups, 'margins become centres'.[41] Crossbones is a sound example of this. Despite some linkage to local art and literature in the form of Constable's work, and occasional media and tourist interest, it remains an eccentric location (the occasional media and tourist interest apparently stemming from this). Hetherington claims that such places 'have a social centrality such that they act like shrines for those who live outside the norms of a society ... because they come to symbolise another set of values and beliefs around which groups can order their identities and the way they want to be identified'.[42] As well as being a place of 'centralised marginality', Crossbones also represents a disruption of time: the outcast dead are remembered (or re-membered) in what Luckhurst describes as one of those 'patterns of disappearance and return that crumple linear time into repeating cycles or unpredictable arabesques'.[43] The site, then, is as heterochronic as it is heterotopic.[44] It should be noted that fieldwork did not indicate that *all* esotericists held this site to be significant. To some, it seemed sleazy or uncomfortably suggestive of female sexual exploitation. Those for whom it held significance were often motivated by ideas of radical sexual liberation – as symbolised by the site's deceased occupants – which are not necessarily shared by everyone involved in city magic. Crossbones is therefore esoterically significant without

[41]   Hetherington, *Expressions of Identity*, p. 214.
[42]   Ibid., p. 107.
[43]   Luckhurst, 'Contemporary London Gothic', p. 531.
[44]   The notion of heterotopia originated with Michel Foucault, in his short essay 'Of Other Spaces', *Diacritics* 16 (1986), 22–7, and has been used by Hetherington (in *Expressions of Identity*, pp. 131–2) and also by Adrian J. Ivakhiv (in *Claiming Sacred Ground: Pilgrims and Politics at Glastonbury and Sedona*, Bloomington, IN, 2001, p. 11). Although neither of the latter scholars was focusing on an urban situation, the people they studied could be described as 'New Age'.

being significant to every esotericist; as with the example of the Richard Budd Memorial, it also relates to the less socially conservative amongst them.

Chaotic cartographies

Whereas sacred spaces in so many traditional religions are limited to quite specific locales, within the esoteric city almost everywhere is potentially sacred space or at least magically meaningful. This final section will examine esoteric practice which does not simply involve working from pre-existing maps, but additionally explores new territory, imbuing it with new and magical meaning. Penczak was one of the first to publish a codified set of specifically urban esoteric practices, introducing the reader to the practice of 'sidewalking'.[45] This word (verbing the American noun for pavement) indicates something very much like what the Surrealists would have termed a *dérive*.[46] On an empirical level, this seems to be simply a stroll through the city, but the journey undertaken is a thoroughly magical one. It is no straightforward journey from A to B however; the end-point is uncertain, if there even is one. The schedule should be open; in Sinclair's words, 'Time on these excursions should be allowed to unravel at its own speed, that's the whole point of the exercise. To shift away from the culture of consumption into a meandering stream.'[47] The route is not precisely planned: intuition will play a significant part in where the journey will lead, though it is generally recommended that one does not get lost (Penczak sensibly advises carrying enough cash for a cab fare home in case of emergency).[48] Moore reports that 'you ... read the street plan's accidental creases and decode the orbit maps left there by coffee cups, then go', thus presenting a 'planning' approach more akin to divination.[49] Fieldwork commonly discovered the consultation of tarot cards. The trek is always preceded by a ritual of protection, the precise nature of which will vary according to the individual or group concerned. It is not considered necessary to wear elaborate ritual clothing (by no means all esotericists would ever do so publically).

---

[45] Penczak, *City Magick*, p. 80.
[46] Even they were not the first to do this. As Hetherington has pointed out (*Expressions of Identity*, p. 65), '[o]ne could go back to others who lived and wrote ... in the eighteenth and nineteenth centuries: to Rimbaud, Baudelaire, Retif de la Breton or Blanqui'. Merlin Coverley (in *Occult London* [Harpenden, 2017], p. 108) mentions Defoe, Blake and De Quincey as examples from the other side of the English Channel.
[47] Iain Sinclair, *Lights Out for the Territory* (London, 1997), p. 7.
[48] Penczak, *City Magick*, p. 80.
[49] Alan Moore and Tim Perkins, *The Highbury Working: A Beat Séance* [CD] (London, 2000), mins/secs 02:00 – 02:10.

However, a specific item of clothing can be worn on such walks; this can be anything, but having pockets in which to place any gathered items is useful, for an urban esotericist may collect found objects to which they feel drawn. A slightly altered state of consciousness is sought: the state of mind one enters is a ludic one, described by Penczak as 'a light trance state'.[50] Then one sets off and, in Penczak's words,

> You will see people and places in ways you have never imagined. ... Buildings will speak out to you. Each home has a spirit. ... By walking by an object, you breathe its energy. You read the vibrations of the objects around you. City gods are speaking through the statues and sculptures. Be prepared for anything.[51]

While it is difficult to do the potential diversity of such *dérives* justice here, a number of significant points present themselves. Ley lines, as we might expect, are part of these walks. Furthermore, while a magical *dérive* is more than just a ghost-hunt, a link with hauntology frequently featured in the fieldwork on which this chapter is based. This is supported by Penczak, who distinguishes between different types of ghost and includes the possibility of 'an event ... so strong that it was recorded into the energy patterns of the area'.[52] This is significant, because it links the idea of hauntology with the esoteric notion of energy. The living are also important to Penczak, because their 'aura' of energy can be seen or at least sensed by a skilled sidewalker.[53] Finally, a negative kind of energy can be perceived as present. This can come from people, politics or history. It can also simply be electro-magnetic pollution, something Penczak warns can have a deleterious impact on physical (and spiritual) health.[54] This is what Davis (writing of the wider population) terms 'powerline paranoia': a fear of actual electro-magnetic energies and anxieties surrounding their transmission.[55] Penczak raises a final interesting quirk of the urban experience for the esotericist: 'Certain messages or signs jump out at you as important. They may come in the form of street signs and billboards, where some words stick out as more important than the others ... '.[56] The urban environment is full of communications. There are advertisements, signs, graffiti and overheard voices and conversations; these all combine in surreal cut-up or collage to

---

[50]   Penczak, *City Magick*, p. 81.
[51]   Ibid.
[52]   Ibid., p. 84.
[53]   Ibid., p. 82.
[54]   Ibid., p. 83.
[55]   Davis, *TechGnosis*, p. 55.
[56]   Penczak, *City Magick*, p. 84.

offer potential esoteric significance. As Moore puts it, the 'peeling letters of the shopfronts are shapes borrowed from some angel lexicon'.[57]

The 'template' for these ambulations is not pilgrimage. As Steve Pile has stated, such undertakings are not a sacred journey in the traditional religious sense of a procession towards particular 'places already known'.[58] Fieldwork revealed that the guiding metaphor is that of exploration in the modern (and, actually, colonial) sense of the traveller going to (and through) wholly or relatively unknown places in order to discover. Some even go beyond discovering what is already latently out there, showing a proactive desire deliberately to imbue an inert cityscape with magical meaning, to re-enchant it. The theoretical point to be underscored here is that this aspect of urban esoteric practice is not following pre-established cartography so much as deliberate, creative recoding of urban spaces to accord with the esoteric worldview and personal experience of the individual in question, who is then left with a unique map of their city. Penczak advises the urban esotericist to 'mark special places that feel particularly powerful [and] … note places that lack power or feel malevolent … Avoid these energies in ritual.'[59]

During fieldwork, it became amply apparent that energy is almost ubiquitous within the magical city. It varies in kind, and it varies in its point of origin. It is in places, in the form of earth energy, place spirits (these are not the same, but separate phenomena) and in locations' 'echoing' of historical events. Furthermore (as Penczak advised, above), it is to be found in buildings and in objects.[60] Moreover, energy is said to be in people, individually and collectively. There is an important diachronic dimension to it: energy is not simply static but in a state of flux. Its flow and its nature can be changed through human agency and it also seems to be prone to changing 'naturally'. Fieldwork revealed a common narrative pattern whereby esotericists would report going to a familiar place or area but finding that, on a certain visit, it did not feel right. They perhaps could not remain there, or at least could not carry out any meditative or ritual activity. The energy, it was said, had changed. Explanations for this were speculative, and ranged from transits and transitions of an astrological nature to something that the esotericist themselves may have done wrong (had they somehow offended the *genius loci*, perhaps by not performing a previous ritual correctly?), or to other human agency, be it mundane urban development or even malign magic. Sometimes such an explanation was

---

[57]   Alan Moore and Eddie Campbell, *Snakes and Ladders* (Paddington, Queensland, 2001), p. 39.

[58]   Steve Pile, *Real Cities* (London, 2005), p. 11.

[59]   Penczak, *City Magick*, p. 83.

[60]   Ibid., p. 81.

found, but this was not always the case. On other occasions, it was just seen as the result of natural and inevitable shifts in the energy of the place or the person(s) concerned, and was simply taken as a sign that it was time to move on. Esotericists see their quest for self-transformation as ongoing, and it thus makes sense that they should hear the call of new places or areas from time to time. For them, it is an expected aspect of an organic, dynamic universe; as they themselves like to put it, 'shift happens'.[61]

Ultimately then, the image presented is rather more complex than one simply consisting of 'city circuits' of ley energy. Instead, co-existing with the physical city is a constantly shifting pattern of many and various energies in flux. It is reminiscent of a meteorological map used to show a television viewer the weather forecast, whereby a territory is superimposed upon by various protean systems which have their own dynamism and, moreover, interact with one another. The real picture is actually more complex still. This chapter has indicated that a high degree of individual specificity is one part of esotericism. Further, a degree of spontaneity or happenstance is also an integral part of the phenomenon: areas for urban exploration are selected by the esoteric equivalent of putting a pin in a map. This personal, idiosyncratic and stochastic nature of city magic is key. Magicians' cities include accidental, aleatory elements which may only have significance to a small group of individuals or one particular person, at one particular time. For example, William Burroughs held that a 'doorway into the nineteenth century' existed in Soho's Peter Street. It seems that this idea was uniquely his until he shared it in print, with the enigmatic comment that 'some doors open and some do not'.[62] It is not known whether the door 'survived' subsequent redevelopment of the area. Another such gateway existed, Burroughs believed, in nearby Brewer Street, but this came to light only recently; Burroughs is not known to have shared that idea widely, if at all, beyond his immediate circle of friends.[63] Even when a group *dérive* takes place, individual experiences vary; during fieldwork, it was common to 'sidewalk' with four or five people who did not all 'feel' an area or place in the same way. The energy of place, it was said, reacts with the unique energy of individuals to produce a unique, personal response.

---

[61]   This is a quip too common to be traced to any one individual. It is a (para-)pun, of course, one which illustrates a certain level of humour often found in esoteric magic.

[62]   William S. Burroughs, 'Treasure Island', in *Architectural Design*, 39/6 (6 June 1969), p. 314.

[63]   Barry Miles, (author of *Call Me Burroughs: A Life* [New York, 2013]); personal communication.

To make sense of this, it helps to note its resonance with certain theoretical developments in human geography which have taken place since around the turn of the millennium. Clearly, a model such as that employed above, in the second section of this chapter, will be of limited value in this context. It is not that such an approach is wrong, because it worked well for fixed places with identifiable, shared meaning; however, the open-ended, unpredictable nature of the *dérive* features neither fixed location (it is nomadic and unstructured) nor predetermined meaning (instead, it is a creation of meaning), and such meanings are not necessarily shared (they could be completely private). Instead, we will need to refer to certain practice-based ideas of place, such as those presented by Thrift.[64] Esoteric urban exploration could be better conceptualised with a stress on practice, focusing on what a group or an individual *do*, in a certain area, within a certain timeframe. This leads on to the idea of the 'assemblage'. This is an 'open' model, which allows for unpredictable things to happen in unpredictable places with some considerable degree of spontaneity. Anderson and McFarlane state that the assemblage

> is often used to emphasise emergence, multiplicity and indeterminacy, and connects to a wider redefinition of the socio-spatial in terms of the composition of diverse elements into some form of provisional socio-spatial formation. … [D]eploying the term assemblage enables us to remain deliberately open as to the form of the unity, its durability, the types of relations and the human and non-human elements involved.[65]

Furthermore, they claim that '[a]ssemblage emphasises spatiality *and* temporality'.[66] This is especially important here, given the diachronic variation and dynamic changes in esoteric energies and circumstances over time. These are a feature of urban magical maps, which are always already unstable and subject to a Heraclitean flow of energies. The idea of assemblage allows for just the kind of coalescent creativity and emergent meanings found in a magical 'sidewalk'.

Conclusion

This study of urban esoteric energies and magical practices suggests that, when approaching urban magic, a 'traditional' model based on a static map will only make partial sense of the phenomenon. The esoteric idea of energy

---

[64] Nigel Thrift, 'The Still Point: Resistance, Expressiveness, Embodiment and Dance', in *Geographies of Resistance*, ed. Steve Pile and Michael Keith (London, 1997), pp. 124–51.

[65] Ben Anderson and Colin McFarlane, 'Assemblage and Geography', *Area* 43 (2011), 124–7 at 124.

[66] Ibid., p. 125 (authors' italics).

describes and prescribes a wide range of multiplicity and unpredictability within the magical city. This leads towards a model of city magic which properly takes into account the polysemic and diachronically unstable nature of socio-cultural reality. In esoteric urbanism, change is the only permanence, and so some familiar ideas need to be refined. Here are found unconventional maps – maps of personal, protean palimpsests, of idiosyncratic, ephemeral assemblages. The cartography of contemporary urban esotericism requires us to take into account the 'fluid' condition of late modernity on the levels of both data and theory. The idea of the modern as an experience of chronic change was famously postulated by Toffler in the 1970s, and later developed by Bauman.[67] In line with such observations, the esoteric urban of late modernity is not merely 'there' in a static sense, but it is volatile, motile and unstable. There are magical maps of the city, yet these are never definitive, never totalised. Instead, one finds a more chaotic cartography, a multiplicity of personalised 'micro-maps' comprising numerous visions and subject to an ongoing process of revision. To return to the opening question, this chapter may not provide a simple answer to the question of 'where is significant, special or sacred' in the mind of an urban esotericist; but it at least explicates why such a question is not one which can or should be answered simply.

Bibliography

Agnew, John A., *Place and Politics in Modern Italy* (Chicago, 2002)

Anderson, Ben and Colin McFarlane, 'Assemblage and Geography', *Area* 43 (2011), 124–7

Bauman, Zygmunt, *Liquid Modernity* (Cambridge, 2000)

Burroughs, William S., 'Treasure Island', in *Architectural Design* 39/6 (6 June 1969)

Bulwer-Lytton, Edward, *The Coming Race* (Edinburgh, 1871)

Campbell, C. B., 'The Cult, the Cultic Milieu and Secularization', in *A Sociological Yearbook of Religion in Britain 5*, ed. Michael Hill (London, 1972), pp. 119–36

Clarke, J. J., *The Tao of the West: Western Transformations of Taoist Thought* (London, 2000)

Constable, John, *The Southwark Mysteries* (London, 1999)

Coverley, Merlin, *Occult London* (Harpenden, 2017)

Cresswell, Tim, *Place: A Short Introduction* (Oxford, 2004)

Davis, Erik, *TechGnosis: Myth, Magic and Mysticism in the Age of Information* (London, 1998)

Evans, Dave, *The History of British Magic after Crowley: Kenneth Grant, Amado Crowley, Chaos Magic, Satanism, Lovecraft, the Left Hand Path, Blasphemy and Magical Morality* (Harpenden, 2007)

[67] See Alvin Toffler, *Future Shock* (London, 1970); Zygmunt Bauman, *Liquid Modernity* (Cambridge, 2000).

Faivra, Antoine and Jacob Needleman (eds), *Modern Esoteric Spirituality* (London, 1993)

Foucault, Michel, 'Of Other Spaces', *Diacritics* 16 (1986), 22–7

Fox, R. G., 'East of Said', in *Edward Said: A Critical Reader*, ed. Michael Sprinkler (Oxford, 1992), pp.144–56

Greenwood, Susan, *Magic, Witchcraft and the Otherworld: An Anthropology* (Oxford, 2000)

Hanegraaf, W. J., *New Age Religion and Western Culture: Esotericism in the Mirror of Secular Thought* (New York, 1988)

Heelas, Paul, *The New Age Movement* (Oxford, 1996)

—— and Linda Woodhead, with Benjamin Steel, Bronislaw Szerszynski and Karin Tusting, *The Spiritual Revolution: Why Religion is Giving Way to Spirituality* (Oxford, 2005)

Hess, David J., *Science and the New Age: The Paranormal, Its Defenders and Debunkers, and American Culture* (Madison, WI, 1993)

Hetherington, Kevin, *Expressions of Identity: Space, Performance, Politics* (London, 1998)

Hodkinson, Paul, *Goth: Identity, Style and Subculture* (Oxford, 2002)

Hughes, Allen and Albert Hughes, *From Hell* [film] (20th-Century Fox, 2001)

Ivakhiv, Adrian J., *Claiming Sacred Ground: Pilgrims and Politics at Glastonbury and Sedona* (Bloomington, IN, 2001)

Lachman, Gary, *Politics and the Occult: The Left, the Right and the Radically Unseen* (Wheaton, IL, 2008)

Lovelock, James, *The Ages of Gaia: A Biography of our Living Earth* (London, 1995)

Luckhurst, Roger, 'The Contemporary London Gothic and the Limits of the "Spectral Turn" ', *Textual Practice* 16 (2002), 527–46

Luhrmann, T. M., *Persuasions of the Witch's Craft: Ritual Magic in Contemporary England* (Cambridge, MA, 1989)

Michell, John, *The View over Atlantis* (London, 1973)

Miles, Barry, *Call Me Burroughs: A Life* (New York, 2013)

Moore, Alan and Eddie Campbell, *From Hell* (London, 2000)

—— and ——, *Snakes and Ladders* (Paddington, Queensland, 2001)

—— and Tim Perkins, *The Highbury Working: A Beat Séance* [CD] (London, 2000)

Muggleton, David and Rupert Weinzierl (eds), *The Post-Subcultures Reader* (Oxford, 2003)

Odier, Daniel, *The Job: Interviews with William Burroughs* (London, 1989)

Penczak, Chris, *City Magick: Urban Rituals, Spells and Shamanism* (York Beach, ME, 2001)

Shanks, Michael, *The Archaeological Imagination* (Walnut Creek, CA, 2012)

Sinclair, Iain, *Lud Heat and Suicide Bridge* (London, 1998)

——, *Lights Out for the Territory* (London, 1997)

Street, Christopher, *Earthstars: The Geometric Groundplan Underlying London's Ancient Sacred Sites and its Significance for the New Age* (London, 1990)

——, *London's Ley Lines: Pathways of Enlightenment* (London, 2011)

——, *London: City of Revelation* (London, 2011)

Sutcliffe, Steven and Marion Bowman (eds), *Beyond New Age: Exploring Alternative Spirituality* (Edinburgh, 2000)

Sutcliffe, Steven J., *Children of the New Age: A History of Spiritual Practices* (London, 2003)

Thrift, Nigel, 'The Still Point: Resistance, Expressiveness, Embodiment and Dance', in *Geographies of Resistance*, ed. Steve Pile and Michael Keith (London, 1997)

Toffler, Alvin, *Future Shock* (London, 1970)

Wallis, Roy, *The Elementary Forms of the New Religious Life* (London, 1984)

Watkins, Alfred, *The Old Straight Track: Its Mounds, Beacons, Moats, Sites and Mark Stones* (London, 1984 [1925])

Wilcock, John, *A Guide to Occult Britain: The Quest for Magic in Pagan Britain* (London, 1976)

York, Michael, *The Emerging Network: A Sociology of the New Age and Neo-Pagan Movements* (London, 1996)

Urban Anxieties

5

The Occultism of the New York Slums: Perceptions and Apparitions *c.* 1850–1930

————◆◆◆————

OLIVER BETTS

I have just finished a new attempt at fiction – the story I told you I would write, with Brooklyn as a setting. The title is *The Horror at Red Hook*, and it deals with hideous cult-practices behind the gangs of noisy young loafers whose essential mystery has impressed me so much. The tale is rather long and rambling, and I don't think it is very good; but it represents at least an attempt to extract horror from an atmosphere to which you deny any qualities save vulgar commonplaceness.[1]

In the above letter to his friend and fellow weird fiction author Frank Belknap Long in the summer of 1925, Howard Phillips Lovecraft, commonly referred to as H. P. Lovecraft, announced a departure from his typical style of writing. Abandoning the quaint New England villages and corrupted seaports that proved so fertile a literary stomping ground for his fantastical tales, he instead turned to a slum at the heart of Brooklyn itself to weave a tale of devil-worshipping cults, strange goings-on, and mysteries too terrible to contemplate. The resulting *The Horror at Red Hook* was not considered by the author one of his best efforts and has divided critics ever since.

---

[1] H. P. Lovecraft, 'To Frank Belknap Long, 2nd August 1925', in August Derleth and Donald Wandrei (eds), *H. P. Lovecraft: Selected Letters, 1911–1924* (Sauk City, WI, 1965), p. 19.

This chapter argues that *The Horror at Red Hook*, written in 1925 and published in *Weird Tales* magazine in January 1927, deserves a more prominent place within the literary canon of Lovecraft's mythos.[2] It also places *The Horror at Red Hook* within its contemporary urban and supernatural context, as it is only through providing that wider context that this tale can truly be appreciated. Although he may have felt that the urban setting was one which paled in comparison with the haunted, otherworldly New England he was soon to enshrine in more famous texts such as *The Dunwich Horror* (1928–29) and *The Shadow Over Innsmouth* (written 1931, published 1936), and was a failed experiment in stepping out of type, the occult slum fancifully depicted in *The Horror at Red Hook* taps a rich vein of horror, anxiety, and cultural misapprehension that governed American attitudes to the inner city, and particularly to New York. Understanding the slum, and how it figured within American social discourse, can rescue *The Horror at Red Hook* from being dismissed simply as among the worst excesses of Lovecraft's 'lurid ethnic diatribes', as one reviewer put it.[3] Half a century of anxious discussion and debate about not just immigration and urban deprivation, but also occultism and the supernatural in New York City were an important backdrop to the story's publication, and *The Horror at Red Hook* is worthy of re-examination as a product of this fractured milieu.

The Horror at Red Hook

Paul Buhle, in attempting to offer an overall conception of Lovecraft's literary universe, pulls no punches when it comes to analysing the author's views on race. Lovecraft was 'an avowed racist for nearly all his life', he asserts.[4] Certainly the creation of *The Horror at Red Hook*, which Buhle touches on, was steeped in Lovecraft's uncomfortable encounters with an ethnically mixed New York. 'The organic things – Italo-Semitico-Mongoloid – inhabiting that awful cesspool', Lovecraft wrote following a trip to Manhattan's Lower East Side in 1922, 'could not by any stretch of the imagination be call'd human.'[5] For Buhle, though, this is but a more overt expression of views commonly

[2]   H. P. Lovecraft, 'The Horror at Red Hook', in *The Complete Fiction of H. P. Lovecraft*, ed. Eric Carl Link (New York, 2016), pp. 335–54.

[3]   Douglas E. Winter, 'Those Eldritch Horrors', *The Washington Post*, 26 October 1997, p. 6.

[4]   Paul Buhle, 'Dystopia as Utopia: Howard Phillips Lovecraft and the Unknown Content of American Horror Literature', in *H. P. Lovecraft: Four Decades of Criticism*, ed. S. T. Joshi (Athens, OH, 1980), pp. 196–210 at 203.

[5]   'To Frank Belknap Long, 21ˢᵗ March 1924', in Derleth and Wandrei (eds), *Lovecraft: Selected Letters*, p. 333.

held in early twentieth-century America. Lovecraft was by no means alone, he observes, in believing that the 'other' beliefs and cultures that existed outside of Western civilisation posed an inherent threat to it, as immigration brought them within the boundaries of America. This was key for Lovecraft, Buhle argues, as 'horror was also fascination' for him.[6]

Others have not been so kind. Seen as an outlier in terms of both its unusual urban setting and its particularly overt racism, *The Horror at Red Hook* has not been among the more celebrated works of the Lovecraft canon. Martyn Colebrook has recently studied the tale from the perspective of alienation in the urban, but the weight of analysis in his study rests firmly on a comparison with China Miéville's supernatural creation of the city of New Crobuzon.[7] James Kneale, delving deeper, has emphasised the importance of pushing beyond the racism of the text to explore 'the *embodied* sense of horror' that blends anxieties about invasion and inbreeding in the slums.[8] In general, though, *The Horror at Red Hook* has been neglected and sidelined, not seen as by any means one of the major contributions Lovecraft is credited with making to American horror and Gothic traditions. S. T. Joshi, perhaps the author's most impassioned biographer, deems the story awful, while many other devoted Lovecraft scholars have struggled to reconcile this particular tale with his wider body of work.[9] Darrell Schweitzer considers it one of those poorer Lovecraft works that seemed to 'gibber from start to finish' with unnecessary detail and a fundamental lack of polish.[10] The popular H. P Lovecraft Literary Podcast, which has analysed each and every literary outpouring of the author on an episodic basis, treated the text with bemusement. Hosts Christopher Lackey and Chad Fifer gently teased that this represented 'H. P. Lovecraft's celebration of diversity' and broached the idea of skipping the 'not very good' text altogether.[11]

Given this comparative neglect, it is perhaps worth offering at this point a brief summary of the plot of *The Horror at Red Hook*. Beginning with former 'Dublin University man' turned police inspector Thomas Malone having a

---

[6]   Buhle, 'Dystopia as Utopia', pp. 198, 204, 207–8.
[7]   Martyn Colebrook, ' "Comrades in Tentacles": H. P. Lovecraft and China Miéville', in *New Critical Essays on H. P. Lovecraft*, ed. David Simmons (New York, 2013), pp. 209–26.
[8]   James Kneale, 'From Beyond: H. P. Lovecraft and the Place of Horror', *Cultural Geographies* 13 (2006), 106–26 at 114–15.
[9]   Kenneth W. Fang Jr and S. T. Joshi, 'H. P. Lovecraft: His Life and Work', in *Lovecraft: Four Decades of Criticism*, ed. Joshi, pp. 1–19 at 14–15.
[10] Darrell Schweitzer, 'Lovecraft and Lord Dunsany', in *Discovering H. P. Lovecraft*, ed. Darrell Schweitzer, rev. edn (Holicong, PA, 2001), pp. 72–87 at 86–7.
[11] H. P. Lovecraft Literary Podcast, http://hppodcraft.com/2010/04/07/episode-38-the-horror-at-red-hook/ (accessed 7 April 2018).

very public breakdown in downtown Pascoag, Rhode Island, at the sight of the tall buildings there, Lovecraft's story slips back in time to the incident that had so terrified Malone. The Red Hook area of Brooklyn, 'a maze of hybrid squalor near the ancient waterfront', occupies much of Malone's attention, and it is through this 'babel of sound and filth' that he becomes aware of the curious behaviour of reclusive old-money scholar Robert Suydam. Suydam has been seen associating with the criminal elements of Red Hook but, fending off speculation about his sanity from relatives, suddenly transforms his life. Leaving Red Hook he begins to move in higher circles, becoming engaged to a society belle, while the police are left with little clue as to either his erstwhile activities in the slum or an ongoing spate of kidnappings in the neighbourhood. Events only climax when Suydam's wedding night on a ship departing New York is disrupted by both his own and his wife's deaths in horrifying circumstances. Involved in a police raid on Suydam's house, Malone is sucked into an underground hellscape, where he witnesses human sacrifice and Sudyam's resurrection by otherworldly entities before something goes wrong and the building above collapses. Malone is found in the rubble, the only policeman to survive, but traumatised – hence his reaction to the similar built-up areas of Pascoeg, related at the beginning of the text. Meanwhile the tunnels and chambers below the collapsed building are sealed with cement – although, as Lovecraft notes, Red Hook's lurking horror remains unperturbed just beneath the surface.

Throughout the text the urban is ever present. From Malone's 'singular lapse of behaviour' on the streets of Pascoeg to the descriptions of the New York waterfront as Suydam's steamer leaves on its ill-fated wedding journey, the city in all its supernatural and unsettling manifestations appears as the constant backdrop. It is Red Hook that is most evident, though, the real neighbourhood that Lovecraft twisted and recast as a hybrid network of chaotic immigration, disorder, and immorality:

> From this tangle of material and spiritual putrescence the blasphemies of an hundred dialects assail the sky. Hordes of prowlers reel shouting and singing along the lanes and thoroughfares, occasional furtive hands suddenly extinguish lights and pull down curtains, and swarthy, sin-pitted faces disappear from windows when visitors pick their way through. Policemen despair of order or reform, and seek rather to erect barriers protecting the outside world from the contagion.[12]

---

[12]   Lovecraft, 'Horror at Red Hook', p. 338.

This was the city as a tangle of unknowable and suspicious places where even policemen, well respected as urban authorities by more well-to-do urban dwellers like Lovecraft, are limited to walling off the district rather than patrolling it. Drawing on contemporary anxieties about slum areas in cities like New York, Lovecraft rendered them as places of horror and subversion of the established urban norm. Properly assessing this text requires a journey deeper into the fin-de-siècle cityscape, for whilst the intense racism displayed in *The Horror at Red Hook* may have been a step more extreme than contemporary racial attitudes in general, his reactions to the shock of the urban, and realisation of the horrifying potential of the slum in particular, were rooted in much more common veins of thought at the time.

Into the slum

In opening his own account of the slums, corrupting and corrupted but not supernatural as Lovecraft's were, the journalist Jacob Riis was careful to ensure his text would not be dismissed as fiction. In introducing his *How the Other Half Lives* (1890) Riis cited the history of slum warrens in New York City, particularly the findings of the commission investigating the causes of the 1863 riots. There was prehistory here, Riis argued, as he laid out a cogent and emotional view into the lives of poor New Yorkers. Evoking the biblical motif of Cain's murder of his brother Abel, the first murder and one for which Cain was permanently cursed by God, Riis conjured a vision where the emergence of slum housing in New York constituted an original sin: 'the first tenement New York knew bore the mark of Cain from its birth, though a generation passed before the writings were deciphered'.[13] His study sent shockwaves through American society, its carefully considered text and evocative photographs burning an image of slumland New York into the national consciousness. Riis had spent years visiting, exploring, and documenting the slums and rookeries of New York with notebook and camera and was determined to make polite society aware of the squalor and deprivation that lurked just below the surface in the major cities of the nation. 'Mr Riis has written a powerful book, which deserves careful and thorough reading', the *New York Times* insisted, entitling it review 'Matters We Ought to Know'.[14] *How the Other Half Lived* was a revelation to American society, serving to raise the level of debate about slums and the poor to the national level.

---

[13] Jacob Riis, *How the Other Half Lives: Studies among the Tenements of New York* (London, 1997 [New York, 1890]), pp. 5–9.

[14] 'Matters We Ought to Know: How the Other Half Lives, Studies among the Tenements of New York. By Jacob A Riis', *The New York Times*, 4 January 1891, p. 19.

Concern over the slum and its inhabitants was not a new phenomenon when Riis published *How the Other Half Lives*. So prominent and heated was the debate and discussion in the printed press about slum neighbourhoods throughout the Western world that Alan Mayne in his classic study has suggested that the slum was, to a great extent, a fictional construct. Slums were not necessarily especially insanitary or criminal, Mayne notes, but just more prominently described as such in the media.[15] Whilst the extent to which Mayne's idea, of the slum as a literary construct, can be taken as wholly representative of the slum experience continues to be debated, there is no denying that certain neighbourhoods in the big cities of the United States were widely considered to be slums by the 1900s.[16] In 1927, residents of Red Hook complained that they were being unfairly singled out as the subject of a city-wide report into juvenile crime. The Rev. Father William L. Long, a local Catholic priest, was quoted in *The New York Times* as pointing out the crass assumptions that he felt dominated the report's description of Red Hook: 'The children are of the nicest kind ... the only complaint I would make of them is that they are too innocent, too much of the Mama boy type', he claimed. 'Those who are responsible for this report are utterly hopeless ... the report is unspeakably false and cruel.'[17] Yet even as defenders of the report protested that objectors had not read or understood its complexity, at least some of the motivation in focusing on Red Hook was clearly that it simply *seemed* like the sort of area in which juvenile delinquents could, or perhaps should, be found. With his suspicion of 'the gangs of noisy young loafers', Lovecraft was by no means alone in the 1920s in casting a wary eye over Red Hook.[18]

It was not just urban decay that led to the unease of outsiders like Lovecraft when they surveyed the slums of New York. By the 1880s, immigrants *en masse*, both from across the United States and increasingly from the wider world, were thronging the city. By 1921, particularly after the upheaval of the First World War, but also following decades of immigration, one *New York Times* columnist was happily describing 'the Old World in New York'. The author saw it as a puzzling but intriguing landscape of shifting immigrant pockets, one where you could step from a Little Athens of Greek immigrants and Italian

[15] Alan Mayne, *The Imagined Slum: Newspaper Representation in Three Cities, 1870–1914* (Leicester, 1993), pp. 1–10.
[16] See David Englander, 'Review: Alan Mayne, *The Imagined Slum: Newspaper Representation in Three Cities, 1870–1914*', *Urban History* 21 (1994), 309–11; also Seth Koven, *Slumming: Sexual and Social Politics in Victorian London* (Oxford, 2004).
[17] 'Red Hook Resents Crime Board Report', *The New York Times*, 21 May 1927, p. 21.
[18] 'To Frank Belknap Long, 2nd August 1925', in Derleth and Wandrei (eds), *Lovecraft: Selected Letters*, p. 19.

shops over into a 'Judea' or 'Israel' around any sharp corner in New York, or where two diners could eat splendidly in a Syrian restaurant for 85 cents, providing they were prepared to deal with a menu 'written in Arabic with letters running from left to right'.[19] Others, however, were far less impressed. From the late 1880s onwards, a rising tide of anxiety about immigration and the 'alien hordes' of the Old World consumed national and civic debate. As historian John Higham has put it, 'a deeper strain and anguish' came to dominate discussion of immigration in the 1890s, fuelled in part by a severe economic depression. Although this ebbed to an extent as fortunes improved in the new century, nativism continued to play a prominent and (sometimes) paranoid part in American political discourse.[20] On the west coast particularly, the anxiety manifested itself as anti-Chinese sentiment; but in the east the increasingly 'polyglot' nature of New York was seen by many as evidence of the growing 'alien' presence immigration brought to America.[21] Ellis Island in Upper New York Bay, where a dedicated facility for processing new arrivals opened in 1892, became a lightning rod for an increasingly polarised debate. When he took up the post of Commissioner General of Immigration at Ellis Island in 1905, Frank P. Sargent was quoted by a *New York Times* reporter as being a fervent opponent of the so-called 'open-door' policy:

> The time has come when every American citizen … must regard with grave misgiving the mighty tide of immigration that, unless something is done, will soon poison or at least pollute the very fountainhead of American life and progress. Big as we are … we cannot safely swallow such an endless-course dinner … without getting indigestion and perhaps national appendicitis.[22]

Lovecraft's categorisation of Red Hook as 'Syrian, Spanish, Italian, and Negro' all jumbled together with, to his mind 'better' bands of 'Scandinavian and American' settlement ringing it in, was part of a wider cultural anxiety about the seemingly unending waves of immigration into New York and its poorer neighbourhoods.

[19] Helen Bullitt Lowry, 'The Old World in New York', *The New York Times*, 3 April 1921, p. 37.

[20] John Higham, *Strangers in the Land: Patterns of American Nativism, 1860–1925*, new edn (New Brunswick, NJ, 1983), pp. 68, 159–60. For a more recent summary of Higham's influential work, see Deirdre Moloney, ' "Strangers in the Land": Gender and Immigration Policy', *The Journal of the Gilded Age and Progressive Era* 11 (2012), 270–5.

[21] Mae M. Ngai, *Impossible Subjects: Illegal Aliens and the Making of Modern America* (Princeton, NJ, 2004), pp. 18–20.

[22] Frank P. Sargent, quoted in Eric Homberger, *The Historical Atlas of New York City: A Visual Celebration of 400 years of New York City's History* (New York, 2005), p. 137.

It is important to place Lovecraft's racism into a context, not to excuse it by arguing that it was merely symptomatic of the time, but rather to emphasise that it became a hook for his horror. The presence of Syrians (often a catch-all term employed for Arab/middle-eastern migrants in the 1900s) in the city provided Lovecraft with an ethnic group into which he could work a supernatural cult. Whilst the cult that Suydam falls in with is never described as exclusively 'Syrian', there is a clear suggestion that older, terrible faiths and superstitions lurked among the immigrant population. Suydam claims to be studying the migrants because he thought their beliefs 'some remnant of Nestorian Christianity', but Malone, in learning they come from Kurdistan, 'could not help recalling that Kurdistan is the land of the Yezidis, last survivors of the Persian devil-worshippers'.[23] This was, and continues to be, a popular misconception of Yazidi beliefs derived from theological and linguistic misunderstandings of the faith's core tenets, and provided a convenient hook for Lovecraft. The slum-dwellers are duplicitous, appearing on the outside to be Christian but harbouring, behind the closed doors and walled-off spaces of the slum they inhabit, far darker ancient rituals and creeds.

This theme of corruption, of the immigrant devil-worshipper transforming the urban landscape of the slum in terrible ways, continues throughout the text. Most notable is the 'Dance-Hall Church' that features as a central point of cult activity in Red Hook. Gangsters, revellers, and all sorts of unsavoury characters – nominally Catholic, although acknowledged by spiritual and secular authorities to be beyond the pale, and including Suydam – flock here each night, until the appearance of a missing child's face at the window prompts a police raid. Inside, the church, already corrupted by its use as a place of revelry, has been transformed. Malone finds 'crudely painted panels ... which depicted sacred faces with peculiarly worldly and sardonic expressions, and which occasionally took liberties that even a layman's sense of decorum could scarcely countenance'. All is corrupted, the older non-Christian traditions replacing the divine (and American), and the 'Greek inscription' on the wall above the pulpit speaks of blood, terror, and ancient and pagan deities appeased only by sacrifice. The familiar has been rendered terrible and 'other' by the intervention of these new arrivals with their corrupted Old World practices and beliefs.[24]

Lovecraft lifted the incantation on the walls of the Dance Hall Church from, of all sources, the 'Magic' pages of the *Encyclopaedia Britannica*. Perhaps a little unsettled by this plunge into a new, urban setting, he admitted that he

---

[23]   Lovecraft, 'Horror at Red Hook', p. 342.
[24]   Ibid., pp. 341–4.

was unsure of 'the right reservoirs to tap' when it came to the occult. 'Are there good translations of any medieval necromancers with directions for raising spirits, invoking Lucifer, and all that sort of thing?', he asked fellow weird-tales author Clarke Ashton Smith in October 1925, confessing himself 'appallingly ignorant' of such issues.[25] Unlike in later works, which increasingly built upon a body of Cthulhu Mythos as imagined in 1928's *The Call of Cthulhu*, and fictional supernatural texts such as the Necronomicon (first mentioned in his short story *The Hound*, published in 1924, but increasingly referenced in later works), composing *The Horror at Red Hook* saw Lovecraft scrabbling for inspiration. Emphasising that he had 'not a shred of credence in any form of supernaturalism', Lovecraft asked his friends whether they could nevertheless recommend some reading material for inspiration: 'If any of the crack-brained cults have free booklets or "literature" with suggestive descriptive matter, I wouldn't mind having my name on their "sucker lists" ', he wrote to Ashton Smith.[26] He had his sinister cult in its decayed urban environment, his 'horrific space' as Kneale dubs it, but struggled to locate the occult hook that would anchor his horror in its urban setting.[27]

Supernatural New York

Lovecraft's struggle to locate the supernatural ambience for his horrific slum cult is all the more intriguing when put into the context of late nineteenth- and early twentieth-century New York, for the city had a considerable pedigree when it came to the supernatural and, especially, the spiritual. Historical convention has held, as Robert S. Cox has recently reiterated, that the genesis of the American spiritualist movement came in upstate New York in the 1840s, with the rhythmic tapping and knocking of the Fox sisters. Claiming to be intermediaries between the spirit world and the mortal one, the sisters spawned enormous public interest in their mediumships, relocating to New York City itself to spread their message. By the time they revealed their fraud in the late 1880s a nation-wide spiritualist craze was already well under way.[28] It was a connection that caused the embers of American spiritualism to settle in the perfect tinder of late nineteenth-century New York.

---

[25] 'To Clarke Ashton Smith, 9th October 1925', in Derleth and Wandrei (eds), *Lovecraft: Selected Letters*, p. 197.

[26] Ibid.

[27] Kneale, 'From Beyond', p. 112.

[28] Robert S. Cox, *Body and Soul: A Sympathetic History of American Spiritualism* (Charlottesville, VA, 2003), pp. 5–6.

Right from the beginning New York's centrality to the developing currents of modern American life made it a perfect location for such a spiritualist movement to grow in strength. The Fox sisters found lodging in Barnum's New York Hotel and worked with Horace Greeley's newspaper empire.[29] In doing, they set a trend for seating the spiritual in New York itself. By the late 1850s, dedicated spiritualist newspapers, including *The Banner of Light* and *Spiritual Telegraph*, were in regular circulation in New York, and in 1856 a conference at the Stuyvesant Institute saw discussion of the central nature of the city as 'one place' where 'the phenomena of Spiritualism' could be properly explained to the people.[30] According to figures collated by David Nartonis, New York was an epicentre of both meetings about spiritualism and of advertised services relating to contacting the beyond in the late nineteenth century.[31] In churches and lecture theatres, in hotels and in their own parlours, New Yorkers and out-of-towners gathered to hear spirits come to share news of the beyond in the urban environment.

Both believers and sceptics mapped the supernatural to the city of New York through their physical and literary interactions. There were, of course, other cities that registered on the spiritual and supernatural geography of the American imagination; Boston was home to *The Banner of Light*, one of the key spiritualist newspapers of the nineteenth century.[32] The entire New England region was of critical importance: the cultural and social influence of the Erie Canal, which traced a line across New York State connecting the Great Lakes to the Hudson river and then on to the Atlantic via New York, has been repeatedly invoked by scholars as vital to creating the fertile ground for an array of beliefs, from Mormonism to Spiritualism.[33] But it was New York that seemed crucial to this sense of otherworldly significance – the city drew national attention but also acted as a place for dissemination of the supernatural.

Mrs M. E. Edwards, one of many mediums plying their trade in late nineteenth-century New York, provides an interesting example of how the spiritual was mapped on to the city in the popular imagination. Edwards conducted séances and other mediumship at her home in Staten Island and was an expert in materialising the spirits of the departed (through a variety of sleights

---

[29]   Ibid, p. 7.
[30]   'New York Conference: Stuyvesant Institute Feb. 27 1857', *Liberator*, 21 March 1856, vol. 26, issue 12, p. 48.
[31]   David K. Nartonis, 'The Rise of 19th- Century American Spiritualism, 1854–1873', *Journal for the Scientific Study of Religion* 49 (2010), 361–73 at 366–70.
[32]   Cox, *Body and Soul*, p. 189.
[33]   See Michael Keene, *The Psychic Highway: How the Erie Canal Changed America* (New York, 2017).

of hands and props) before both delighted and sceptical audiences.[34] But she also published, during the 1880s, a short-lived newspaper that promoted her mediumship regionally. In it, the voices of those who had 'passed' sought out their loved ones through her intermediary skill. 'We are all here,' Mary Louisa Simmons informed her father of Andalusia, Pennsylvania. 'I have tried to send a message to my friends in Cincinnati, Ohio, on two occasions.' John Clenending's ghost announced in print, 'I find my wife is opposed to my coming in public.'[35] It is clear that Edwards presented herself as a New York conduit to the other world for those grieving families who consulted her from all over the Atlantic seaboard. She was certainly not alone in this practice. For example, *The Banner of Light* had a regular 'Spirit Message Department' purporting to detail messages from beyond the veil of death, and in each case the purpose of the column was to centre attention on the services of the medium.

This idea of the importance of place to the medium became distinctly clear in the sceptical investigations of the Seybert Commission. In an effort to uncover fraudulent practices, academics from the University of Pennsylvania investigated well-known mediums between 1884 and 1887. The records of the Commission offer an insight into spiritual practice in New York and elsewhere. During the investigation, Horace Howard Furness, a respected Shakespearean scholar and a critic of spiritualism, contacted Edwards supposedly for advice. She in turn suggested he contact another New York medium, John Caffray, who could teach Furness to become a self-practising medium at home. An amused Furness reported to the Commission that the process of being taught automatic writing by Caffray required the purchase of special slates:

> The first step was the purchase of two slates from Caffray, for which I gave him several dollars. They were common enough to look at, but ah! they had been for months in his Materializing Cabinet and had absorbed Spiritual power to the point of saturation, and fairly exuded it. I brought them carefully from New York, and folded them in black muslin, and laid them away in a dark drawer.[36]

Although Furness's purpose was to expose Caffray as a fraud, the exchange does highlight the significance of New York as a centre of supposed spiritual power, where the slates Caffray sold were imbued with their potency to connect to the

---

[34] 'She's Minnie's Spook: Real "Bright Eyes" is Operating on Staten Island', *The Washington Post*, 3 September 1907, p. 11.

[35] *Beacon Light*, 12 December 1885, p. 4.

[36] H. H. Furness (ed.), *Preliminary Report of the Commission Appointed by the University of Pennsylvania to Investigate Modern Spiritualism in Accordance with the Request of the Late Henry Seybert* (Philadelphia, 1920), pp. 124–5.

afterlife. Like hundreds of others whose records can be found scattered across the often fleeting explosion of spiritualist newspapers and periodicals from the 1850s onwards, the Commission focused direct attention on mediums in major cities like New York, a place to which visitors could travel but also where communication could be sought by those able to pay the medium's fee.

But what of the poor immigrants that Lovecraft fictionalised, Riis investigated, and large swathes of middle-class America agonised about? The image of spiritualism, with its parlour settings and genteel séances, seems somewhat removed from Lovecraft's grimy tale of slum occultism. Like the publicity image for New York's latest spiritualist-inclined play that appeared in *The Spur* in 1920, which featured an actress in a tasteful gown looking out of a high-rise window as she imagines telepathic communion with her London-based sister, much of the settings and apparatus of the spiritualist movement seem unconnected to the purported horrors of Red Hook.[37] The reality was that despite New York's immigrant population representing an array of beliefs and customs, some traditional and brought from overseas, others newer or adapted to the realities of American and urban life, little of this was known by Lovecraft, nor did that lack of knowledge matter. Like many slum travellers, Lovecraft took what he wanted from Red Hook and the Lower East Side; touring these areas confirmed already held beliefs rather than informing new ones. The individual, he noted in a 1924 letter recalling a trip to the Lower East Side two years prior, was lost to him in a morass of terrible overall impressions: 'From that nightmare of perverse infection I could not carry away the memory of any living face,' he wrote, adding that, 'the individually grotesque was lost in the collectively devastating.'[38] The geography of the slum was important – a 'realistic' portrayal of the discomfort of the urban that he found himself in – but the people and their cultures were empty vessels for Lovecraft to fill with his imagination.

Robert Suydam and H. P. Lovecraft

In his study of Lovecraft's urban writings, Kneale highlights the importance of spaces of horror to Lovecraft, in that in creating a contrast between 'banality and fantasy' the author located a deeply unsettling landscape. In this connection, Kneale touches on *He*, the other story Lovecraft set in New York, often read as an autobiographical piece.[39] Written during the same summer as *The*

---

[37] 'Telepathic Communication with London', *The Spur*, 15 November 1920, p. 47.

[38] 'To Frank Belknap Long, 21st March 1924', in Derleth and Wandrei (eds), *Lovecraft: Selected Letters*, p. 333.

[39] Kneale, 'From Beyond', 115–17, 120.

Horror at Red Hook (1925), *He* is a very different and, in some ways, more traditional horror narrative. An anonymous narrator, a New Englander disaffected by life in New York, encounters on his nocturnal ramblings through the city a strange elderly man. This man, revealed to be in eighteenth-century garb, leads the narrator deeper into the older, more authentic New York that he craves. Back at his house, the old man shows the narrator terrifying visions of the past and future, before being murdered by the spirits of those from whom he had stolen the secrets of his immortality, as the narrator flees in horror into the nocturnal streets.[40] The love of the narrator for a pre-modern, uncorrupted New York is so clearly linked to Lovecraft's own attitudes towards the city that biographical interpretations seem obvious. In August 1924, Lovecraft and friends, inspired by a pocket guide called *Little Old New York*, ended their dinner-party at 1.30 AM with a wander into the streets in search of 'the real stuff' of 'old-world' New York.[41] Kneale does not dispute this, but expresses 'unease' at a biographically oriented study of the New York texts as mere 'expressions' of Lovecraft's personal beliefs, precluding serious analysis of the 'fantastic ideas within strong narratives' that dominate his work.[42]

One vein of biographical interpretation remains to be explored, however, in *The Horror at Red Hook*. Kneale is right to argue that an over-concentration on such forms of analysis undervalues the horrific geography at play in the text and, as argued above, an insistence on reading *The Horror at Red Hook* purely as a product of Lovecraft's xenophobia is extremely limiting when exploring the supernatural elements of the text. Malone – a police officer with a dynamic presence in the narrative (and one presented in the third person) – does not conform to the typical first-person perspectives of those scholars and travellers whom Lovecraft selected as his semi-autobiographical representations in his fiction.[43] Robert Suydam, however, the secretive patrician figure at the centre of events, deserves a critical second look. Suydam, first assumed to be insane by relatives who cannot understand his fascination with the slums of Red Hook and their corrupt inhabitants, is transformed by the occult forces unleashed in the narrative. Yet leaving aside the demonic marriage and supernatural corruption, there are particular parallels between Lovecraft and his ill-fated academic. Both are interlopers in Red Hook, exhibiting a horrified fascination with the local people and sights, although Suydam is more directly

---

[40] H. P. Lovecraft, 'He', in *Complete Fiction*, ed. Link, pp. 355–64.
[41] 'To Mrs F. C. Clark, 20th August 1924', in Derleth and Wandrei (eds), *Lovecraft: Selected Letters*, pp. 345–6.
[42] Kneale, 'From Beyond', pp. 116–17.
[43] Compare Malone to the central character in *The Shadow over Innsmouth* (in *Complete Fiction*, ed. Link, pp. 866–923), for example.

involved than Lovecraft was. Both are fascinated by the suspicion of darker and more corrupt cultures at play amongst the immigrants. Although it is Malone who mentions the work of anthropologist and folklore expert Margaret Murray (of which Lovecraft was a devoted admirer), it is clear from Suydam's defence of his actions when his sanity is questioned that he shares this intense interest in human tradition.[44] The reclusive scholar claims to be 'engaged in the investigation of certain details of European tradition which required the closest contact with foreign groups and their songs and folk dances' – an ethnography that Lovecraft himself may have found appealing.[45] There are also more minor shared connections, less significant, but by no means superficial. Suydam comes from the sort of patrician old-money family that Lovecraft saw himself as having an affinity with: 'a lettered recluse of ancient Dutch family'.[46] As Suydam gains supernatural powers through his unholy dealings with the supernatural in the slums, he is transformed in looks, emerging from Red Hook clean-shaven and no longer 'deformed' by 'corpulence' as he leaves the slums and re-enters conventional society; similarly, Lovecraft's wife's departure to work in Cincinnati saw him lose weight as he began to arrange his own meals for the first time in his life during his residence in Brooklyn.[47] Most significantly, both Suydam and Lovecraft find themselves drawn into the horrifying spaces of the city.

The analogy has limits. It is doubtful that Lovecraft deliberately wrote himself into the Suydam character, although it is worth noting the similarities between Suydam – educated, withdrawn, but with an explorer's passion for uncovering the truth – and the comparable protagonists of Lovecraft's later and more celebrated works, such as Robert Olmstead (anonymous in the original text) in *The Shadow over Innsmouth* and Henry Armitage in *The Dunwich Horror*. But it is an analogy that offers a clearer contextual understanding of this complicated text. Crucially, like Suydam, Lovecraft was an urban explorer of Brooklyn and, in the best traditions of the urban wanderer out of place in the slums, the bustle, and the mixed immigrant population, the author projected his own fantastic understandings of society, space, and the supernatural. Sometimes this could be potentially delightful, as with the antiquarian tour that begins *He*; but very often Lovecraft's active imagination took darker turns. Inspired by the presence of the immigrant populations that troubled

---

[44] 'To Clark Ashton Smith, 9th October 1925', in Derleth and Wandrei (eds), *Lovecraft: Selected Letters*, p. 27.

[45] Lovecraft, 'Horror at Red Hook', p. 341.

[46] Ibid., p. 339.

[47] 'To Maurice W. Moe, 15th June 1925', in Derleth and Wandrei (eds), *Lovecraft: Selected Letters*, pp. 17–18.

him so deeply and were a constant feature in the local and national press, he attempted in his fictional efforts to impose an order and purpose upon what he saw as the slum-dwellers' loafing and idleness. Their haunts became places of cult worship, their families and connections networks of malicious trafficking and occultism, and Red Hook itself became a warren of depravity with hidden caverns filled with their otherworldly summonings. Lovecraft, like so many urban wanderers, sought an overarching reason for what he perceived as the chaos of urban life and, in his fiction at least, this manifested itself in super-natural terms.

The urban wanderer, the *flâneur* of nineteenth-century society, has received much historical and literary attention. The sexualised, thrill-seeking motives of some urban explorers has been studied in depth by Seth Koven, who draws out the titillation that could come from the abrasive cultural clash of descend-ing into the slums.[48] Judith Walkowitz's celebrated *City of Dreadful Delight* explores the more troubling side of the violent and sexualised narratives that came out of the East End of London in the final decades of the nineteenth cen-tury, the Whitechapel murders, and W. T. Stead's sensational *Maiden Tribute of Modern Babylon*: tales that Lovecraft would certainly have been aware of.[49] As Joachim Schlör notes, nocturnal rambling through the city was (and is) a creative act: 'perception is as marked by the attraction of the forbidden as by the fear of it', he argues.[50] Vision was key; urban wandering was making sense of the landscape through one's own eyes, interpreting it in ways that made sense to oneself, rather than an act of objective reasoning. Thus, like so many writers, reformers, journalists, and missionaries who had gone before him and would come after, Lovecraft was part of a tradition of recasting the slum in line with his own occult imaginings.

The genesis of *The Horror at Red Hook*, particularly its unusual detective-tale style, may derive from the shifting editorial policy of Lovecraft's chosen recip-ient for his stories, *Weird Tales* magazine. In a letter to fellow author Frank Belknap Long in 1924, he noted that rumours of a potential editorial shift towards the emerging genre of supernatural fiction would make it much more receptive to his 'Poe-Machen shudders'. 'Right in my line,' Lovecraft remarked optimistically.[51] Aware (albeit dismissive) of the spiritualism that swirled around New York at the time, alarmed by the mixed-race crowds that thronged

---

[48]   Koven, *Slumming*, pp. 1–14.
[49]   Judith R. Walkowitz, *City of Dreadful Delight: Narratives of Sexual Danger in Late Victorian London* (Chicago, 1992), pp. 1–14.
[50]   Joachim Schlör, *Nights in the Big City: London, Paris, Berlin* (London, 1998), p. 246.
[51]   'To Frank Belknap Long, 21st March 1924', in Derleth and Wandrei (eds), *Lovecraft: Selected Letters*, p. 330.

Brooklyn and had provoked social anxiety in white America for at least thirty years, and searching around for a way to channel his desperate desire to publish, Lovecraft focused on Red Hook, warping it into a chaotic and corrupt version of the real-life sense of horror he himself experienced there.

This twisting of the real into the imaginary, creating tension between fixed geographies and lived spaces noted by Kneale, is most evident in *The Horror at Red Hook*'s dramatic conclusion. The menace of urban unrest, a concern that shaped attitudes to urban space in Lovecraft's time, has drawn Malone and the police to Red Hook.[52] Battering in the doors of Suydam's basement flat, the police descend into his collection of curios and, as a crack opens up, Malone is sucked into a subterranean world of horror. Here the story arguably begins to unravel, as it is never entirely clear what Malone is witness to. Certainly the demonic marriage that Lovecraft suggests ties in with Gina Wisker's study of his understanding of women as 'liminal figures … powerful, subtle, and in the main uncrushable', and empowered as 'living vehicles through which monstrous aliens can be reproduced'.[53] Whether it really is the biblical Lilith that Malone sees through the unnatural lights of the cave, or something more akin to Lovecraft's evolving concept of the Elder Gods, matters little; the supernatural is revealed as just below the surface of Red Hook, broken into with the merest of occult dabbling from the now-damned Suydam. Like the underground sewers that had been at the centre of much public attention and action at the turn of the century, the surface manifestations of horror appear in Red Hook as a bubbling over of the evil beneath. Lovecraft's text was one of many that hinted at an underlying evil beneath the apparent chaos of the slums: an explanation in terms of a supernatural purpose behind the slum's apparent moral malaise. Gustave Lening's *The Dark Side of New York Life and its Criminal Classes*, of 1873, had taken a similarly suspicious, but less occult-laden angle. It identified a more 'realistic' horror, in exposing everything from séances to lunatic asylums that, it claimed, were 'hidden' just out of sight in New York, in its slums and rookeries, peopled, often, by the new waves of migrants arriving from abroad.[54] When Lovecraft first came to New York, he was stepping into a city steeped in both the real-life misery and social anxiety

---

[52] Riis's study of New York's poverty had opened with the report into the 1860s draft riot which had cited the terrible rookeries where the unrest began. See Riis, *How the Other Half Lives*, p. 5.

[53] Gina Wisker, ' "Spawn of the Pit": Lavinia, Marceline, Medusa, and All Things Foul: H. P. Lovecraft's Liminal Women', in *New Critical Essays*, ed. Simmons, pp. 32–3, 52.

[54] Gustave Lening, *The Dark Side of New York Life and its Criminal Classes from Fifth Avenue down to the Five Points, A Complete Narrative of the Mysteries of New York* (New York, 1873), pp. 509–39.

of the slums and a supernatural heritage more than half a century in the making. Much like his native New England, Brooklyn was fertile ground for his imagination of the supernatural.

Like many of his critics and subsequent readers, Lovecraft was not convinced that *The Horror at Red Hook* represented a successful foray into new territory. By late 1925, he was already regretting his move to New York and was working on the manuscript that was to become *The Call of Cthulhu*, a story that would see his writing shift decisively into a more otherworldly and almost dream-like direction. The following year, his return to Providence signalled a similar shift into the horror spaces of his native New England, that 'lonely and curious country' that suffused later texts such as *The Dunwich Horror*.[55] As his marriage broke down and he became more reclusive, he never again returned in his work to the theme of supernatural cities. Horror was, instead, located in the ruinously inbred fishing settlements and isolated villages overshadowed by terrible old native-American monuments that dominated his vision of the New England landscape he once again called home.

Yet Lovecraft did not emerge unscathed from his time in New York; it had a profound influence on his writing style for the next, critical decade to come. His return to Providence saw him alarmed by the continuing destruction and renovation of the historic urban fabric that, as Kenneth Fang and S. T. Joshi note, had already marked his early years.[56] His works continued to delve into concepts of human degeneration and the corruption of spaces somehow tainted by the occult and the supernatural.[57] *The Horror at Red Hook*, for all its faults, should be seen as part of this trajectory. Rather than being merely an unusual and unaccomplished outlier, the text at its core represents Lovecraft's early struggles with concepts of underlying horror, of peopled spaces of decay, and the history of places and their present manifestations. In time this would lead to the looming church on Federal Hill, set amid 'a vast Italian quarter' where 'most of the houses were remnants of older Yankee and Irish days', that so lures writer Robert Blake to his destruction in *The Haunter of the Dark* (1936); to 'dying and half-deserted Innsmouth' with its crawling and creeping fisher-folk in *The Shadow over Innsmouth* (1936); to rural Dunwich, where one dreaded 'to trust the tenebrous tunnel of the bridge' and struggled with the 'faint, malign odour about the village street, as of the massed mould and decay of centuries' in *The Dunwich Horror* (1929). Each of Lovecraft's

[55]   H. P. Lovecraft, 'The Dunwich Horror', in *Complete Fiction*, ed. Link, pp. 674–717.
[56]   Fang and Joshi, 'Lovecraft: Life and Work', pp. 14–15.
[57]   Gerry Carlin and Nicola Allen, 'Slime and the Western Man: H. P. Lovecraft in the Time of Modernism', in *New Critical Essays*, ed. Simmons, pp. 73–5; Buhle, 'Dystopia as Utopia', p. 198.

celebrated centrepieces of horror, as it wrestles with horrifying landscapes and their initially hidden and terrifying inhabitants, carries the taint of *The Horror at Red Hook*.[58] Like poor Malone, terrified by the small cluster of high-rises in downtown Pascoag at the story's opening, Lovecraft carried the supernatural city with him when he left New York, imprinted on his literary psyche.

As this chapter has endeavoured to show, however, this was an influence that was by no means exclusive to Lovecraft and his particular brand of weird fiction. New York was a magnet for intense social concern, and although Lovecraft's motives, ideology, and literary output were very different from those of Jacob Riis, for instance, or the editors of spiritualist papers, both *The Horror at Red Hook* and *He* reflect these wider social issues. Rendering him expert at deriving horror from the ordinary, at inverting the daily reality of life and revealing a terrifying underside of hidden supernatural forces, Lovecraft's experience of New York reveals the supernatural city as the reflection of the myriad influences of the urban environment through the prism of individual perception. Whereas Riis saw the danger of social decay, for example, Lovecraft imagined lurking cults; both writers were inspired by the slums, albeit in very different ways. The peculiarities of the supernatural world of *The Horror at Red Hook* were all Lovecraft – his own unique blend of occult and otherworldly imagination. But it drew upon the broader potential of the city for such supernatural manifestations – contemporary concerns that had gotten under his skin as an author. Like it or not, in *The Horror at Red Hook* Lovecraft was exorcising his own urban demons.

Bibliography

Primary sources

Beacon Light [spiritualist newspaper], 12 December 1885

Lowry, Helen Bullitt, 'The Old World in New York', *The New York Times*, 3 April 1921

'Matters We Ought to Know: How the Other Half Lives, Studies among the Tenements of New York. By Jacob A Riis', *The New York Times*, 4 January 1891

'New York Conference: Stuyvesant Institute Feb. 27 1857', *Liberator*, 21 March 1856, vol. 26, issue 12

'Red Hook Resents Crime Board Report', *The New York Times*, 21 May 1927

'She's Minnie's Spook: Real "Bright Eyes" is Operating on Staten Island', *The Washington Post*, 3 September 1907

'Telepathic Communication with London', *The Spur*, 15 November 1920

---

[58] See H. P. Lovecraft, 'The Haunter of the Dark', in *Complete Fiction*, ed. Link, pp. 1075–94; 'The Dunwich Horror', in ibid., pp. 674–717; 'Shadow over Innsmouth'.

Secondary sources

Buhle, Paul, 'Dystopia as Utopia: Howard Phillips Lovecraft and the Unknown Content of American Horror Literature', in *H. P. Lovecraft: Four Decades of Criticism*, ed. S. T. Joshi (Athens, OH, 1980), pp. 196–210

Carlin, Gerry and Nicola Allen, 'Slime and the Western Man: H. P. Lovecraft in the Time of Modernism', in *New Critical Essays on H. P. Lovecraft*, ed. David Simmons (New York, 2013), pp. 73–90

Colebrook, Martyn, ' "Comrades in Tentacles": H. P. Lovecraft and China Miéville', in *New Critical Essays on H. P. Lovecraft*, ed. David Simmons (New York, 2013), pp. 209–26

Cox, Robert S., *Body and Soul: A Sympathetic History of American Spiritualism* (Charlottesville, VA, 2003)

Derleth, August and Donald Wandrei, *H. P. Lovecraft: Selected Letters, 1911–1924* (Sauk City, WI, 1965)

Englander, David, 'Review: Alan Mayne, *The Imagined Slum: Newspaper Representation in Three Cities, 1870–1914*', *Urban History* 21 (1994), 309–11

Fang, Kenneth W., Jr and S. T. Joshi, 'H.P. Lovecraft: His Life and Work', in *H. P. Lovecraft: Four Decades of Criticism*, ed. S. T. Joshi (Athens, OH, 1980), pp. 1–19

Furness, H. H. (ed.), *Preliminary Report of the Commission Appointed by the University of Pennsylvania to Investigate Modern Spiritualism in Accordance with the Request of the Late Henry Seybert* (Philadelphia, 1920)

H. P. Lovecraft Literary Podcast, http://hppodcraft.com/2010/04/07/episode-38-the-horror-at-red-hook/

Higham, John, *Strangers in the Land: Patterns of American Nativism, 1860–1925*, new edn (New Brunswick, NJ, 1983)

Homberger, Eric, *The Historical Atlas of New York City: A Visual Celebration of 400 years of New York City's History* (New York, 2005)

Keene, Michael, *The Psychic Highway: How the Erie Canal Changed America* (New York, 2017)

Kneale, James, 'From Beyond: H. P. Lovecraft and the Place of Horror', *Cultural Geographies* 13 (2006), 106–26

Koven, Seth, *Slumming: Sexual and Social Politics in Victorian London* (Oxford, 2004)

Lening, Gustave. *The Dark Side of New York Life and its Criminal Classes from Fifth Avenue down to the Five Points, A Complete Narrative of the Mysteries of New York* (New York, 1873)

Lovecraft, H. P., 'He' in *The Complete Fiction of H. P. Lovecraft*, ed. Eric Carl Link (New York, 2016), pp. 355–64

——, 'The Dunwich Horror', in ibid., pp. 674–717

——, 'The Haunter of the Dark', in ibid., pp. 1075–94

——, 'The Horror at Red Hook', in ibid., pp. 335–54

——, 'The Shadow over Innsmouth', in ibid., pp. 866–923

Mayne, Alan, *The Imagined Slum: Newspaper Representation in Three Cities, 1870–1914* (Leicester, 1993)

Moloney, Deirdre, ' "Strangers in the Land": Gender and Immigration Policy', *The Journal of the Gilded Age and Progressive Era*, 11 (2012), 270–5

Nartonis, David K., 'The Rise of 19th-Century American Spiritualism, 1854–1873', *Journal for the Scientific Study of Religion* 49 (2010), 361–73

Ngai, Mae M., *Impossible Subjects: Illegal Aliens and the Making of Modern America* (Princeton, NJ, 2004)

Riis, Jacob, *How the Other Half Lives: Studies among the Tenements of New York* (London, 1997 [New York, 1890])

Schlör, Joachim, *Nights in the Big City: London, Paris, Berlin* (London, 1998)

Schweitzer, Darrell, 'Lovecraft and Lord Dunsany', in *Discovering H. P. Lovecraft*, ed. Darrell Schweitzer, rev. edn (Holicong, PA, 2001), pp. 72–87

Walkowitz, Judith R., *City of Dreadful Delight: Narratives of Sexual Danger in Late Victorian London* (Chicago, 1992)

Winter, Douglas E., 'Those Eldritch Horrors', *The Washington Post*, 26 October 1997

Wisker, Gina, ' "Spawn of the Pit": Lavinia, Marceline, Medusa, and All Things Foul: H. P. Lovecraft's Liminal Women', in *New Critical Essays on H.P. Lovecraft*, ed. David Simmons (New York, 2013), pp. 31–54

6

Manila-as-Hell: Horror, Geopolitics and Religious Orientalism in Anglo-American Literary Constructions of an Asian City, 1946–2013

TOM SYKES

The most heinous sinners tormented by the flames raging forever within Dante's 'unhappy city of Dis'. Shakespeare's Troy, Vienna, Athens and Rome, where 'disloyalty and disease thrive ... where love is sold for gold, and syphilis eats away the human body'.[1] The grubby, pestilential and penury-cursed Paris of Victor Hugo and Eugène Sue, or the London of Charles Dickens and George Reynolds. Other, more mythical visions of an infernal London; grotesque apparitions and fantastic happenings symbolising social, historical and psychic crisis, in the work of China Miéville, Michael Moorcock, Will Self and Angela Carter. In novels by Toni Morrison, Amiri Baraka, James Baldwin, Carlos Bulosan and Sergio de la Pava, the formally or informally segregated American city of the twentieth century, a Babylon – in the Afrocentric or Rastafarian sense – where the devil is invariably white and his evil is projected through racial supremacism, neo-imperialism and state violence against, and economic subjugation of, ethnic minorities. Cities ripped apart by

---

[1] Leslie Fiedler, 'Mythicizing the City', in *Literature and the American Urban Experience: Essays on the City and Literature*, ed. Michael C. Jaye and Ann Chalmers Watts (Manchester, 1981), p. 116.

war, the fire of bombs and shells standing in for the biblical 'furnace of fire';[2] Tolstoy's Borodino of cannonball and grenade explosions, Kurt Vonnegut's Dresden gutted by incendiaries and high explosives, Sarah Waters's Blitz-era London of air raid sirens and blazing buildings.

Western writers have been imagining the city as a version of hell since at least the Middle Ages. As is evident from the terse descriptions above, these urban textual spaces have occupied various points on a sliding scale of metaphorical intensity. At one end are cities vaguely analogous to hell or possessing hell-like characteristics which can be explained rationally in cases of what Tzvetan Todorov, inspired by Freud, has termed 'the Uncanny'. At the other end of the scale are cities that constitute a more exact reproduction – as in Dante's *Inferno* – of hell as it has been described in religious texts, and that are therefore closer to Todorov's concept of 'the Fantastic', wherein persons and events in narratives are only comprehensible in outlandishly supernatural terms.[3] Given that, with any other literary convention, there is a risk of defining the city-as-hell motif too generally, the critic Simon Kemp has helpfully proposed a number of its variants in French fiction over the last three centuries, formulations which are also relevant to the British and American texts I will be scrutinising in this chapter. The urban hell of the literary imagination is, Kemp argues, 'a repository for the darkest and most extreme imaginings, where violence and cruelty run unchecked by any moral sense; where the body, in its sinful lust and exquisite torture, banishes the mind from the essence of self; and where all order and reason is overwhelmed by fiery chaos. It is a place beyond understanding.'[4] Further to this, each textual city-as-hell is determined by cultural and material factors specific to its historical moment of origin. For example, the literary critic Joan M. Ferrante has conjectured that the prevalence of heresy in Dis is due in part to that sin being 'intimately associated with politics for Dante's audience', an audience who would have been aware of contemporary events such as Pope John XXII's persecution of his rivals for disputing Christian dogma and the elision of religious dissent and sedition that the Holy Roman Emperor Frederick II used as a rationale for executing his opponents.[5]

[2]   Matthew 13:50, *New International Version* (Biblica, 2011), https://www.biblegateway. com/versions/New-International-Version-NIV-Bible/#booklist (accessed 27 June 2018).

[3]   Tzvetan Todorov, *The Fantastic: A Structural Approach to a Literary Genre* (Ithaca, NY, 1975), p. 25.

[4]   Simon Kemp, 'Urban Hell: Infernal Cities in Modern French Literature', in *Imagining the City, Volume 1*, ed. Christian Emden, Catherine Keen and David Midgley (Bern, 2006), pp. 95–6.

[5]   Joan M. Ferrante, *The Political Vision of Dante* (Princeton, NJ, 1984), pp. 41–2.

This chapter analyses how, since the Second World War, the city-as-hell conceit has been mobilised by Anglo-American fiction and narrative nonfiction set in Manila, the capital city of the Philippines. As with the other instances outlined above, these representations can be explained by reference to their wider social, economic and political contexts. Moreover, they cohere with Orientalist *idées fixes* about the inferiority of Eastern religious beliefs, social mores and political-economic structures, as articulated by Edward Said in his pioneering study *Orientalism* (1978) and, more recently, by Chris Goto-Jones, who regards Western power-knowledge discourses on Asia as 'mechanism[s] of self-reflection (i.e. the invention of a society that represents the instantiation of values opposite to those that the Orientalist would like to see as characteristic of his or her own society)'.[6] I have chosen to consider texts situated in the city of Manila rather than other parts of the Philippines, because the vast majority of Anglo-American writing on this part of the world has focused to some degree or other on the capital city, and much of it exclusively so. The preoccupation with Manila can be ascribed to its significance in regional and global history: it was in many respects the site of certain pivotal junctures in the development of Western imperialism, amongst them the extinction of the Spanish empire and the ascent of the United States to global hegemony. Control of Manila was also a strategic desideratum for both sides in the Pacific theatre of the Second World War, and the city underwent such heavy fighting that, by February 1945, 'an American investigation team thought Manila was the second most devastated city after Warsaw'.[7] During the Cold War, when the Philippines shifted from being an official US possession to a key satellite of America's 'informal empire ... shown up by military bases, economic pressures and military coups', Manila became the epitome of a Third World urban space in the clutches of 'dollar-imperialism', both as a source of profitable land, labour and capital resources, and as a market for US-manufactured commodities.[8] From the last decades of the twentieth century up to the present day, Manila has been something of a bellwether for what Niall Ferguson has characterised as 'the descent of the West' and the 'reorientation of the world' towards Asia; the city's economic ties to the US and Europe have loosened as the Philippines has established trading relationships with China, Japan, South

---

[6] Chris Goto-Jones, *Conjuring Asia: Magic, Orientalism and the Making of the Modern World* (Cambridge, 2016), pp. 104–5.

[7] José S. Arcilla, *An Introduction to Philippine History* (Manila, 1998), p. 124.

[8] See Pankaj Mishra, *From the Ruins of Empire: The Revolt against the West and the Remaking of Asia* (London, 2013), p. 7; Jan Romein, *The Asian Century: A History of Modern Nationalism in Asia* (Berkeley, CA and Los Angeles, 1962), p. 228.

Korea and other emergent regional powers.[9] As we will see, these geopolitical events since 1945 have informed dominant Western attitudes to the Philippines which in turn have, to a lesser or greater extent, shaped Western literary visions of Manila-as-hell.

The Manila-as-hell model originated long before the Second World War, in the mid-nineteenth century, when Britain, France, Germany and the United States were expanding their imperial influence over parts of Africa, Asia and the Americas while the Spanish empire was rapidly disintegrating. Portugal had annexed Spain's West African colonies in 1778 and the US captured Spanish territories in North America, including West Florida, in the 1810s and 1820s. By 1865, all of Spain's colonies in Latin America save Cuba and Puerto Rico had gained their independence. In the Philippine context, the Cavite Mutiny of 1872 was the fifth major anti-Spanish revolt to have occurred that century.[10] These defeats and losses informed a consensus amongst British and American Orientalist writers of the 1800s that Spain was losing its grip over its prized Philippine possession – which it had ruled since the late 1500s – through a combination of anachronistic fiscal policies, administrative incompetence and authoritarian oppressiveness. A crucial supposition undergirding this Hispanophobia was that the Roman Catholic church – which then dominated the culture and politics of the Spanish Philippines – was backward, profane and atavistic to the core. In the tradition of literary adumbrations of cities 'whose forms are systematically distorted to convey a particular mood or quality', expatriate writers, including the American sailor Charles Wilkes and the British coffee merchant Nicholas Loney, construed Manila as an othered, impenetrably mystical space ruled by medieval Catholic superstitions that were forbiddingly alien to the rational Protestant mind.[11] According to Loney's correspondence from the 1850s, 'shadows flit … about' the old walled Spanish quarter of Intramuros 'like unearthly things' and the lurid paintings of the Inferno inside a church had been designed to scare the public into 'properly attending to their religious duties'.[12]

Writing after the US annexed the Philippines from Spain in 1898 and had established a new colonial state headquartered in Manila, travel writers such as

---

[9] Niall Ferguson, *The War of the World: Twentieth-Century Conflict and the Descent of the West* (New York, 2007), p. 14.

[10] Renato Constantino, *A History of the Philippines: From Spanish Colonization to the Second World War* (New York, 2010), pp. 133–42.

[11] Kevin McNamara, 'Introduction', in *The Companion to the City in Literature*, ed. idem (Cambridge, 2013), pp. 1–13 at 3.

[12] Nicholas Loney, *A Britisher in the Philippines; or, the Letters of Nicholas Loney* (Manila, 1964), p. 6.

George A. Miller and Walter Robb drew upon dark and foreboding imagery to demonstrate how far the capital had advanced from being a retrograde Hispanic-Catholic outpost to a modern Protestant-American metropolis. *Interesting Manila* (1929) was Miller's portentously toned account of his peregrinations around Intramuros' 'old convents' and 'old monasteries' which, from his perspective, harboured 'mysteries as dark as the black robes' and 'deeds of lust and blood'.[13] However, he was non-specific about the nature of these mysteries and deeds, alluding only to Spanish-era 'political plotting' and 'ecclesiastical intrigue'.[14] In Miller's mind, perhaps there was no need to elaborate, given the fundamental incompatibility of this religious and cultural milieu with the mindset of the 'American … [who] usually turns up his nose because the way of doing things is different from his own'.[15] By way of final analysis of this issue of cultural impenetrability, he declares, 'The Anglo-Saxon lives in the concrete, the Oriental in the shadows'.[16] Moreover, Miller implies, although its influence had been greatly curtailed since the Spanish were ousted, the Catholic church's opaque ideas and doctrines lingered on like a ghostly presence in the new, modernising Manila that was now open to international business and tourism: 'The globe trotter … has no idea that he treads on the bones of a vanished empire'.[17] For Walter Robb, in his travel chronicle *The Khaki Cabinet and Old Manila* (1926), America's new, supposedly more just and enlightened approach to colonial dominion – 'a course [that] would entail no injustice upon anyone else, Filipinos least of all' – was bound to rescue a civic infrastructure that had, under the Spanish, been persistently menaced by fires, earthquakes and other, almost biblical *forces majeures*.[18]

Western novels and memoirs published during and shortly after the Second World War amplified these religious metaphors, except that their target was now, perhaps predictably, Japan's empire rather than Spain's. While American foreign correspondent Clark Lee's wartime memoir *They Call it Pacific* (1943) castigated the racism of the American colonial state in Manila, and evaluated Japan's material motivation for invading the Philippines ('[t]o go on playing power politics, they had to gain free access to certain raw materials') with a degree of empathy unusual amongst Orientalists of the time, his descriptions of Japanese air-raids on Manila fell squarely within the conventions of both

---

[13] George A. Miller, *Interesting Manila* (Manila, 1929), pp. 48, 26.
[14] Ibid., p. 48.
[15] Ibid., p. 27.
[16] Ibid., p. 51.
[17] Ibid., p. 79.
[18] Walter Robb, *The Khaki Cabinet and Old Manila* (Manila, 1926), pp. iii, 126.

faith-driven Orientalism and the city-as-hell canon.[19] If a proposition such as 'there was not a time when the night skies of Manila were not brilliant with fires' appeared to be borne of a professional journalist's obligation to record accurately and straightforwardly the events he had witnessed, it recalled at the same time the prototypical burning city of Dis, not to say numerous other literary cities-as-hell that had been set alight by military violence. Later in the same paragraph, Lee likened the 'death and ruin' caused by the attacks to 'Genghis Khan and his hordes of terror'.[20] This harked back to Ernest Renan and other nineteenth-century Western intellectuals, whose 'view of European superiority over Muslims', contends Felix Konrad, led them to the conviction that Genghis was a savage infidel who would never have succeeded had Christian 'progress' reached the East in the thirteenth century.[21] *Perla of the Walled City* (1946) by the American – and avowedly Christian – novelist John Bechtel limned war-wrecked Manila in an even more apocalyptic vernacular: 'blocks – yes, miles – of twisted ruins and grotesque concrete skeletons'.[22] The scene was, in Bechtel's bombastic simile, as if 'Mars, the mighty god of War, had tramped down his iron heel and had ground unmercifully The Pearl of the Orient into the dust'.[23] Since Manila – and, more specifically, the church-filled sanctuary of Intramuros – had been desecrated by the heathen Japanese occupiers, the modern 'Pearl of the Orient' that the American colonial regime had developed between 1898 and 1941 was no more. The special sense of hurt and loss in relation to Manila's fate in the war was possibly due to the fact it had been, unlike Singapore, Nanking or any other Asian city conquered by the Japanese, the nexus of American colonial power in Asia. Indeed, DeLouis Stevenson in *Land of the Morning* (1956), a memoir of accompanying her clergyman husband on a post-war mission to the Philippines, regretted how this 'daughter of the American republic' was now a wasteland of 'bombed-out buildings' because the Japanese had blasphemed against the Christian creed by obliterating '80% of church buildings' and had converted 'churches [into] ... fortresses during the war'.[24] Stevenson was silent, though, about American connivance in the carnage: the historical record shows that the 'liberation' of Manila in 1945 killed 120,000 and ravaged its built environment, whereas the Japanese

---

[19] Clark Lee, *They Call It Pacific: An Eyewitness Story of Our War against Japan from Bataan to the Solomons* (New York, 1943), pp. 4, 24.
[20] Ibid., p. 47.
[21] See Felix Konrad, *From the 'Turkish Menace' to Exoticism and Orientalism: Islam as Antithesis of Europe (1453–1914)?* (Mainz, 2011), p. 40.
[22] John Bechtel, *Perla of the Walled City* (Grand Rapids, MI, 1946), p. 1.
[23] Ibid., p. 2.
[24] DeLouis Stevenson, *Land of the Morning* (St Louis, MO, 1956), pp. 10, 14, 144.

invasion of Manila in 1941–42 resulted in considerably fewer casualties and little structural damage.[25] When we consider such an omission – whether wilful or not – alongside Western literary representations of European cities ruined by the Second World War (London, Paris and Berlin for example) that were palpably not rooted in religious distaste or partisanship, it would seem that authors like Bechtel and Stevenson were imbuing Manila with their own fantasies of hell and damnation. Such a reflex is typical of Orientalist discourses for, as Said observes, 'designation of geographical space to the east of Europe as "Oriental" ' does not depend on 'actual experience of the Orient'.[26] Rather, 'the imaginative demonology of "the mysterious Orient" ' derives more from a long tradition of Orientalists cleaving to 'unshakeable abstract maxims about the "civilization" … [they] had studied; rarely were Orientalists interested in anything except proving the validity of these musty "truths" by applying them, without great success, to uncomprehending, hence degenerate, natives'.[27] In like fashion, Stevenson's commitment to the redemptive power of her evangelical faith obliged her to present the US church and state in Manila as positive forces for renewal, conjuring order from chaos, as in the case of the Union Theological Seminary on Taft Avenue, now 'completely rehabilitated'.[28] It is hard not to uncouple Bechtel's and Stevenson's impressions of Manila as a city doomed by its retreat from Western-Christian hegemony from the historical fact that, as Damon L. Woods avers, 'After World War II, there was an influx of fundamentalist missionaries to the islands' who, taking a classically Orientalist stance of cultural condescension, 'came to the conclusion that Filipinos were incapable of ecclesiastical leadership'.[29] This attitude, too, would appear to be a figment of the American Orientalist imagination given that in 1902, Filipinos had established the *Iglesia Filipina Independente*, a large, influential and successfully administrated independent church.[30]

When the US granted the Philippines its formal independence in 1946, leading American politicians were concerned about the new republic gaining too much autonomy over its economy, armed forces and foreign policy. US legislation such as the 'Bell measure' and the Tydings Rehabilitation Act imposed harmful quotas on Philippine exports while granting preferential treatment to

[25] Arcilla, *Introduction to Philippine History*, p. 124.
[26] Edward Said, *Orientalism* (London, 1985), p. 210.
[27] Ibid., pp. 26, 52.
[28] Stevenson, *Land of the Morning*, p. 16.
[29] Damon L. Woods, *The Philippines: A Global Studies Handbook* (Oxford, 2006), p. 125.
[30] Luis H. Francia, *A History of the Philippines: From Indios to Bravos* (New York, 2014), pp. 59–60.

American importers. Such initiatives encouraged unfair competition between national and foreign banks which 'hindered economic development' and 'established the basis of a neo-colonial control of the economy'.[31] Furthermore, the two nations agreed treaties on war veterans' benefits, the absorption of the Philippine military into the US armed forces and the retention of American military bases in the country.[32] As the Cold War was commencing, the stage was set for the new, nominally independent Philippine republic to become a strategic and economic client state of the US, forming a link in the Asian *cordon sanitaire* around communist China and the USSR, and occupying a subordinate role in the 'dollar-imperialist' world order in which '[developing nations] suffered from a degree of dependence on trade with the dollar area'.[33]

In the 1950s and 1960s, numerous personal accounts of the Second World War in the mould of Clark Lee's were published in the USA and Britain, which either constructed Manila in much the same fashion as Lee or avoided the city entirely, concentrating instead on significant military flashpoints elsewhere in the Philippines.[34] While a number of relatively apolitical Anglo-American guidebooks, histories and memoirs referencing Manila appeared during the same period, they tended to favour symbolic modes other than the city-as-hell.[35] It is possible that the optimistic write-ups of Manila as a vibrant and rapidly developing – if still socially fragmented – urban centre, in texts such as Raymond Nelson's travelogue-cum-history book *The Philippines* (1968), were sparked by a melioristic impulse to see the new American-led world order as benefiting and uplifting the Global South.[36]

However, in life writing of the 1970s and 1980s by P. J. O'Rourke, Ian Buruma, Maslyn Williams and others, the city-as-hell trope was resurrected and infused with what Mary-Louise Pratt terms 'third world blues', a tendency within Western travel writing to depict non-Western 'cityscapes' as 'grotesque' and 'joyless', driven by pessimism and unacknowledged guilt towards societies

---

[31]   Samuel K. Tan, *A History of the Philippines* (Manila, 1987), pp. 82–3.

[32]   Frank Hindman Golay, *Face of Empire: United States–Philippine Relations, 1898–1946* (Manila, 2010), pp. 454–77.

[33]   Romein, *The Asian Century*, p. 228.

[34]   These texts include Benjamin Appel, *Fortress in the Rice* (New York, 1951); John Benjamin Howell, *42 Months of Hell: My Life as a Prisoner of the Japanese, World War II* (Muskogee, OK, 1969); Wanda Liles Kellett, *Wings as Eagles* (New York, 1954); Norman Mailer, *The Naked and the Dead* (New York, 1948); Blanche Palmer, *Pilgrim of the Night* (Nashville, TN, 1966).

[35]   These texts include Bernard Bancroft, *Bread upon the Waters* (Des Plaines, IL, 1959), Albert Roland, *The Philippines* (New York, 1967) and David Joel Steinberg, *The Philippines: A Singular and Plural Place* (Boulder, CO, 1969).

[36]   Raymond Nelson, *The Philippines* (London, 1968).

that had freed themselves from Western colonial oppression, though not from indirect manipulation.[37] Pratt holds that two prime exponents of third world blues, the travel writers Paul Theroux and Alberto Moravia, were oblivious to the global roots of the local problems they explored in their respective works, because they refused the 'history tying the North American Theroux to Spanish America or the Italian Moravia to Africa, despite the fact that much of what they are lamenting is the depredations of western-induced dependency'.[38] The more recent research of the urban theorist Tom Angotti elucidates the dynamics of this dependency and how they impact upon Global Southern cities such as Manila: 'Urbanization', he writes, 'responds to the demand for cheap labor and raw materials in the developed nations of the North' and is at the mercy of 'debt to Northern banks, reliance on oil and other exports, and increasing dependency on food and other products made in the North'.[39] The resulting 'unequal, inefficient sprawled metropolitan growth', Angotti claims, is misunderstood by 'urban orientalist' scholars and experts as a problem to be solved by 'the expansion and accumulation of capital in cities' and the 'global marketplace for land and resources', whereas the problem is in actuality produced by those same economic processes.[40]

In the same spirit of denial, P. J. O'Rourke, in *Holidays in Hell* (1989), portrayed a slum in northern Manila as a hell-like 'pile of rotting, burning trash', before holding the actions of President Corazon Aquino, who had recently succeeded the despotic Ferdinand Marcos, responsible for both the regression of living conditions in the slum and for Manila more generally remaining 'the same squalid mess it's always been'.[41] (This comment is a rather pithy demonstration of Said's contention about Orientalism's 'dogmatic views of "the Oriental" as a kind of ... unchanging abstraction').[42] At no point in his narrative does O'Rourke suggest that the blame for the 'mess' could be spread more widely, to the Philippines' subordinate position in the world economic system, which was an epiphenomenon of his own country's global capitalist-imperialist policies.

In his collection of personal essays on Asia, *God's Dust* (1989), Ian Buruma offered a diagnosis of Manila's social defects that owed something to his

---

[37] Mary Louise Pratt, *Imperial Eyes: Travel Writing and Transculturation* (London, 1991), p. 217.
[38] Ibid., p. 218.
[39] Tom Angotti, *The New Century of the Metropolis: Urban Enclaves and Orientalism* (New York, 2013), p. 11.
[40] Ibid., pp. 12, 17.
[41] O'Rourke, P. J., *Holidays in Hell* (New York, 1989; repr. 2012), Amazon Kindle e-book, ch. 9, para. 15, loc. 1708; ch. 8, para. 2, loc. 1675.
[42] Said, *Orientalism*, p. 8.

anti-Catholic antecedents in the previous century. After a curt discussion of the Filipino intellectual Reynaldo C. Ileto's research, which 'traces the forms of peasant rebellion back to folk versions of the [Christian] passion', Buruma argued that modern Manileños remained beholden to 'ancestor worship', 'a succession of messiahs' and other primitive customs and beliefs.[43] This was, he hinted via the observations of a taxi driver he paraphrased by way of a conclusion to his chapter on the Philippines, one reason for the prevalence of 'the politicians' quarrelling, the crime, the communists, the lack of any change in the country'.[44]

While James Fenton's book of reportage *All the Wrong Places* (1988) was more critical of American complicity in Manila's political predicaments – he upbraided US foreign policy for making 'the Philippines a nuclear target' and found President Reagan's Machiavellian stance towards the dictatorial Marcos administration 'absolutely wicked' – his critique of that regime and its opponents revived a number of religious and supernatural tropes from his literary forebears of the late 1800s/early 1900s.[45] Before he went to the Philippines, he was minded by Western press reports to think it a 'strange and fascinating place', where a 'holy war' was being waged by Muslim *Moro* separatists in the south against the Roman Catholic central government in Manila.[46] As with other textual cities-as-hell, vice and corrosive carnality defined urban identity, for 'Manila was a brothel'.[47] When Fenton travelled to the capital, he discovered that Manileños rich and poor, powerful and powerless, were fettered by superstition. A group of opposition protestors who 'quite expected to be shot' took a detour into the Church of Our Lady in Binondo in order to rest 'under the crucified figure of the Black Nazarene', a dark-skinned model of Jesus believed by Filipinos to bestow good fortune.[48] When Fenton met the First Lady, Imelda Marcos, she told him that her spiritual guide had warned of the occurrence of three omens before the government would collapse: an earthquake that would ravage a church, a volcanic eruption and the seizure of a major bridge by anti-government marchers. After he interrogated the rational validity of this theory – 'some people said … [the condition] had already been fulfilled … Others said no'[49] – Fenton asserted his atheism during a conversation with his

[43] Ian Buruma, *God's Dust: A Modern Asian Journey* (London, 1991), p. 170.
[44] Ibid., p. 107.
[45] James Fenton, *All the Wrong Places: Adrift in the Politics of Southeast Asia* (London, 2005), pp. 164, 172.
[46] Ibid., p. 113.
[47] Ibid.
[48] Ibid., p. 124.
[49] Ibid., p. 121.

peasant host, a self-described Christian, in Ilocos Norte province. The conversation concluded with his host saying 'firmly: "If you don't believe in religion at all, then there is no reason to discuss these things." '[50] The implication here, perhaps, was that, while Fenton had tried hard, or at least harder than O'Rourke and Buruma, to arrive at a holistic understanding of the political situation in Manila and the Philippines, his Western, rational subjectivity would always prove a barrier to the kind of cross-cultural communication that would permit him to see things as a Manileño or Filipino would. His host appeared to acknowledge this quandary when, after their *tête-a-tête* about religious belief, he said, '*You* must now start a new subject and we will talk about that.'[51] Thus, it would appear that the Manila-as-hell type is easily conjured by outsiders, but not ultimately conceivable or knowable to them. We will see shortly how this tension is exacerbated in texts published in the 1990s and 2000s.

The work of the Anglo-Australian writer Maslyn Williams was a notable exception to the above authors' simultaneous fetish for and distrust towards local superstition, not to say their silence (at least in the cases of O'Rourke and Buruma, if not Fenton) about the neo-colonial damage done to Manila. As told in his 1979 travelogue *Faces of My Neighbour*, Williams visited Manila a decade before O'Rourke, Buruma and Fenton, when Marcos was secure in his position and still very much 'America's boy'.[52] Wary of the Manichaean binaries of Orientalist thought, Williams critiqued the West's failure to live up to its own religious ideals: 'We are excellent pretenders. We pretend to believe in a Christian style of democracy to feel for the underprivileged.'[53] He was equally biting about the West's conduct on the world stage, which was contributing to the construction and sustentation of Global Southern cities-as-hell: 'I am also aware that the West is in large part responsible for the fact that countries like the Philippines are going through a time of internal political conflict, and that our economic policies are aggravating the poverty and inequality that create these conflict situations.'[54]

However, Williams was not entirely free of Orientalist cognition; his perception of Manila was, like those of O'Rourke, Buruma and Fenton, dominated by 'strongmen' and 'corrupt and egomaniacal' officials fawned over by

---

[50]   Ibid., p. 163.
[51]   Ibid.
[52]   James Hamilton-Paterson, *America's Boy: The Marcoses and the Philippines* (London, 1998), p. 160.
[53]   Maslyn Williams, *Faces of My Neighbour: Three Journeys into East Asia* (Sydney, 1979), p. 129.
[54]   Ibid., p. 21.

adoring subjects.[55] When Williams met Marcos he noted how people 'gaze up at him and wait expectantly to be moved, amused, inspired, and made to feel pleased that they have him as their leader'.[56] Similarly, the literary journalist Mark Kram's article on the 'Thrilla in Manila' boxing match from 1975 characterised Marcos as a 'small brown derringer of a man' whose presence at the Joe Frazier–Muhammad Ali fight compelled '28,000' Manileños to brave 'packed and malodorous' public transport to join him there.[57] Many of the same postulations can be found within a discourse of reactionary Western historiography preoccupied with what Reynaldo C. Ileto calls 'cacique democracy'.[58] Ileto has argued that mainstream American scholars of the Philippines from the 1950s to the 1990s, such as Stanley Karnow and Alfred McCoy, overstated and exaggerated the issues of 'repressive, manipulative' governance, election-rigging, graft, 'clientilism' and clannish 'factionalism'[59] in order to assert that 'the tragedies and problems of the present are the consequence not so much of American intervention as of the tenacity of Philippine traditions'.[60] In keeping with the 'third world blues' hypothesis, the figure of the tyrannical, passion-driven cacique leader at once embodies Western cynicism about Filipinos' fitness to govern themselves in the post-colonial era and vindicates Western neo-imperialist meddling in Philippine affairs.

While Kram, Williams, O'Rourke and the other life writers of the 1970s and 1980s did not make explicit comparisons between the cacique and the Christian Devil, common characteristics are observable. According to Christian demonology, the Devil intimidates mortals into doing his evil bidding or, as in the myth of Faust, manipulates them with offers of magical powers.[61] This dialectic of rule by terror and rule by inducement is, from an Orientalist perspective, not too remote from the mechanics of the cults of personality propagated by Marcos and the other demonic lords of textual Manilas-as-hell.

---

[55]   Buruma, *God's Dust*, p. 75; O'Rourke, ch. 7, para. 2, loc. 1625.

[56]   Williams, *Faces of My Neighbour*, p. 19.

[57]   Kram, Mark, 'Lawdy, Lawdy, He's Great', Sports Illustrated Online, 13 October 1975, https://www.si.com/boxing/2012/01/17/muhammad-ali-70th-kram   (accessed   28 September 2017).

[58]   Reynaldo C. Ileto, *Knowledge and Pacification: On the US Conquest and the Writing of Philippine History* (Manila, 2017), p. 289.

[59]   Ibid., pp. 267–87.

[60]   Ibid., p. 268.

[61]   See Matthew 26:56, *New International Version* (Biblica, 2011), www.biblegateway.com/versions/New-International-Version-NIV-Bible/#booklist, (accessed 11 July 2018); David Hawkes, *The Faust Myth: Religion and the Rise of Representation* (Basingstoke, 2007).

'Third world blues' may also help to illuminate why the city-as-hell trope intensified within the discourse after 1989. After Cold War rivalries ceased, the Philippines' geopolitical value to the US lessened and Japan superseded the US as the country's primary trading partner.[62] That Manila's descent into an even more hellish condition may be a consequence of that departure from the Western sphere of influence was hinted at by one of the Filipino characters in Alex Garland's thriller novel *The Tesseract* (1998). He states that the Spanish conquistadors of the 1570s had God on their side when they colonised the islands; the concomitant point here, perhaps, being that God may be displeased now that the Spanish – and other Western powers – have relinquished explicit political control over the territory.[63]

Compared to the caciques or cacique-like characters in Fenton, Buruma and O'Rourke, the protagonists of *The Tesseract* and other Western fictions of the 1990s are inordinately cruel, crooked and vicious. Informed by the intertextual and ahistorical conventions of postmodernism, these caricatures belong firmly to the Western pulp horror/thriller genre. The pages of *The Tesseract* presented maladroit, Quentin Tarantino-esque hitmen, while in Timothy Mo's graphically violent picaresque *Renegade or Halo²*, a Manileño mobster looked like a 'Mexican bandido, El Jefe from a Sam Peckinpah movie'.[64] These symbolic standards, selected from fifty years of Hollywood film and more than a century of lowbrow paperbacks, revealed more about the political climate and means of cultural production of late twentieth century Britain and the US than anything of import about Manila. Fredric Jameson, in his study of American 'nostalgia films' of the 1980s, has argued that the crime movie *Body Heat*'s (1981) blending of a 1930s aesthetic with 'a contemporary setting' demonstrates that Westerners are 'unable to focus our own present, as though we have become incapable of achieving aesthetic representations of our own experience. But if that is so, then it is … an alarming and pathological symptom of a society that has become incapable of dealing with time and history'.[65] Transposing Jameson's thesis to Mo and Garland, we might propose that these writers were incapable of expressing much of value or meaning about the real 'time and history' of Manila because they fixated on projecting on to the city idioms cannibalised from representational schemes that were firmly

---

[62]   Daniel Workman, *Philippines Top Trading Partners* (2017), http://www.worldstop-exports.com/philippines-top-import-partners (accessed 25 September 2017).

[63]   Alex Garland, *The Tesseract* (London, 1998; repr. 2007), Amazon Kindle e-book, ch. 2, para. 1, loc. 363.

[64]   Timothy Mo, *Renegade or Halo²* (London, 1999), pp. 57–8.

[65]   Fredric Jameson, *The Cultural Turn: Selected Writings on the Post-modern, 1983–1988* (London, 1998), pp. 9–10.

embedded in Western popular culture and had little or no connection to the Philippines or Asia. So, while Mo's and Garland's postmodernist approach marked a new stylistic direction for the canon in one sense, in another it was far from new because, as we have seen, previous generations of Anglo-American writers on Manila had also plundered the Western cultural imagination for concepts such as the Judeo-Christian city-as-hell itself.

Furthermore, these 1990s narratives were decidedly less naturalistic and more imaginative in their depictions of the supernatural than any of their (fictional or nonfictional) predecessors. In Garland's Manila, hotels appeared 'undead' or reminded his protagonist, Sean, of 'concrete corpses'.[66] A graveyard was infested with 'an army of ancestral spirits, seething in the still air around the tomb, peering out of the statues' eyes'.[67] Like a merciless Devil type, the mobster-cacique character Don Pepe 'moves in mysterious ways' in a turbid moral universe when ordering the maiming of one lieutenant for a petty offence and then forgiving another for the mass murder of innocents.[68] Various faiths and religions have posited hell as a zone subject to physical laws almost inconceivably different from those of the phenomenal world, including unending time.[69] Thus, Sean in *The Tesseract* felt as if he is waiting for an eternity in confused anguish to rendezvous with the criminals he has wronged, and that Manila's otherworldly temporality can never be comprehended, at least not by a Western outsider: 'What about ten minutes ago? Or was it fifteen? Whatever. Ten, fifteen, he'd been a headless chicken.'[70] Ultimately, the entire textual time and space of *The Tesseract* is an unfathomable puzzle articulated by the guiding motif of the novel: 'A tesseract is a four-dimensional object – a hypercube – unravelled ... We can see the thing unravelled, but not the thing itself.'[71]

In the same vein, 'Everything [is] thrown into question' in *Ghosts of Manila* (1994), James Hamilton-Paterson's arguably eerier conception of the city.[72] Like a splatter movie script, the novel began with a cinematic sweep across the gruesome preparation of corpses for the illegal trade that, 'smacking of Burke and Hare', supplied skeletons to medical researchers: 'Two of the men now take down butcher's knives from a magnetic rack ... One takes the upper half of the body, the other lower. Deftly they remove the arms and legs.'[73] The environs of

---

[66] Garland, *The Tesseract*, ch. 5, para. 3, loc. 679.
[67] Ibid., ch. 4, para. 1, loc. 1005.
[68] Ibid., ch. 3, para. 2, loc. 565.
[69] Thomas A. Smith, 'The Pleasure of Hell in *City of God*', *Augustinian Studies* 30 (1999), 195–2014 at 197.
[70] Garland, *The Tesseract*, ch. 4, paras 4–6, loc. 287.
[71] Ibid., ch. 1, para. 5, locs 3152–56.
[72] James Hamilton-Paterson, *Ghosts of Manila* (London, 1994), p. 43.
[73] Ibid., pp. 5, 8.

Hamilton-Paterson's Manila-as-hell were reminiscent of the farthest circles of Dante's hell, with 'water … bubbling fiercely'[74] in place of the river Styx where 'Beneath the water people are who sigh / And make this water bubble at the surface';[75] and the 'perpetual slime of the squatter areas' and 'noxious black estuaries'[76] in lieu of the Styx's 'putrid water'.[77] Furthermore, like the nightmarish metropolis of Dis, Hamilton-Paterson's Manila was a holding tank for every Dantean sinner imaginable: thieves, liars, pederasts and murderers. Whereas in the post-war novels of Bechtel and Stevenson Manila was faintly redolent of hell, and its hellish incidents and topographical features are situated within the parameters of reason, the Manila of both *The Tesseract* and *Ghosts of Manila* was a more direct, thoroughgoing signifier for the Place of Torment. As Alberto Manguel put it in his review of *Ghosts of Manila*, 'Hell is the present-day Philippines'.[78] That 'sane people chose' to believe in paranormal creatures such as a hybrid bat-woman who sucks the livers out of babies suggests that, like *The Divine Comedy*, Hamilton-Paterson's fictional universe fell into the Todorovian category of the 'Fantastic', since it often framed supernatural phenomena as natural and self-evident.[79] At the same time, Hamilton-Paterson's persistent questioning of the reliability of characters who observed or reported on preternatural events, such as journalists who wrote 'vampire stories' in the popular press as a means of 'character assassination' of local politicians, places *Ghosts of Manila* in the 'Marvellous' camp because, as the Todorovian scholar Andrzej Wicher notes, 'the reader, and sometimes also the acting characters, cannot feel certain as to the nature of the narrated, or observed, events: they may be supernatural, but this remains only a supposition or hypothesis'.[80] Either way, the novel marked a significant departure from the more realist fictions of Bechtel and Stevenson, which deployed hell and the mystical as ciphers for ideas or emotions, as is more typical of 'Uncanny' narratives.[81]

---

[74] Ibid., p. 4.
[75] Dante, *Inferno*, trans. Henry Wadsworth Longfellow (Mineola, NY, 2005), p. 49.
[76] Hamilton-Paterson, *Ghosts of Manila*, p. 1.
[77] Dante, *Inferno*, p. 204.
[78] Alberto Manguel, 'Gouging Out Hell's Entrails: Ghosts of Manila – James Hamilton-Paterson', *Independent Online*, 3 June 1994, http://www.independent.co.uk/arts-entertainment/books/book-review-gouging-out-hells-entrails-ghosts-of-manila-james-hamilton-paterson-jonathan-cape-pounds-1420229.html (accessed 25 September 2017).
[79] Hamilton-Paterson, *Ghosts of Manila*, p. 103; Todorov, *The Fantastic*, p. 25.
[80] Hamilton-Paterson, *Ghosts of Manila*, p. 257; Andrzej Wicher, 'Introduction', in *Basic Categories of Fantastic Literature Revisited*, ed. Andrzej Wicher, Piotr Spyra and Joanna Matyjaszcyk (Newcastle upon Tyne, 2014), p. 3.
[81] Todorov, *The Fantastic*, p. 103.

These later writers' invocations of religious argot are greatly at odds with contemporary Western literary and cinematic portrayals of other Asian cities, particularly those in China and Japan. 'Whereas Orientalism as a strategy of representational containment, arrests Asia in traditional, and often premodern imagery,' averred David S. Roh, Betsy Huang and Greta A. Nui, 'Techno-Orientalism presents … an "Orient" undergoing rapid economic and cultural transformations.'[82] In its arresting of Manila in such pre-modern metaphors as hell, sin, curses and mythical beasts, the system of signification to which Garland and Hamilton-Paterson referred is in an arrested state itself, in not having evolved in step with parallel Techno-Orientalist modes. As with previous iterations of the Manila-as-hell paradigm, the disparity might be ascribed to transformations in the power relationship between not only the US/UK and the Philippines, but between East and West over the last thirty years. As Martin Jacques contends, China, Russia, Japan and India have been growing in prosperity, military strength and scientific capability at a rate that poses a substantial threat to US and Western European hegemony.[83] The Philippines lacks the material means to join that order of nations – as yet, anyway – and therefore has not been imagined in terms of Techno-Orientalism, which often fetishizes and exaggerates progress in the East.

If I may be permitted to end this survey on a bathetic note, after mention of Dante, Shakespeare and others in the high literary canon, it is worth noting that Dan Brown's lowbrow, cliché-crowded potboiler *Inferno* (2013) – the title an obvious reference to Dante – has recently fused many of these past iterations of city-as-hell into a single imagined geography. Subtlety is not a priority for Brown. Manila is, he declares, 'the gates of hell',[84] and as soon as his British doctor character, Sienna Brookes, enters them she is shocked and appalled by every urban Orientalist boilerplate in the cupboard: the 'shantytown – a city made of corrugated metal and cardboard',[85] the 'masses of people',[86] 'the young men approaching, salivating like wolves',[87] 'the stench of human excrement

---

[82] David S. Roh, Betsy Huang and Greta A. Nui, 'Technologizing Orientalism', in *Techno-Orientalism: Imagining Asia in Speculative Fiction, History, and Media*, ed. David S. Roh, Betsy Huang and Greta A. Nui (New Brunswick, NJ, 2015), p. 3.

[83] Martin Jacques, *When China Rules the World: The End of the Western World and the Birth of a New Global Order* (London, 2012), pp. 1–89.

[84] Dan Brown, *Inferno* (New York, 2013), Amazon Kindle e-book, ch. 79, para. 2, loc. 6151.

[85] Ibid., para. 4, loc. 6151.

[86] Ibid., para. 1, loc. 6147.

[87] Ibid., para. 1, loc. 6155.

[hanging] … in the air',[88] 'the six-hour traffic jams, suffocating pollution, and a horrifying sex trade'.[89]

In this chapter I have examined variations on the city-as-hell motif as they have been overlaid on Manila, from violence of both the interpersonal and large-scale military varieties to sin, corruption, poverty, urban decay, incoherent religiosity and supernatural menace. In accordance with Said's discourse of Orientalism, these ideologically informed constructions 'are particularly valuable as a sign of European-Atlantic power over the Orient'.[90] While the exact extent to which these constructions have 'enabled' – to use another of Said's designations – hostile and/or exploitative Western policy in Manila and the Philippines is difficult to ascertain, clearly they have provided an 'accepted grid for filtering through the Orient into Western consciousness'.[91]

It is important not to overstate the political and societal influence of the texts I have analysed. That said, they are components of a popular cultural discourse that was hegemonic and therefore stood more chance than other, competing discourses of shaping public opinion about the Philippines. After reading DeLouis Stevenson, for example, a voting member of the American polity may have been more inclined to support their government's intentions to reconstruct the post-war Philippines in America's image, as a semi-dependent, Christianised, laissez-faire capitalist democracy. Forty years later, having read *The Tesseract*, a British man or woman of a certain ideological bent might well have felt a pang of colonial nostalgia for the days when Western empires dominated cities like Manila, given how the city had deteriorated so dramatically since that time, at least according to Garland's depiction. In the case of Dan Brown's *Inferno*, the impact was more verifiable, and caused controversy in the Philippines amongst Manila-based politicians, writers and intellectuals. The chairman of the Metro Manila urban region, Francis Tolentino, accused Brown of an 'inaccurate portrayal of our beloved metropolis … We are displeased [by] how you have used Manila as a venue and source of a character's breakdown and trauma, much more her disillusionment in humanity.'[92]

As we have seen, Brown was by no means the first Western author to render Manila as a psychogeographical hell. Indeed, the acuteness and severity of *Inferno*'s imagery shows that neither literary history nor actual history have

---

[88] Ibid., para. 1, loc. 6152.
[89] Ibid., para. 3, loc. 6141.
[90] Said, *Orientalism*, p. 6.
[91] Ibid.
[92] Francis Tolentino, quoted in Kate Hodal, 'Manila less than thrilled at Dan Brown's Inferno', 24 May 2013, https://www.theguardian.com/world/2013/may/24/manila-thrilled-dan-brown-inferno (accessed 13 July 2018).

changed as significantly as some might have hoped. That ethnocentric fear, anxiety, contempt and condescension continue to animate Manilas-as-hell after all these years is partly because some literary conventions die hard, but also because, while we are no longer living in the 'Age of Empires', through the Cold War or under the 'New World Order' of the 1990s and early 2000s, Global Northern countries like Britain and the United States continue to exploit Global Southern countries like the Philippines.[93] According to the political theorist M. G. E. Kelly, this 'parasitical' arrangement contributes to the 'pitiful conditions' of many Third World cities blighted by hunger, 'environmental devastation' and 'inadequate medical and educational systems'.[94] All of which suggests that the Orientalist city-as-hell is unlikely to disappear from Western letters until these political and economic relations between North and South alter drastically.

Bibliography

Angotti, Tom, *The New Century of the Metropolis: Urban Enclaves and Orientalism* (New York, 2013)

Appel, Benjamin, *Fortress in the Rice* (New York, 1951)

Arcilla, José S., *An Introduction to Philippine History* (Manila, 1998)

Bancroft, Bernard, *Bread upon the Waters* (Des Plaines, IL, 1959)

Bechtel, John, *Perla of the Walled City* (Grand Rapids, MI, 1946)

Brown, Dan, *Inferno* (New York, 2013), Amazon Kindle e-book

Buruma, Ian, *God's Dust: A Modern Asian Journey* (London, 1991)

Constantino, Renato, *A History of the Philippines: From Spanish Colonization to the Second World War* (New York, 2010)

Dante, *Inferno*, trans. Henry Wadsworth Longfellow (Mineola, NY, 2005)

Ferrante, Joan M., *The Political Vision of Dante* (Princeton, NJ, 1984)

Fiedler, Leslie, 'Mythicizing the City', in *Literature and the American Urban Experience: Essays on the City and Literature*, ed. Michael C. Jaye and Ann Chalmers Watts (Manchester, 1981), pp. 113–22

Ferguson, Niall, *The War of the World: Twentieth-Century Conflict and the Descent of the West* (New York, 2007)

Fenton, James, *All the Wrong Places: Adrift in the Politics of Southeast Asia* (London, 2005)

Francia, Luis H., *A History of the Philippines: From Indios to Bravos* (New York, 2014)

Freedman, Lawrence, 'The Gulf War and the New World Order', *Survival* 33 (1991), 195–209

Garland, Alex, *The Tesseract* (London, 1998; repr. 2007), Amazon Kindle e-book

---

[93] George H. W. Bush, quoted in Lawrence Freedman, 'The Gulf War and the New World Order', *Survival* 33 (1991), pp. 195–209 at 195–6.

[94] M. G. E. Kelly, *Biopolitical Imperialism* (London, 2015), pp. 65, 93, 123.

Golay, Frank Hindman, *Face of Empire: United States–Philippine Relations, 1898–1946* (Manila, 2010)

Goto-Jones, Chris, *Conjuring Asia: Magic, Orientalism and the Making of the Modern World* (Cambridge, 2016)

Hamilton-Paterson, James, *America's Boy: The Marcoses and the Philippines* (London, 1998)

——, *Ghosts of Manila* (London, 1994)

Hawkes, David, *The Faust Myth: Religion and the Rise of Representation* (Basingstoke, 2007)

Hodal, Kate, 'Manila less than thrilled at Dan Brown's Inferno', 24 May 2013, https://www.theguardian.com/world/2013/may/24/manila-thrilled-dan-brown-inferno

Howell, John Benjamin, *42 Months of Hell: My Life as a Prisoner of the Japanese, World War II* (Muskogee, OK, 1969)

Ileto, Reynaldo C., *Knowledge and Pacification: On the US Conquest and the Writing of Philippine History* (Manila, 2017)

Jacques, Martin, *When China Rules the World: The End of the Western World and the Birth of a New Global Order* (London, 2012)

Jameson, Fredric, *The Cultural Turn: Selected Writings on the Post-modern, 1983–1988* (London, 1998)

Kellett, Wanda Liles, *Wings as Eagles* (New York, 1954)

Kelly, M. G. E., *Biopolitical Imperialism* (London, 2015)

Kemp, Simon, 'Urban Hell: Infernal Cities in Modern French Literature', in *Imagining the City, Volume 1*, ed. Christian Emden, Catherine Keen and David Midgley (Bern, 2006), 95–108

Konrad, Felix, *From the 'Turkish Menace' to Exoticism and Orientalism: Islam as Antithesis of Europe (1453–1914)?* (Mainz, 2011)

Kram, Mark, 'Lawdy, Lawdy, He's Great', Sports Illustrated Online, 13 October 1975, https://www.si.com/boxing/2012/01/17/muhammad-ali-70th-kram

Lee, Clark, *They Call It Pacific: An Eyewitness Story of Our War against Japan from Bataan to the Solomons* (New York, 1943)

Loney, Nicholas, *A Britisher in the Philippines; or, the Letters of Nicholas Loney* (Manila, 1964)

Mailer, Norman, *The Naked and the Dead* (New York, 1948)

Manguel, Alberto, 'Gouging Out Hell's Entrails: Ghosts of Manila – James Hamilton-Paterson', *Independent Online*, 3 June 1994, http://www.independent.co.uk/arts-entertainment/books/book-review-gouging-out-hells-entrails-ghosts-of-manila-james-hamilton-paterson-jonathan-cape-pounds-1420229.html

McNamara, Kevin, 'Introduction', in *The Companion to the City in Literature*, ed. idem (Cambridge, 2013), pp. 1–13

Miller, George A., *Interesting Manila* (Manila, 1929)

Mishra, Pankaj, *From the Ruins of Empire: The Revolt against the West and the Remaking of Asia* (London, 2013)

Mo, Timothy, *Renegade or Halo²* (London, 1999)

Nelson, Raymond, *The Philippines* (London, 1968)

New International Version (Biblica, 2011), www.biblegateway.com/versions/New-International-Version-NIV-Bible/#booklist

O'Rourke, P. J., *Holidays in Hell* (New York, 1989; repr. 2012), Amazon Kindle e-book

Palmer, Blanche, *Pilgrim of the Night* (Nashville, TN, 1966)

Pratt, Mary Louise, *Imperial Eyes: Travel Writing and Transculturation* (London, 1991)

Robb, Walter, *The Khaki Cabinet and Old Manila* (Manila, 1926)

Roh, David S., Betsy Huang and Greta A. Nui, 'Technologizing Orientalism', in *Techno-Orientalism: Imagining Asia in Speculative Fiction, History, and Media*, ed. David S. Roh, Betsy Huang and Greta A. Nui, (New Brunswick, NJ, 2015), pp. 1–20

Roland, Albert, *The Philippines* (New York, 1967)

Romein, Jan, *The Asian Century: A History of Modern Nationalism in Asia* (Berkeley, CA and Los Angeles, 1962)

Said, Edward, *Orientalism* (London, 1985)

Smith, Thomas A., 'The Pleasure of Hell in *City of God*', *Augustinian Studies* 30 (1999), 195–204

Steinberg, David Joel, *The Philippines: A Singular and Plural Place* (Boulder, CO, 1969)

Stevenson, DeLouis, *Land of the Morning* (St Louis, MO, 1956)

Tan, Samuel K., *A History of the Philippines* (Manila, 1987)

Todorov, Tzvetan, *The Fantastic: A Structural Approach to a Literary Genre* (Ithaca, NY, 1975)

Wicher, Andrzej, 'Introduction', in *Basic Categories of Fantastic Literature Revisited*, ed. Andrzej Wicher, Piotr Spyra and Joanna Matyjaszcyk (Newcastle upon Tyne, 2014), pp. 1–7

Williams, Maslyn, *Faces of My Neighbour: Three Journeys into East Asia* (Sydney, 1979)

Woods, Damon L., *The Philippines: A Global Studies Handbook* (Oxford, 2006)

Workman, Daniel, *Philippines Top Trading Partners* (2017), http://www.worldstopexports.com/philippines-top-import-partners

7

The Goatman and Washington, D.C.: Strange Sightings and the Fear of the Encroaching City

—◆◇◆—

DAVID J. PUGLIA

On the border of Washington, D.C., a humanoid cryptid has menaced Prince George's County for over half a century. The creature haunted Lottsford Road, Fletchertown Road or Tucker Road and emerged from either the tuberculosis sanitarium at Glenn Dale Hospital or a science experiment mishap at the Beltsville Agricultural Research Center.[1] Or he may have been a goatherd who lived isolated among his goats for so long that he began to resemble them. Others say teenagers mistreated him, killed his herd and drove him insane, and the deranged herder has stalked the woods as Goatman ever since, preying on teenagers as revenge. In addition to the many legendary accounts of his origin, the Goatman has documented, identifiable historical origins. Regional newspapers show the Goatman mass panic began with a series of newspaper reports in the early 1970s, transforming Goatman into the region's most notorious local monster.[2] According to oral tradition, the

---

[1] The Beltsville Agricultural Research Center origin story is so common that the Center's spokesperson was forced to deny it publicly. See Andy Wright, 'Maryland's Goatman is Half Man, Half Goat, and Out for Blood', *Modern Farmer*, 16 September 2013.

[2] For more specific information about the Goatman legend, its creations and its diffusion, see Trevor J. Blank and David J. Puglia, *Maryland Legends: Folklore from the Old Line State* (Charleston, SC, 2014); David J. Puglia, 'Getting Maryland's Goat:

homicidal Goatman of the 1970s skulked in the Washington metropolitan area's woods, surfacing only to victimise salacious teenagers and beloved domestic animals.[3] Goatman's portrayal differed from legend to legend, but a common pattern held among the various accounts. Goatman's combined characteristics were reminiscent of the folk image of Lucifer. His gaze threatened, and his stance intimidated. That he brandished a blade, often an axe, only added to an already murderous appearance.[4] If he lacked his blade, he tossed bricks and rocks. In the most common depiction, his legs were bent, hairy and hooved like a goat, but his upper body was humanoid. Prominent serpentine horns protruded from his goat-like head, and a billygoat's beard sprouted from his face, which had shades of both human and goat.

The choice of the goat as monster reflected the region's cultural history. To make religious sense in the Middle Atlantic region of the United States, the Goatman legend subtly incorporated Christian symbolism into its core narrative. The half-man, half-goat suggested Baphomet of Christian lore. The horns, too, recalled past and present popular portrayals of Satan.[5] To make secular cultural sense, the legend incorporated the local agricultural symbolism of goats. Goats have been on Maryland's cultural landscape since the seventeenth century, when John Smith and other settlers transported goats, man's first domesticated animal, to the Virginia Colony (which included present-day Maryland) to supply milk and meat for the colonists. Marylanders continue to

---

Diffusion and Canonization of Prince George's County's Goatman Legend', *Contemporary Legend: The Journal of the International Society for Contemporary Legend Research* 3 (2013), 63–77.

[3]   There are several Goatmen across North America, but these are not cognates to Maryland's Goatman. Some are cryptids. Another was an itinerant preacher who travelled the Upland South evangelising, his cart pulled by goats. For more on this, see J. Nathan Couch, *Goatman: Flesh or Folklore?* (North Charleston, SC, 2014).

[4]   The axe is probably due to conflation with another local legend, of the Bunnyman. More often associated with nearby Virginia, the Bunnyman is also known in Maryland and Washington, D.C. See Brian A. Conley, 'The Bunny Man Unmasked: The Real Life Origins of an Urban Legend' (2002), https://research.fairfaxcounty.gov/c.php?g=713238&p=5229327 (accessed 2 June 2019).

[5]   Goats play an important role in Biblical narrative, especially in the Sermon on the Mount. The Lord promises to divide humanity into 'the sheep' and 'the goats'. The sheep, placed at His right hand, will be rewarded by God. But He will condemn the goats, placed at His left hand, saying 'also unto them on the left hand, Depart from me, ye cursed, into everlasting fire, prepared for the devil and his angels'. Catholic priest and former Prince George's County resident Father Joe Jenkins has written on the theological ramifications of the Goatman. See Joe Jenkins, 'The Goatman of Prince George's County', in *Father Joe: From Silly to Sacred, A Priest Speaks* (1998), http://fatherjoe.wordpress.com/stories/the-goatman-of-prince-georges-county/ (accessed 2 June 2019, restricted site).

husband goats, but cultural prejudices unfairly vilify them. Cultural geographer David Siddle has documented the West's prevalent and persistent scorn for goats. In some 'deep dark places of our collective cultural subconscious', Siddle writes, the goat has 'been associated with fear of peripheries: woods and forests' and 'represented similar murky and deep sexually dangerous relationships with the outer edge, the periphery, the unknown'.[6] In fact, the word "goat" itself has faint connotations beyond the animal, as a type of licentious man. For example, in its less common forms, 'goat' is listed in the *Oxford American Writer's Thesaurus* as a synonym for lecher, libertine, womaniser, seducer and ladykiller. Siddle argues that these subconscious aversions towards goats 'persist to this day and are still evident in cartoons, cinema, and many cultural references' – such as the Goatman legend.[7]

The legendary Goatman's purported fiefdom was significant. He lived on the fringes of Prince George's County, which itself borders the United States' urban federal capital, The District of Columbia, better known as Washington, D.C., this habitat being an important element of the Goatman legend. As this chapter will demonstrate, Goatman arose as a socio-cultural and historical symbol that paralleled the perceived threats associated with Washington D.C. and its encroachment into the surrounding suburbs. Living outside the boundaries of humanity both morally and geographically, Goatman's monstrous characteristics and deeds imitated the daily horrors that newspapers and rumour-mongers reported about Washington, D.C. An antisocial personality who killed, vandalised properties, abused animals and purposefully frightened residents, Goatman was the locus for the transference of fears associated with the proximate and encroaching metropolitan area into this once bucolic setting.

Goatman's heyday predated the advent of social media, his legend travelling instead via a combination of newspapers and oral transmission. Folklorists have examined this dynamic relationship between legends and newspapers. In 1973, Linda Dégh and Andrew Vázsonyi argued that 'legend makes a part of its way – presumably the lesser – on foot and continues on the longer trail through the speedy modern vehicle' of the mass media.[8] Attempting to define the American folk legend, folklorist Richard M. Dorson found it necessary to 'distinguish legends perpetuated through town histories, tourist brochures, local-color literature, Sunday supplements and similar printed channels from

---

[6]   David Siddle, 'Goats, Marginality, and the "Dangerous Other" ', *Environment and History* 15 (2009), 521–36 at 530.
[7]   Ibid., p. 531.
[8]   Linda Dégh and Andrew Vázsonyi, *The Dialectics of the Legend*, Folklore Preprint Series 1, no. 6 (Bloomington, IN, 1973), p. 37.

spoken legends'.[9] He coined the term 'popular legend' to refer to legends that are neither exclusively oral nor purely literary, but rely on the synergy between the two. Paul Smith, too, encouraged legend scholars to consider all possible transmission channels. By looking only at oral channels, scholars constructed legend as a unique phenomenon disconnected from everyday life. In truth, Smith argued, legends are transmitted through any means available. He agreed with Dégh and Vázsonyi that, beyond oral tradition, 'the major disseminators of contemporary legend are the news gathering agencies'.[10] Newspapers allowed the Goatman legend to flourish across Prince George's County and across the state in ways that it had not done in oral tradition.

Goatman existed in Prince George's County oral tradition prior to newspaper coverage in 1971, but the legend spread rapidly only after media attention. It may have started as Dorson's 'folk legend', circulating primarily through oral transmission, but, as Dégh and Vázsonyi argued legends are prone to do, Goatman travelled his greatest distance on the backs of the media. Rather than trivialising the legend, this moment marked the pinnacle of its importance. Goatman became Dorson's 'popular legend', and through the 1970s the interplay of folk and popular sources gave the legend its strength. By acknowledging both the oral sources and the newspaper sources, as Smith and Roger E. Mitchell have encouraged scholars to do, researchers can interpret Goatman as locals did, grasping the legend's full regional significance.[11]

Was there really a Goatman lurking about the Prince George's County woods? Considering reports of large, hairy bipeds like Sasquatch or Bigfoot, David Hufford argued against folklorists perfunctorily labelling supernatural creatures like Goatman as fictional.[12] These accounts, he argued, may come from an 'objectively real referent' that has subsequently developed into

[9] Richard M. Dorson, 'Defining the American Folk Legend', in *American Folklore and the Historian*, ed. idem (Chicago, 1971), pp. 157–72 at 160.

[10] Paul Smith, ' "Read All About It! Elvis Eaten by Drug-Crazed Giant Alligators": Contemporary Legend and the Popular Press', *Contemporary Legend* 2 (1992), 41–71 at 42.

[11] See Roger E. Mitchell, 'The Press, Rumor, and Legend Formation', *Midwestern Journal of Language and Folklore* 5, nos 1/2 (1979 special issue). In an earlier Goatman article, I considered how oral and journalistic sources overlapped and diverged. Newspaper sources fed on oral sources and reflected the diversity of oral rumour. While newspaper sources spread the legend generally across a large geographic area, they were not as successful in feeding the legend's particular motifs to new tellers. See Puglia, 'Getting Maryland's Goat'.

[12] See David Hufford, 'Humanoids and Anomalous Lights: Taxonomic and Epistemological Problems', *Fabula* 18 (1977), 234–41.

legendary form.[13] From the standpoint of a candid narrator, the legend is 'simple facts accurately reported'.[14] It is plausible that creatures repeatedly reported over the years but never verified do exist, Hufford argues, and, therefore, such phenomena should not be analysed from a purely psychological perspective. Following this line of inquiry elsewhere, I have attempted to chronicle the rise of Goatman as a reaction to honest reports that were then embellished by later legend tellers and journalists.[15] However, a community-based, symbolic and psychological interpretation seems more useful in this instance to explain why Goatman was seized upon and kept alive by media and locals alike. Specifically, this chapter will consider how Goatman served as an unconscious symbol for the psychological discontent the encroaching city had evoked in the surrounding rural area, especially in the 1970s when reports of rising crime, an expanding city and rapidly changing demographics had increased local anxieties.[16] Reports of crime took on a life of their own, turning legendary. It is in this situation that a symbolic and psychological interpretation of Goatman reveals the cultural unease of the specific era that spawned him.

The rise of Goatman

Student and Prince George's County local George Lizama had begun investigating 'The Goatman of Tucker Road' as an undergraduate folklore project while attending the University of Maryland. On 18 May 1971, he submitted his final project. Unknown to him at the time, his research would vault Goatman into the forefront of Prince George's County's community consciousness. Lizama's project eventually landed in the Maryland Folklore Archives, the final

---

[13] Ibid., p. 238.

[14] Ibid.

[15] The most important of these reports was repudiated by its teller, decades later, as a hoax that got out of hand. See Sean Daley, 'The Legend of Goatman', *Washington City Paper*, 18 September 1998.

[16] Several scholars have used the psychological concepts of 'transference' and 'projection' as methods of analysis in folklore studies, most notably Alan Dundes and Simon J. Bronner. See, for example, Alan Dundes, 'Earth-Diver: Creation of the Mythopoeic Male', *American Anthropologist* 64 (1962), 1032–51; idem, 'Into the Endzone for a Touchdown', *Western Folklore*, 37 (1978), 75–88; idem, 'Projection in Folklore: A Plea for Psychoanalytic Semiotics', in *Interpreting Folklore*, ed. idem (Bloomington, IN, 1980), pp. 33–61; Simon J. Bronner, ' "This is Why We Hunt": Social-Psychological Meanings of the Traditions and Rituals of Deer Camp', *Western Folklore* 63 (2002), 11–50; idem, *Explaining Traditions: Folk Behavior in Modern Culture* (Lexington, KY, 2011); idem, 'Toward the Formulation of a Folkloristic Theory of Mind: The Role of Psychoanalysis and Symbolist Approaches to Tradition', *Millî Folklor* 27, (2015), 18–30.

resting place for all University of Maryland student folklore assignments at the time. Of the eight legends Lizama collected, he considered Patricia Isidro's version the most common and representative of the Goatman cycle:

> Yes I've heard of the Goatman. Of course he died a long time ago. He was killed in a fire and burned to crisp [*sic*]. I'll tell you what I know. Tucker Road is a long tree laden road that is very, very narrow. A lot of the kids go out there to park and I think that's how the legend got started. It seems there lived an old man who had the face of a goat and the body of a man. At the time of a full moon he would come out onto the bridge to ward off people, because it was his bridge. He always had a kind of wicked grin on his faced [*sic*] and called out like a real goat would. I've heard where cars have gone off the road because of the Goatman and that a few people a couple of years back were even killed and no trace of them was found.
>
> Kids say that he always carries bricks and that lots of cars have come off the bridge with busted windshields and the strangest thing is that not a sound was heard of bricks hitting glass or the shattering of glass. He only comes out at night and when the moon is bright. People say that he used to be a goat herder and that after all his goats died he almost turned into one. Some of my friends say they saw his eyes glowing at them at one time or another, but no one has really seen him.[17]

Later that same year, *Prince George's County News* reporter Karen Hosler found Lizama's fieldwork while rummaging through the Maryland Folklore Archives for inspiration for a macabre Halloween-season feature. The only Goatman file in the Archives at the time, Lizama's folklore project became Hosler's first 'Goatman' article for the *Prince George's County News*, published on 27 October 1971:

> The woods around Fletchertown Road have other strange inhabitants, folklore records indicate. One is a Goatman, half-man, half-goat who supposedly once was a researcher at the Beltsville Agricultural Farm. The story goes that the man experimented on goats. One day he went insane and ran into the woods. He grew all his hair until it covered his body ... other accounts say he lives in an old shack and beats upon parked cars with an axe.[18]

Instead of locating Goatman on Tucker Road in Clinton, Maryland, Hosler decided to place Goatman on Fletchertown Road in Bowie, Maryland, a

---

[17] George Lizama, 'The Goatman of Tucker Road', Maryland Folklore Archives (College Park, MD, 1971).

[18] Karen Hosler, 'University Archives Reveals: Boaman, Goatman, and Ghosts Still Haunt Area', *Prince George's County News*, 27 October 1971.

similar dark wooded stretch of road commonly associated with Goatman, approximately twenty miles to the north. The article had an immediate real-world effect two weeks later. On the night of 3 November 1971, Bowie resident April Edwards claimed she heard odd sounds outside her house on the edge of the woods. Edwards, Willie Gheen and John Hayden described witnessing 'an animal … six-foot, something like that, and hairy, like an animal … it was on two feet'. The next morning, noting Edwards's dog Ginger was missing, Gheen and Hayden searched the woods. There they discovered Ginger's severed head and body beside the Penn Central Railroad tracks. Hosler published an account of the gory events in a subsequent article.[19]

Hosler had thus reported the existence of Goatman, and then followed up with her own real-world evidence. In response, Bowie's teenagers embraced the Goatman legend with a youthful exuberance, embarking on legend trips hoping to capture the notorious monster.[20] Two weeks after reporting the discovery of the decapitated dog, Hosler wrote again to chastise raucous and destructive Goatman hunts in yet another Goatman article, 'Pranksters and Thrill-Seekers: The Real Monsters of Fletchertown Road'.[21] The pandemonium caught the attention of *Washington Post* reporter Ivan G. Goldman, who announced the existence of Goatman to a much larger audience.[22] The Goatman legend would soon proliferate in a third Maryland location, in addition to Tucker Road in Clinton and Fletchertown Road in Bowie: Lottsford Road in Mitchellville.

Bowie, Mitchellville and Clinton form a roughly fifty-mile stretch immediately east of Washington, D.C., all three sharing the cultural context that made Goatman a suitable psychological symbol for fears of the encroaching city. In fact, the three towns lie immediately east of the Capital Beltway (completed in 1964, only a few years before the Goatman reports). The Capital Beltway encircles Washington, D.C., creating a boundary that both confines and defines the city, while also connecting it to the surrounding suburban communities. The advent of the beltway precipitated a drastic increase in the movement of outsiders from the city in, out and through these communities, and an influx of new residents as the suburbs became more convenient and commutable,

---

[19] Hosler, 'Residents Fear Goatman Lives: Dog Found Decapitated in Old Bowie', *Prince George's County News*, 10 November 1971.
[20] Files in the Maryland Folklore Archives document the rapid increase in Goatman collections in the years immediately following the news reports. See the section 'Folklife Archives Files' for the full list of Goatman collections from this era.
[21] Karen Hosler, 'Pranksters and Thrill-Seekers: The Real Monsters of Fletchertown Road', *Prince George's County New*, 24 November 1971.
[22] See Ivan G. Goldman, 'A Legendary Figure Haunts Remote Pr. George's Woods', *Washington Post*, 30 November 1971.

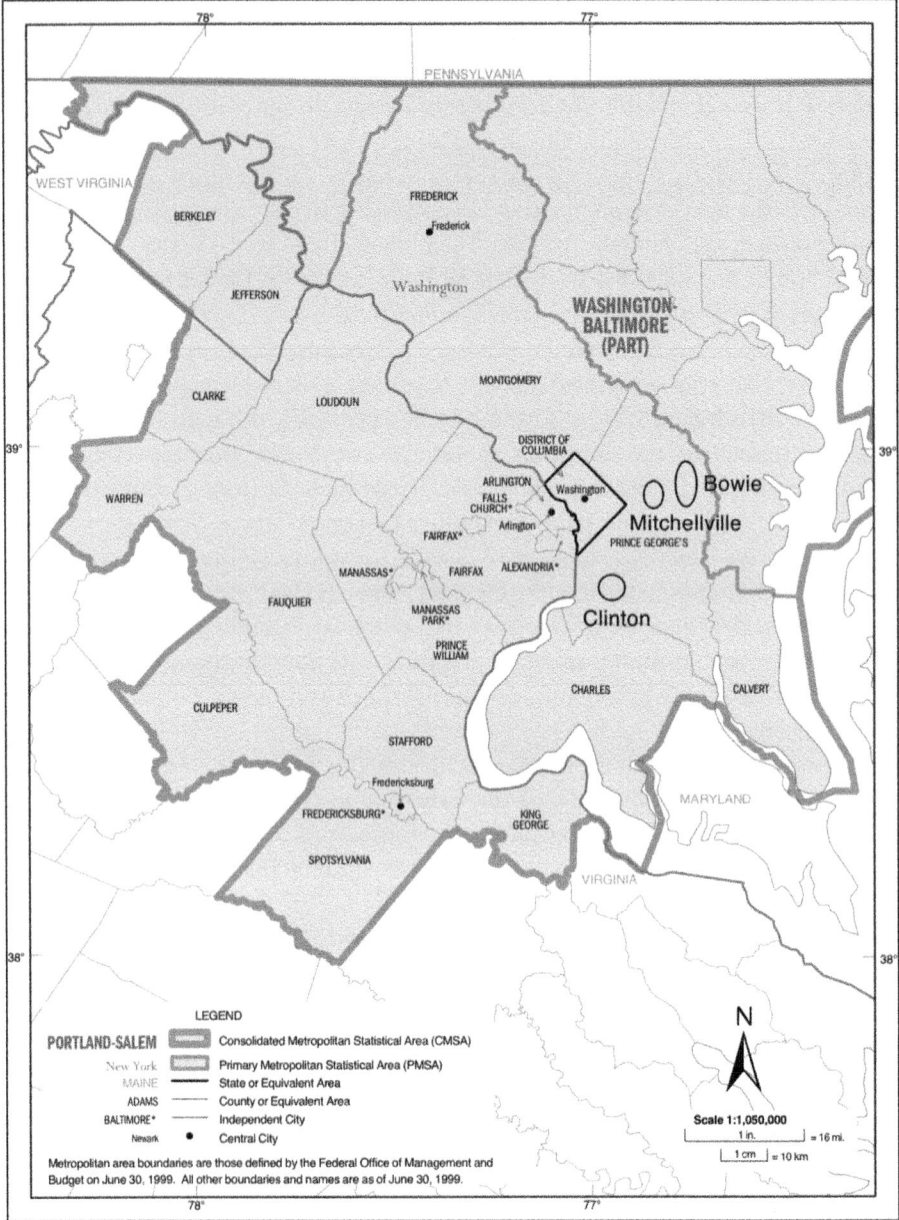

Fig. 4. Map of Washington, D.C. and the Goatman's three Maryland haunts to the east: Bowie, Mitchellville and Clinton. Map Courtesy of U.S. Census Bureau.

to jobs in the city. This rapid change threatened to transform community life, increasing cultural anxiety among the local populace.

Previously, Prince George's County had been connected to Washington, D.C. geographically, but remained culturally separate. Indeed this geographic relationship is a major theme in Prince George's County's own history of itself.[23] As Prince George's County residents faced rapid change, they transferred their anxiety about an encroaching city and shifting demographics to the form of the fiendish Goatman. Washington, D.C., bordering Goatman's territory, is colloquially known as the 'Murder Capital of [the] Country' or the 'Crime Capital of the World'.[24] Over only a few decades in the mid-twentieth century, intensive development transformed the once-rural farming community surrounding the city into one of the most heavily populated in Maryland and one of the most multicultural in the country. Catholic priest, former Prince George's County resident and fellow Goatman theorist Father Joe Jenkins recalled Prince George's County in the Goatman frenzy era as being 'in the early stages of a transition wherein unchecked construction of homes, businesses, and roads were encroaching'.[25] In the *Washington Post*, Ivan G. Goldman wrote of Prince George's County during the Goatman craze as 'a long-settled, but still sparsely populated area – a place inherently apart from the Washington metropolitan area – yet within its geographical boundaries'.[26] In his folklore project that sparked the Goatman craze, George Lizama mentioned that the legends he collected came from 'sections of the county being developed into modern residential and commercial areas', shaping 'one of the few regions where the past and present live side by side'.[27] All agreed the city had catalysed rapid change, the reverberations of which were felt in the surrounding suburbs.

The threat of the city

Researchers have investigated the Goatman phenomenon, and their explanations have been cryptozoological, journalistic, theological or folkloristic. None

---

[23] For a full discussion of the rapid demographic change in Prince George's County in the twenty-first century, see Alan Virta, 'Prince George's County: Over 300 Years of History', *Prince George's County History*, http://www.pghistory.org/PG/PG300/history.html (accessed 3 June 2019).

[24] Debbie M. Price, ' "Murder Capital" Label Has Long Stalked D.C.', *Washington Post*, 4 April 1989.

[25] Jenkins, 'The Goatman of Prince George's County'.

[26] Goldman, 'A Legendary Figure'.

[27] Lizama, 'The Goatman of Tucker Road'.

as yet has attempted a psychological inquiry.[28] A psychological interpretation of socio-cultural transference reveals Goatman as a symbolic manifestation of the threat of the encroaching city. County residents felt this transformation especially at the beginning of the second half of the twentieth century, when the population increased tenfold and demographics began to shift from white and rural to black and urban.[29]

Rapidly changing demographics led to the creation of new legends, ones that met the needs of Prince George's County residents.[30] In the early 1970s, precisely the time that the Goatman legend came to prominence, the legend seemed to link Goatman to the purported crime wave that was sweeping the country and creating public safety panics. The Federal Bureau of Investigation's Uniform Crime Reporting shows a total of 4,230 violent crimes in Washington, D.C. in 1960. That total remained approximately steady for the first half of the 1960s, but then rose rapidly, more than tripling by the end of the decade to 17,038 violent crimes in 1969. While the total had receded by the end of the 1970s, in the first half of that decade – the early Goatman era – violent crimes remained near the annual high of 16,084. Murders, too, rocketed from 81 in 1960, to 148 in 1965, to a high of 287 in 1969. They again approached this figure, at a total of 275, in 1971, during the Goatman craze.[31] According to the

---

[28] For various interpretations, see Daley, 'The Legend of Goatman'; Jenkins, 'The Goatman of Prince George's County'; Mark Opsasnick, 'Horror on Fletchertown Road', in idem, *The Real Story Behind the Exorcist: A Study of the Haunted Boy and Other True-Life Horror Legends from Around the Nation's Capital* (Bloomington, IN, 2007), pp. 67–80; Puglia, 'Getting Maryland's Goat'.

[29] The United States Census Bureau's data show racial demographics changed quickly in the mid-twentieth century, from 517,865 white and 280,803 black in the 1950s to 345,263 white and 411,737 black in the 1960s, to 209,272 white and 537,712 black in the 1970s. Other racial groups constituted approximately 1 per cent or less of the city population during these decades.

[30] While there are prior hints of the Goatman legend, only in the 1970s does the Goatman become a household figure. Earlier Maryland folklorists do not broach the topic of the Goatman in their earlier general-purpose Maryland folklore books: see Madeline Vinton Dahlgren, *South Mountain Magic: Tales of Old Maryland* (Maple Shade, NJ, 2002 [1882]); Annie Weston Whitney and Caroline Canfield Bullock, *Folk-Lore from Maryland* (New York, 1925); George Carey, *Maryland Folklore and Folklife* (Centreville, MD, 1970) and *Maryland Folk Legends and Folk Songs* (Centreville, MD, 1971). In contrast, the Goatman's current renown placed an artist's depiction of him on the title page of Matt Lake's *Weird Maryland*, and afforded him two separate chapters. See Matt Lake, *Weird Maryland: Your Travel Guide to Maryland's Local Legends and Best Kept Secrets* (New York, 2006).

[31] The Federal Bureau of Investigation provides these data through its Uniform Crime Reporting Statistics, https://www.ucrdatatool.gov/. The Washington, D.C. data are found by searching by state (District of Columbia) and year range.

Maryland crime data provided by the Governor's Office of Crime Control and Prevention, despite the pessimistic outlook, violent crime in Prince George's County remained steady in the 1970s, as likely to decrease slightly one year as it was to increase the next. It was the fear of urban crime spreading to the county, not actual local crime events, that stirred Prince George's County residents' anxiety. Each suburban community had its own way of dealing with crime and the fearsome new invasion by city ills. Legends about the deeds of Goatman paralleled news of conditions and the occurrence of violent crimes in the city: homelessness and poverty, murder and disposal of corpses, destruction of property and random assaults. And newspapers appeared more than happy to exploit gory headlines and correspondingly increase their readership.

News stories about Goatman, drawn from oral tradition, were similar to other violent news stories on urban stations. For example, newspapers frequently reported on mutilated corpses found on Lottsford Road, supposedly drug dealers from Washington, D.C., but whose fate was identical to that of Goatman's alleged victims.[32] News outlets are often accused of privileging sensational anecdotes over scientific evidence and accurate reporting.[33] From the beginning, the Goatman reporting was classic fear-based 'if it bleeds, it leads' journalism. The stories were gruesome, and the follow-up coverage was equally bloody, featuring severed puppy heads and haphazardly dumped corpses. As psychologist Deborah Serani explains, 'Fear-based news stories prey on the anxieties we all have and then hold us hostage'.[34] Because it is difficult to ignore death and destruction, such stories succeed in securing the reader's or viewer's attention. Profiting more from fear than from hope, the media habitually portray certain subjects as redolent of danger, and promote unique occurrences as examples of terrifying trends. Such depictions of events make people 'feel their neighborhoods and communities are unsafe', 'believe that crime rates are rising', 'overestimate their odds of becoming a victim' and 'consider the world to be a dangerous place'.[35]

32 Eugene L. Meyer, 'Lottsford Road: Local Legend Says It's a Trail of Terror', *Washington Post*, 1 October 1984.
33 See David L. Altheide, *Creating Fear: News and the Construction of Crisis* (New York, 2002); Barry Glassner, *The Culture of Fear: Why Americans are Afraid of the Wrong Things: Crime, Drugs, Minorities, Teen Moms, Killer Kids, Mutant Microbes, Plane Crashes, Road Rage, & So Much More* (New York, 2010).
34 See Deborah Serani, 'If It Bleeds, It Leads: Understanding Fear-Based Media', *Psychology Today* (2011), https://www.psychologytoday.com/us/blog/two-takes-depression/201106/if-it-bleeds-it-leads-understanding-fear-based-media (accessed 3 June 2019).
35 Deborah Serani, 'If It Bleeds, It Leads: The Clinical Implications of Fear-Based Programming in News Media', *Psychoanalysis and Psychotherapy* 24 (2008), 240–50 at

In this unpleasant media milieu, how did the Goatman legend help residents cope with prevailing anxieties about urban crime coming to their suburban oasis? Across the United States, sceptics often attribute fantastical and crypto-zoological sightings to misinterpretations of mundane occurrences. Michael Taft argues that such sightings, regardless of the mythic canon from which they derive, must make local cultural and environmental sense.[36] In Maryland, the goat had the requisite cultural and religious familiarity to make Goatman an acceptable, if unusual, being. Funneling anxieties into a single manageable monster was preferable to visualising the vast array of violent criminals on the nearby landscape. In addition, the fear-based, anxiety-producing stories offered not only a source for anxiety but also an ostensible protection against it, requiring only that the potential victim be aware and prepared.

Stories of murder, assault and property destruction, once rare in Prince George's County, had by the 1970s become commonplace. Local media embraced the sensational news. Whereas during the previous decade the predominant threat had been that of nuclear annihilation, that threat, unresolved, was now combined with perceptions of the rise of the Black Power movement, with loss of faith in political leaders and government due to the Vietnam war, with soaring oil prices, racial discord and the proliferation of aircraft hijackings. For the United States, the 1970s was an understandably anxiety-producing period.[37] Goatman, it would seem, was a symbol of these anxieties, a way of expressing and handling, through the unconscious religious and cultural symbolism of the goat, fear that could not otherwise be managed.

Goatman as symbolic manifestation of urban crime

Woods-living itinerants were likely Hufford's 'objectively real referent' that sparked the subsequent Goatman legends. Disconcerting men – hermits, transients, vagrants – had drifted into the area from the city. Father Joe Jenkins recalls from his childhood in Prince George's County itinerant trappers traversing the woods toting threatening trapping tools. Because of the thick hide coats the trappers wore in all seasons, some children called them 'coat-men', which possibly later morphed into 'Goatman'.[38] The Prince George's

---

249.

[36]   See Michael Taft, 'Sasquatch-like Creatures in Newfoundland: A Study in the Problems of Belief, Perception, and Reportage', in *Manlike Monsters on Trial: Early Records and Modern Evidence*, ed. Marjorie Halpin and Michael Ames (Vancouver, 1980), pp. 83–96.

[37]   See Joel Best, *Random Violence: How We Talk about New Crimes and New Victims* (Berkeley, CA, 1999).

[38]   See Jenkins, 'The Goatman of Prince George's County'.

County Police themselves believed there really had been a Goatman. Captain Lawrence Wheeler, commander of the Prince George's County Police Department's Bowie District, told the *Washington Post* that he 'had heard there really was an old man who used to live in a shack in the woods'. The captain remembered, 'Kids would come around and once in a while he would come out and scare them.'[39]

The Maryland Folklore Archives hold additional clues that roaming indigents may have served as the Goatman legend's inspiration. For example, student Frank Caherty proposed a project involving the collection of tales of 'goat-men' and 'murderous woodsmen'.[40] However, the results of his study ultimately recorded not a supernatural Goatman, but an plethora of destitute hermits residing in the Prince George's County woods, sporadically emerging to frighten children. A self-sustaining, elderly African American with a long white beard served as the inspiration for at least one of the variants of this legend. He lived in a small shack near a bridge, and children knew him as 'Goatman':

> Yes I've heard of the Goatman from time to time. You know that the road isn't very far from here. The legend is only partly a story some of it is true. There really is a Goatman of Tucker Road. He is an old man, an old black man with a real long white beard – like a goat. He's a hermit who lives by the bridge in a little shanty. He grows all his food and hunts for his meat and in order to do so must cross the narrow bridge from time to time. This is probably when everyone sees him and as they pass he smiles and then everyone in the car gets bent-out-of-shape and goes around screaming Goatman. I've gone down the road and never met up with him, but relatives have and they're all still alive.[41]

Suburban Prince George's County at the time of the Goatman legend was perceived as threatened from all sides. The city was coming to the county, but the wild areas also threatened. Both the woods and the 'urban jungle' could be chaotic, menacing places. Suburban communities not only feared a more urban future, but also harboured anxieties about the wilderness on their doorstep. Simultaneously with fears generated by the influx of urban newcomers, Goatman could in addition represent anxieties about rural life for urban dwellers who had moved into the suburbs. The men living in the woods were just as incomprehensible, and thus as threatening, as the urban criminal.

[39]   Goldman, 'A Legendary Figure'.
[40]   See Frank Caherty, 'Goat-men, Hermits, & Murderous Woodsmen: Strange Tales and Curious Happenings', Maryland Folklore Archives (College Park, MD, 1977).
[41]   Lizama, 'The Goatman of Tucker Road'.

The late 1960s had been an era of violent and destructive rioting. In 1968, four days of riots followed the assassination of Martin Luther King Jr. The violence and destruction affected hundreds of cities, including Chicago and Baltimore, but no city was more affected than Washington, D.C. George Marvin Fletcher had been stabbed to death in a confrontation with eight African American youths, and a seventy-eight year-old was also allegedly beaten to death by a group of African Americans: he was found unconscious and later succumbed to his injuries. Property damage was extensive and suspected of motivating subsequent white flight to the suburbs.[42] As mentioned above, violence hit a record high in 1969.[43] The threat of random violence seems to be reflected in the stories of Goatman's actions:

> The goatman is a man who lives on Lottsford Road and protects a bridge on the road called Crybaby Bridge. He lives in the woods beside the road and tries to keep all trespassers away from his home. If you happen to be walking down the road anywhere near the bridge, the goatman will smell you and come out to kill you. There are some stories about people in broken down cars who have gotten killed by the goatman, but I don't know them, I've just kind of heard of them.[44]

The murder rate increased drastically in the 1960s and did not abate until the mid-1990s – precisely the time when instances of the Goatman legend ceased to be collected in Prince George's County. Sociologist Joel Best identifies 1960 to 1975 as the period that brought a new level of attention to victims, indiscriminate violence and fears of arbitrary victimisation.[45] Popular culture was inspired by these themes, and slasher films such as *Black Christmas* (1974), *Halloween* (1978) and *Friday the 13th* (1980) were products of this era.[46]

Murder and the subsequent disposal of corpses was further aspect of real-world anxiety about crime symbolised by Goatman and his offences. That Lottsford Road in Mitchellville, for example, was a prime area for the dumping of Washington, D.C. murder victims *and* one of the standard haunts of

---

[42]   Although I do not dwell on it here, property damage is another theme that seems to be embroiled in the Goatman legend, which indicts the Goatman for numerous acts of malicious destruction of property, especially automobiles.

[43]   See the statistics previously quoted and FBI website cited in note 31.

[44]   Ian McKeller, 'The Goatman and Crybaby Bridge: Local Legends of Lottsford Road', Maryland Folklore Archives (College Park, MD, 1986).

[45]   Best, *Random Violence*, p. 96.

[46]   See Adam Rockoff, *Going to Pieces: The Rise and Fall of the Slasher Film, 1978–1986* (Jefferson, NC, 2002)

Goatman seems more than mere coincidence.[47] Goatman became a symbol of urban crime's arrival in suburban Maryland. Girded by woodland, the sylvan, constricted, gloomy Lottsford Road provided fertile ground for the Goatman legend, because of its notorious reputation. The 1984 *Washington Post* article cited above described the road's 'macabre reputation as a dumping ground for bodies'.[48] Shirley Hutchinson, one of the local townsfolk living along the road, grumbled, 'It's a damper finding dead bodies in the road and all.'[49] Police found that Bernard Carter, for example, had been violently murdered and 'thrown over a guardrail of a small bridge that crossed the stream' on Lottsford-Vista Road. Four bodies in the years leading up to the Goatman craze, and fourteen more in the years to follow, were dumped from bridges into streams on Lottsford Road. Former Lottsford Road patrolman Dennis Husk (now Mount Rainier police chief) recalled that '[E]very time [we]'d turn around, [we] were finding either a prostitute from the District or a dope dealer from downtown.'[50]

The Maryland Folklore Archive also includes numerous instances of Goatman legends from Lottsford Road at this time. Unsurprisingly, student collector Mark McGuigan spoke to a man on Lottsford Road who told him the road's reputation as a 'common dumping ground for bodies' led him to believe that Goatman may exist.[51] The grim space encouraged local stories and legends. Goatman was an extreme version of the murdering psychopath that residents feared – a singular, if fantastical, threat. Numerous others told of murderous happenings on Lottsford Road, all attributed to Goatman. For example:

> This happened on Lottsford Road. A friend of mine saw him last year. Anyway, this girl and guy's car broke down and the girl stayed in the car while the guy went to get some help. She locked all the doors and then hears pounding on the roof. Later the cops came and shine lights all around. They told her not to look back — her boyfriend was hanging over the car. They blamed it on Goatman. It's supposed to be true.[52]

---

[47] See Carolyn Hoffman, 'Local Legends of Lottsford Road Area', Maryland Folklore Archives (College Park, MD, 1974); Meyer, 'Lottsford Road'; McKeller, 'The Goatman and Crybaby Bridge'.

[48] Meyer, 'Lottsford Road'.

[49] Ibid.

[50] Ibid.

[51] Mark McGuigan, 'Local Legends'. Maryland Folklore Archives (College Park, MD, 1984).

[52] Rose Ann Duley, 'Goatman Tales', Maryland Folklore Archives (College Park, MD, 1975).
This is a local variant of the 'Boyfriend's Death' legend. See Jan Harold Brunvand, *The Vanishing Hitchhiker: American Urban Legends and their Meanings* (New York, 1981), pp. 5–10 for a more thorough overview of the 'Boyfriend's Death'.

Perhaps more than being simply an embodiment of the common criminal, the Goatman figure had connections to the fear of urban serial killers that was on the rise in the 1970s. Some accounts demonstrated Goatman's similarity to serial killers, or the frighteningly motiveless killers associated with random urban violence:

> I know the goatman is supposed [sic] a freak of nature. He is half man and half goat. He has the head of a man and the neck of a man, but the rest of him is goat. He has four legs with hooves and a tail, and he is covered with hair. He guards Lottsford from trespassers and enjoys killing people. If he catches you he is supposed to chop you up however he feels like it.[53]

Goatman committed only the most abhorrent crimes. He terrorised communities, mistreated animals, abused children, vandalised property and murdered without emotion or pity, much like a classic serial killer.[54] Goatman rejected mankind's physical and ethical boundaries, living in the woods and killing as he pleased. In his violent deeds, he was a burlesque amplification of the very men most feared by society. From a psychological perspective, Goatman may have been fictional, but what he symbolised was very real indeed.

Cryptids as suburban projections of urban anxieties

Creatures such as Goatman serve as rural projections of urban anxieties. This chapter has argued that Goatman was a symbolic psychological transference of concerns about the encroachment of the city, Washington, D.C., into the once pastoral Prince George's County setting, offering residents a means of managing their anxiety. This argument embraces Hufford's notion that Prince George's County residents did encounter phenomena in the 1970s and honestly reported them. However, a psychological approach has suggested ways in which the characteristic concerns regarding Goatman in fact mirrored

---

[53]   McKeller, 'The Goatman and Crybaby Bridge'.
[54]   Many serial killers began their reigns of terror by abusing animals. Similarly, people who abuse animals are more likely to commit violence against humans. See Susan McDonald, 'Childhood Animal Abuse and Violent Criminal Behavior: A Brief Review of the Literature', report prepared for the Office of Strategic Planning and Research, Department of Correction, Commonwealth of Massachusetts (2011). The Goatman legend cycles include numerous tales of violence against animals, especially dogs. See Hoffman, 'Local Legends of Lottsford' for examples of the Goatman mutilating dogs or hanging them from trees. Other renditions such as Brian Murphy's in Duley's collection directly or indirectly reference Hosler's news article 'Residents Fear Goatman Lives', cited above, about April Edwards and her decapitated dog Ginger.

shifting demographics and advancing urban threat. A closer examination of the legend and corresponding crime trends demonstrates how these symbolic projections paralleled the concerns associated with neighbouring Washington, D.C., especially in the crime-ridden 1970s. In the guise of tradition, the community could express its feelings publicly in terms of a single threat rather than a vague feeling of an ever-present amorphous unease. While the Goatman legend varied from telling to telling, an analysis of the legend's patterns in its historical context allows researchers to deduce the psychological impetus underpinning the legend's rapid rise and spread across this particular geographic landscape.

Goatman became the 'scapegoat', the accused, symbolic manifestation representing the many real and frightening individuals who lived on the fringes of civilisation, unwilling to conform but seemingly willing to carry out atrocities at random. Goatman came out of this historical moment and fulfilled the psychological need of the community, focusing amorphous anxieties by directing them towards a single, ferocious, evil being. Washington, D.C. thrust Goatman upon Prince George's County, and he galloped into the collective psyche as the embodiment of growing anxieties about the city.

Occasional Goatman sightings continue, but fears of Goatman seem to have receded from folk and popular consciousness as Prince George's County has fully transformed into its previously projected quasi-urban, majority-minority county and become widely acknowledged as a satellite territory of Washington, D.C. [55] This has forced Goatman to recede into the shadows. This case suggests that folklorists should perhaps embrace and undertake more psychological investigations of such legendary creatures. These beings, whose purported existence often arises from honest reports of encounters with natural phenomena, reveal the fears, anxieties and cultural discontents of the community and particular historical moments. The legends these creatures spawn bring those dark anxieties into the light, providing opportunities for the discussion of community unease. In the case of the Goatman legend, a psychological approach has demonstrated how 1970s urban violence fed the suburban imagination, and revealed the anxiety associated with crime, fluid and ever-fluctuating urban and suburban borders and local demographics.

---

[55] In 2016, *WBAL TV* received multiple reports and a photograph taken in Montpelier Park in Laurel, Maryland, showing what resembled a particularly hairy Goatman. (*WBAL TV*, 'What is this?! Is it the Goatman?'). 'Majority-minority' is the term used in the United States for geographic areas where a racial or ethnic minority, in comparison to the total composition of the country, constitutes the majority of residents.

Bibliography

Primary sources

News articles

Daley, Sean, 'The Legend of Goatman', *Washington City Paper*, 18 September 1998

Goldman, Ivan G., 'A Legendary Figure Haunts Remote Pr. George's Woods', *Washington Post*, 30 November 1971

Hosler, Karen, 'University Archives Reveals: Boaman, Goatman, and Ghosts Still Haunt Area', *Prince George's County News*, 27 October 1971

——, 'Residents Fear Goatman Lives: Dog Found Decapitated in Old Bowie', *Prince George's County News*, 10 November 1971

——, 'Pranksters and Thrill-Seekers: The Real Monsters of Fletchertown Road', *Prince George's County New*, 24 November 1971

Meyer, Eugene L., 'Lottsford Road: Local Legend Says It's a Trail of Terror', *Washington Post*, 1 October 1984

Price, Debbie M., ' "Murder Capital" Label Has Long Stalked D.C.', *Washington Post*, 4 April 1989

'What is this?! Is it the Goatman?' *WBAL TV*, 25 April 2016

Wright, Andy, 'Maryland's Goatman is Half Man, Half Goat, and Out for Blood', *Modern Farmer*, 16 September 2013

Folklore Archives files

The following lists the complete collection of Goatman files in the Maryland Folklore Archives, located in the Maryland Room at the Hornbake Library, along with the rest of the University of Maryland Special Collections. To review any of the following files, scholars must write in advance, requesting files by name and location. Each collection contains numerous Goatman variants, totalling upwards of one hundred Goatman legends.

Caherty, Frank, 'Goat-men, Hermits, & Murderous Woodsmen: Strange Tales and Curious Happenings', Maryland Folklore Archives (College Park, MD, 1977)

Duley, Rose Ann, 'Goatman Tales', Maryland Folklore Archives (College Park, MD, 1975)

Hoffman, Carolyn, 'Local Legends of Lottsford Road Area', Maryland Folklore Archives (College Park, MD, 1974)

Lawler, Mark, 'Legends of Bowie Maryland', Maryland Folklore Archives (College Park, MD, 1983)

Lizama, George, 'The Goatman of Tucker Road', Maryland Folklore Archives (College Park, MD, 1971)

McGuigan, Mark, 'Local Legends', Maryland Folklore Archives (College Park, MD, 1984)

McKeller, Ian, 'The Goatman and Crybaby Bridge: Local Legends of Lottsford Road', Maryland Folklore Archives (College Park, MD, 1986)

Schofield, Clay, 'Legends of Bowie', Maryland Folklore Archives (College Park, MD, 1972)

Wilson, Trish, 'Bowie Legends', Maryland Folklore Archives (College Park, MD, 1990)

Secondary sources

Altheide, David L., *Creating Fear: News and the Construction of Crisis* (New York, 2002)

Best, Joel, *Random Violence: How We Talk about New Crimes and New Victims* (Berkeley, CA, 1999)

Blank, Trevor J. and David J. Puglia, *Maryland Legends: Folklore from the Old Line State* (Charleston, SC, 2014)

Bronner, Simon J. ' "This is Why We Hunt": Social-Psychological Meanings of the Traditions and Rituals of Deer Camp', *Western Folklore* 63 (2002), 11–50

——, *Explaining Traditions: Folk Behavior in Modern Culture.* (Lexington, KY, 2011).

——, 'Toward the Formulation of a Folkloristic Theory of Mind: The Role of Psychoanalysis and Symbolist Approaches to Tradition', *Millî Folklor* 27 (2015), 18–30

Brunvand, Jan Harold, *The Vanishing Hitchhiker: American Urban Legends and their Meanings* (New York, 1981)

Couch, J. Nathan, *Goatman: Flesh or Folklore?* (North Charleston, SC, 2014)

Carey, George G., *Maryland Folklore and Folklife* (Centreville, MD, 1970)

——, *Maryland Folk Legends and Folk Songs* (Centreville, MD, 1971)

Conley, Brian A., 'The Bunny Man Unmasked: The Real Life Origins of an Urban Legend' (2002), https://research.fairfaxcounty.gov/c.php?g=713238&p=5229327

Dahlgren, Madeline Vinton, *South Mountain Magic: Tales of Old Maryland.* (Maple Shade, NJ, 2002 [1882])

Dégh, Linda and Andrew Vázsonyi, *The Dialectics of the Legend.* Folklore Preprint Series 1, no. 6 (Bloomington, IN, 1973)

Dorson, Richard M., 'Defining the American Folk Legend', in *American Folklore & the Historian*, ed. idem (Chicago, 1971), pp. 157–72

Dundes, Alan, 'Earth-Diver: Creation of the Mythopoeic Male', *American Anthropologist* 64 (1962), 1032–51

——, 'Into the Endzone for a Touchdown', *Western Folklore* 37, (1978), 75–88

——, 'Projection in Folklore: A Plea for Psychoanalytic Semiotics', in *Interpreting Folklore*, ed. idem (Bloomington, IN, 1980), pp. 33–61

Glassner, Barry, *The Culture of Fear: Why Americans are Afraid of the Wrong Things: Crime, Drugs, Minorities, Teen Moms, Killer Kids, Mutant Microbes, Plane Crashes, Road Rage, & So Much More* (New York, 2010)

Hufford, David, 'Humanoids and Anomalous Lights: Taxonomic and Epistemological Problems', *Fabula* 18 (1977), 234–41

Jenkins, Joe, 'The Goatman of Prince George's County', in *Father Joe: From Silly to Sacred, A Priest Speaks* (1998), http://fatherjoe.wordpress.com/stories/the-goatman-of-prince-georges-county/

Lake, Matt, *Weird Maryland: Your Travel Guide to Maryland's Local Legends and Best Kept Secrets* (New York, 2006)

McDonald, Susan, 'Childhood Animal Abuse and Violent Criminal Behavior: A Brief Review of the Literature', report prepared for the Office of Strategic Planning and Research, Department of Correction, Commonwealth of Massachusetts (2011)

Mitchell, Roger E., 'The Press, Rumor, and Legend Formation', *Midwestern Journal of Language and Folklore* 5, nos 1/2 (1979 special issue)

Opsasnick, Mark, 'Horror on Fletchertown Road', in idem, *The Real Story Behind the Exorcist: A Study of the Haunted Boy and Other True-Life Horror Legends from around the Nation's Capital* (Bloomington, IN, 2007), pp. 67–80

Puglia, David J., 'Getting Maryland's Goat: Diffusion and Canonization of Prince George's County's Goatman Legend', *Contemporary Legend: The Journal of the International Society for Contemporary Legend Research* 3 (2013), 63–77

Rockoff, Adam, *Going to Pieces: The Rise and Fall of the Slasher Film, 1978–1986* (Jefferson, NC, 2002)

Serani, Deborah, 'If It Bleeds, It Leads: The Clinical Implications of Fear-Based Programming in News Media', *Psychoanalysis and Psychotherapy* 24 (2008), 240–50

——, 'If It Bleeds, It Leads: Understanding Fear-Based Media', *Psychology Today* (2011), https://www.psychologytoday.com/us/blog/two-takes-depression/201106/if-it-bleeds-it-leads-understanding-fear-based-media

Siddle, David, 'Goats, Marginality, and the "Dangerous Other" ', *Environment and History* 15 (2009), 521–36

Smith, Paul, ' "Read All About It! Elvis Eaten by Drug-Crazed Giant Alligators":
Contemporary Legend and the Popular Press', *Contemporary Legend* 2 (1992), 41–71

Taft, Michael, 'Sasquatch-like Creatures in Newfoundland: A Study in the Problems of Belief, Perception, and Reportage', in *Manlike Monsters on Trial: Early Records and Modern Evidence*, ed. Marjorie Halpin and Michael Ames (Vancouver, 1980), pp. 83–96

Virta, Alan, 'Prince George's County: Over 300 Years of History', *Prince George's County History*, http://www.pghistory.org/PG/PG300/history.html

Whitney, Annie Weston, and Caroline Canfield Bullock, *Folk-Lore from Maryland* (New York, 1925)

8

Horror Stories of Young Ural Cities

—◆◇◆—

NATALIA VESELKOVA, MIKHAIL VANDYSHEV
AND ELENA PRYAMIKOVA

The supernatural is usually associated with places with long histories, and it is often propagated and legitimised through the replication of fairy tales and folkloric knowledge accumulated over many generations. However, even young cities have their own ghosts, their own haunting legacies and lingering fears. These represent something repressed and shifted to the edge of the collective consciousness. This chapter explores the urban and environmental anxieties of young Russian settlements built in the Urals in the twentieth century. Following a short theoretical and methodological introduction, it moves on to a description of the Urals with its Bazhov-influenced mythology, as well as the paradoxical lack of that mythology in its young towns. The next two sections explore the role of water and other non-human actants in local urban horror stories.[1] These stories suggest that the inhabitants of the Urals' young industrial towns engage with the supernatural or preternatural in unusual ways, incorporating into their histories and local understandings of place seemingly superhuman feats of effort, a sense of the natural environment as a non-human but near sentient force and a shadowy unease about potential industrial, environmental and urban disaster.

---

[1] These stories were gathered through a series of interviews conducted as part of a larger project on social memory and industrialisation in young Ural towns. See 'Scaling of Social Memory of Generations in the Cities of "Old" and "New" Industriality' project (The Russian Foundation for Basic Research, No. 18-011-00456 A, 2018).

The theoretical foundations for understanding different aspects of the supernatural can be located in a number of disciplines and classical works.[2] In this study, we draw upon the terminology of classical Freudian psychoanalysis, in particular as it has been used by geographers.[3] Alongside this, this chapter also draws upon Actor-Network Theory, with its appreciation of omnipresent non-humans and assemblages. John Law defines these assemblages as 'a process of bundling, of assembling, or better, of recursive self-assembling in which the elements put together are not fixed in shape, do not belong to a larger pre-given list but are constructed at least in part as they are entangled together'. For our analysis, we stress two other properties of assemblage – coherency and the feasible bundling of human and non-human elements. Assemblage is understood here as a fairly constant but at the same time flexible network of relationships, which can involve both man-made and 'natural', human and non-human components.[4]

Young cities are defined here as settlements built from scratch in the Soviet era and therefore characterised by relatively 'short histories'.[5]

[2] See, for example, key sociological and anthropological works such as Émile Durkheim, *The Elementary Forms of Religious Life* (Oxford, 2001); Marcel Mauss, *A General Theory of Magic* (London, 2001); Henry Hubert and Marcel Mauss, *Sacrifice: Its Nature and Functions* (Chicago, 1981); Lucien Lévy-Bruhl, *Primitive Mentality* (London, 1923); idem, *Primitives and the Supernatural* (New York, 1935); James George Frazer, *The Golden Bough: A Study in Magic and Religion* (New York, 1959). The phenomenological ideas of Edmund Husserl and Maurice Merleau-Ponty have also been developed in a very inspiring way, which correlates with our interest in the sites of memory, in Dylan Trigg, *The Memory of Place: A Phenomenology of the Uncanny* (Athens, OH, 2012).

[3] See Sigmund Freud, *The 'Uncanny'* (London, 2003); also Paul Kingsbury and Steve Pile (eds), *Psychoanalytic Geographies* (Farnham, 2014). Particularly relevant to this chapter is Mark Lipovetsky's consideration of P. P. Bazhov's tales through the prism of Freud's theory of the uncanny. See Mark Lipovetsky, 'Pavel Bazhov's *skazy*: Discovering the Soviet Uncanny', in *Russian Children's Literature and Culture*, ed. Marina Balina and Larissa Rudova (London, 2008), pp. 263–84 at 263–4.

[4] See John Law, *After Method: Mess in Social Science Research* (London, 2004), p. 42. For human/non-human relationships, see Bruno Latour, 'Where are the Missing Masses? The Sociology of a Few Mundane Artifacts', in *Technology and Society: Building our Sociotechnical Future*, ed. Deborah J. Johnson and Jameson M. Wetmore (Cambridge, 2008), pp. 151–80.

[5] Philosopher Elena Trubina, from whom we borrowed the expression, relegates not only new cities of the twentieth century to this category (because they have not yet gained sufficient legacies and histories), but also Ekaterinburg, even though it was founded in the eighteenth century. This was the period when the Urals started to be explored intensively, by Royal Decree. Historians Jo Guldi and David Armitage also reference the short and long time scales by matching Braudel's *longue durée* to

Krasnoturyinsk was founded in the 1940s in connection with the construction of the Bogoslovsky Aluminum Plant. Kachkanar and Zarechny were founded in the 1950s to service the Kachkanar Mining and Processing Combine and the Beloyarsk Nuclear Power Plant.[6] In comparison with special studies in line with the 'spectral turn', there were in our interviews no particular questions about weird, uncanny or supernatural experiences in these cities.[7] Rather, various aspects of the supernatural intruded into our study in an organic way, encouraging the view that the extraordinary and the paranormal are not sharply separated from secular mundanity, even if they do penetrate into all aspects of our everyday life, as Barbara Walker supposes.[8] Through our interaction with residents and our own acquaintance with the settlements under discussion, past and present (past views were accessed via archival documents, mass media publications and specialist literature), we learned of horror stories that could not be described as simple urban legends: fish-mutants in a city pond; a drowned house that still contained its inhabitant after the filling of the reservoir; the threat of collapsing buildings predicted by clairvoyants.[9]

---

contemporary *short termism*. See Elena Trubina, 'To Reconcile with the Decline: Ruins 2.0', *Neprikosnovennyy Zapas* 3 (2013), 175–94 (in Russian); Jo Guldi and David Armitage, *The History Manifesto* (Cambridge, 2014).

[6] The settlements were selected as young Ural towns that vary: (a) in socio-economic status (Krasnoturyinsk experienced a decline; Kachkanar and Zarechny were relatively stable) and (b) in distance from the regional centre (Ekaterinburg, 1.4 million?). Krasnoturyinsk (population 58,600) is located 400 km to the north of Ekaterinburg, Kachkanar (population 40,000) 260 km to the north-west and Zarechny (population 27,600) 50 km to the east.

[7] See, for example, María del Pilar Blanco and Esther Peeren (eds), *The Spectralities Reader: Ghosts and Haunting in Contemporary Cultural Theory* (London, 2013); James McClenon, 'Supernatural Experience, Folk Belief, and Spiritual Healing', in *Out of the Ordinary: Folklore and the Supernatural*, ed. Barbara Walker (Logan, UT, 1995), pp. 107–21. McClenan specifically surveyed more than a thousand American, Chinese and Japanese students and American scientists about their experiences of the paranormal and observed and interviewed over thirty healers from different countries.

[8] See Walker, *Out of the Ordinary*, pp. 2–3.

[9] We communicated with informants aged between five and seventy-seven, using maximum variation sampling and accompanying interviews as a primary field method. Empirical data were collected in 2013–14 as part of the research project 'The Sites of Memory in the Young Ural Towns: Identity Construction' (Russian Foundation for Humanities and Government of Sverdlovsk Region, 13-13-66010 a (p)) and later supplemented with new material. For more details, see Natalia Veselkova, Elena Pryamikova and Mikhail Vandyshev, *Sites of Memory in Young Towns* (Ekaterinburg, 2016) (in Russian); eadem, Mikhail Vandyshev and Elena Pryamikova, 'The Discourse of Nature in Young Towns', *The Russian Sociological*

On the one hand, these stories are local, related to particular locations or circumstances. On the other, such stories have links far beyond their local aspects and necessitate an appreciation of differing temporal and spatial scales. Temporally, this can best be exemplified by the Braudelian concept of plural temporalities, from the 'almost timeless history' (*longue durée*) to the 'time with slow but perceptible rhythms', to 'a history of brief, rapid, nervous fluctuations'.[10] With regard to spatial scales, recent discussions have focused on urban changes as interconnections of global, regional and local processes, with attendant issues of what have been termed (multi)scalar politics, strategies and effects.[11] These multiple temporal and spatial scales inform our work and analysis.[12] In this chapter, we shall take the Urals scale as the basis, but look at specific towns too, while historically we will focus on the Soviet and especially late Soviet period (1960s–1980s), but also consider links to the longer historical context. Our approach aims to tease out the intersection of these multiscalarities, something especially important for young towns which appear to lack layers of historical depth.

The severe *genius loci* of the Urals

The Urals are usually associated with an abundance of natural resources: low, weathered mountains dominate this mining-industrial region and its urban civilisation.[13] Pavel Bazhov's *The Malachite Casket* (1939) offers an important

Review 15 (2016), 112–33 (in Russian); eidem, 'Young Towns: Scaling Sites of Memory', *The Russian Sociological Review* 16 (2017), 36–65 (in Russian).

[10]   See Fernand Braudel, *The Mediterranean and the Mediterranean World in the Age of Philip II*, vol. I (Berkeley, CA, 1995), pp. 20–1.

[11]   See Elena Trubina, 'International Events in the Non-Capital Post-Soviet City: Between Place-Making and Recentralization', *Region: Regional Studies of Russia, Eastern Europe, and Central Asia* 1 (2012), 231–53; Päivi Rannila, 'Scale and the Construction of Urban Space: Temporary Re-Scaling in Lahti, Finland, during the European Union Meeting of 2006', *NorskGeografiskTidsskrift – Norwegian Journal of Geography* 65 (2011), 93–103; Harran Shin, Se Hoon Park and Jung Won Sonn, 'The Emergence of a Multiscalar Growth Regime and Scalar Tension: The Politics of Urban Development in Songdo New City, South Korea', *Environment and Planning C: Politics and Space* 33 (2015), 1618–38; Massimo Giovanardi, 'A Multi-Scalar Approach to Place Branding: The 150ᵗʰ Anniversary of Italian Unification in Turin', *European Planning Studies* 23 (2015), 597–615. For a more detailed review, see Veselkova et al., 'Young Towns'.

[12]   Veselkova et al., 'Young Towns'; eidem, *Sites of Memory*.

[13]   See Alexey Ivanov, *Mining Civilization: Album* (Moscow, 2014) (in Russian), p. 11 for reference to the 'academic formula' created by A. Bogoslovsky.

contribution to how we imagine this region.[14] As Tatyana Kruglova had aptly phrased it, 'Bazhov predetermined the mythology of the place where people are not born from "soil" (a favourite metaphor of Russian thinkers), as in many Russian places, but they are made of rock'.[15] Bazhov's *skazy* (tales) intertwined fantastic characters such as the Mistress of Copper Mountain, Great Poloz the snake and Silver Hoof the deer with real plant owners like the Turchaninovs, combining the supernatural with local toponyms and events from the recent past.[16] This mythology has become very distinctive, if not central 'to the Ural's cultural imaginary'.[17] Nowadays it is reflected and reconsidered in such works of art as Olga Slavnikova's novel *2017*, and in paintings by Ekaterina Poedinshchikova.[18]

In terms of spatial scale, the places and legendary figures depicted by Bazhov came to represent the Ural region in general. For example, Bazhov's *skazy* originally located the legend of the Mistress of the Copper Mountain around the small, Middle Ural towns of Polevskoy and Sysert, but the character came to

[14] Pavel Bazhov, *The Malachite Casket: Tales from the Urals* (Amsterdam, 2002); see also Lipovetsky, 'Pavel Bazhov's *skazy*'.

[15] National Centre for Contemporary Arts, Ural Branch, Ekaterinburg, ' "Rough Urals Nature" and its Miners: Bazhov, Ryzhy, Kolyada, Shakhrin [Announcement of lecture by Tatyana Kruglova, 4 August 2016]', http://www.ncca.ru/events.text?filial=5&id=3652 (in Russian; accessed 17 March 2018). There has been a new surge of interest in Bazhov: see National Centre for Contemporary Arts, Ural Branch, Ekaterinburg 'Bazhov fest-2016: The New Ural Mythologies', http://www.ncca.ru/events.text?filial=5&id=3615 (accessed 17 March 2108); Yeltsin Centre, 'Bazhov's Urals: The Power of Place' Exhibition (2018), https://m.yeltsin.ru/affair/otkrytie-vystavki-ural-bazhova-sila-mesta/ (accessed 17 March 2018); EverJazz, 'Melodramatic reading and singing of P. P. Bazhov's stories in improvisation and synthesis, 8 April 2018', http://www.everjazz.ru/playbill/item/3660/ (in Russian; accessed 18 June 2019).

[16] Lipovetsky, 'Pavel Bazhov's *skazy*'. See also Marina Balina, 'Introduction', in *Politicizing Magic: An Anthology of Russian and Soviet Fairy Tales*, ed. eadem, Helena Goscilo and Mark Lipovetsky (Evanston, IL, 2005), pp. 114–16.

[17] See Sharae Deckard, 'Ghost Mountains and Stone Maidens: Ecological Imperialism, Compound Catastrophe, and the Post-Soviet Ecogothic', in *Global Ecologies and the Environmental Humanities: Postcolonial Approaches*, ed. Elizabeth DeLoughrey, Jill Didur and Anthony Carrigan (New York, 2015), pp. 286–386 at 295–6.

[18] See Olga Slavnikova, *2017*, trans. Marian Schwartz (London, 2010); Elena Givental, 'Three Hundred Years of Glory and Gloom: The Urals Region of Russia in Art and Reality', *SAGE Open* 3 (2013), 1–9, (http://journals.sagepub.com/doi/abs/10.1177/2158244013486657) (accessed 17 March 2018); Deckard, 'Ghost Mountains'; Tatiana Kruglova, 'Bazhov's Werewolves and Ovid's Metamorphoses: Uncanny versus Marvellous', Exhibition Hall. Kamensk-Uralsky City, 9 January 2016, http://v-zal.ru/oborotni-bazhova-i-metamorfozyi-ovidiya-zhutkoe-protiv-chudesnogo/ (in Russian; accessed 17 March 2018).

represent the entire region. With regard to historical depth, one might speak of a combination of long- and short-term temporal scales. Bazhov's world of fairytales, myth and magic seems to stand outside any specific time, especially if we take into account the affiliation of the main characters to the cthonian gods.[19] At the same time, however, Bazhov vividly describes the life of factory settlements in the late nineteenth and early twentieth centuries. Historian Paul Dukes, who introduced Urals history from the sixteenth century to the present to the English-speaking public, sees the Mistress of the Copper Mountain as 'a palpable ancestor of today's Mistress of the Copper Mountain, a *zlata baba*, a golden old woman or witch'.[20] This connects these modern tales to a far longer time scale, one that stretches back over at least seven hundred years.

Despite the intense presence of Bazhov's mythical reading of the Urals landscape, our selected towns seem to be completely devoid of such folkloric colouring. Kachkanar and Zarechny were founded after the storyteller's death. However, neither this nor the relatively short histories of these newly built settlements is likely to be the reason for the lack of a localised mythology. The present authors' own acquaintance with these towns convincingly testifies that there is no place without any history. This is not so obvious as it might seem, if we take into account discourses of young towns as founded in 'empty spaces', in culturally blank terrains, a discourse which remains strong up to the present. Given this, young towns are perhaps compelled to develop their symbolic connections and historical baggage even more extensively than the older towns.[21]

For example, the mid-twentieth century settlements that form the focus of this research were constructed as socialist cities (*Sotsgoroda*). In this, their creation was informed by utopian socialist ideas that drew upon a long (literary) history, encompassing Thomas More's *Utopia*, Tommaso Campanella's *The City of the Sun* and conceptions of social reform promoted by the likes of Charles Fourier and Robert Owen.[22] Yet it was also informed by the concept of the

---

[19]   The theme of the chthonic forces in the Ural art is developed in Tatyana Kruglova, 'Self-Representation of the Ural Industrialism: From Marxism to Mythology', in *1st Ural Industrial Biennale of Contemporary Art, Special Projects* (Ekaterinburg, 2010), p. 66; eadem, 'Bazhov's Werewolves'.

[20]   See Paul Dukes, *A History of the Urals: Russia's Crucible from Early Empire to the Post-Soviet Era* (London, 2015), pp. 7, 102, 114, fig. 19; also Alexey Burykin, 'Golden Baba: An Idol or a Place Name?', *Siberian Zaimka: History of Siberia in Scientific Publications*, 27 February 2012, http://zaimka.ru/burykin-zolotaya-baba/ (in Russian; accessed 17 March 2018).

[21]   See Veselkova et al., *Sites of Memory*; eidem, 'Young Towns'.

[22]   Works by More, Campanella, Fourier and Owen were studied in Soviet universities as emblematic examples of utopian socialism: see Thomas More, *Utopia*

designed industrial towns of the nineteenth century: those practical attempts to improve society by creating places such as Saltaire, Port Sunlight and Pullman. Closer still, in terms of historical connections and layering, these towns also comprised a twentieth-century chapter of progress and industrialization, with Soviet overtones. Young towns were represented as arising necessarily 'from scratch', with fabulous, fairytale-like speed, the product of human will and the enthusiasm of freed labour. This narrative glorified the heroism and romanticism of creation, not only of the urban and industrial, but of a new world and a new pioneering man.[23] This task of the conquest of nature and construction of the new world reminds us of Herculean labours, Ilia of Murom and other heroes of myths and Russian epic. Limited human, material and technical resources were combined with hugely ambitious goals to result in heroic hyper-efforts to dominate the environment.

This presupposes inevitable sacrifice. As people in Krasnoturyinsk say, 'This dam was built on bones' (KrM34).[24] This familiar image from the mid-twentieth century (and, Valentine Blazhes suggests, from far older legends) turned out to be a stable meme in this town.[25] As a local newspaper noted, when discussing Ivan F. Weiss's work on memorialising the German Labour Army members who died there in the 1940s, 'Every resident of Krasnoturyinsk knows that the dam at the Turya River was built on bones.'[26] The same wording was used in

---

(Cambridge, 2002); Tommaso Campanella, *The City of the Sun: A Poetical Dialogue between a Grandmaster of the Knights Hospitallers and a Genoese Sea-Captain, his Guest* (Auckland, 2009); Charles Fourier, *The Theory of the Four Movements* (Cambridge, 1996); Robert Owen, *The Book of the New Moral World* (New York, 1969)). During the 1940s and 1950s, when our young towns were founded, Russian architect Ivan Leonidov was developing his 'The City of the Sun' project. For more on the connection between new socialist towns and utopian visions, see Barbara Engel, 'Public Space in the Blue Cities in Russia', *Progress in Planning* 3 (2006), 147–239.

[23] See Veselkova et al., *Sites of Memory*.

[24] '(KrM34)' refers to interviews with residents of the cities. The following codes are used: K – Kachkanar; Z – Zarechny; Kr – Krasnoturyinsk; the second capital letter indicates the informant's sex (M or F); the figures indicate age. Thus (KF17), for example, means a seventeen year-old female resident of Kachkanar.

[25] See Valentine Blazhes, *The Folklore of the Urals: The National Story about Yermak* (Ekaterinburg, 2002) (in Russian), p. 23.

[26] Olga Isakova, 'Give a Bow to Ancestries', *Dawn of the Urals*, 10 June 2005, http://krasnoturinsk.me/cgi-bin/news/index.pl?id=2206#.WrUkxB3FLDc (in Russian). Members of the Labour Army, including the builders of Krasnoturyinsk, lacked adequate food, shelter, clothing and medical care, and many died from malnutrition, disease and exposure. See J. Otto Pohl, 'Hewers of Wood and Drawers of Water: The Russian-Germans in the Labour Army', *The Eurasia Studies Society Journal* 2 (2013), 1–17. On the extremely harsh conditions in the Labour Army during the Second World War, and special settlers in the Urals after it, see also Viktor Krieger,

discussion in support of the proposed development of a cathedral rather than entertainment centres in 2011: 'The dam was built on bones. Thousands died here.'[27] The dark image is used again in publications at 'Proza.ru' (a Russian literary internet portal): 'The dam is built on bones. As many people died here as there are stones in the dam.'[28] Elaboration is provided by the author Alexander Merker: he quotes the words of a former political prisoner, noting that before Labour Army members arrived, 'the pond bottom was studded with our bones'.[29] However, our informant clearly became confused regarding the origin of the 'bones', attributing them to prisoners of war and not to the Soviet Germans, even though the events took place only seventy years ago.

Thus, the memories of these heroic efforts on the part of previous generations are gradually acquiring folkloric features without (yet) generating supernatural beings, preserved in the forms of sketchy stories and the ordinary embodiments of cultural memory, such as place names, monuments and memorial plates. As Michel de Certeau wrote, the population of the supernatural 'traverses time, survives the wearing away of human existences, and articulates a space'.[30] Such town spaces as those discussed here, with their focus on the rational and industrial, cannot get rid of those ghosts. They reappear at times in very unexpected places, not least during interviews in which the topic of discussion was unconnected with ghostly issues.

The power and unpredictability of water

Local horror stories are mainly related not to Bazhov's rocks (though rocks play their role), or heroes, but to water. Water is the link that one should explore in order to solve the tangle of meanings in these curious stories. Being a modern 'quasi-object', neither purely 'natural' nor purely 'human', water remains a marker of otherness, and marks the transition between the secular

---

Bundesbürger russlanddeutscher Herkunft: historische Schlüsselerfahrungen und kollektives Gedächtnis (Münster, 2013); A. A. German and O. Ju. Silantjewa (eds), *'Auf ewig, ohne Recht auf Rückkehr': Augenzeugen und Wissenschaftler über das Sondersiedlungsregime der Deutschen in der UdSSR: Sammelband mit wissenschaftlichen Aufsätzen und Erinnerungen* (Moscow, 2015) (in Russian and German).

27   'New Cathedral in Krasnoturyinsk?', *Evening Krasnoturyinsk*, 25 February 2011, http://krasnoturinsk.info/2011-02-25-08-47-05/ (in Russian; accessed 17 March 2018).

28   Alexander Merker, 'North Ural. Krasnoturyinsk', *Prose.ru*, 2015. See https://www.proza.ru/2015/12/23/1325 (accessed 17 March 2018).

29   Ibid.

30   Michel de Certeau, 'Ghosts in the City', in idem, Luce Giard and Pierre Mayol, *The Practice of Everyday Life*, vol. 2: *Living and Cooking* (Minneapolis, 1998), p. 136.

and sacral worlds.[31] In our stories, collected in the towns, water is presented as part of the myth of origin.

An account in the memoirs of Nikolay Tukmachev, the senior survey technician at the Kachkanar Mining and Processing Combine, shows the response of residents of the nearby settlements in 1957: 'Upon hearing about forthcoming construction, some of them started to feel regret for meadows and hunting lands. One old grandma wished to scare us, and said gloomily, "There is a lake on the Kachkanar mountain. As soon as you make a pit – it will wash you away" '.[32] Tukmachev explained, more prosaically, that local residents in the late 1950s were former gold miners, workers who 'used to look for their luck alone in ravines and swamps'.[33] Their previous livelihood, based on the rare chance of a lucky find, was contrasted with future 'employment and permanent wages'.[34] Thus many people embraced commissioned work; yet for those who were not enthusiastic about industrialisation, nature seemed to be their protector. As the grandma's warning suggests, the mountain could exact revenge upon the conquerors, fighting back, not from its depths, in the style of Bazhov's stories, but with water.

The pioneers' memories are filled with pride in their victory, including their success against the rigidity and non-belief of some of the old-timers. The construction of new industrial settlements was presented as the apotheosis of the conquest of nature, the triumph of Soviet scientific and technological progress and social justice. Yet while the new industrial cities were considered a symbol of successful opposition to natural forces, their horror stories express existing fears about the uncontrollability and unpredictability of the elements. People attempted to conquer nature, but nature refused to be tamed. Thus the inhabitants of these industrial towns were aware that their urban centres had been developed and existed in a potentially threatening environment. Perhaps somewhat unwillingly, the pioneers documented a story in which water embodied powerful elemental forces, thereby serving as a reminder of human weakness and decrying attempts at environmental domination. As Bazhov's

---

[31] For more on these ideas see Maria Kaika, 'Interrogating the Geographies of the Familiar: Domesticating Nature and Constructing the Autonomy of the Modern Home', *International Journal of Urban and Regional Research* 28 (2004), 265–86 at 267–72; Olga Andreeva, 'Ontological and Semantic Constituents of Eastern Slavs' Cultural-Language Picture of the World (by the Example of Ritual Complexes with Sacred-Semantic Component "Water")', *Philological Sciences. Issues of Theory and Practice* 6 (2013), 23–6 (in Russian), at 25.

[32] Nikolay Tukmachev, 'The Early Days', in *The Source: Memories of Kachkanar Pioneers*, ed. Gennady A. Ponomarev (Kachkanar, 2000) (in Russian), pp. 81–115 at 81.

[33] Ibid.

[34] Ibid.

tales taught, one had to come to agreement with the chthonic forces, and only skill and a respectful approach in communication could sometimes win them over and make them help, and then, only for chosen ones.[35]

Given that the city of Kachkanar rests on the Dolgaya mountain, the locals are confident that they 'would never be flooded. This is an advantage of Kachkanar [laughs] – when it rains all water runs off' (KM59). Although the informant laughs when he speaks about rainwater, flooding is mentioned, and thus the prophecy of the 'grandma' from Tukmachev's story still haunts these modern accounts. We were told about an accident at a sludge repository 'some fifteen to twenty years ago'.[36] The accident was created by water interacting with the artefacts of industrial colonisation, including the dam and sludge repository at the Kachkanar facility: 'The dam was broken and all the way down to the Tura, about thirty kilometres … all the forests, everything was flooded with sludge' (KM59). The informant explained in detail how sludge appeared in the technological chain and described its main features: 'sludge, what is its main problem … it is a creeping substance. When it is saturated with water, it's like a landslide, [it] starts creeping at once … you can't hold it' (KM59). As the informant suggests, the sludge acted as a non-human entity with its own agency.

A young resident of Kachkanar told us about a more recent event, when the Kachkanar 'sea' (city pond) 'broke its banks and flooded everything. There in the tenth [block, part of the town] everything was flooded' (KF17). When she spoke about the origin of the pond, the girl added one more element to the narrative assemblage – the river: 'It used to be the Vyja river. And later the canal was made, which was called Verkhnevyjsky, Verkhnevjskoye Sea, as people call it for some reason'.[37] The Kachkanar reservoirs, as well as the Beloyarsk water storage facility in Zarechny, were constructed in the 1960s. In comparison with the building of the Krasnoturyinsk dam, these later projects took place in peaceful times, with the aid of heavy construction machinery. Residents of Kachkanar always stress that there was no forced labour in the 'town of their youth', and therefore no tales of 'bones' are mentioned in connection with them.

The erection of dams, in any version, becomes a powerful symbol of modernisation, and expressively marks its 'starting point' in the region.[38] Dams,

---

[35] See Bazhov, *Malachite Casket*; Lipovetsky, 'Pavel Bazhov's *skazy*'.

[36] A sludge repository is a hydrotechnical construction for storing production waste.

[37] Informants get confused with names because the water system consists of several reservoirs. In this case they meant the Nuzhnevyjsk reservoir.

[38] Maria Kaika, 'Dams as Symbols of Modernization: The Urbanization of Nature between Geographical Imagination and Materiality', *Annals of the Association of*

pumping stations and water towers could be considered what Maria Kaika and Korinna Thielen have termed 'secular shrines'. From the second half of the nineteenth century, these constructions, not cathedrals, came to 'dominate the urban skyline and the public imagination', heralding the enthronement of industrial society.[39] In young Soviet towns, these new technological shrines represented modernisation, secularisation and industrialisation, but they never competed with the old religious sites and, unlike equivalents in the West, they never symbolised the power of money. Nevertheless, sometimes the 'conquered' water can still demonstrate that it is a real power and, in asserting itself, expose the imperfections of (and arrogant assumptions behind) man-made creations. When our informant refers to the above-mentioned sludge repository as a 'great hydrotechnical construction', he interprets the accident as a failure of technology: 'pipes failed and were blocked. And the whole mass [o sludge] ran off' (KM59). Thus, the mysterious prediction of 'the grandma' comes true in a certain sense: although the fluid substance does not collapse from the top of the Kachkanar mountain, it intrudes into the town and its suburbs.

The dam in the town of Zarechny is a massive construction with three attractive ochre-yellow towers. The town guide reasonably considers this place to be the town's most picturesque spot, and the locals like to promenade there.[40] In an account from an eighteen year-old interviewee, flooding and submersion generates a myth of creation. The dam in her story is present from the 'start of Zarechny history' (ZF18), although, chronologically, construction of the hydrotechnical facilities in the 1960s started about ten years after the town's initial establishment in 1955. During the interview, the girl pointed at the old bed of the Pyshma river: 'The river bed was changed and they started to flood it. There used to be houses there. People used to live there, but all of them were relocated.' She also pointed at the recently relocated settlement: 'The dam here may break any time and everything will be flooded! No one lives there now.' If the theme of bursting, uncontrolled water was intended simply to create a sense of narrative threat, the climax of the informant's story leaves no doubts concerning the flood. The girl remembers that once (when 'we were little') 'a man, our city historian, came to school and told a story of Zarechny's development and dam construction. He also told us a horror story,

American Geographers 96 (2006), 276–301; Veselkova et al., *Sites of Memory*, pp. 105–10.

[39] Maria Kaika and Korinna Thielen, 'Form Follows Power: A Genealogy of Urban Shrines', *City* 10 (2006), 59–69 at 60.

[40] '[The] Beloyarsk Reservoir', *The Sverdlovsk Region Tour Guide* (n. d.), http://got-oural.com/tourist_attractions/402 (in Russian; accessed 17 March 2018).

Fig. 5. The dam in Zarechny. Photograph by Mikhail Vandyshev

that they flooded a house, a wooden two-storeyed one. And that somebody was staying there'.

While these horror stories may not feature in the town's formal history, it is worth mentioning that in 2013 a local newspaper published a similar story:

> There are legends that a small chapel and a few graves of monks rest at the bottom of the Beloyarsk storage reservoir. Men say that not far from the dam the structure of the former Ryabov mill still remains under water, at a depth of several metres. This mill was named after its first owner, the merchant Ryabov, before [the] revolution.[41]

Referencing the local regional history museum, the paper reprinted the memories of one of Zarechny pioneer builders:

> When the Ryabov mill was flooded, one could see the worker's house under water. And it was an entertainment for the locals. They could run a boat at high speed and try to slip through the window. People liked boating there and when the mill drowned some people called it 'our Atlantis'.[42]

[41] Alyona Arkhipova, 'Undiscovered Zarechny', *Zarechensky Fair*, 10 October 2013, http://zar-yarmarka.ru/2013/41/Neizvestny_Zarechny (in Russian).
[42] Ibid.

While mention of the monks' graves encourages expectations of a dark story, talk of boating fun draws the mood away from any hint of melancholy. The newspaper's report may be spiced with the mystery of legends, but it has nothing to do with a horror story. In our informant's narrative, on the contrary, an archetypal story frame distinctly emerges – the flooding of the old world and the transition into a new world order. For the short industrial history of young towns an allusion to the final scene of *The Cherry Orchard* would probably be more apt. The unknown character remaining in the big flooded house from the interview in Zarechny is reminiscent of old Firs from Chekhov's play, locked in the old house until spring. The old world may have disappeared, but in its ruins, and in the stories attached to them, it still lingers. It is here that one really senses the horrifying, haunting overtones.

Nowadays, the reservoirs are involved in different practices, and are widely used as sites of leisure, fun and fishing. Without any hint at horror stories, the participants in a group interview in Kachkanar discussed the fact that 'crayfish disappeared from the pond ... No more crayfish for three years now. All at once. It was when the water had a smell. At that moment the crayfish disappeared' (KM30). The extended fragment of this conversation below, captured while travelling by car in a ride-along group interview, is illustrative of 'discursive veiling' of environmental issues; that is, when these issues are subconsciously avoided and mostly talked around:

Anton: ... last year [I caught] a pike, couldn't fit it across the *chetvyorka* [Lada 2104] trunk. Unbelievable! ...

Maria: It's some sort of radioactive ...

Anton: Well, no. Just an old fish. There are a lot of them here. Divers say they swam there and found such monsters.

Maria: Where is the green pond ...? Haven't [we] reached it yet? Men say there are ... what kind of fish are there? In general, there are monstrosities here in this storage reservoir.

Julia: This is a technical reservoir.

Maria: Water is green there. They dump water from the quarry there.

Anton: I don't think there is anybody there.

Maria: Somebody said there were mutants there. (KM30, KF29, KF28)

As a rule, the informants mention the environmental situation casually, emphasising the favourable ecological situation in their towns. For example, although Zarechny has a nuclear power plant, we were told a lot about the abundance of greenery: 'as for ecology, well, hedgehogs are everywhere around, especially in summer' (ZF20). In response to direct questions, residents of Zarechny habitually mock the fears of laypersons:[43]

Interviewer: Are people concerned about the nuclear power plant?

Svetlana: No, no one is afraid of anything. [Both informants laugh]

Interviewer: I am asking just in case …

Svetlana: It [Beloyarsk nuclear power plant] produces no radiation. It never happened that anything was released. People feel safe.

Anna: Well, but people from other cities always ask about it.

Svetlana: 'Do you glow at night?' [laughs]. (ZF33, ZF36)

Our research participants express the local relationship between humans and nature, along with changes that occur. Thus, a young resident of Kachkanar thinks that the man-made reservoir used to be saline, and now is not. He notes, 'Our pond in Kachkanar? There had been no pond. It's man-made. Before, it was called the Kachkanar Sea, because water was saline, and now the salt is [gone]' (KM15). On the one hand, our informants always stress the environmental safety of their settlement, making light of other peoples' fears about radiation leaks or pollution. On the other, they discuss the accident in the sludge repositories reluctantly. Perhaps the reason for this lies in their local patriotism and their desire to demonstrate the best of their town.[44] Nevertheless, environmental horror stories serve as a kind of valve that regulates hidden concern. Stories about mutant fish are more likely to be a joke, explained away rationally, such as by claiming they are just very old fish; but the very presence of stories of this type, and the desire to tell them, indicates the prominence of environmental anxieties.

Insidious non-humans and what to do with them

It is not only natural objects that are endowed with seemingly preternatural qualities. As non-human actants, cities, buildings and roads can possess similar qualities. A human desire to transform the environment is not automatically accompanied by an ability to control it. Non-human components can be seen to take on a life of their own, and perhaps even take revenge for changes to the environment. In Krasnoturyinsk, this was

---

[43] We have examined this plot in Veselkova et al., 'Discourse of Nature', p. 127.

[44] We address these issues in Veselkova et al., *Sites of Memory*; eidem, 'Discourse of Nature'.

painfully demonstrated in a situation when the shutting down of the industrial enterprise that had fostered the creation of the town overlapped with the emergence there of retail chains, and the consequent marginalisation of small businesses. Significantly, we were told a horror prediction about a collapsing shopping mall:

> [P]eople from Moscow built Stolichny [the shopping mall in Krasnoturyinsk]. There was a TV show with those people who see everything ... clairvoyants. And they say that our Stolichny was built in a very wrong way, and that in winter it would collapse. About three hundred people would die. Heavy show would come soon. They did not say it would be in our city for certain. They just said that it would be Stolichny built in a town in the Sverdlovsk region. It seems like this is the one. All [the] girls who work there are scared. But the cracks already began to appear on the ceiling in some places. (KrF45)

The lake that is ready to crash down the mountain and the shopping mall with cracks on the ceiling, ready to collapse on peoples' heads, seem to be variants of the same narrative. Both these stories articulate the fear of payback for something very wrong, be it the alleged engineering or construction errors in the case of Krasnoturyinsk's shopping mall, or the violation of a traditional way of life in the case of Kachkanar. Unpronounced threats crowd around in the form of horror stories and jocular tales. The stories about floods and mutant fish create a discursive and therefore controlled space, allowing communities to embroider the past and enrich their present. At the same time, they help to dilute the industrial and environmental anxieties produced by the activities of the town-formation enterprises in the settlements under research.[45] These towns are often heavily reliant on a particular industrial organisation – a factory, plant or pumping station. If these fail, the whole town is placed at risk, economically, and perhaps environmentally too. These anxieties form the fearful underside to the heroic efforts that created the towns in the first place. Often kept at a distance by the use of humour, these muted concerns are typical and quite understandable in the case of mono-towns that are dependent upon their core factories and power plants to sustain them. Despite their many unsolved problems, however, such towns

---

[45] In Krasnoturyinsk, Kachkanar and Zarechny there have been no large-scale accidents, but like all industrial areas, they have a certain level of environmental pollution. For more on large-scale industrial accidents in the Urals, including the 1957 disaster at Mayak nuclear waste storage facility, see Dukes, *History of the Urals*, pp. 141–82.

remain habitable places, and their horror stories do not detract from the relatively comfortable urban lives lived within them.[46]

This chapter has demonstrated that the horror stories of young towns have a modality different from that of towns with longer histories. They have no castle ghosts, no occultural alterity, no dark tourism practices.[47] The horror stories of the settlements studied here offer us insight into some of the fears that accompanied or grew from the various optimistic drives behind the towns' initial formation. These include both the social utopianism of *Sotsgoroda* in the USSR and other socialist countries, and the nineteenth and twentieth centuries' modernising conquest of nature through the erection of giant industrial facilities and the urban settlements that serviced them.

This chapter has sought to differentiate between several aspects of the supernatural and preternatural with regard to new town settlements in the Urals. Firstly, these industrial towns owe their origin to heroic efforts that appeared to exceed the limits of the possible. While not supernatural, these herculean achievements do appear almost superhuman. Rather than transmitting this heroism to remote myths and legends, the brevity of the history of the towns require that it be utilised in (folkloric) memories of ancestors, relatives, friends and fellow residents. This is reflected and symbolised within the town's spaces as monuments, and reinforced through locals retelling stories about their urban origins in a heroic but relatively recent past. Secondly, in the stories collected during our research, the supernatural does not have anthropomorphic features or figures (such as witches and vampires). In the young Ural towns, nature itself becomes a source of the uncanny. Although rendered a hostage and a victim of industrialisation, it is not rendered

---

[46] See Jeremy Morris, 'Notes on the "Worthless Dowry" of Soviet Industrial Modernity: Making Working-Class Russia Habitable', *Laboratorium: Russian Review of Social Research* 7 (2015), 35–48.

[47] See Christopher Partridge, *The Re-Enchantment of the West: Alternative Spiritualities, Sacralization, Popular Culture, and Occulture*, vol. 1 (London, 2004); vol. 2 (London, 2005); Pavel Nosachev, 'Sociology of the Occult', *St. Tikhon's University Review. Series I: Theology. Philosophy. Religious Studies*, 70 (2017) (in Russian), 110–26. For more on dark tourism, see Richard Sharpley and Philip R. Stone (eds), *The Darker Side of Travel: The Theory and Practice of Dark Tourism*, (Bristol, 2009); Leanne White and Elspeth Frew (eds), *Dark Tourism: Place and Identity: Managing and Interpreting Dark Places* (London, 2013); Ekaterina Rybakova, 'Dark Tourism in Russia: State-of-the-Art, Problems of Investigation', *Theory and Practice: Economy, Social Sphere and Technology* 3/17 (2013) (in Russian), 180–7; Lea Kužnik, 'Typology of Dark Tourism Heritage with its Implications on Slovenian Future Dark Tourism Products', *Research in Social Change* 7 (2015), 318–48; Philip R. Stone, Rudi Hartmann, Tony Seaton, Richard Sharpley and Leanne White (eds), *The Palgrave Handbook of Dark Tourism Studies* (London, 2018).

unresponsive, and is capable of striking; for example, in the form of flooding.[48] Thirdly, it has been argued that the supernatural is involved in the production of symbolic capital of place and regional identity. Drawing upon the work of Bazhov, Ural folklore is infused with strong regional specifics, embodied in such entities as the Mistress of Copper Mountain, Great Poloz the snake and Silver Hoof the deer.[49] Acknowledging Bazhov's tales as a literary substitute for folk culture, a recent publication has suggested that he did something

> almost impossible for the Urals: he gifted the region with … myths, determined the main parameters of history and pre-history, and introduced residents of the region to the world. Not existing before silent Urals masters, their wives and children opened their mouths, it turned out that their thoughts are profound, [their] language … strange but charming and expressive.[50]

Finally, the supernatural of these young, mono-industrial towns is marked with an imprint of post-industrial future phobia. Vengeful mountains, rivers and man-made reservoirs, mutant fish and pollution, the lingering inhabitant of a village submerged in the name of industrial progress; the active and passive actants of this late industrial assemblage create a hybrid of the real and non-real, paradoxically intensifying the topophilia of the towns' urban inhabitants. While these young towns are supposed to represent the bold, conquering spirit of modern industrial settlement, their horror stories continue to recognise the power of nature and natural forces, especially water. Despite their seemingly short histories, these towns are haunted by a long tradition of utopian ideals, by fears of the environment they sought to tame and by anxieties about the potential hazards of their own industrial might.

Acknowledgements

We would like to thank Karl Bell, Dmitriy Chulakov and Julia Podlubnova for their helpful comments and recommendations.

---

[48] Veselkova et al., 'Discourse of Nature'.

[49] See Andrey Bobrikhin, 'Contribution of P. P. Bazhov to the Urals Identity', in *New Word in Science: Development Perspectives: IV International Conference*, 29 May 2015, ed. O. N. Shirokov et al. (Cheboksary, 2015) (in Russian), pp. 46–8.

[50] Yeltsin Centre, 'Bazhov's Urals.

Bibliography

Andreeva, Olga, 'Ontological and Semantic Constituents of Eastern Slavs' Cultural-Language Picture of the World (by the Example of Ritual Complexes with Sacred-Semantic Component "Water")', *Philological Sciences. Issues of Theory and Practice* 6 (2013), 23–6 (in Russian)

Arkhipova, Alyona, 'Undiscovered Zarechny', *Zarechensky Fair*, 10 October 2013 (in Russian), http://zar-yarmarka.ru/2013/41/Neizvestny_Zarechny

Balina, Marina, 'Introduction', in *Politicizing Magic: An Anthology of Russian and Soviet Fairy Tales*, ed. eadem, Helena Goscilo and Mark Lipovetsky (Evanston, IL, 2005), pp. 105–21

Bartolini, Nadia, Sara MacKian and Steve Pile, 'The Place of Spirit: Modernity and the Geographies of Spirituality', *Progress in Human Geography* 41 (2017), 338–54

Bazhov, Pavel, *The Malachite Casket: Tales from the Urals* (Amsterdam, 2002)

'[The] Beloyarsk Reservoir', *The Sverdlovsk Region Tour Guide* (n. d.) (in Russian), http://gotoural.com/tourist_attractions/402

Blanco, María del Pilar and Esther Peeren (eds), *The Spectralities Reader: Ghosts and Haunting in Contemporary Cultural Theory* (London, 2013)

Blazhes, Valentine, *The Folklore of the Urals: The National Story about Yermak* (Ekaterinburg, 2002) (in Russian)

Bobrikhin, Andrey, 'The Contribution of P. P. Bazhov to the Urals Identity', in *New Word in Science: Development Perspectives: IV International Conference*, 29 May 2015, ed. O. N. Shirokov et al. (Cheboksary, 2015) (in Russian), pp. 46–8.

Burykin, Alexey, 'Golden Baba: An Idol or a Place Name?', *Siberian Zaimka: History of Siberia in Scientific Publications*, 27 February 2012 (in Russian), http://zaimka.ru/burykin-zolotaya-baba/

Braudel, Fernand, *The Mediterranean and the Mediterranean World in the Age of Philip II*, vol. 1 (Berkeley, CA, 1995)

Campanella, Tommaso, *The City of the Sun: A Poetical Dialogue between a Grandmaster of the Knights Hospitallers and Genoese Sea-captain, his Guest* (Auckland, 2009)

Certeau Michel de, 'Ghosts in the City', in idem, Luce Giard and Pierre Mayol, *The Practice of Everyday Life*, vol. 2: *Living and Cooking* (Minneapolis, 1998), pp. 133–43

Deckard, Sharae, 'Ghost Mountains and Stone Maidens: Ecological Imperialism, Compound Catastrophe, and the Post-Soviet Ecogothic', in *Global Ecologies and the Environmental Humanities: Postcolonial Approaches*, ed. Elizabeth DeLoughrey, Jill Didur and Anthony Carrigan (New York, 2015), pp. 286–306

Dukes, Paul. *A History of the Urals: Russia's Crucible from Early Empire to the Post-Soviet Era* (London, 2015)

Durkheim, Émile, *The Elementary Forms of Religious Life* (Oxford, 2001)

Engel, Barbara, 'Public Space in the Blue Cities in Russia', *Progress in Planning* 3 (2006), 147–239

EverJazz, 'Melodramatic reading and singing of P.P. Bazhov's stories in improvisation and synthesis, 8 April 2018' (in Russian), http://www.everjazz.ru/playbill/item/3660/

Freud, Sigmund, *The 'Uncanny'* (London, 2003)

Fourier, Charles, *The Theory of the Four Movements* (Cambridge, 1996).

Frazer, James George, *The Golden Bough: A Study in Magic and Religion* (New York, 1959)

German, A. A. and O. Ju. Silantjewa (eds), *'Auf ewig, ohne Recht auf Rückkehr': Augenzeugen und Wissenschaftler über das Sondersiedlungsregime der Deutschen in der UdSSR: Sammelband mit wissenschaftlichen Aufsätzen und Erinnerungen* (Moscow, 2015) (in Russian and German)

Giovanardi, Massimo, 'A Multi-Scalar Approach to Place Branding: The 150th Anniversary of Italian Unification in Turin', *European Planning Studies* 23 (2015), 597–615

Givental, Elena, 'Three Hundred Years of Glory and Gloom: The Urals Region of Russia in Art and Reality' *SAGE Open* 3 (2013), 1–9, (http://journals.sagepub.com/doi/abs/10.1177/2158244013486657)

Guldi, Jo and David Armitage, *The History Manifesto* (Cambridge, 2014)

Hubert, Henry and Marcel Mauss, *Sacrifice: Its Nature and Functions* (Chicago, 1981)

Isakova, Olga, 'Give a Bow to Ancestries', *Dawn of the Urals*, 10 June 2005 (in Russian), http://krasnoturinsk.me/cgi-bin/news/index.pl?id=2206#.WrUkxB3FLDc

Ivanov, Alexey, *Mining Civilization: Album* (Moscow, 2014) (in Russian)

Kaika, Maria, 'Interrogating the Geographies of the Familiar: Domesticating Nature and Constructing the Autonomy of the Modern Home', *International Journal of Urban and Regional Research* 28 (2004), 265–86

——, 'Dams as Symbols of Modernization: The Urbanization of Nature Between Geographical Imagination and Materiality', *Annals of the Association of American Geographers,* 96 (2006), 276–301

—— and Korinna Thielen, 'Form Follows Power: A Genealogy of Urban Shrines', *City* 10 (2006), 59–69

Kingsbury, Paul and Steve Pile (eds), *Psychoanalytic Geographies* (Farnham, 2014)

Krieger, Viktor, *Bundesbürger russlanddeutscher Herkunft: historische Schlüsselerfahrungen und kollektives Gedächtnis* (Münster, 2013)

Kruglova, Tatyana, 'Self-Representation of the Ural Industrialism: From Marxism to Mythology', in *1st Ural Industrial Biennale of Contemporary Art, Special Projects* (Ekaterinburg, 2010), pp. 58–66

——, 'Bazhov's Werewolves and Ovid's Metamorphoses: Uncanny versus Marvellous', *Exhibition Hall. Kamensk-Uralsky City* Exhibition Hall. Kamensk-Uralsky City, 9 January 2016 (in Russian), http://v-zal.ru/oborotni-bazhova-i-metamorfozyi-ovidiya-zhutkoe-protiv-chudesnogo/

Kužnik, Lea, 'Typology of Dark Tourism Heritage with its Implications on Slovenian Future Dark Tourism Products', *Research in Social Change* 7 (2015), 318–48

Latour, Bruno, 'Where are the Missing Masses? The Sociology of a Few Mundane Artifacts', in *Technology and Society: Building our Sociotechnical Future*, ed. Deborah J. Johnson and Jameson M. Wetmore (Cambridge, 2008), pp. 151–80

Law, John, *After Method: Mess in Social Science Research* (London, 2004)

Lévy-Bruhl, Lucien, *Primitive Mentality* (London, 1923)

——, *Primitives and the Supernatural* (New York, 1935)

Lipovetsky, Mark, 'Pavel Bazhov's *skazy*: Discovering the Soviet Uncanny', in *Russian Children's Literature and Culture,* ed. Marina Balina and Larissa Rudova (London, 2008), pp. 263–84

Mauss, Marcel, *A General Theory of Magic* (London, 2001)

McClenon, James, 'Supernatural Experience, Folk Belief, and Spiritual Healing', in Walker (ed), *Out of the Ordinary*, pp. 107–21

Merker, Alexander, 'North Ural. Krasnoturyinsk', *Prose.ru* (2015) (in Russian), https://www.proza.ru/2015/12/23/1325

More, Thomas, *Utopia* (Cambridge, 2002)

Morris, Jeremy, 'Notes on the "Worthless Dowry" of Soviet Industrial Modernity: Making Working-Class Russia Habitable', *Laboratorium: Russian Review of Social Research* 7 (2015), 35–48

National Centre for Contemporary Arts, Ural Branch, Ekaterinburg 'Bazhov fest-2016: The New Ural Mythologies', http://www.ncca.ru/events.text?filial=5&id=3615

——, ' "Rough Urals Nature" and its Miners: Bazhov, Ryzhy, Kolyada, Shakhrin [Announcement of lecture by Tatyana Kruglova, 4 August 2016]' (in Russian), http://www.ncca.ru/events.text?filial=5&id=3652

'New Cathedral in Krasnoturyinsk?', *Evening Krasnoturyinsk*, 25 February 2011 (in Russian), http://krasnoturinsk.info/2011-02-25-08-47-05/

Nosachev, Pavel, 'Sociology of the Occult', *St. Tikhon's University Review. Series I: Theology. Philosophy. Religious Studies* 70 (2017), 110–26 (in Russian)

Owen, Robert, *The Book of the New Moral World* (New York, 1969)

Partridge, Christopher, *The Re-Enchantment of the West: Alternative Spiritualities, Sacralization, Popular Culture, and Occulture*, vol. 1 (London, 2004); vol. 2 (London, 2005)

Pohl, J. Otto, 'Hewers of Wood and Drawers of Water: The Russian-Germans in the Labour Army', *The Eurasia Studies Society Journal* 2 (2013), 1–17

Rannila, Päivi, 'Scale and the Construction of Urban Space: Temporary Re-Scaling in Lahti, Finland, during the European Union Meeting of 2006', *NorskGeografiskTidsskrift – Norwegian Journal of Geography* 65 (2011), 93–103

Rybakova, Ekaterina. 'Dark Tourism in Russia: State-of-the-Art, Problems of Investigation', *Theory and Practice: Economy, Social Sphere and Technology* 3 (2013), 180–7 (in Russian)

Sharpley Richard and Philip R. Stone (eds), *The Darker Side of Travel: The Theory and Practice of Dark Tourism* (Bristol, 2009)

Shin, Harran, Se Hoon Park and Jung Won Sonn, 'The Emergence of a Multiscalar Growth Regime and Scalar Tension: The Politics of Urban Development in Songdo New City, South Korea', *Environment and Planning C: Politics and Space* 33 (2015), 1618–38

Slavnikova, Olga, *2017*, trans. Marian Schwartz (London, 2010)

Stone, Philip R., Rudi Hartmann, Tony Seaton, Richard Sharpley and Leanne White (eds), *The Palgrave Handbook of Dark Tourism Studies* (London, 2018)

Trigg, Dylan, *The Memory of Place: A Phenomenology of the Uncanny* (Athens, OH, 2012)

Trubina, Elena, 'International Events in the Non-Capital Post-Soviet City: Between Place-Making and Recentralization', *Region: Regional Studies of Russia, Eastern Europe, and Central Asia* 1 (2012), 231–53

——, 'To Reconcile with the Decline: Ruins 2.0', *Neprikosnovennyy Zapas* 3 (2013), 175–94 (in Russian)

Tukmachev, Nikolay, 'The Early Days', in *The Source: Memories of Kachkanar Pioneers*, ed. Gennady A. Ponomarev (Kachkanar, 2000) (in Russian), pp. 81–115

Veselkova, Natalia, Elena Pryamikova and Mikhail Vandyshev, *Sites of Memory in Young Towns* (Ekaterinburg, 2016) (in Russian)

——, Mikhail Vandyshev and Elena Pryamikova, 'The Discourse of Nature in Young Towns', *The Russian Sociological Review* 15 (2016), 112–33 (in Russian)

——, —— and ——, 'Young Towns: Scaling Sites of Memory', *The Russian Sociological Review* 16:3 (2017), 36–65 (in Russian)

Walker, Barbara (ed.), *Out of the Ordinary: Folklore and the supernatural* (Logan, UT, 1995)

White, Leanne and Elspeth Frew (eds), *Dark Tourism: Place and Identity: Managing and Interpreting Dark Places* (London, 2013)

Yeltsin Centre, 'Bazhov's Urals: The Power of Place' Exhibition (2018), https://m.yeltsin.ru/affair/otkrytie-vystavki-ural-bazhova-sila-mesta/

9

The London Underground:
A Supernatural Subterranean Heterotopia

—◆◇◆—

ALEX BEVAN

Subterranean spaces have a rich and culturally varying history. For Christians, the biblical Book of Revelation describes a subterranean pit known as hell, which contains a 'lake of fire' in which 'the devil, the beast, and false prophet' will be 'tormented day and night for ever and ever'.[1] Discourses of hell secure the underworld as a space of terror, beneath life on the surface. Throughout history, from Neanderthals to the nineteenth-century homeless, underground caverns have been used as shelters and homes, whilst the earth underground is used as a place of burial for the dead. Yet the nineteenth century also saw a move towards utilising underground space for modernisation and technological innovation. In 1858, Joseph Bazalgette designed a modern subterranean sewage system for London which diverted waste to the Thames estuary. As chief engineer for the Metropolitan Board of Works, Bazalgette utilised subterranean space by installing over one hundred miles of sewage pipes, attempting to rid London of the disease and despair caused by free-flowing human waste at street level. Shortly after the installation of the sewage pipes, building works on the London Underground rail network began in 1863, with the intention of revolutionising urban travel. Due in part to the fact that the underground is typically a place for the dead, and given the subterranean biblical connotations of hell, superstition surrounding 'the Tube' began to grow.[2] Far from quashing supernatural beliefs, the urbanisation of

---

[1] Revelation 20:10 (AV)

[2] The London Underground is colloquially referred to as 'the Tube'.

subterranean London gave rise to an increasingly Gothic space which, since its inception, has reflected the socio-cultural anxieties of contemporary society, particularly in relation to increasing modernity. The Gothic is, as David Punter notes, 'a voice: it is restless, questioning, never silent: it may be, or seem, melodramatic, exaggerated, lacking in subtlety', but 'above all [it is] a literature of transgression'.[3]

The chapter will begin by examining the history of the Tube and its accumulation of eerie and supernatural tales, which position the Underground as an uncomfortable or hostile space. These Gothic narratives and their ghosts each serve as expressions of anxiety towards the London Underground as a signifier of urban modernity. The chapter will then analyse the Underground as a space that is heterotopic, due to the unusual presence of utopian narratives, which position it as a symbol of modern industrial triumph, alongside supernatural and Gothic narratives which threaten and undermine that image. This section will also consider the passenger experience in light of these competing narratives; specifically how the increasingly Gothic perception of the London Underground may impact upon how contemporary travellers experience this subterranean urban space. The final part of the chapter turns to contemporary Gothic fiction that engages with the Underground. In doing so, it positions the issue of twenty-first century cultural anxieties within a historicist frame of haunting, thereby offering new insights into our contemporary relationship with the London Underground.

The first part of the London Underground, known as the 'Metropolitan Railway', was constructed in 1863. Following the initial construction, it was noted that surface-level land was expensive and saturated, and this led to the construction of the first deep-level, electric tube in 1890, known as the 'City and South London Railway'. Deep-level tube construction was preferred as this did not disrupt the complex networks of sewers and underground pipework. Since the London Underground's inception in the Victorian era, it has been under development and expansion, throughout the twentieth century and into the present day.[4] The *Transport for London* website informs visitors that the Underground currently comprises 270 stations and eleven lines

---

[3]   David Punter, *The Gothic Condition: Terror, History and the Psyche* (Cardiff, 2016), p. 4.

[4]   For further information on the history of the London Underground, see Peter Ackroyd, *London Under* (London, 2011); Christian Wolmar, *The Subterranean Railway: How the London Underground was Built and How it Changed the City Forever* (London, 2004).

which transport millions of passengers each year.[5] Despite assumptions that supernatural beliefs have, over time, faded alongside modernity, the Victorian urban expansion 'underground' soon became entangled with Gothic narratives. In 1845, before the construction of the London Underground began, a preacher named Reverend Cumming protested against the plans for underground travel. Cumming famously pronounced that 'burrowing into the infernal regions' would 'disturb the devil'. He added, it is 'better to wait for the devil than to make roads down into hell', exemplifying the way in which biblical, and mythological depictions of the underworld still shaped perceptions of subterranean spaces in the nineteenth century.[6] Evoking further religious superstition, the excavation works at Liverpool Street station, which was built in 1875, disrupted around eight bodies per cubic metre, as the station was built upon a mass burial site.[7] The bones of the dead were tactlessly dug up and moved to make way for the Tube system, creating widespread unease amongst Victorian Londoners. The practice of disturbing the bones of the dead signalled the horrors of modernity, as the urbanisation of London travel literally unearthed the past to make way for the future.

The London Underground is physically positioned amidst earth, sewers and the street level. Lynda Nead describes contemporary photographs of the London Underground under construction during the 1860s:

> In these images, the full wonder of the London Underground could be displayed; an apparently normal street above the ground and then, below the gas pipes and sewers, another, parallel world of passengers, locomotives and airy tunnels illuminated by gas. … This was a new urban aesthetic built around the forms of the tunnel, the trench, the vault and scaffolding.[8]

Nead discusses the various layers of London, existing parallel to one another; yet the increasingly Gothic narratives being ascribed to the Tube insist upon these parallels becoming obscured, as fears surrounding subterranean London, so evident in these narratives, began to be felt at street level. The physical layers of London are also symbolically obscured through the black grime present in the Tube, which enters the noses of passengers, altering the colour of their mucus following tube travel, suggesting that the Tube does not occupy a

---

[5]   See 'London Underground', *Transport for London*, https://tfl.gov.uk/corporate/about-tfl/what-we-do/london-underground (accessed 14 June 2019).

[6]   David Long, *The Little Book of the London Underground* (Stroud, 2014), p. 29.

[7]   See London Paranormal, 'Haunted London Underground', *London Paranormal*, http://www.londonparanormal.com/underground/ (accessed 14 June 2019).

[8]   Lynda Nead, *Victorian Babylon: People, Streets and Images in Nineteenth-Century London* (New Haven, CT, 2005), p. 39.

space in its own right, but is connected to the industrial layers by which it is surrounded. In the nineteenth century, this smog that began to pass through subterranean London's various industrial layers was considered a symbol of production and industry, but in the twenty-first century, polluted air is disliked and, of course, environmentally damaging. Throughout its history, and even today, grime from the Underground's air impinges on the bodies of the passengers, affecting their cleanliness. As Peter Hutchings notes, 'this dirt can also be considered in terms of its relation to London's history, and indeed it is frequently presented ... as a trace or residue of that city's long history'.[9] The dirty air today can therefore be understood through Hutchings's analogy as a 'residue' of the Underground's Victorian roots, and is perhaps symbolic of the traveller's journey into its dark, historic, subterranean realm.

The Underground's networks of tunnels are from surface level unseen, secretive and mysterious. One is entirely reliant on London Underground maps in order to visualise the space. However, the first such map, drawn in 1908, was geographically based, overcrowded, difficult to read, and could not present the rail network in its entirety.[10] In 1931, Harry Beck's iconic topological map replaced earlier designs, and this design, albeit modified, is still in circulation today. Beck's map is simple in design and does not reflect the relationship between the London Underground and the city of London, perhaps securing the Underground as 'other' to the city, a Gothic, separate entity. Les Roberts explains that the 'topological map became a standard means of visualizing the space-time compression of urban modernity'.[11] Roberts implies that the scale of urban modernity in the form of the London Underground's vast subterranean network is somewhat overwhelming for its users, and the map offers a form of visual comfort to the anxious urban traveller. The map is, therefore, a mediator between the traveller and the subterranean labyrinth, forging a connection between ground level and the tunnels beneath the surface. Large Underground maps are positioned throughout the Tube system's subterranean passageways. Interwoven symbolically within these maps is the promise of order, control and eventual escape from the menacing, mysterious tunnel networks which could be read as a variant of the Gothic trope of entrapment within a carceral edifice.

Contributing to supernatural beliefs, the London Underground possesses a dark history of deaths, including accidental deaths, suicides and murders.

---

[9]   Peter Hutchings, 'Horror London', *Journal of British Cinema and Television* 6 (2009), 190–206 at 204.

[10] Richard Tames, *London: A Cultural History* (Oxford, 2006), p. 92.

[11] Les Roberts, *Mapping Cultures: Place, Practice, Performance* (Basingstoke, 2012), p. 59.

As Drew D. Gray has noted, 'the late Victorian period had witnessed a gradual rise in criminality after a steady decline from the mid-century', a trend
that interestingly coincided with the development of deep-level tubes on the
London Underground, suggesting that the city's subterranean expansion provided opportune environments for crime.[12] The Victorian stations were poorly
lit by 'gas flames in glass globes' which would burn yellow due to impurities
in the atmosphere, further rendering platforms and passageways fertile environments for such criminality.[13] Even with today's closed-circuit television
systems, criminal activity underground is rife. Most disturbingly, there are
approximately fifty suicides recorded each year on the London Underground.[14]
The manner in which suicides are dealt with in the London Underground is
cold and practical. As Wynford Hicks notes, ' "passenger action" is the current
euphemism [for "suicide"] on the London Underground for what used to be
called "a person under a train" '.[15] This pragmatic approach to suicide in the
London Underground extends to the modifications of the tracks, as what are
known as 'suicide-pits' have been installed at many stations. Martha Jane Smith
and Derek Blaikie Cornish explain that these pits 'run under the length of the
central electrified rail', adding that 'those attempting suicide at such stations
may be pushed into the pit upon impact with the front of the train'.[16] Peculiarly,
there is a noticeably low level of shock surrounding tube deaths if compared
to railway deaths at ground level. One very rarely hears about 'Underground
deaths' in the media – it is almost as if the hidden, subterranean space so akin
to the grave absorbs the trauma that would be felt at surface level, and the
bodies of the dead are swept under the carpet, or in this instance, the tracks.

Unsurprisingly, after the many dark and tragic events which have taken
place in the Underground, it is renowned for a multitude of ghost stories, both
historical and contemporary. David Long states, 'The London Underground is
said by many to be haunted and several hundred sightings have been reported
by staff and passengers alike over the years.'[17] Akin to folkloric tales, most
spatial ghost stories develop over time and have many authors. Elephant and
Castle station is famed for possessing the ghost of a woman who boards trains

---

[12] Drew D. Gray, *London's Shadows: The Dark Side of the Victorian City* (London,
      2010), p. 231.
[13] Andrew Martin, *Underground, Overground: A Passenger's History of the Tube* (Lon-
      don, 2012), p. 37.
[14] Evi Routoula, *London Tube: 7 Stations, 7 Stories* (London, 2013), p. 135.
[15] Wynford Hicks, *Quite Literally: Problem Words and How to Use Them* (London,
      2004), p. 169.
[16] Martha Jane Smith and Derek Blaikie Cornish, *Secure and Tranquil Travel: Prevent-
      ing Crime and Disorder on Public Transport* (Abingdon, 2012), p. 179.
[17] Long, *Little Book*, p. 160.

and then mysteriously disappears. This is perhaps emblematic of travellers' fears surrounding the safety of the Underground, and of whether they will indeed surface from the subterranean depths. The website known as *Ghost Story* claims to have a 'genuine testimony from a tube driver on the London Underground who has actually seen the ghost' at Elephant and Castle station:

> At around 6 pm at a Bakerloo line Underground Station, I was in pursuit of my duties as an employee of London Underground. I join the train at the terminus at Elephant and Castle and walk forward to the front of the train with a view to travelling with the driver. At this point the driver has not arrived so I put my bag down and move to the rear door to wait for him. While I am waiting a girl gets into the carriage – she walks straight through the carriage and I have to move aside making some muttered apology – I sort of have to do this since I was in uniform! A minute or so later the driver turns up, and we move toward the front of the train. I notice that the girl is not in the carriage and this is a rather immediate cause for concern – she could not have left the train without passing me – I had full view of the carriage and platform at the time. My reaction was to inform the driver – the only place she could have gone was to have walked down the tunnel – not really what we want! The driver's response was unusual: 'Oh, her. We hear about her all the time – she's even been in the papers.'[18]

Other haunted tube stations include Aldwych, Farringdon and Bethnal Green, although, as one might expect, there are many other famous ghosts throughout the Tube system. The Royal Strand Theatre was demolished in 1905 in order for Aldwych station to be built, and legend has it that an actress still performs in this former theatre space.[19] This ghost story further echoes the early unease felt towards modernising the underground spaces of London, especially surrounding the tube's disruption to the people of London: this woman's professional identity was erased in the wake of the theatre's demolition. The story of the Aldywch station ghost serves to highlight the way in which people invest their identities and sense of purpose in places, and how change, often in the form of modernisation, can threaten such identity formation. Farringdon station is similarly haunted by the occupiers of the buildings which formerly stood on the land. In 1758, Annie Naylor, a thirteen year-old apprentice hat-maker, was brutally murdered by her master and his

---

[18] 'London Underground Ghosts: London, England', *Ghost Story*, http://www.ghost-story.co.uk/index.php/haunted-houses/276-london-underground-ghosts-london-england (accessed 14 June 2019).

[19] David Brandon and Alan Brooke, *Haunted London Underground* (Stroud, 2009), pp. 22–4.

wife. The hat-shop was demolished in 1863 for Farringdon station to be built. People have reported hearing the girl in the Underground station, and she has become known as the '*screaming* spectre'.[20]

Larger-scale tragic events which have occurred on the London Underground have led to collectives of ghosts being spotted. During the Second World War, Bethnal Green station was used as an air raid shelter, and as crowds flocked to the entrance of the station during an attack on 3 March 1943, 173 people died as a result of overcrowding. Consequently, Bethnal Green station is reportedly haunted by groups of children who can be heard crying in the tunnels. Similarly, at Lewisham station people have reported hearing the screams of the formerly trapped passengers who were involved in a Tube crash in 1957. Ninety people died and over a hundred were injured in the accident.[21] Although no ghost stories have arisen specifically from the terrorist attacks on the London Underground on the 7 July 2005, these have contributed to the Tube's history of tragedy and dark atmosphere. In these attacks, fifty-two passengers were killed and over seven hundred people were injured.[22] In 2005, the first explosion actually took place between Aldgate and Liverpool Street, two notoriously haunted stations. All of the three explosions took place on sub-surface trains, marking the subterranean rail network as a targeted space of terror. From tales of a supposed ghostly man with a hat and cloak at Covent Garden station, to the Black Nun at Bank station, subterranean legends of haunting dominate every corner of the Tube.[23] Whilst space does not permit discussion here of all of the ghost stories in circulation, it is worth noting that many of them appear to reveal long-standing cultural apprehensions and anxieties surrounding the development of the Underground as a signifier of urban modernity, and, indeed, the subterranean space itself. These apprehensions are also manifest in travellers' Underground behaviours and experiences, along with Underground-based literature, both of which will be explored below.

Travelling on the London Underground is an iconic experience for visitors to London, and, indeed, a gateway for tourists navigating the cityscape. According to the *Transport for London* website, 1.37 billion people travel on

---

[20] Stephanie Clarke, *Down, Dirty and Divine: A Spiritual Ride through London's Underground* (Kibworth, 2012), p. 39 [my italics].

[21] Brandon and Brooke, *Haunted*, pp. 29–31.

[22] Lucy Rodgers, Salim Qurashi and Steven Connor, '7 July London bombings: What happened that day?' *BBC News Online*, 3 July 2015, http://www.bbc.co.uk/news/uk-33253598 (accessed 14 June 2019).

[23] Alex Landon, 'The Horror, The Horror! London's Most Haunted Underground Stations', *Secret London*, https://secretldn.com/haunted-underground-stations/ (accessed 14 June 2109).

the underground each year, indicating the enormous scale of its utilisation.[24] Today, there are in the region of forty abandoned, disused London Underground stations, which have been colloquially termed 'ghost stations', and, in the course of my fieldwork, I resolved to try to catch sight of these ghost stations while travelling on the Underground. They are uncanny, strange-yet-familiar spaces which have fallen into disrepair. Although these disused stations are often difficult to see, trains carrying thousands of tourists each day pass through them when connecting with the operational stations. My research led me to an amateur website run by a London Underground enthusiast, Hywel Williams, which has a dedicated page with guidance for tourists on how to catch a glimpse of the ghost stations, indicative of the long-standing cultural desire to scratch beneath the surface of the Tube's supposedly modern structure. Providing a table that features many of the known ghost stations and precisely how to find them, the website's page is proactively entitled 'What can I see …?'. Williams states,

> A lot of people have said that they've printed out these pages to go on a tour to try to see some of the things I've mentioned. Some also suggested a page with an outlined 'tour' that could be printed out and taken, with all the things visible from the public sections of the network outlined.[25]

He reveals the significant number of people fascinated by the idea seeing London's unseen historical stations who embark on self-guided 'tours' of them. Despite being closed to the public, and in some cases deliberately hidden from plain sight, the ghost stations are generating Underground Gothic tourism. Following Williams's advice, that the abandoned South Kentish Town station on the Northern Line 'can be seen in both directions by looking out of the right hand window of the train', I eagerly placed myself with a clear view from the window and directed my gaze at the walls while travelling through the tunnels.[26] As promised, I caught a fleeting glimpse of an open area where the former platform would have stood. Following Williams's instructions, I was able to experience the London Underground in a new way, through the lens of its Gothic past. South Kentish Town station is a shadow of its former self, gutted and torn apart. Many other ghost stations have been bricked over, preventing travellers from seeing the former station's (absent) platform area. I decided to take a tour of the Piccadilly Line in order to pass through Brompton

---

[24] 'Facts & figures', *Transport for London*, https://tfl.gov.uk/corporate/about-tfl/what-we-do/london-underground/facts-and-figures (accessed 14 June 2019).
[25] Hywel Williams, 'What can I see …?' *Underground History*, https://underground-history.co.uk/see.php (accessed 14 June 2109).
[26] Ibid. See 'South Kentish Town' in Williams's table.

Road and Down Street stations, in order to see further examples of the hidden stations to which Williams refers. He notes that when passing both stations, the tunnel walls 'change from cast iron to brick for the bricked off platforms', and I clearly saw the brickwork covering these ghost stations.[27] The bricks permanently encase the platforms, sealing off the station's former identity.

Although I sighted them only momentarily, the experience of seeing remnants of the ghost stations was exciting, even more so as I was 'touring' under the guidance of a website page intended for the select few fascinated by portions of abandoned subterranean London. David Ashford describes the ghost stations thus:

> These abandoned stations excite our imagination because we see in them the working of forces hitherto unsuspected in the modern city, but which we are aware of in some remote corner of our own being: they speak to our condition as ghosts in the machine, our sense that we *haunt* rather than *inhabit* the modern city.[28]

The ghost stations capture the multi-layered narratives of *haunting* within the London Underground. As one glimpses the abandoned stations, there is a sense that these derelict stations are haunting the lively operating ones, reminding passengers of the Tube's forgotten past. In addition to the haunting by the ghost stations, the passengers on board the trains can themselves be deemed to haunt this forgotten territory, the 'No Man's Land of the Tube', as they momentarily pass previously occupied platforms, almost becoming the ghosts one assumes inhabit these spaces. Serving as symbols of derelict industry, the ghost stations may be considered urban Gothic *ruins*. Jamieson Ridenhour defines urban Gothic as expressing 'the fear that the progressive metropolis is actually just a shell over a corrupt and threatening past that could savagely erupt at any time';[29] the ghost stations no longer possess urban Gothic status, as they are no longer part of the 'progressive metropolis'. When discussing the ghosts of industrial ruins, Tim Edensor states,

> Because of imperatives to bury the past too swiftly in search of the new, modernity is haunted in a particularly urgent fashion by that which has been consigned to irrelevance but which demands recognition of its historical impact.[30]

---

[27] Ibid. See 'Brompton Road' and 'Down Street'.

[28] David Ashford, *London Underground: A Cultural Geography* (Liverpool, 2013), p. 169.

[29] Jamieson Ridenhour, *In Darkest London: The Gothic Cityscape in Victorian Literature* (Lanham, MD, 2013), p. 132.

[30] Tim Edensor, 'The Ghosts of Industrial Ruins: Ordering and Disordering Memory in Excessive Space', *Environment and Planning D: Society and Space*, 23 (2005),

The derelict status of the ghost stations captures the shortcomings of urban development, a post-urban Gothic consciousness which stands to highlight the stations' former 'historical impact' along with the modern impulse to *attempt* to 'bury the past too swiftly'.

Whilst the London Underground can thus be explored as a form of independent Gothic experience – one which enables tourists to navigate its decades of Gothic narratives comprising ghost stories, legends, literary works and real-world tragedies – various offerings of organised Gothic tourism within the Underground should also be mentioned. First, 'The Old London Underground Company', founded in 2009 by director Ajit Chambers, previously ran ghost tours of some of the abandoned stations. The objective of the company was eventually to redevelop some of the abandoned London Underground stations and use them for corporate hire, while in the meantime the tours would gain the company revenue and increase public interest in subterranean London. Sadly, the tours ceased to operate in 2012. When available, however, they included access to the abandoned station at Brompton Road, allowing people to explore the station's disused platforms and offices. The abandoned stations are eerie, because some stations remain unaltered, still housing original papers, signage and artefacts. The tours were popular because they featured an opportunity to explore the 'secret', the off-limits. As Mark S. Madoff notes, 'The locked-room mystery is characteristic of the Gothic. It nearly is the Gothic.'[31] The Gothicised, sealed-off ghost station, in this sense like the locked door, was opened and accessed by the tourist.

As an alternative to Chambers's ghost tour, one can embark upon the 'London Underground and Tube Tour'. This runs five days per week, meeting at Paddington Mainline concourse. The *London Insider* describes the tour thus:

> Travel across 150 years in just two hours ... from learning about the Tube's origins, construction and design, to catching a glimpse of one of London's abandoned 'ghost stations', this experience is perfect for getting under the skin of the world's oldest iconic underground system.[32]

The evocation of time-travel interestingly situates the tour as a means of defending the Underground as a revolutionary space of architectural triumph, imbued with discourses of utopian modernity since its inception. The tour

---

829–49 at 829.

[31] Mark S. Madoff, 'Inside, Outside, and the Gothic Locked-Room Mystery', in *Gothic Fictions: Prohibitions/Transgressions*, ed. Kenneth Graham (New York, 1989), pp. 49–62 at 49.

[32] See 'London Underground and Tube Tour', *London Insider*, http://www.insider-london.co.uk/product/london-underground-and-tube-tour/ (accessed 14 June 2109).

permits the tourist merely to 'glimpse' the ghost stations, and appears deliberately to distance itself from the macabre and supernatural aspects of the Tube's history. The use of the word 'iconic' further emphasises that this tour aims to revive the perhaps fading image of the London Underground as a signifier of modern industrial achievement.

As the London Underground's trains are, literally, the vehicles in which one navigates the Tube, it is worth exploring the train as an entity in its own right, and specifically Michel Foucault's spatial analysis of the train in his article 'Of Other Spaces':

> A train is an extraordinary bundle of relations because it is something through which one goes, it is also something by means of which one can go from one point to another, and then it is also something that goes by.[33]

Foucault insists that 'we live inside a set of relations that delineates sites which are irreducible to one another and absolutely not superimposable on one another', and goes on to argue that 'one might attempt to describe these different sites by looking for the set of relations by which a given site can be defined'.[34] The train is therefore a useful symbolic device to capture Foucault's 'sets of relations' which make up the spaces in which we encounter. The trains operating within the London Underground possess more complex sets of relations than the ground-level trains which connect cities, towns and villages, because they travel through abandoned 'ghost stations', former burial sites and the realms of the dead. Whether the London Underground traveller is a conscious ghost-station tourist or an individual using the Tube as a means of touring London, s/he is on board the largest ghost train network in operation, over 250 miles (400 km) in length. Foucault's observation that the train is a 'means [by] which one can go from one point to another' thus takes on new meaning here, as the traveller passes through *other* spaces which are interwoven with narratives of haunting. The complicated sets of relations at work on these ghost trains connect the industrial past with the contemporary present and the living with the dead. The tourists' glimpses of abandoned ghost stations function as Gothic visual stimuli, uncannily frozen in time, unlike traditional ghost train props which 'come to life' and startle the passengers. Rather than producing screams, the London Underground is therefore a silent ghost train, wherein the tourist absorbs these extraordinary sets of relations.

[33]   Michel Foucault, 'Of Other Spaces', trans. Jay Miskowiec, *Diacritics* 16 (1986), 22–7 at 23–4.
[34]   Ibid., p. 23.

Having established space(s) as sets of relations, Foucault argues that he is 'interested in certain [spaces] that have the curious property of being in relation with all the other sites, but in such a way as to suspect, neutralize, or invert the set of relations that they happen to designate, mirror, or reflect'.[35] He identifies these forms of space as embodying two distinct types: utopias and heterotopias, loosely categorising utopias as having 'no real place' and heterotopias being locatable within a society.[36] The London Underground, a 'real' and locatable space, can be said to embody many of Foucault's properties of the heterotopia. The Underground marks an attempt to bring ground-level technological civilisation underground, representing a revolution of subterranean space and, in particular, a stark shift between the sets of relations that previously delineated subterranean space. Spaces underground were formerly recognised as sacred locations of burial for the dead. The London Underground therefore occupies a new form of space, which inverts these former sets of relations, placing living people underground as part of their everyday lives. For this reason, it can be identified as, in the Victorian era, a heterotopia of deviation, which for Foucault contains 'individuals whose behavior is deviant in relation to the required mean or norm'.[37] The dominant religious view at the time determined the underground as a pathway leading to the devil: long-standing superstition by default rendered early underground travellers as exhibitors of deviant behaviour.

Although the London Underground can now no longer be considered a deviant heterotopia, it has evolved into a different form of the phenomenon. Foucault explains how heterotopias can shift over time:

> The *second principle* of this description of heterotopias is that a society as its history un-folds, can make an existing heterotopia function in a very different fashion; for each heterotopia has a precise and determined function within a society and the same heterotopia can, according to the synchrony of the culture in which it occurs, have one function or another.

In the present day, the London Underground finds itself entangled in a multitude of Gothic narratives; from accounts of tragic deaths to ghost stories, it is riddled with historical and contemporary dark tales. The Tube's gradual accumulation of Gothic events and narratives, along with the decay of many of its former stations, has rendered the it an uncanny space for the tourist, embodying competing narratives of hope and loss, prosperity and ruin. Foucault observes,

[35] Ibid., p. 24.
[36] Ibid.
[37] Ibid., p. 25.

> There are ... in every civilization, real places – places that do exist ... which are something like counter-sites, a kind of effectively enacted utopia, in which the real sites, all the other real sites that can be found within the culture, are simultaneously represented, contested, and inverted.[38]

The London Underground therefore remains a heterotopic space in the twenty-first century: its status as an architectural triumph positions it is an 'effectively enacted utopia', yet it is riddled with counter-narratives which undermine this. This heterotopic space is thus loaded with competing narratives, specifically Gothic narratives, where sites such as the ghost stations are 'contested' and 'represented'. As Foucault goes on to argue, 'the heterotopia is capable of juxtaposing in a single real place several spaces, several sites that are in themselves incompatible'; and this statement is highlighted by the experience of the modern-day tourist who is subjected to incompatible fleeting images of industrial triumph and industrial ruin while aboard the Tube.

As Foucault notes, the heterotopia is always under threat of collapse, and the sustained Gothicisation of the Underground over time signals a long-standing anxiety about, or at least suspicion towards, urbanisation. The fire at King's Cross station in 1987, which led to the deaths of thirty-one travellers, further subverted the perception of the London Underground as a site of progressive modernity, and the Tube gained a reputation for being unsafe. John Drury and Clifford Stott note that the fire 'is believed to have started when a lighted match was dropped between the moving stairway and the escalator side', which was made out of wood.[39] Ironically, it is said to have spread quickly owing to the inadequate, dated, wooden structure of the stairways, combined with vast amounts of rubbish and grime beneath the steps. Therefore, the fire marks a locatable moment in which the (false) promise of utopian modernity was undermined, and the hidden deprivation of the Tube was exposed. The King's Cross fire also connotes hell-like images, echoing the Underground's former status as a deviant heterotopia, marking an inward journey into the bowels of an underworld eerily akin to that portrayed by Reverend Cumming. In this sense, the competing narratives – the ghost stories, the subterranean tragedies, the aged and abandoned infrastructure – threaten the heterotopic properties of the London Underground, and it becomes an uncanny amalgamation of hope and despair, modernity and decay. It is, therefore, the array of competing narratives that makes travelling on the London Underground a Gothic experience for the tourist, as s/he will likely be aware of the its notoriously dark

---

[38] Ibid., p. 24.
[39] John Drury and Clifford Stott, *Crowds in the 21st Century: Perspectives from Contemporary Social Science* (Abingdon, 2013), p. 87.

history; one which is further cemented into popular culture in particular by the literary texts which will be explored in the final part of this chapter.

The contemporary heterotopic space of the London Underground is further experienced via the reflections offered in the glass windows of the trains. Foucault uses the metaphor of the mirror in order to capture the competing states experienced within a heterotopic environment:

> The mirror functions as a heterotopia in this respect: it makes this place that I occupy at the moment when I look at myself in the glass at once absolutely real, connected with all the space that surrounds it, and absolutely unreal, since in order to be perceived it has to pass through the virtual point which is over there.[40]

As the trains speed through the dark and mysterious tunnels, the passengers view their reflections in the glass, simultaneously identifying themselves both as passengers in the carriage and as fleeting images caught in the suction of the wind tunnels. Passing through the 'virtual point' of the tunnel, the passenger experiences the uncanny Gothic temporality of the Underground. Furthermore, the travellers symbolically encounter the various modes of Gothic doubling there at play: the seen and the unseen (the material train and the mysterious tunnel), the technological and the urban decay, and finally one's own shifting subjectivity between physical states of being and the projected ghostly states observed in the window, signifying the dislocation of the contemporary subjects occupying the heterotopia.

The changing perception of the London Underground thus impacts upon how it is experienced by passengers. Early users of the Tube were experiencing a deviant yet revolutionary mode of transport which many would have never believed to be possible – it inspired awe and the promise of utopian modernity. These perceptions were interlaced with negative anxieties surrounding religious superstition and safety in the wake of the many tragic events endured on the Underground rail network. Travellers were, and continue to be, simultaneously experiencing a mixture of emotions fuelled by storytelling, folklore and historical events. For this reason, it is worth exploring the psychogeography of the London Underground. In 1955, Guy Debord defined psychogeography as 'the study of the specific effects of the geographical environment, whether consciously organized or not, on the emotions and behaviour of individuals'.[41] Debord was specifically interested in urban space and the impact urban

---

[40] Foucault, 'Of Other Spaces', p. 24.

[41] Guy-Ernest Debord, 'Introduction to a Critique of Urban Geography', in *Situationist International Anthology*, ed. and trans. Ken Knabb (Berkeley, CA, 2007), pp. 8–11 at 8.

environments have upon groups of people, and the London Underground is the archetypal crowded urban space, notorious for affecting the emotions of its users. Peter Ackroyd intuitively identifies the emotions which the London Underground can conjure:

> Certain people are afraid of the Underground. The journey under the earth inspires panic and claustrophobia. It induces dreams of fire and suffocation. You may experience what has been called the fear and madness of the crowds. Once you are immersed in this other-land, removed from the familiar world, you may suffer from inexplicable terrors.[42]

Ackroyd's reference to 'dreams of fire' demonstrates how the users of the Tube are likely to forge experiences and emotions in response to historical events and/or storytelling practices such as the fire at King's Cross Station and religious superstition surrounding the underworld. It is also widely acknowledged that passengers on the Tube are unusually quiet, afraid of making eye contact with or speaking to others. In this sense, the passengers are as lifeless as the abandoned stations through which they pass. Prior to boarding the ghost train, travellers descend into the subterranean realm via large one-way escalators, which lead to the roaring, seemingly unstaffed trains which disappear into the black tunnels ahead. The train's headlights dazzle passengers and disguise the driver, appearing as if the train is self-operational: a monstrous machine.

Users of the London Underground are comparable to the lemmings from the video game *Lemmings* (1991). This is a platform game in which the player has to clear obstacles in order for the lemmings (troll-like creatures) to descend. The lemmings move in a line, and should the path become obstructed, they pile up and move forwards and backwards in an attempt to clear the space. The users of the Tube descend in monotonous fashion through tunnels which dictate their path, and subsequently experience 'blockages' upon attempting to enter trains, leading to temporary retreats until the next train arrives. Only when passengers 'surface' at their destination is their game complete, and they are released from 'lemming mode'. The lemming-like crowds are similar to the Morlocks in H. G. Wells's *The Time Machine* (1895), forming a subterranean pseudo production-line, producing only repetition and higher volumes of movement. Tatiana Pogossian argues that 'the city [London] resembles a body gone wrong, which cannot be prevented from expanding', and it is the herding of human bodies in the London Underground that instantiates Pogossian's metaphor.[43] The crowds are pumped in volumes underground and dispelled

---

[42]   Peter Ackroyd, *London Under* (London, 2011), p. 138.
[43]   Tatiana Pogossian, 'Dislocations and Ecologies: The Disruption of the Urban Experience of London in Peter Ackroyd, Iain Sinclair and Gilbert & George', *European*

to the surface, creating unease at street level. This symbolic reading serves to highlight the way in which the subterranean Tube system is both a Gothic travel experience and a journey which mysteriously affects the way in which travellers behave.

Whilst this chapter has explored some of the historical and folkloric Gothic narratives that permeate the London Underground, literary works also play a pivotal role in it becoming recognised as a Gothic space and, indeed, in capturing the Gothic atmosphere of the Tube. Jeanette Winterson's novel *Tanglewreck* (2006), which is set in the London Underground, tells the adventure of a girl named Silver, who is on a quest to understand 'strange disruptions in the fabric of time'.[44] Silver is hunting for the 'Timekeeper', which allegedly enables the user to control time. Winterson depicts a group of people living in the tunnels of the London Underground, whom she calls the 'Throwbacks', who 'never celebrated birthdays, nor did they follow a calendar or clock, like Updwellers'.[45] The fact that the Throwbacks exist in a subterranean realm which exists outside 'time' renders the Underground as a timeless space. The timelessness which Winterson conveys symbolises how the Underground's multitude of competing narratives and its Gothic heterotopic properties distort present time, creating a vortex of stories and events within which the contemporary tourist becomes enveloped. A Throwback named Gabriel describes the trains of the London Underground: 'Updwellers use him [the train] when they come down here. They fear to walk here by themselves. They come all together in the Long Wagon.'[46] Gabriel personifies the train, emblematising it as an autonomous entity – a ghost train, as I argued above. Furthermore, 'wagon' usually denotes a vehicle which is designed to carry goods, rather than people, which intriguingly de-personifies the Updwellers. As pedestrians, the Updwellers 'fear' walking the tunnels, highlighting the train's role as technological mediator between the supernatural subterranean labyrinth and the passenger.

Another key London Underground-based novel is Conrad Williams's *London Revenant* (2004). As the title suggests, Williams is concerned with depicting the ghostliness of London. 'Revenant', another term for 'ghost', derives from Latin *reveniens* ('returning').[47] Williams's title captures the ways in which a multitude of narratives 'return' to the passengers in the London Underground, the Tube's opposing narratives of utopian modernity and

---

Journal of Literature, Culture and Environment 2 (2011), 99–110 at 102.

[44] Jeanette Winterson, *Tanglewreck* (London, 2006), p. 16.

[45] Ibid., p. 177.

[46] Ibid., p. 112.

[47] June Michele Pulliam, 'Revenant', in *Ghosts in Popular Culture and Legend*, ed. eadem and Anthony J. Fonseca (Santa Barbara, CA, 2016), pp. 272–5 at 272.

Gothic tales co-occupying the space through which they pass, rendering it a heterotopic mode of literary Gothic tourism. Furthermore, the cover of the novel features the London Underground logo with the word 'Underground' replaced by 'Revenant', accompanied by a ghostly figure, suggesting a quite deliberate attempt by Williams to Gothicise London's subterranean space and perhaps even intertextually allude to the Underground's many well-known ghost stories.

London Revenant is written in the first person, narrated by 'Adam Buckley', a young man who has moved from Manchester to London in the hope of finding success in the city. Buckley has narcolepsy, a condition which can cause patients to experience 'black-outs' and memory loss due to regularly slipping into unconsciousness. After the sudden death of his mother, Buckley is caught up in a pursuit of happiness, but London does not deliver:

> London was less than 20 minutes away. I could feel its suck; it was a starving, ruined baby, looking for nourishment from any quarter. Defiled, indiscriminate, blind. It devoured us all, digested us in its poisonous juices for years and then spat out the bones.[48]

Williams suggests that the city is a poisonous, even monstrous space. Ackroyd has interpreted London 'as a human body', and Nead similarly claims that Victorian London was designed to function like a 'wholesome body [with] sewers and drains carry[ing] away the waste of the metropolitan body and streets and subways facilitat[ing] the circulation of trade and production'.[49] Nead's identification of the 'circulation' of London's transport with waste-removal systems reinforces the co-dependency of such a 'wholesome body', and this brings the Gothic potential for mutation. In this sense, one can read the London Underground symbolically as part of the internal organs of London's abhuman, mutated body. The trains thus 'flow' with the blood of the city (people), whilst the sewers are considered London's bowels. Williams is thus exploring the effects of London's abhuman, subterranean body and, more specifically, how London's Underground *consumes* its tourists, linking death and monstrosity with London travel.

Death is a strong theme in *London Revenant*. The novel centres on locating a mysterious murderer, 'the pusher', in the London Underground, a figure one cannot help but recognise as a metaphor for what drives around fifty people per year to commit suicide in the Tube. This pusher is initially considered to be a single person pushing passengers to their deaths beneath oncoming

[48] Conrad Williams, *London Revenant* (San Francisco, 2006), p. 147.
[49] See Peter Ackroyd, *London: The Biography* (London, 2001), p. 1; Nead, *Victorian Babylon*, p. 163.

trains, 'forcing up to a dozen people a day onto the rails'.[50] Later in the novel, the reader discovers that the pusher(s) are a group of people who have abandoned what they term 'topside living' and formed a cult of 'unders'. Williams is therefore playing with the notion of the Gothic 'double', by deliberately failing to expose the actual number of pushers. The pack of unders can be considered zombie-like, as the term 'unders' suggests that these people have been buried and have risen from the dead, from 'under' the earth's surface. Moving beyond the traditional parameters of the zombie, which is without conscience, Williams depicts a herd of sentient pseudo-zombies rising from the grave of the London Underground, symbolising the Tube's potential to 'feast' upon and mutate its visitors.

The act of pushing is a method of disrupting the 'circulation' of people through subterranean London. The pushers are pseudo-Grim Reapers, or rather, the personification of the suicidal impulse in the Underground. Ackroyd has described the way in which many interpret the thunder of the trains as an 'invitation to leap' on to the rails.[51] Williams's narrator further personifies death as an underground entity: 'Death queued up with everyone else at the ticket booths. It hung around the platforms like a busker without any tunes to play. Sometimes it picked a train to travel on, with no particular destination in mind.'[52] The novel addresses the fears felt by passengers travelling on the Underground, in the wake of its history of tragic deaths, and the language Williams uses suggests that the travellers' fates are sealed from the moment they obtain their tickets: one-way tickets 'under'. *London Revenant* positions the Underground as a space which chooses its victims at random; perhaps the 'pushers' represent deeply disenfranchised Londoners trying to restore order, albeit macabrely, to the deadly Underground.

Subterranean spaces might easily be dismissed in assessing the key urban properties or characteristics of the city; but it is evident that, certainly in the case of London, subterranean urban spaces can house and symbolise the greatest advances in modern technology. The London Underground represents a revolution of subterranean space, a modern, technological metropolis beneath the streets of London, expanding the project of modernity at subsurface level. The Gothic superstition and folklore at work in the Underground has meanwhile evolved into Gothic fiction, whereby recognition of the Tube as a supernatural space in turn proliferates. The long history of subterranean Gothic narratives, with biblical and mythological depictions of the underworld, in combination with widespread anxieties surrounding urban modernisation,

---

[50] Williams, *London Revenant*, p. 192.
[51] Ackroyd, *London Under*, p. 146.
[52] Williams, *London Revenant*, p. 106.

has rendered the London Underground a heterotopic space. While it could be said to be held together by a utopian framework – a triumph of modern engineering representative of the endless industrial and technological possibilities of the future of urban life – that image is, however, under constant threat from competing Gothic histories which posit that same space as being a site of mourning and decay. The experiences of contemporary users of the Tube are therefore framed by over a century's-worth of supernatural narratives that have attached themselves to it. Due to the fact that urban modernisation continues to be a cause for widespread anxiety, moreover, the Tube retains its supernatural identity in the twenty-first century. Despite their largely unseen and overlooked locations, we must re-position subterranean urban spaces at the forefront of our researches into urban cityscapes. As this chapter's exploration of the London Underground has tried to suggest, such spaces are, through their very positioning, saturated with the supernatural, housing the city's underbelly of narratives and offering key insights into urban dwellers' deepest and darkest fears and emotions.

Bibliography

Ackroyd, Peter, *London: The Biography* (London, 2001)
——, *London Under* (London, 2012)
Ashford, David, *London Underground: A Cultural Geography* (Liverpool, 2013)
Brandon, David and Alan Brooke, *Haunted London Underground* (Stroud, 2009)
Clarke, Stephanie, *Down, Dirty and Divine: A Spiritual Ride through London's Underground* (Kibworth, 2012)
Debord, Guy-Ernest, 'Introduction to a Critique of Urban Geography', in *Situationist International Anthology*, ed. and trans. Ken Knabb (Berkeley, CA, 2007), pp. 8–11
Drury, John and Clifford Stott, *Crowds in the 21st Century: Perspectives from Contemporary Social Science* (Abingdon, 2013)
Edensor, Tim, 'The Ghosts of Industrial Ruins: Ordering and Disordering Memory in Excessive Space', *Environment and Planning D: Society and Space* 23 (2005), 829–49
'Facts & figures', *Transport for London*, https://tfl.gov.uk/corporate/about-tfl/what-we-do/london-underground/facts-and-figures
Foucault, Michel, 'Of Other Spaces', trans. Jay Miskowiec, *Diacritics* 16 (1986), 22–7
Gray, Drew D., *London's Shadows: The Dark Side of the Victorian City* (London, 2010).
Hicks, Wynford, *Quite Literally: Problem Words and How to Use Them* (London, 2004)
Hutchings, Peter, 'Horror London', *Journal of British Cinema and Television* 6 (2009), 190–206
Landon, Alex, 'The Horror, The Horror! London's Most Haunted Underground Stations', *Secret London*, 12 October 2017, https://secretldn.com/haunted-underground-stations/
'London Underground', *Transport for London*, https://tfl.gov.uk/corporate/about-tfl/what-we-do/london-underground

'London Underground and Tube Tour', *London Insider*, http://www.insider-london.co.uk/product/london-underground-and-tube-tour/

'London Underground Ghosts, London, England', *Ghost Story*, http://www.ghost-story.co.uk/index.php/haunted-houses/276-london-underground-ghosts-london-england

Long, David, *The Little Book of the London Underground* (Stroud, 2014)

Madoff, Mark S., 'Inside, Outside, and the Gothic Locked-Room Mystery', in *Gothic Fictions: Prohibitions/Transgressions*, ed. Kenneth Graham (New York, 1989), pp. 49–62.

Martin, Andrew, *Underground, Overground: A Passenger's History of the Tube* (London, 2012)

Nead, Lynda, *Victorian Babylon: People, Streets and Images in Nineteenth-Century London* (New Haven, CT, 2005)

Pogossian, Tatiana, 'Dislocations and Ecologies: The Disruption of the Urban Experience of London in Peter Ackroyd, Iain Sinclair and Gilbert & George', *European Journal of Literature, Culture and Environment* 2 (2011), 99–110

Pulliam, June Michele, 'Revenant', in *Ghosts in Popular Culture and Legend*, ed. eadem and Anthony J. Fonseca (Santa Barbara, CA, 2016), pp. 272–5

Punter, David, *The Gothic Condition: Terror, History and the Psyche* (Cardiff, 2016)

Ridenhour, Jamieson, *In Darkest London: The Gothic Cityscape in Victorian Literature* (Lanham, MD, 2013)

Roberts, Les, *Mapping Cultures: Place, Practice, Performance* (Basingstoke, 2012)

Rodgers, Lucy, Salim Qurashi and Steven Connor, '7 July London bombings: What happened that day?', *BBC News Online*, 3 July 2015, http://www.bbc.co.uk/news/uk-33253598

Routoula, Evi, *London Tube: 7 Stations, 7 Stories* (London, 2013)

Smith, Martha Jane, and Derek Blaikie Cornish, *Secure and Tranquil Travel: Preventing Crime and Disorder on Public Transport* (Abingdon, 2012)

Tames, Richard, *London: A Cultural History* (Oxford, 2006)

Williams, Conrad, *London Revenant* (San Francisco, 2006)

Williams, Hywel, 'What can I see...?', *Underground History*, https://underground-history.co.uk/see.php

Winterson, Jeanette, *Tanglewreck* (London, 2006)

Wolmar, Christian, *The Subterranean Railway: How the London Underground was Built and How it Changed the City Forever* (London, 2004)

10

The Uncanny City: Delving into the Sewers and Subconscious of Tokyo in Haruki Murakami's *Hard-Boiled Wonderland and the End of the World*

——◄◇◇►——

DEIRDRE FLYNN

In *Hard-Boiled Wonderland and the End of the World*, Haruki Murakami alternates the narrative between a dystopian urban Tokyo of the future filled with secret underground tunnels, and a subconscious walled town. His protagonist becomes an uncanny resident of both simultaneously, as his conscious and subconscious explore the anxieties of both unknown locations. The unnamed protagonist is split between the two worlds. He lives in a technological dystopian future where each individual is commodified and adapted to be of greatest value to the system, while also exploring a Baudrillardian world within his subconscious, created and edited by the same system. This space is populated from his own experience, based on representations of what is 'real', on simulations of real life. Described by Susan Napier as archetypal fantasy for contemporary Japan, *Hard-Boiled Wonderland and the End of the World* creates two phantasmagorical urban spaces that compete for control of the mind of the protagonist.[1] And in accordance with Todorov's definition of the

---

[1] Susan Napier, *The Fantastic in Modern Japanese Literature: The Subversion of Modernity*, London, 1995), p. 4.

fantastic, the events that happen cannot be explained by 'the laws of this same familiar world'.[2]

This spatial hybridity and fragmentation creates a postmodern and Gothic urban experience that explores the cultural anxieties of late twentieth-century Japan. The postmodern and the Gothic merge here because of their complementary concerns. As Maria Beville explains, '[S]ome of the issues that are explored separately in Gothic and postmodernist fiction, are one and the same, namely: crises of identity, fragmentation of the self, the darkness of the human psyche, and the philosophy of being and knowing.'[3] These are the issues explored throughout *Hard-Boiled Wonderland and the End of the World*. The protagonist's experience of the fragmentation of self is mirrored in the topography of the city around him, and the urban space he creates in his subconscious.

This chapter explores the uncanny nature of the urban spaces in Murakami's dystopian world in relation to the postmodern anxieties that it represents. The urban spaces of the novel are filled with strange, spectral uncanny features. The city, through its Gothic layering, becomes a postmodern space. Through the fragmented narrative that moves between Tokyo and a subconscious town in the mind of the protagonist, Murakami heightens the uncanny simulacra atmosphere of the novel. Looking first at the 'Hard-Boiled Wonderland' section and then at 'the End of the World', this chapter will discuss the uncanny and postmodern elements of the novel that speak to the cultural anxieties of contemporary urban life.

Postmodernity

Published in 1985, *Hard-Boiled Wonderland and the End of the World*, Murakami's fourth novel, is an eclectic mix of Eastern and Western references, a postmodern hard-boiled detective style narrative that addresses contemporaneous concerns. Through the alternating stories, Murakami manages to speak to debates on post-humanism, AI, and the inability to know the city or the self. The 'Hard-Boiled Wonderland' section features an unnamed narrator whose brain has been commodified by the 'system' to shuffle data. He has become a machine for the system, estranged from his city and his self. As a result of the system's experimentation on his brain a new world has been created inside his subconscious: a walled town called The End of the World. It is not obvious that these two worlds are related, apart from the uncanny references that feature

---

[2]   Tzvetan Todorov, *The Fantastic: A Structural Approach to a Literary Genre* (Ithaca, NY, 1975), p. 25.

[3]   Maria Beville, *Gothic-Postmodernism: Voicing the Terrors of Postmodernity* (Amsterdam, 2009), p. 53.

in both worlds, until later in the novel. The protagonist in the Hard-Boiled section of the novel is hired by a renegade professor to shuffle or launder data, and learns, as he travels through tunnels and caves under Tokyo, that he has just days until his mind will turn over to his subconscious world. There is a constant negotiation between these two urban spaces, both of which are filled with uncanny representations of his life. These layered worlds are haunted by spectral images that the protagonist cannot decipher, or even originate. Are these his own memories or are they created by the system? The anxiety of his present, his life in this dystopian future, causes his subconscious to force him to abandon the city and its strange creatures through Alice-in-Wonderland rabbit holes, and retreat further into the walls of his subconscious, populated by ghosts.

He must enter the darkness of his own mind, and the tunnels below Tokyo, in order to be and know. His world order has been challenged by the city space that reveals new labyrinthine qualities to him. Susan Napier suggests that the protagonist 'ultimately decides to leave the outer high tech world of modern late twentieth-century Japan to retreat into a fantasy Utopia inside his own mind.'[4] His current isolated existence in Tokyo has fragmented his self and his city, and the crisis of knowing either leads him to withdraw completely into fantasy. The genre of fantasy has always been an important mode within Japanese literature, and developed as a 'powerful means of coming to terms with the anxieties triggered by the acquisition of new technologies, new institutional and social structures and new notions of selfhood.'[5] Rebecca Suter suggests that fantasy in Japanese literature has played an important role in exploring the self and Other, and here in this novel Murakami is critiquing Japanese society: 'its conformism, its capitalist competition, or the encroachment of technology onto human life.'[6] This novel also fits with the *Encyclopedia of Fantasy* description of 'Urban Fantasy' as the city makes it 'difficult to determine the extent and nature of the surrounding reality.'[7] The novel becomes a space 'where fantasy and the mundane world intersect and interweave throughout a tale which is significantly *about* a real city.[8]

For the Japanese reader, the differentiation between the two worlds is much more obvious, as the unnamed protagonist of the Hard-Boiled section

---

[4]   Napier, *The Fantastic*, p. 4.
[5]   Rebecca Suter, 'Critical Engagement through Fantasy in *Hard-Boiled Wonderland and The End of the World*', in *Haruki Murkami: Challenging Authors*, ed. Matthew C. Strecher and Paul Thomas (Rotterdam, 2016), pp. 59–71 at 63.
[6]   Ibid., p. 67.
[7]   John Clute and John Grant (eds), *The Encyclopedia of Fantasy* (London, 1997).
[8]   Ibid.

is written as the formal I, the Japanese word 'watashi'. The I of The End of the World section is the informal I, 'boku'. This is what one of Murakami's transla-tors calls a 'psychological bifurication'.[9] This separation of the self mirrors the Japanese phenomenon highlighted by another contemporary Japanese author, Ryu Murakami: that of 'Hikikomori'.[10] Roughly translated, *hikikomori* means to 'socially withdraw', and Ryu Murakami's article discusses how this 'state of anomie' has impacted large numbers of younger people since the 1970s, esti-mating in 2000 that one million young people are affected. He suggests that the rapid improvement of the economy after the Second World War left people without goals or aims:

> [B]y the 1970s, we had already achieved the national goal. We had worked hard to restore the country from the ruins of World War II, develop the economy and build a modern technological state. When that great goal was attained, we lost much of the motivating force that had knit the nation so tightly together. Affluent Japanese do not know what kind of lifestyle to take up now. That uncertainty has pulled people further apart and caused a whole raft of social problems. Hikikomori is naturally one of them.[11]

In order to fulfil this hikikomori, the protagonist of Murakami's novel will be forced to socially withdraw. Watashi already lives an isolated, technologised life in Tokyo, but this bifurcation allows him to retreat further. The town that boku chooses does not allow for connection, love, or extremes of emotion. The End of The World takes hikikomori to the next level by removing the technology and allowing the protagonist to withdraw completely from life. As Ryu Murakami points out 'technology … fixes people in their individual space. In this information society, none of us can be free from being somewhat socially withdrawn'.[12] For watashi, technology ties him to the system, connects him, while at the same time creating the space in his subconscious that allows him to completely withdraw, socially and consciously. Murakami's protagonist retreats to the 'black box' inside his brain, making his 'state of anomie' from the urban uncanny complete.

The fragmented and unknowable nature of the protagonist is matched by the urban spaces of the novel. The translation of the word 'watashi', the

---

[9]   Jay Rubin discusses the formal/informal 'I' and the issues in translation in *Haruki Murakami and the Music of Words* (London, 2005). See p. 117.

[10] See Ryu Murakami, 'Japan's Lost Generation', *Time*, Asian edn, 1 May 2000, p. 49. [Online: http://edition.cnn.com/ASIANOW/time/magazine/2000/0501/japan.es-saymurakami.html (accessed 8 July 2018).]

[11] Ibid.

[12] Ibid.

formal 'I', is the perfect term for the postmodern individual: a shop front-like facade, a public image, a creation, a re-representation, a simulacrum. This is what Tokyo becomes for the protagonist. The city space he has known is a facade, because underneath is another world filled with Gothic tunnels and creatures that haunt the dark space. And like a Gothic narrative, these tunnels and labyrinthine spaces hold the key to secrets that have been kept hidden from the protagonist. The Gothic merges with the postmodern in this novel, to deal with contemporary fears. As Fred Botting explains, '[G]othic forms are reinvented for postmodern interrogations as well as for the accompanying freedoms of consumerist, corporate, creative and post-industrial orders.'[13] In this hard-boiled late-capitalist Tokyo, the Gothic elements parallel the postmodern concerns. As Nick Bentley puts it, the 'postmodern metropolis represents a labyrinthine enigma that metaphorically stands in for the dizzying plurality of contemporary urban living'.[14] This postmodern city is the representation of what Bentley calls 'hyper-urban living': an excess of consumer culture, control, ambiguity, and simulacra.

What is created is a fragmented and layered city that is matched through Murakami's narrative, where references from both Eastern and Western culture merge; the Beach Boys and Levi jeans with Shinto shrines. It becomes a Lyotardian 'anything goes' reference, where 'eclecticism is the degree zero of contemporary general culture', where you 'listen to reggae; you watch a western; you eat McDonald's at midday and local cuisine at night; you wear Paris perfume in Tokyo and dress retro in Hong Kong; knowledge is the stuff of TV game shows'.[15] This eclecticism is transferred to the fictional cartographies in Murakami's world. It is layered, fragmented, and decentred. As Yomoto explains, the 'cultural sensibility that [Murakami] draws on ... the urban way of life that he depicts are all of a nature that cannot be attributed to any single place or people, drifting and circulating as they do in this globalised world.[16] Toshiko Ellis calls Murakami's writing 'expressive of a postmodern cultural trend' that is representative of the 'critical issues related to Japanese culture today'.[17] Ellis finds the 'used-up-ness ... pastiche, the dominance of

[13] Fred Botting, *Gothic*, 2nd edn (London, 2013), p. 14.

[14] Nick Bentley, 'Postmodern Cities', in *The Cambridge Companion to The City in Literature*, ed. Kevin. R. McNamara (Cambridge, 2014), pp. 175–87 at 175.

[15] Jean-François Lyotard, *The Postmodern Condition: A Report on Knowledge* (Minneapolis, 1984), p. 8.

[16] Inuhiko Yomota, 'How to View the "Haruki Boom" ', in *A Wild Haruki Chase: Reading Murakami around the World*, ed. The Japan Foundation (Berkeley, CA, 2008), pp. 34–5.

[17] Toshiko Ellis, 'Literature: Questioning Modernism and Postmodernism in Japanese Literature', in *Japanese Encounters with Postmodernity*, ed. Yoshi Sugimoto and

nostalgia themes and of historical amnesia' in Murakami's writing reminiscent of 'Jameson's description of the postmodern'.[18] Furthermore it is the sense of place, or, more accurately, the lack of a sense of place that Ellis suggests sets Murakami apart from the modernist tradition, 'because these images are too fragmented to construct a three-dimensional picture of a real place'.[19] There is a heterogeneity to the worlds that Murakami creates, because of the fragmentation of postmodernity. As Jolanta A. Drzewiecka and Thomas K. Nakayama explain in relation to postmodernity and urban space, it is 'no longer possible to maintain ... a fixed configuration of culture, nation, and space'.[20] The Tokyo that watashi thought he knew is not the real city. Through his work with the Professor, he comes to realise the city is much more layered and fragmented; he becomes decentred in his own urban space. It is, to borrow David Harvey's term, a 'palimpsest' or a 'collage' of 'forms superimposed upon each other'.[21]

Urban anxieties

In their introduction to *Urban Space and Representation*, Maria Balshaw and Liam Kennedy suggest that the city 'resonates' with conscious and unconscious impulses and as a result 'repressed material erupts in paranoid or obsessional form' because of the displacement or dislocation of the uncanny city. They also suggest that the literary mapping and representation of the city projects the 'fears and fantasies of the urban living'.[22] They aver that the postmodern condition of late capitalism, including elements such as the simulacrum and the hyperreal, has the potential to remove a sense of place. However, they add that we cannot deny that places 'are sites of spatial contiguity, of interdependence and entailment, which take on contours of identity and location through representation'.[23] The contested and porous borders of space and place represented in literary or cultural texts demonstrate how the urban responds 'to the lived intersections of urban social relations'.[24]

Johann P. Arnason, (London, 1995), pp. 133–53 at 143–6.

[18] Ibid., p. 146.
[19] Ibid., p. 147.
[20] Drzewiecka, Jolanta A. and Thomas K. Nakayama. 'City Sites: Postmodern Urban Space and the Communication of Identity', *Southern Communication Journal* 64 (1998), 20–31 at 20.
[21] David Harvey, *The Condition of Postmodernity* (Oxford, 1990), p. 66.
[22] Maria Balshaw and Liam Kennedy, *Urban Space and Representation* (London, 2000), p. 6.
[23] Ibid.
[24] Ibid., p. 7.

Myles Chilton suggests that Tokyo is an important location in the formation of Japanese cultural identity, and that Murakami's work articulates the range of meanings that Tokyo might have for the Japanese in the present age of globalisation.[25] The narrative creates a divided spatiality; it is not just the protagonist that is layered, but the city. This layering is a trope of Murakami fiction, repeated in *The Wind-up Bird Chronicle* (1995), which Myles Chilton describes as an urge to render the everyday spaces of Tokyo 'fantastic'.[26] Tokyo is also the urban focus of this later novel, published ten years after *Hard-Boiled Wonderland*. The hidden urban spatiality of the cityscape allows Murakami to explore the cultural anxieties of the contemporary moment. Through this uncanny mapping of the city, Chilton suggests Murakami is trying to

> displace the material reality of Tokyo into controllable discursive realms … that reflects how, in the globalized present where Tokyo has grown to global-city strength, its multiplicity of powers – economic, political, social, cultural, and geographic – take over every aspect of literary production and reception, and re-negotiate the relationship between place and experience.[27]

Chilton adds that Murakami's blending of 'the real with unreal … articulates the sense of how global Tokyo estranges subjects from the city. The "real" city spaces are tied by the narrative to mundane city functions, the production of capital and the circulation of anonymity'.[28] The city becomes a site of exploration of the relationship of late capitalist urban space to the urban dweller, commenting on the social anxieties that have led to the growth of the hikikomori phenomenon. This is also true of *Hard-Boiled Wonderland and The End of The World*. Watashi is so estranged from his city, so isolated, so socially withdrawn that he does not recognise the city that he explores. The underground tunnels open up an uncanny space that is at once fantastic and unexplainable. The city and his contemporary moment seem to isolate him further, pushing him to retreat further into the aptly entitled 'End of the World'. Susan Napier contends that *Hard-Boiled Wonderland and The End of The World* represents Tokyo as "a bleak and alienating city, a world based on mindless consumption of products that range from Italian food to data information".[29]

Murakami's Tokyo becomes what Fredric Jameson would categorise as 'high-tech paranoia'. The novel is filled with 'labyrinthine conspiracies of

---

[25]   Myles Chilton, 'Realist Magic and the Invented Tokyos of Murakami Haruki and Yoshimoto Banana', *Journal of Narrative Theory* 39 (2009), 391–495 at 393.

[26]   Ibid., p. 392.

[27]   Ibid., p. 393.

[28]   Ibid., p. 398.

[29]   Napier, *The Fantastic*, pp. 211–12.

autonomous but deadly interlocking and competing information agencies in a complexity often beyond the capacity of the normal reading mind'.[30] In true postmodern style, it refuses to be categorised neatly, and contains parodies and pastiche from hard-boiled detective fiction, neo-noir, sci-fi, cyberpunk, and fantasy, to name a few. Jameson suggests that 'high-tech paranoia' has been 'crystallized' in what he calls 'a new type of science fiction, called cyperpunk, which is fully as much an expression of transnational corporate realities as it is of global paranoia itself'.[31] Stephen Snyder explains that Murakami's novel 'attempts to give utterance to the dilemmas of his times and imagine a coping mechanism to deal with this particular brand of paranoia'.[32] Snyder suggests that it is 'conceivable' to understand the 'walled, amnesia stricken community … as a metaphor for a Japan that hesitates to come to terms with its past or actively define a global role for its future' – a metaphor for Jameson's postmodern condition in Japan.[33]

Hard-Boiled Wonderland

The formal I or 'watashi' section of the novel is set in a futuristic Tokyo, what Steffan Hantke calls 'neo-noir'.[34] The watashi, or protagonist, is a divorced, isolated individual who works for the 'system' as a 'calcutec': a data shuffler. Information is the commodity in this post-industrial future, and two competing forces, the System and the Factory, are vying for control. Watashi works for the system, which was originally a private conglomerate, but it now has quasi-governmental status. The Factory was seen as the other, as the opposite of the System, very little being known about it; it was referred to as 'data mafia', but watashi comes to realise that everything has been monopolised: 'The System monopolizes everything under the info sun, the Factory monopolizes everything in the shadows. They don't know the meaning of competition. What ever happened to free enterprise?'[35] Information has become a very important

---

[30]   Fredric Jameson, *Postmodernism, or, The Cultural Logic of Late Capitalism* (Durham, NC, 1991), p. 38.

[31]   Ibid.

[32]   Stephen Snyder, 'Two Murakamis and Marcel Proust: Memory as Form in Contemporary Japanese Fiction', in *In Pursuit of Contemporary East Asian Culture*, ed. Xiaoping Tang and Stephen Snyder (Boulder, CO, 1996), pp. 69–83 at 73.

[33]   Ibid., p. 75.

[34]   Steffan Hantke 'Postmodernism and Genre Fiction as Deferred Action: Haruki Murakami and the Noir Tradition', *Critique: Studies in Contemporary Fiction* 49 (2007), 3–24 at 16.

[35]   Haruki Murakami, *Hard-boiled Wonderland and The End of The World* (London, 2003 [1985]), p. 137.

commodity, and watashi has to be careful of 'semiotecs' who work for the Factory and want to steal his data. The streets can become a dangerous place for those in the data industry. Watashi is careful to stay on public transport, as the semiotecs have 'fake taxis' to kidnap calcutecs after a job and steal their data.

The novel opens with watashi taking an Alice-in-Wonderland elevator ride through an office block in Tokyo, on the way to a meeting:

> The elevator continued its impossibly slow ascent. Or at least I imagined it was an ascent. There was no telling for sure: it was so slow that all sense of direction simply vanished. It could have been going down for all I knew, or maybe it wasn't moving at all. But let's assume it was going up. Merely a guess. Maybe I'd gone up twelve stories, then down three. Maybe I'd circled the globe. How would I know?[36]

Immediately, the world is decentred, as the laws of physics are challenged inside this elevator. This foreshadows the forthcoming journeys this watashi will take through the subterranean tunnels of Tokyo. The city that he knows, and has spent all his life in, is revealing new layers. Once inside the office, he goes through an opening into a closet into the unknown: 'What was going on here?', he asks. 'A closet in an office building with a river chasm at the bottom? And smack in the middle of Tokyo! The more I thought about it, the more disturbed I got.'[37] As he is 'plunged into darkness', watashi imitates Alice's fall into the rabbit hole once again, climbing down the stairs and walking alongside the underground river, in a space known as a 'media well'.[38] The purpose of this secret space is unknown to anyone other than the Professor and his grand-daughter and 'the construction crew was told it was a "media well", a communications cortex that would house fibre-optic networks later'.[39]

This is Tokyo, but not as watashi knows it. Both familiar and strange; Murakami is creating an uncertainty that resembles Freud's discussion of the uncanny in the figure of the Sandman 'by not letting us know … whether he is taking us into the real world or into a purely fantastic one of his own creation'.[40] There is a duality to the space here, not only because of the dual narratives, and dual perspectives, of the protagonist, but also because of this hidden and emerging Tokyo. Freud's uncanny and Todorov's fantastic combine in this space, as the boundaries between the layered worlds become more fluid

---

[36] Ibid., p. 1.
[37] Ibid., p. 21.
[38] Ibid.
[39] Ibid., p. 191.
[40] Sigmund Freud, *The Uncanny* (1919), http://web.mit.edu/allanmc/www/freud1.pdf (accessed 5 June 2019), p. 7.

and liminal. There is, as Julian Wolfreys points out, an 'endless juxtaposition of differing liminalities' in the uncanny city, and these competing pluralities create a defamiliarisation.[41] As watashi climbs down into this underground world, a new layer is added to Tokyo and to his ability to experience his city. He describes this underground cavern as an 'abyss'. There is a river with a swift current flowing through the space, which branches off into tunnels, each tunnel a 'fissure' or a 'black hole'. The Professor meets him and brings him through a waterfall into a cave with an iron door which leads to a laboratory.[42] The Professor has discovered a way to control sound, and this discombobulates watashi further: 'With the sound turned down, I had gotten confused by the sheer discrepancy between the non-sounds and the reality that would have produced them had they been audible.'[43] The familiar, the expected, is now strange, and becomes as Wolfreys describes Venice in the film *Don't Look Now*: 'neither wholly solid nor liquid, but a precarious amalgam', because the 'identity of place is transmogrified' by aural and visual defamilarisation.[44] Watashi's Tokyo, his home, his urban space, has become uncanny to him. It is, like Wolfreys's Venice,

> an abyss in which the iterability of the self-same only serves as a reminder that nothing is the same, and that each and every street is wholly other, in which one comes to find oneself adrift, without bearings, lost … nothing is to be found, nothing known, and anxiety twinned with obsession is exponentially generated in the face of the uncanny persistence of resistance to any epistemological mode that will comfort or make familiar.[45]

Watashi is unable to get his bearings, and when he is brought into the laboratory he is once again faced with a place both familiar and strange. The laboratory is exactly the same as the first office he was brought to in the building: 'The carpet, the walls, the lighting, everything was the same. On the coffee table in front of the sofa was an identical smoking set, on the desk an identical appointment book and an identical scattering of paperclips. Had I been led around in a circle back to the same room? Maybe in fact I had; maybe in fact I hadn't.'[46] It is the uncanny doppelganger, unsettling watashi, and making him

---

[41] Julian Wolfreys, 'The Urban Uncanny: The City, the Subject and Ghostly Modernity', in *Uncanny Modernity: Cultural Theories, Modern Anxieties*, ed. Jo Collins and John Jervis (London, 2008), pp. 168–80 at 168.
[42] Murakami, *Hard-boiled Wonderland*, pp. 23–5.
[43] Ibid., p. 25.
[44] Wolfreys, 'The Urban Uncanny', p. 168.
[45] Ibid, p. 170.
[46] Murakami, *Hard-boiled Wonderland*, p. 26.

question what he has believed to be real. Tokyo has become the postmodern metropolis as discussed by Maria Beville: a decentred, labyrinthine, discontinuous urban site that thrives on tension between order and chaos, presence and absence, reason and imagination.[47] This space, this layer, needs to be mapped, as it is a site of resistance to the order, or to the system that watashi works for; it needs Jameson's cognitive mapping. This space does not conform to traditional mapping; it is as Kevin Lynch (quoted in Jameson) describes, a space of 'urban alienation' that is 'directly proportional to the mental unmappability of local cityscapes'.[48] The chaos of this uncanny space decentres watashi, making him feel ill at ease in the urban space. The geography does not compute; he is unable to place himself either in this laboratory or in the tunnels, unmapped as they have been to him.

This unknowability and plurality of the city feeds into the hard-boiled detective style of the novel.[49] Watashi has discovered a hidden and dangerous element to his city that hints at Murakami's homage to Raymond Chandler.[50] Matthew Strecher calls this 'sinister characterisation of the city as a beautiful shell, teeming with evil and danger' a 'defining characteristic' of the hard-boiled genre.[51] Strecher adds that this style is suited to exploring those cultural anxieties about the city and social structures where the 'allure of the urban landscape is replaced by a dark, pervasive sense of danger' in postmodern, late capitalist society. Like watashi, the system has stripped 'the individual of his identity', and replaced it 'with an artificial, externally constructed indemnity designed for optimum state control'.[52]

INKlings

Adding to the Gothic and supernatural feeling of this subterranean space are the strange INKlings.[53] These unseen creatures lurk and live in the shadows of this underground realm and feed on sewage and human flesh, their tunnel

---

[47]   Maria Beville, 'Zones of Uncanny Spectrality: The City in Postmodern Literature', *English Studies* 94 (2013), 603–17 at 604.

[48]   Fredric Jameson, 'Cognitive Mapping', in *Marxism and the Interpretation of Culture*, ed. C. Nelson and L. Grossberg (Champaigne, IL, 1990), pp. 347–60 at 351.

[49]   For more on this, see Hantke, 'Postmodernism and Genre Fiction'.

[50]   Murakami has translated many of Raymond Chandler's novels into Japanese, and the hard-boiled detective trope features in many of his own.

[51]   Matthew Strecher, *Dances with Sheep: The Quest for Identity in the Fiction of Murakami Haruki* (Ann Arbor, MI, 2002), p. 41.

[52]   Ibid.

[53]   For research into the name INKling, its links with the writer's circle, which included fantasy writers such as J. R. R. Tolkien and C. S. Lewis, its ties to the *Alice in Wonderland* references, and the postmodern hypertextuality of the novel, see

network extending to the subway system of Tokyo. Stefan Hankte describes them as 'nightmare creatures out of horror or fantasy fiction, explicable only in reference to the supernatural'.[54] In true Todorovian fashion, these unseen creatures can be 'sensed' by watashi as he travels through the underground tunnels and they move around or near him. He can smell their presence. They become what Todorov describes as the fantastic: 'that hesitation experienced by a person who knows only the laws of nature, confronting the supernatural event'.[55] Watashi has neither 'total faith or total incredulity', but a sustaining hesitation that maintains the fantastic nature of these creatures.[56] His hesitation stems from his postmodern hikikomori, the acceptance that his city will always be unknowable, hidden, defamiliarised.

Watashi learns from the system's henchman, Junior, that the Government are fully aware of these creatures living underground in Tokyo, but will not do anything about it or warn people: 'It'd upset too many people … any trouble and they crawl up at night and drag people under. Japan would be upside-down.'[57] The city is kept from chaos through the systematic estrangement of the urban dweller from the actuality of the urban space. The issue of the INKlings will not be acknowledged and as watashi travels through the underground with the Professor's grand-daughter he is warned not to look at the monsters: 'You must never, ever, look at an INKling, if you set eyes on an INKling, you'll never look away.'[58] Once seen, they can never be unseen, their existence denied or ignored. Those who encounter the INKlings have the choice to acknowledge them. These monsters play with the nature of watashi's reality; they highlight how the contemporary city dweller can become unsettled and alienated by their city. Watashi is not only cognitively unmapped by the city, but also physically unsettled by its supernatural elements lurking below the streets: 'INKling voices. More like a ringing in my ears, actually. Cutting through the drill bits of high-pitched sound, like the humming of insects gone wild, the sound careened off the walls and screwed into my eardrums.'[59] Their unseen qualities just add to the terror as they slip between Todorov's uncanny and marvellous, never committing to either, thereby remaining fantastic.

Judith Caesar, 'Murakami, the Inklings, and the Uses of Fantasy', *Critique: Studies in Contemporary Fiction* 52 (2011), 41–54.

[54] Hantke, 'Postmodernism and Genre Fiction', p. 18.

[55] Todorov, *The Fantastic*, p. 25.

[56] Ibid., p. 31.

[57] Murakami, *Hard-Boiled Wonderland*, p. 128.

[58] Ibid., p. 304.

[59] Ibid., p. 303.

Typical of urban fantasy, these monsters fit with Stefan Ekman's research on the unseen in this genre. The INKlings live in a 'dark, labyrinthine, or subterranean setting' and are 'fantastical beings that hide out of sight'.[60] These characteristics are also emblematic of Gothic horror, as Ekman explains: 'The prominent Gothic component of urban fantasy thus emphasizes the thematic concern with the Unseen, by creating a milieu dominated by concealment, obscurity, and places where things can hide.'[61] Gothic literature has long been known as a genre that addresses the hidden concerns or fears of the time, and watashi becomes aware of these INKlings that haunt the tunnels of Tokyo as he uncovers the hidden corruption of the system.[62] As Strecher points out, 'This portrayal of the System/State as all-powerful, omniscient, and danger-ous, is typical of Murakami's literature, but more importantly for the formula, it locates an evil presence throughout the urban landscape of Tokyo.'[63] The INKlings hide behind the façade of the city, suggesting the danger that lurks under the surface of this late-capitalist system.

End of the World

It's a peaceful world. Your own world, a world of your own makin'. You can be your self there. You've got everythin' there. And at the same time, there is nothin' ... it's your consciousness that's created it.[64]

The protagonist of the novel comes to realise that experiments were conducted on his brain when he became a calcutec. The system put him 'on ice for two weeks to conduct comprehensive tests on my brainwaves, from which was extracted the epicentre of encephalographic activity, the "core" of my con-sciousness'.[65] They named this re-inputted data 'End of the World', and his 'conscious mind' was 'completely restructured'. 'First there was the overall chaos of my conscious mind, then inside that, a distinct plum pit of condensed chaos as the centre.'[66] As a result, a subconscious world was created in his mind, and because of a fault with the experiment his consciousness will move to that world. The Professor, who hired him at the start of the novel, is also the

---

[60]   Stefan Ekman, 'Urban Fantasy: A Literature of the Unseen', *Journal of the Fantastic in the Arts* 27 (2016), 452–69 at 463.

[61]   Ibid., p. 464.

[62]   See Jerrold E. Hogle, 'Introduction', in *The Cambridge Companion to Gothic Fiction*, ed. idem (Cambridge, 2002); Botting, *Gothic*.

[63]   Strecher, *Dances with Sheep*, p. 38.

[64]   Murakami, *Hard-Boiled Wonderland*, p. 286.

[65]   Ibid., p. 113.

[66]   Ibid.

one responsible for the experiment. This new subconscious world is created from memory and experience in the real world.

The End of the World narrative uses the informal 'I' in Japanese, 'boku', a more private 'I' than the formal, public-facade 'watashi' of the Hard-Boiled Wonderland section. This world is a walled town containing hills, forests, canals, and a central urban space around a clock tower that does not tell the time. Jay Rubin notes it is 'like a post-nuclear (or perhaps simply post-war) world with ruined reminders of a past that cannot quite be remembered'.[67] Here the observant reader is rewarded, as references from the other world are repeated and appear in different and uncanny forms. As boku notes, 'Everything here is a part of me – the Wall and Gate and Woods and River and Pool. It is all my self'.[68] The book actually includes a map of the walled town, described by Judith Caesar as being 'like a human brain, with a river bisecting the two hemispheres and the wall around the town and its environs representing a skull'.[69] This uncanny visual mapping offers a reminder of the plurality of the world Murakami has created. Like the Tokyo of watashi's conscious world, the 'End of the World' town becomes what Beville would call 'a ghostly locus of the uncanny: decentred, fragmented and defined by … the simulacra of signs that swarm our field of perception'.[70]

The world of the narrator's subconscious is constructed through images from the actual world, which implies that his whole existence will be based on a simulation of real life:

> The food here is different than elsewhere. We use only a few basic ingredients. What resembles meat is not. What resembles eggs is not. What resembles coffee only resembles coffee. Everything is made in the image of something.[71]

Boku is left with no option but to live within this representation, fabricated from his own ideas combined with images which have been stolen from his subconscious, selected by the system, and edited together by the Professor. His subconscious uses this amalgam to create an entirely new world within which he will be forced to live for eternity when his real life comes to an end. His actual, real-world life is ending because of the dominance of his imagined world, which is growing and strengthening. This subconscious world has managed to involve boku to such an extent that he adds reproductions of his

---

[67] Rubin, *Haruki Murakami*, p. 122.
[68] Murakami, *Hard-Boiled Wonderland*, p. 369.
[69] Caesar, 'Murakami', p. 44.
[70] Beville, 'Zones of Uncanny Spectrality', p. 616.
[71] Murakami, *Hard-Boiled Wonderland*, p. 224.

own view of the world in order to make the new 'world' a direct representation of the old. It becomes a Baudrillardian simulacrum. For Baudrillard, it is the image, the simulation of the real, and the hyperreal that are the most important aspects of the postmodern experience. In *Simulations*, Baudrillard's most explicit theorisation of the term 'hyperreality', he talks about 'the four successive phases of the image'. These phases relate to the sign's or image's distancing from the object of representation until the final phase when it bears no relation to any reality whatever: it is its own pure simulacrum.[72] This final stage represents the world of the protagonist's subconscious, a pure simulacrum, a creation which Strecher describes as a world constructed through 'different modes of consciousness'.[73]

However, the town is not a mirror image of Tokyo, but also not an 'Other' to the cityscape. It is an uncanny doppelganger: different, strange, but containing so many of the same references. The Professor tells him, 'Everythin' that's in this world here and now is missin' from that world. There's no time, no life, no death. No values in any strict sense. No self. In that world of yours, people's selves are externalized into beasts'.[74] The song *Danny Boy*, unicorns, skulls, paper clips, digging holes, librarians all feature in both narratives. It becomes what Freud would call 'an involuntary return to the same situation'.[75] Boku is subconsciously taking references from his life and work in Tokyo to use here in the Town, and as Freud points out, this also results in an expansion of this uncanny feeling:

> the same feeling of helplessness and of something uncanny ... it is only this factor of involuntary repetition which surrounds with an uncanny atmosphere what would otherwise be innocent enough, and forces upon us the idea of something fateful and inescapable where otherwise we should have spoken of 'chance' only.[76]

The protagonist, the boku, of the End of the World section is a newcomer to this town. He explains that he arrived in spring and it is now autumn, but the walled town is still being discovered and revealed to him. Boku decides to make a map of the End of the World, because even from the top of the Western Hill he can 'gain only the most general sense of the Town'.[77] There are also parts of this town that are unknown and dangerous to him. The Gatekeeper tells him

---

72 Jean Baudrillard, *Simulations* (New York, 1983), p. 11.
73 Strecher, *Dances with Sheep*, p. 39.
74 Murakami, *Hard-Boiled Wonderland*, p. 270.
75 Freud, *The Uncanny*, p. 11.
76 Ibid.
77 Murakami, *Hard-Boiled Wonderland*, p. 117.

not to venture far from inhabited areas and to be careful of the wall that sur-rounds the town: 'the Wall shuts the Town in. It is impenetrable and it encloses it irrevocably. The Wall sees everything that transpires within,' he warns.[78] As in the Hard-Boiled Wonderland section, there are secrets in this urban space. Even as boku tries to map it, he must come to realise that this place is his core consciousness, but how much is his? And how much has been interfered with by the experiments of the System and the Professor? It is a mapping of his cognitive space, but limited in space, unlike the never-ending layers appearing in the Tokyo of his real life.

The beasts

Strange creatures also inhabit the Town, but on this occasion they roam the cobbled streets. The beasts, which have the skull of a unicorn and develop a golden coat in autumn, are another fantastic element that create a Todorovian hesitation for boku. The beasts create an uncanny link between the conscious and subconscious worlds. Described as having a 'single horn protruding from the middle of their forehead', the beasts are a reminder of the gift of the uni-corn skull that watashi received from the Professor in the Hard-Boiled section of the novel.[79] The beasts are allowed to roam through the town during the day, and each evening the Gatekeeper calls them with three short notes on a horn back to their enclosure outside the walls.[80]

As they wander through the Town, the unicorns absorb the minds of the people. As critic Fuminobu Murakami explains, 'they then ferry them to the outside world where they die in the winter with the residue of people's selves inside them'.[81] These beasts facilitate the complete social withdrawal of the residents, allowing them to isolate themselves from meaningful interaction, extremes of emotion and even memory. When boku's shadow realises boku is the dreamreader, he tells him that the beasts die because of 'the weight of self forced upon them by the Town'.[82] When they die their skulls are buried for one year, before they are brought to the library. There they are given to the dreamreader where the shadow explains that the dreamreader's hands 'release the last glimmers of mind into the air ... where it diffuses and dissipates'.[83] Each new resident of the town is made a dreamreader, until their shadow dies.

[78] Ibid., p. 146.
[79] Ibid., p. 13.
[80] Ibid., p. 14.
[81] Fuminobu Murakami, *Postmodern, Feminist and Postcolonial Currents in Contem-porary Japanese Culture* (London, 2005), p. 27.
[82] Murakami, *Hard-Boiled Wonderland*, p. 335.
[83] Ibid., p. 336.

When their shadow dies, they are unable to read the dreams of the Town any more. Each town dweller submits their self to the creatures, and allows the weight of contemporary living to be lifted from them.

As watashi's existence comes to an end in the Hard-Boiled Wonderland section, the unicorn skull he received begins to glow with supernatural light, just as the skulls in the town glow for the dreamreader. It produces a light that 'no manmade energy source could produce', and the warmth and heat emanating from the skull seem 'purposeful' to watashi: 'An attempt to convey a signal, to offer a touchstone between the world I would enter and the world I was leaving … there was nothing to fear'.[84] These creatures play with the boundaries between the worlds, and as Rebecca Suter points out, create more Todorovian fantastical suspension.[85]

Casting off his shadow

In order to enter the town, boku had to cast off his shadow, which Chiyoko Kawakami describes as 'the last residue of watashi's consciousness'.[86] The Gatekeeper severs the shadow from boku as he enters the walls of the town. His shadow must stay outside the wall, and becomes weaker without boku. As Kawakami points out, it is the Gatekeeper who prevents boku's shadow from entering the town and who ensures that boku loses his last sense of self: 'Severing it from boku's physical body, he confines it in the basement of his hut to let it die. He then attempts to eradicate the concept of the self that lingers within boku in an ambiguous way.'[87] In order to live in this town, boku must leave behind not only his shadow, but music, memory, emotion; all of the things that make up his self. He must assimilate to become part of this 'utopian' urban space. Here he is guided by another, older man, the Colonel. As boku tries to recall half remembered memories, he is fearful of losing his mind, but the Colonel tells him to surrender to the loss: 'You are fearful now of losing your mind, as I once feared myself. Let me say, however, that to relinquish your self carries no shame … . Lay down your mind and peace will come.'[88] Just as in the Hard-Boiled Wonderland section, the protagonist is searching for identity in an unreliable world. The Professor there has already told him that the mind and identity are the same: 'And what is identity? The cognitive system arising from the aggregate memories of [an] individual's past experiences. The

[84] Ibid., p. 372.
[85] Suter, 'Critical Engagement', p. 70.
[86] Chiyoko Kawakami, 'The Unfinished Cartography: Murakami Haruki and the Postmodern Cognitive Map', *Monumenta Nipponica* 57 (2002), 309–37 at 328.
[87] Ibid.
[88] Murakami, *Hard-Boiled Wonderland*, p. 318.

layman's word for this is the mind.'[89] This is where the protagonist now resides. If he 'relinquishes' his mind he can live a peaceful life, without ever knowing the self.

Throughout the End of the World section, the shadow tries to convince boku that he must find a way of escaping. It is for this reason that the shadow encourages him to map the landscape inside the wall. He tells boku, 'Maybe you can't die here, but you will not be living. You will merely exist.'[90] He explains that without love, without the full expanse of feeling, boku can never really live in this town:

> You tell me there is no fighting or hatred or desire in the Town. That is a beautiful dream, and I do want your happiness. But the absence of fighting or hatred or desire also means the opposites do not exist either. No joy, no communion, no love. Only where there is disillusionment and depression and sorrow does happiness arise; without the despair of loss, there is no hope.[91]

Relinquishing the mind, and choosing to live here as an isolated being, without a shadow or consciousness, means that boku can create a limited, controlled life. The wall will keep out any of the concerns of contemporary Tokyo, or the semiotecs, or the INKlings. However, it also means that he will forgo music, memory, love, emotion. He will be incomplete, as his shadow explains.

The shadow's wish for boku to have a complete life adds another doppelganger to the narrative. The double here is interesting from a Freudian perspective, as an insurance against death. In his discussion of Hoffman and the uncanny, Freud suggests through doubling or dividing, 'the self becomes confounded, or the foreign self is substituted for his own',[92] which is the case for the protagonist of Murakami's novel. He is interchanging the self, switching places with his internal self. Freud goes on to say that the invention of doubling was a preservation against extinction, and boku's shadow fights for him to live. He tells boku that as long as he is 'sealed inside' himself he will be trapped in the walled town, 'existing' rather than living.[93] Boku refuses to follow his shadow into the pool, into the unknown, and chooses to stay in the hope that he 'may find the key to my own creation, and to its undoing'.[94] He believes that here, in this controlled and protected environment, he can begin to recall the

---

[89]   Ibid., p. 255.
[90]   Ibid., p. 399.
[91]   Ibid., p. 334.
[92]   Freud, *The Uncanny*, p. 9.
[93]   Murakami, *Hard-Boiled Wonderland*, p. 399.
[94]   Ibid.

emotions and memories of his life; but his shadow does not agree, and leaps into the unknown alone. As he watches his shadow leave, boku realises that he is 'alone at the furthest periphery of existence. Here the world expires and is still.'[95] At the same time, in his car in the Hard-Boiled Wonderland section, watashi sits parked beside a deserted warehouse at the waterfront, listening to Bob Dylan's *A Hard Rain's A-Gonna Fall*, waiting for his life to end. Boku is the only one who will avoid extinction in the walled town, but it will be an isolated life without the ability to experience. He feels a responsibility to this town, to its inhabitants:

> 'I have responsibilities,' I say. 'I cannot forsake the people and places and things I have created. I know I do you a terrible wrong. And yes, perhaps I wrong myself, too. But I must see out the consequences of my own doings. This is my world. The Wall is here to hold me in, the River flows through me, the smoke is me burning. I must know.'[96]

His desire to know, but in a controlled way, is in vain, but represents the difficulty faced by the postmodern individual in keeping up with the rapidly changing world around them.

Conclusion

Kawakami describes *Hard-Boiled Wonderland and the End of the World* as articulating 'the radically changing nature of society and the impossibility for individuals to grasp this change through "conflict and struggle." '[97] The alternating narrative between the worlds highlights the lack of stability the protagonist feels and the internal struggle he has as a result of the fragmented, unknowable nature of this society. These cultural anxieties lead him to create a secure, controlled environment inside his mind. The fragmentation and self-isolation stem from this fear for what Kawakami calls the 'individual's precarious social position in contemporary Japan.'[98] He moves from the real urban space of Tokyo, a layered urban space that represents the ambiguity he fears, to a digital-free isolated walled town inside his mind. The fragmented postmodern protagonist chooses a world that he can control, that he can make, and hopefully know. This walled town will keep contemporary society out, and allow the protagonist to retreat fully into his subconscious, and isolate himself into Ryu Murakami's hikikomori. Watashi's contemporary society has caused

---

95 Ibid., p. 400.
96 Murakami, *Hard-Boiled Wonderland*, p. 399.
97 Kawakami, 'Unfinished Cartography', p. 330.
98 Ibid.

him to feel disconnected from his city and even from his physical self, and the decentring effect of urban life has caused the protagonist to retreat further into his subconscious.

Susan Napier tells us that in *Hard-Boiled Wonderland* the 'protagonist feels that his responsibilities are to himself, not to a wider society or history'.[99] Wider society is an unknown for the protagonist. The streets of the city are filled with dangerous spectres, and roaming underneath are the INKlings. However, rather than become totally isolated in the city, the protagonist re-creates an urban space that is safe for him, filled with uncanny references from his life in the 'real' world. As Kawakami explains, there is a dilemma here. The individual longs for 'bonds with some structure/system on one hand', while also having a 'deep suspicion of its authenticity on the other'.[100] In the walled town, he can filter his world, he can control what he allows in and out. It is a technology-free space that does not contain the 'System' or the 'Factory', but the structure of urban life remains. The pluralisation of the city space, represented in the fragmented and layered narrative, highlights the difficulty the individual has in negotiating the complexity of the uncanny and postmodern city. As a result, the protagonist chooses to move from the multi-layered Tokyo to a simulacrum of the urban, because the opportunity to find a fixed perspective is lost, but the re-representation is still available.

Bibliography

Balshaw, Maria and Liam Kennedy, *Urban Space and Representation* (London, 2000)

Baudrillard, Jean, *Simulations* (New York, 1983)

Bentley, Nick, 'Postmodern , in *The Cambridge Companion to The City in Literature*, ed. Kevin R. McNamara (Cambridge, 2014), pp. 175–87

Beville, Maria, *Gothic-Postmodernism: Voicing the Terrors of Postmodernity* (Amsterdam, 2009)

——, 'Zones of Uncanny Spectrality: The City in Postmodern Literature', *English Studies* 94 (2013), 603–17

Botting, Fred, *Gothic*, 2nd edn (London, 2013)

Caesar, Judith, 'Murakami, the Inklings, and the Uses of Fantasy', *Critique: Studies in Contemporary Fiction* 52 (2011), 41–54

Chilton, Myles, 'Realist Magic and the Invented Tokyos of Murakami Haruki and Yoshimoto Banana', *Journal of Narrative Theory* 39 (2009), 391–415

Clute, John and John Grant (eds), *The Encyclopedia of Fantasy* (London, 1997)

Drzewiecka, Jolanta A. and Thomas K. Nakayama, 'City Sites: Postmodern Urban Space and the Communication of Identity', *Southern Communication Journal* 64 (1998), 20–31

---

[99] Napier, *The Fantastic*, p. 3.
[100] Kawakami, 'Unfinished Cartography', p. 331.

Ekman, Stefan, 'Urban Fantasy: A Literature of the Unseen', *Journal of the Fantastic in the Arts* 27 (2016), 452–69

Ellis, Toshiko, 'Literature: Questioning Modernism and Postmodernism in Japanese Literature', in *Japanese Encounters with Postmodernity*, ed. Yoshi Sugimoto and Johann P. Arnason (London, 1995), pp. 133–53.

Freud, Sigmund, *The Uncanny* (1919), http://web.mit.edu/allanmc/www/freud1.pdf

Hantke, Steffan, 'Postmodernism and Genre Fiction as Deferred Action: Haruki Murakami and the Noir Tradition', *Critique: Studies in Contemporary Fiction* 49 (2007), 3–24

Harvey, David, *The Condition of Postmodernity* (Oxford, 1990)

Hogle, Jerrold E., 'Introduction', in *The Cambridge Companion to Gothic Fiction*, ed. idem (Cambridge, 2002), pp.1–20

Jameson, Fredric, 'Cognitive Mapping', in *Marxism and the Interpretation of Culture*, ed. C. Nelson and L. Grossberg (Champaigne, IL, 1990), pp. 347–60

——, *Postmodernism, or, The Cultural Logic of Late Capitalism* (Durham, NC, 1991)

Kawakami, Chiyoko, 'The Unfinished Cartography: Murakami Haruki and the Postmodern Cognitive Map', *Monumenta Nipponica* 57 (2002), 309–37

Lyotard, Jean-François, *The Postmodern Condition: A Report on Knowledge* (Minneapolis, 1984)

Murakami, Fuminobu, *Postmodern, Feminist and Postcolonial Currents in Contemporary Japanese Culture* (London, 2005)

Murakami, Haruki, *Hard-Boiled Wonderland and The End of The World* (London, 2003 [1985])

Murakami, Ryu, 'Japan's Lost Generation', *Time*, Asian edn, 1 May 2000, p. 49; online: http://edition.cnn.com/ASIANOW/time/magazine/2000/0501/japan.essaymurakami.html

Napier, Susan J., *The Fantastic in Modern Japanese Literature: The Subversion of Modernity,* (London, 1995)

Rubin, Jay, *Haruki Murakami and the Music of Words* (London, 2005)

Snyder, Stephen, 'Two Murakamis and Marcel Proust: Memory as Form in Contemporary Japanese Fiction', in *In Pursuit of Contemporary East Asian Culture*, ed. Xiaoping Tang and Stephen Snyder (Boulder, CO, 1996), pp. 69–83

Strecher, Matthew, *Dances with Sheep: The Quest for Identity in the Fiction of Murakami Haruki.* (Ann Arbor, MI, 2002)

Suter, Rebecca, 'Critical Engagement through Fantasy in *Hard-Boiled Wonderland and The End of the World*', in *Haruki Murkami: Challenging Authors*, ed. Matthew C. Strecher and Paul Thomas (Rotterdam, 2016), pp. 59–71

Todorov, Tzvetan, *The Fantastic: A Structural Approach to a Literary Genre* (Ithaca, NY, 1975)

Wolfreys, Julian, 'The Urban Uncanny: The City, the Subject and Ghostly Modernity', in *Uncanny Modernity: Cultural Theories, Modern Anxieties*, ed. Jo Collins and John Jervis (London, 2008), pp.168–80

Yomota, Inuhiko, 'How to View the "Haruki Boom" ', in *A Wild Haruki Chase: Reading Murakami around the World*, ed. The Japan Foundation (Berkeley, CA, 2008), pp. 33–7.

Urban Spectrality

11

Ghosts on the Goldfields:
Ballarat as a Haunted City

DAVID WALDRON AND SHARN WALDRON

BALLARAT GHOST TOURS!!!

*Earning itself the reputation as Australia's most haunted city, Ballarat has
seen more than its share of blood, tears and misery – from the hazards of the
Gold Rush, the Eureka Stockade massacre, to the many souls who discovered
mortality in the town's 150 year history.*[1]

The history of Ballarat, situated at the heart of the goldfields of central Victoria, Australia, is closely tied to the colonial experience. As the site of the Eureka Stockade rebellion, its history is linked to the foundation myths of Australian democracy. It boasts both the Museum of Australian Democracy at Eureka (M.A.D.E), situated on one of the suspected sites of the rebels' stockade, and Australia's premier open air museum, the theme park of Sovereign Hill, which re-enacts life on the goldfields of the 1850s and 1860s. In Ballarat itself many of the businesses utilise symbols of the goldfields in their advertising and trademarks, as do many of the street names, festivals and public events. The Victorian architectural heritage is highly prized and showcased to the thousands of visiting tourists on Sturt and Lydiard Streets, and particularly those who come each year for Ballarat's Heritage Weekend festival held in May. Yet there is a dark side to this history. The prosperity of the gold

---

[1] Advertisement for one of Ballarat's many ghost tours, by the company Eerie Tours. See https://www.eerietours.com.au/ballara-ghost-tours (accessed 14 April 2018).

rush was built on the land of the Wathawurrung Aborigines who were displaced and marginalised, and suffered under the weight of colonial occupation and environmental devastation. Likewise, despite the prominence of stories surrounding those who became wealthy on the goldfields of central Victoria, many who came to Ballarat during the Victorian era found themselves displaced and living in extreme poverty, facing disease, hunger and vulnerability to crime, prostitution and dangerous working conditions.[2] It is these stories from the underbelly of Ballarat's heritage that form the fodder of a thriving dark tourist industry, expressed in popular ghost tours and supplemented by a rich heritage of ghost stories in folklore and popular culture. In the tension between these two discordant narratives Ballarat has become, in popular imagination, a haunted city.

It is the hiddenness of this darker, submerged history which has motivated our Jungian approach to this exploration of Ballarat's haunted heritage. Jungian analyst James Hollis argues that this sense of being 'haunted' and of ghostly experiences is fundamentally a psychic projection generated by the deeper suppressed workings of a person's psychological state within their broader social and cultural context. He argues that we are all influenced by the presence of invisible forms, spirits, parental influences, dreams and impulses as a reflection of the untold stories, synchronicities and complexes which permeate us in our lived social experience.[3] The framework he proposes indicates that a 'ghostly' experience, whether it is encountered as an event which comes upon a person unbidden or even as a deliberately perpetrated falsehood, is nevertheless an indicator of much deeper stirrings within the psyche of the individual in his or her cultural context. Ghosts, in whatever manifestation they are encountered, are a window into the internal workings of the society and the individual. As such, this window requires an exploration of what it

---

[2]   Ballarat's class divide in the Victorian era is perhaps best exemplified by the division between the prosperous Ballarat West, centred on the government and banking centres of Lydiard and Sturt Streets, and the poverty-stricken Ballarat East, centred on Eureka Street, site of the Eureka Stockade rebellion. This division is well covered in the literature from even the earliest histories of Ballarat and the goldfields. See, for example, William Bramwell Withers, *The History of Ballarat: From the First Pastoral Settlement to the Present Time* (Ballarat, 1887). The desperate experience of women on Ballarat's goldfields is well studied in Clare Wright, *The Forgotten Rebels of Eureka* (Melbourne, 2013), and Christina Twomey, ' "Without natural protectors": Responses to Wife Desertion in Gold-Rush Victoria', *Australian Historical Studies* 27 (1997), 22–46.

[3]   James Hollis, *Hauntings: Dispelling the Ghosts Who Run Our Lives* (Asheville, NC, 2013), p. 84.

reveals if we are to comprehend the dynamics that are at work in the emerging Victorian *Weltanschauung* on the goldfields.[4]

Carl Jung theorised that the more anxiety resides within the unconscious, the more it is likely to generate negative and traumatic impacts on the psyche. The unconscious aspect of a person's or community's psyche can only be utilised positively if there is a conscious recognition and expression of its existence, and an integration of this comprehended reality into functional operations, individually and corporately. For this to occur, the individual or community must acknowledge the content of the unconscious, encounter it, live it and suffer it. The power of the unconscious is problematic if it remains unacknowledged and silenced. The buried aspects of the psyche will find ways of signifying and making known their suppressed content; they will erupt into the conscious life in an unmediated and often violent way, unless integrated.[5]

Ballarat's haunted past is arguably the unconscious eruption of the hiddenness of its unnamed traumas. The strength of this haunted urban imagination is the direct counterpart to the obfuscation of the city's violent heritage. The romancing of the era, expunging from the narrative the displacement of black and white, the myriad infants buried in children's cemeteries, the brutal hardship of survival against the natural predations of heat, pollution and pestilence, all serve to suppress that which must find expression. It is in this context that the broader psychological context of ghosts and hauntings begins to become apparent. In the psyche of the individual and/or community, the phenomenon of ghosts and spectres is a kind of 'entanglement' between history and the unconscious which is given expression through experiences connected to unsettlement, displacement, transgression, repressed anxiety and loss of security. On behalf of the community, ghosts and paranormal activity enact the fear, the displacement, the dislocation and the unspoken.[6] As the ghost researcher John Sabol argues, 'What emerges (or materializes) is a re-assemblage of what still remains; the "ghost". The use of a creative experiential, entangled, and relational archaeology in the present can engage in those spaces in which the past intervenes today in the present "haunted sites".'[7]

---

4   Ibid., p. 85.
5   Carl Jung, 'Analytical Psychology and Weltanschauung', in *The Collected Works of C. G. Jung*, 2nd edn, vol. 8, ed. Herbert Read, Michael Fordham and Gerhard Adler (London, 1991), p. 367.
6   See Carl Jung, 'The Shadow', in *The Collected Works of C. G. Jung*, Bollingen series 20, vol. 9, ed. Herbert Read, Michael Fordham and Gerhard Adler (Princeton, NJ, 1979), part 2, pp. 8–10; idem, 'Archetypes and the Collective Unconscious', in ibid., part 1, pp. 3–41.
7   John Sabol, *Haunting Presences, Ruins, and Ghostly Entanglements: Excavations at the Edge of Performance* (Charleston, SC, 2015), p. 13.

This was particularly pertinent in colonial Australia, especially the south-east, where systemic efforts were being made to construct Australia in the image of 'the old country' – often specifically England, given the cultural prejudices held against Irish immigrants – through the introduction of flora and fauna and through the literal reconstruction of the landscape, as well as culturally, through borrowing traditions from the European immigrants' past to create a homage to what they had lost. At the same time, respect for and trust in spiritual authority was weak and distant across the sea, and the traditional custodian of spiritual verity, the Church, appeared similarly disempowered in an alien landscape.[8] The effects of physical displacement were echoed in the events overtaking the world in the spiritual sphere, with the development of science and its challenge to long-held truths that could no longer be relied upon. In its colonial Victorian context, this global phenomenon is perhaps best exemplified in the challenges posed to traditional Christian eschatology and the fate of the dead wrought by new religious movements originating in the Victorian goldfields, and the rise of spiritualism into the cultural mainstream during the late nineteenth century.[9]

In this light, ghosts, while often a subject for ridicule by sceptics, fulfil important functions that reflect social anxieties as manifested in the uncanny experiences of the supernatural. In 'The Uncanny', Freud discusses the means by which the psyche achieves disentanglement of the conscious from the unconscious, the modern from the primal. While his focus is primarily on the function of the psyche, his work also pertained to fundamental existential questions regarding one's sense of being in the world. He describes the uncanny through the use of the oppositional terms *heimlich* and *unheimlich*: *heimlich* referring to the sense of the comforting and familiar and, in contrast, *unheimlich* referring to the strange and inaccessible.[10] Thus, for Freud, uncanny experiences occur when the comforting and familiar become entangled with the strange, rendering them both familiar and alienated. In this experience there occurs a duality in which one has a sense of being in and out of place at the same time. In an experience of haunting, this dichotomy characterises

---

8   For further reading on colonial attempts to grapple with an unfamiliar and alien environment, see Eric C. Rolls, *They All Ran Wild: The Story of Pests on the Land in Australia* (Melbourne, 1969).

9   See Greg Young, 'Spiritualism in Nineteenth-Century Ballarat', in *Goldfields and the Gothic: A Hidden Tradition of Heritage and Folklore*, ed. David Waldron (Melbourne, 2016), pp. 3–18; Diana Carroll, 'Talking to the Dead: An Ethnographic Study of Contemporary Spiritualism in Australia' (PhD thesis, University of South Australia, 2013).

10   Sigmund Freud, 'The Uncanny', in *The Penguin Freud Library*, vol.14: *Art and Literature*, ed. Richard Wollheim (Harmondsworth, 1990), pp. 339–76 at 340.

precisely the moment when repressed tensions and anxieties of the past return to haunt the present.

By themselves, psychological approaches to the uncanny can fail to do justice to the rich complexities surrounding both experiences of haunting and the perpetuating of ghost stories in local folklore. As Bath and Newton argue in their research into popular beliefs on haunting and the supernatural in seventeenth-century England, functionalist perspectives have a tendency to write out the complexities of existing eschatological beliefs and the complex web of symbolism in which people both share stories and have phenomenological experiences of the supernatural.[11] In 1860s Ballarat, folklore surrounding ghost appearances tied to traumatic events in the community was already enmeshed with the fabric of popular culture, mass media and Gothic literature. Even today, Federation University's SMB campus, located in the former Ballarat gaol built in 1861, is often claimed by staff to be haunted.[12] A figure of a small child is reported to have been seen by security guards in the G building; a woman in a plain grey dress is claimed to inhabit the former women's work area (now C building) and the spirit of Dennis Murphy, executed in 1867 and still interred under the north-east corner of the library, is believed to haunt the premises.[13] Dennis Murphy's was one of the more contested executions in Ballarat's history, it being widely suspected that he was innocent, on account of his close friendship with the victim, his purported good character and the circumstantial nature of the evidence presented. Suspicions were raised that his conviction was a product more of anti-Irish sentiment than of robust policing.[14] Many of the others executed at the gaol had more notorious pasts, however, and have their own associated ghost stories, one such being the convicted rapist Jim Ashe. There is also a story told of a young serving girl on Bath Lane, in the higher floors of the TNG building on the corner of Lydiard and Sturt Streets, who committed suicide after being revealed as pregnant out of

[11] Jo Bath and John Newton, 'Sensible Proof of Spirits: Ghost Belief during the Later 17th Century', *Folklore* 117 (2006), 1–14.
[12] The information derives from personal communication with many staff members at the University, and especially staff in the library, under which are located isolation cells, kitchen and laundry of the former goal. These are technically inaccessible to the public, though students from the former mining school have indicated that access to the underground complex was possible via the old gaol's ventilation shaft, as was confirmed when the site was opened in May 2018 for digital VR filming and tours were conducted by the one of the authors at Ballarat's Heritage Weekend. This suggests many of the sounds heard in the library from underground may in fact have been made by local youths.
[13] Personal communication with staff and students at SMB campus Ballarat.
[14] *Melbourne Leader*, 20 April 1867, p. 2.

wedlock by her employer, her dreams of marrying out of poverty dashed by fate.[15] Likewise, the ghost story of Kitty Beatchley, murdered with a hatchet in public on Lydiard Street by her former husband, is still often told by students at Federation University's Camp Street campus (next to the alley in which the murder occurred).[16]

These stories saturated the newspaper reports of the day and were frequently recirculated through the print media. They were also very quickly shaped by the expectations of Gothic popular culture and detective fiction, and were subject to telling and retelling through ghost tours, local fiction and print media retrospectives. Today they are also retold through the popular *Dr Blake* television series, similarly featuring darker more unsavoury parts of Ballarat's past. The context surrounding haunting experiences and ghost stories was a complex pastiche of myths, popular culture and sources of societal anxiety, enmeshed in a mutually formative network of popular fiction, experience and folklore. The multi-cultural melting pot of colonial Victoria is extremely pertinent in this context.

Ballarat as a supernatural melting pot

Colonial Victoria was, from its very inception, an immigrant community. After the discovery of gold, people from across the British Empire and beyond came to central Victoria in the pursuit of gold. While gold mining remained the primary industry during the 1850s and 1860s, a wide variety of businesses developed to support the mining industry in terms of food, transport and housing. The chaotic nature of this rapidly developing community, the complexity of administering the colony and the exploitation and police corruption so common to the goldfields led to a number of conflicts, of which the Eureka Stockade rebellion is the most famous.[17] Yet there were also conflicts between ethnic communities, conflicts with the original Wathawurrung inhabitants and an enormous disparity between the rich and the poor, all of which was exacerbated by a lack of infrastructure in terms of water, healthcare and policing. By the 1870s, the industrial focus had shifted from alluvial to large-scale deep lead gold mining, and Ballarat rapidly began to industrialise with the advent of rail links to Melbourne and Geelong in 1866 and the establishment

---

[15] The story features prominently in the Eerie Tours Ballarat Ghost Tour. It is cited in numerous newspaper reports from the era. See, for example, *Geelong Advertiser*, 4 June 1896, p. 1.

[16] *Ballarat Star*, 17 October 1904, p. 2.

[17] As a critical event in the formation of Australian democracy, the Eureka Stockade rebellion is a key foundational myth in Australian history and is beyond the scope of this chapter. See John Lynch, *The Story of the Eureka Stockade* (Ballarat, 1999).

of telegraph lines. This led to another demographic shift, as the fragmented networks of alluvial miners and small businesses became absorbed into an industrial working class and globalised links with Britain and the United States. Despite this, the inherent ethnic diversity remained, with communities of Irish, Scandinavians, Americans, Chinese, Canadians and others still prominent in the local community.

The migrants who came to Australia in the 1850s and 1860s brought their own rich traditions of folklore and heritage with them, from places as diverse as the British Isles, France, China, the United States, Canada, Germany, Italy and the European colonies in Africa, Asia and Latin America. Many traces of these can be seen in the rich legacy of ghost stories, monstrous legends and the strange ritual marks left in old homesteads and blue stone work.[18] Some of the most pervasive examples of these lie within nineteenth-century Victoria's tradition of 'Baen-Sidhe', or Banshee, legends, tales of headless horsemen, and many other examples of prolific ghost stories.[19] There was also an established traditional understanding of the supernatural among the indigenous population that met the first settlers in Victoria, featuring the ubiquitous Bunyip, emu-footed witch women, hairy men and the serpent Mindai, plus a complex mélange of spirits and supernatural beings.[20]

Commonly, the experience of migration to the Australian colonies was etched in grief; the immigrants knew they might never see their home or loved ones again. As one plaintive convict song runs, 'Oh had I the wings of a turtle dove / Far over the seas I would fly / Flap-bang to the arms of my Polly love / And in her sweet presence I'd die.'[21] Moreover, immigrants were unlikely to receive the news of the death of a loved one until months after the event, if at all, given the time it took for letters to travel from Europe to Australia and the precarious nature of the voyage. Holding on to old beliefs and practices, in the face of ridicule from the intelligentsia and admonition from religious authorities, was a means by which people could hope to be reconciled to their grief

---

[18] George Ewart Evans, *The Pattern Under the Plough* (London, 1966), pp. 232–54.
[19] See Jill Blee, 'Banshees', in *Goldfields and the Gothic*, ed. Waldron, pp. 43–54. There are many examples in Australian print media of headless horseman stories, across rural Australia. Of these, arguably the most famous, with its own monument, is that of the Headless Horseman of Black Swamp. For a rich synopsis of the legend, see *The Land*, 21 December 1951, p. 22.
[20] See Ian Clark, 'Indigenous Folklore of the Northern Wathawurrung Peoples', in *Goldfields and the Gothic*, ed. Waldron, pp. 151–64.
[21] This iconic Australian folksong has numerous variations and iterations. See the National Library of Australia record, https://catalogue.nla.gov.au/Record/1399842 (accessed 18 June 2019).

and sense of loss against the background of this traumatic sense of separation from homeland and culture.

This deep, pervasive sense of loss was also clearly evident in the burgeoning spiritualist movement of the 1860s, through which grief-stricken people were able to reconcile themselves with the spirits of departed loved ones overseas through séances (most notably via James Curtis, Ballarat's most noted and published spiritualist).[22] Like nearby Castlemaine and Bendigo, Ballarat became known internationally as a 'Mecca' for spiritualism, and attracted numerous high-profile spiritualists, performing to packed audiences and in exclusive private sessions.[23] Likewise, at a more folkish level, rituals such as 'keening' by Irish migrants were a common feature of nineteenth-century Ballarat. Integrated with stories of encounters with Baen-sidhe or Banshees and other supernatural creatures, such practices became part of Ballarat's folk heritage. Reid and Mannigan, for example, recorded the ritual of a 'keening circle', held in the 1850s to commemorate the spirits of the dead and missing loved ones in the members' homeland of Ireland: 'Yesterday was devoted to Keening, that is, to deploring their fate, old Ireland, and their friends and relations. Seven or eight would get together in a little circle and keep up a dismal howling, without any distinct words that I could catch.'[24] This grief, loss and displacement was arguably a result of Britain wanting to divest itself of its unwanted 'dross' by sending it overseas. In this sense, the colonies represented a physical expression of the shadow of Britain; unconscious, unacknowledged, unintegrated and brutal. That brutality and displacement, psychologically speaking, had to find a target for its projection, and the loci of this projection were the Aborigines, the Chinese, the convicts, the environment.

The gold rush also attracted thousands of immigrants from Southern China, divided into the Si Yup and Macau factions. They too brought with them rituals, traditions and a rich legacy of ghost stories and beliefs. The stories themselves, and European fascination with their rituals, beliefs and medical practices, commonly featured in print media discussions and in local fiction. In the 1860s, Si Yi headman and Chinese interpreter Hugh Ah Coon was a focal point of these stories. He claimed encounters with spirits allowed him to locate the bodies of his murdered compatriots. On one occasion he claimed the spirit of a man murdered at Long Gully in nearby Creswick possessed the body of his cat, and wrote a message in Chinese characters on an ash-stained tray; on another, that the spirits of deceased members of the Chinese community

---

[22] See Young, *Spiritualism*, pp. 3–18
[23] Ibid.
[24] Richard Reid and Cheryl Morgan, '*A Decent Set of Girls*': *The Irish Famine Orphans of the Thomas Arbuthnot 1849–1850* (Yass, 1996), p. 39.

haunted Ballarat due to the absence of appropriate funeral facilities, which Ah Coon later campaigned to build into Ballarat Old Cemetery.[25]

The indigenous people of western Victoria had their own deeply entrenched folkloric traditions tied to landscape, culture and heritage, and these also profoundly shaped the cultural terrain of the goldfields of colonial Victoria. In indigenous culture, the landscape was richly and deeply imbued with meaning through stories, songs, artwork, rituals and the perceived occupation of the land by a rich tapestry of spiritual beings. It was also a landscape ordered by a vast array of folklore surrounding animals, plants, sacred sites and the deeds of great ancestors, which persists to the present. Yet the attempts at systematic destruction of this rich heritage were hardly acknowledged until very recently. It remained another hidden grief, unspoken and part of the shadow. As Philip Clarke comments,

> Spirit and ghost beliefs contain encoded knowledge about culture and landscape … Even in landscapes transformed by European settlement, contemporary Aboriginal people use knowledge of Dreaming Ancestors, ghosts and spirits, to help them to make sense of events occurring in their environment. The syncretism of tradition has led to the demarcation between indigenous and non-indigenous folklores in Australia becoming blurred.[26]

Thus the landscape of Victoria's goldfields was on the one hand marked by cultural vibrancy arising out of this cultural synergy and hopes for a better future, but on the other underscored by darkness and tragedy from occupation, poverty and loss. Beneath the stories of success, wealth and opportunity of the gold rush, typified by today's patriotic veneration of Eureka Stockade, the 'Golden Triangle' of Ballarat, Bendigo and Castlemaine was very much a haunted landscape. Within this spectrum, ghost stories, mysteries and monster stories proliferated in the vibrant cultural melting pot that was Victoria's goldfields, with tales drawn primarily from indigenous Australia, China, the British Isles, Europe and the Americas.

Much of the literature of ghost stories and hauntings has focused on the notion of trauma, because nineteenth-century Australia was a traumatic place to be. Convicts and their gaolers were removed from their homes and families; brutality was endemic to both the European population and the indigenous peoples they displaced. The goldfields were primitive places to live, with only the most rudimentary accommodation and sanitation. Disease and death rates were very high. Even if chosen as a way of life, it was a precarious and traumatic

---

[25] *Melbourne Leader*, 15 July 1871, p. 20.
[26] Philip A. Clarke, 'Indigenous Spirit and the Folklore of Settled Australia', *Folklore* 118 (2007), 141–61 at 141.

existence. Typhoid and diphtheria, caused by pollutants in the water and the lack of adequate sewerage facilities, claimed the lives of hundreds of Ballarat children each year. Medical facilities were dependent on charitable donations, and this made treatment extremely difficult, especially when combined with the difficulties inherent in regulating patent medicines and medical practitioners. As a result, many families were forced to rely on traditional folk remedies and Chinese herbalists. Crime was also rampant, and the lack of a trained police force until the late 1860s meant there was very little protection against those who preyed upon the weak. Troopers were renowned for their heavy-handed tactics. The lack of meaningful welfare and support networks similarly drove many women to precarious employment as prostitutes, opium den staff and ad hoc workers wherever they might be employed. In one case, frustration at working conditions and poor pay led to a strike by Ballarat's prostitutes in protest over being undercut by imported immigrant labour.[27] Workplace safety was close to non-existent, with a high incidence of mining accidents and 'black lung disease'. In some cases there was mass loss of life, such as the 1882 Creswick mining disaster in which twenty-three miners lost their lives and others their health and sanity, as they remained in a flooded mine for nearly two days in the pitch black after hitting an underground stream.[28] These experiences and the horrors they represented for those who 'fell through the cracks' or suffered accident and misfortune made ample fodder for ghost stories and hauntings: the newspapers were filled with stories of haunted mines and homes across the Ballarat goldfields.

It was in this melting pot of supernatural belief, obscured realities and deep grief that the ghost hoaxing or 'playing the ghost' arose. Enterprising men (and more rarely women) would venture out at night, dressed in outlandish costumes and phosphorescent paint, and scare people, especially women, and sometimes engage in petty crime. These characters became legend, and were opposed by enthusiastic vigilantes who went out to 'lay the ghost', leading to many cat-and-mouse games across Ballarat from the 1850s to the early 1900s. These were a frequent occurrence, and some of the more renowned individuals involved were given titles by the media and went to extraordinary efforts in their costuming and hoaxing:

[27] George Bennett, 'Prostitution in Victoria: The Role of Local Government: An Inner City Perspective', in *Sex Industry and Public Policy*, conference proceedings, May 1991, https://aic.gov.au/publications/proceedings/14 (accessed 20 July 2018).

[28] See Leonard Murton Williams and the New Australasian Commemoration Committee, *Diary of Disaster: The New Australasian Mine Tragedy, Creswick, 1882* (Creswick, 1982).

A ghost scare is again on in Ballarat, where a number of females have been frightened by the pranks of stupid jokers. At Brown Hill a man with a loaded fowling piece, while playing the part of a phantom, was seized by one of his neighbours, and during the struggle the gun went off, harmlessly. In Ballarat East on Tuesday night several Europeans and Chinese met an unearthly figure in Humffray Street, which gave forth a phosphorescent light, causing the Chinese to collapse in terror. At Redan a local 'push' is roaming after dark in glowing white garments, to the great alarm of women and children.[29]

In some more high-profile cases 'ghosts' took on names and personas to play cat-and-mouse games with police and vigilantes. Herbert Patrick McLennan, for example, led the people of Ballarat on chases for months before his eventual capture, causing the city council to offer a bounty of five pounds for information leading to the arrest of the 'Ballarat Ghost'.[30]

The goldfields of central Victoria thus formed a fertile ground for belief in ghosts, exorcisms and superstition. As an editorial by the *Argus* commented,

It is a noticeable symptom of the reactionary movement against the materialistic philosophy so much in vogue at the present day that ghosts, after having been objects of contempt to the educated and intelligent classes for some generations, are beginning to grow again into favour ... But outside the obscure regions tenanted by this creed, there are distinct signs that ghosts, which we thought were laughed out of existence by the robust common sense of the eighteenth century, are creeping back into the world, revisiting again the glimpses of the moon, in these rather sickly times of the moribund nineteenth century.[31]

---

[29] *Kyneton Observer*, 10 June 1899, p. 1.
[30] While a full discussion of the phenomenon of ghost hoaxing or 'playing the ghost' is beyond the scope of this chapter, it should be noted that there are unique qualities to the Ballarat experience, notwithstanding the widespread proliferation of the phenomenon throughout the British Empire. In contrast to the English perception of it being the work of dilettante noblemen playing pranks on the working class, in Australia the usual target of community outrage was working-class Irish larrikins eager to embarrass the anti-supernaturalist and enlightened values of the Protestant British intelligentsia. The proliferation of the 'ghost nuisance' was seen to be an outgrowth of widespread belief in ghosts that could be rectified by education. There was also a particular proliferation of ghost hoaxing centred on the goldfields region, which gave it a unique role. See David Waldron and Sharn Waldron, 'Playing the Ghost: Ghost Hoaxing and Supernaturalism in Late Nineteenth-Century Victoria, Australia', *Folklore* 127 (2016), 71–90.
[31] *The Argus*, 3 March 1884, pp. 8–9.

Ghost stories and supernatural mysteries proliferated so strongly in these tumultuous kinds of cultural and social environment because of their role in memorialising traumatic experiences via the medium of storytelling. They tied together place, events, people and experiences with sources of anxiety, grief and horror. This folklore gave a sense of authenticity to the popular Gothic literature of the period, yet this popular culture also shaped and defined the folklore and expectations of those engaged in ghostly experiences. This is very much apparent when one examines the lyrical style and appropriation of Gothic flourishes in newspaper coverage of haunting experiences, from local tales of Ballarat and Melbourne haunted houses to the ubiquitous tale of 'Fisher's ghost', repeated across the country, concerning an Englishman, Frederick Fisher who was murdered by his friend George Warrell. In the story, police are alerted by tales of the ghost of Fisher pointing to the location of his body to passers-by at midnight, leading to the arrest of the perpetrator and the final 'laying of the ghost'. This tale, familiar across the country and the subject of numerous theatrical adaptations, became a common theme in Australian folklore.[32] Likewise the tradition of campfire outback ghost stories, drawing on Australian storytelling traditions, became a common theme in the retelling of tragic tales of colonial Australia.[33]

The stories of Haunted Gully, with its multiple murders, of Ballarat's haunted Old Gaol and Camp Street Barracks and even of the ghost of Bath Lane all speak to these sites associated with trauma and horror, remembered through communal storytelling.[34] The emotional power of the stories also unsettles and disturbs, undermining Enlightenment notions of reason, predictability and the illusion of control.[35] Although it is distinctly uncomfortable for those of us raised in a scientific and 'enlightened' education system, these emotionally powerful stories remain deeply entrenched in our unconscious and are closely tied to our sense of place.[36]

The goldfields of central Victoria continued to thrive for decades, although the focus of the mining shifted from alluvial to deep lead. Much of the population established in the 1850s remained as the communities became more urban; concomitant and supportive industries flourished, including an ever more influential free press. By the 1890s, the ghost stories, along with routine

---

[32] See *Illawarra Mercury*, 24 December 1908, p. 4; *Wagga Wagga Advertiser*, 21 August 1875, p. 4.

[33] See *Cairns Post*, 21 February 1922, p. 3.

[34] For more on Haunted Gully, see *Melbourne Punch*, 8 December 1908, p. 21.

[35] See Avery Gordon, *Ghostly Matters: Haunting and the Sociological Imagination* (Minneapolis, 2008), pp. 7–8.

[36] See Michael Bell, 'The Ghosts of Place', *Theory and Society* 26 (1997), 813–36.

supernaturalist pranks and hoaxing, had become increasingly popular subjects in the print media and were being referred to as the 'ghost nuisance'.[37] While many of these discussions surrounding ghost beliefs and haunting treated these proliferating stories with scepticism and ridicule, the same papers often exhibited a fascination by the Gothic; they relished the skill of storytelling and the sensationalist aspects of these reports. The two primary Ballarat papers of the 1850s to 1870s, the conservative *Ballarat Courier* and the progressive *Ballarat Star*, frequently played against each other in reporting of these stories. The hauntings made excellent copy for papers eager to increase their readership. In many cases, the reports were clearly presented with an eye to humour at the expense of the gullible believers. One example featured the story of a headless hound, revealed to be a cat with its head trapped in a lobster tin.[38] Another told the story of a Castlemaine farmer who returned to town in hysterics, terrified after an encounter with a headless horsewoman. The article repeated the farmer's claim of how the ghost was seen 'with a fine body', and then revealed it to be a misidentification of an abandoned draper's dummy lying next to an old log.[39] What is common in these more frivolous reports is a disconnect between the story and darker events in the local community history. Divorced from trauma, they could be dismissed as mere flights of fancy and exaggerated Gothic imagination.

In contrast other reports, relating to murders, assaults and tragedy were treated in a more serious, though no less sensationalist manner, such as that of the ghost of a young man believed to be a Castlemaine murder victim.[40] In Ballarat, the story of the 'Burnt Bridge Ghost', where people were said to be so struck with fear upon entering the site of a brutal murder in nearby Lal Lal that they became paralysed, unable to move, was taken seriously as a real and deeply concerning series of events at the (by then abandoned) homestead.[41] While often these cases could be later reframed as Irish superstitions or the work of larrikinism, other stories, such as the aforementioned ghost story concerning Ballarat headman and Chinese interpreter Hugh Ah Coon, were taken quite seriously. Its complex, interwoven story of Chinese and English folklore tied to the apparent murder of a man in Creswick curiously omitted the

---

[37] Reference to the problems raised by hauntings and ghost hoaxing on the goldfields as the 'ghost nuisance' was well entrenched in print media reporting during the late nineteenth century. See, for example, *Telegraph and St Kilda, Prahran and South Yarra Guardian*, 1 July 1871, p. 3, and 3 August 1878, p. 3; *Bendigo Advertiser*, 4 August 1891, p. 2; *Sydney Evening News*, 2 August, 1898, p. 5; *Mercury*, 9 July 1904, p. 6.

[38] *Bendigo Advertiser*, 24 August 1861, p. 3.

[39] *Ballarat Star*, 27 September 1861, p. 3.

[40] *Singleton Argus and Upper Hunter General Advocate*, 20 January 1977, p. 4.

[41] See *Bendigo Advertiser*, 8 July 1871, p. 3; *The Country*, 11 July 1871, p. 2.

horrific fate of Ah Coon's adoptive daughter, Rachel Mon Sing, on account of which he was disgraced and imprisoned.[42] Such an account illustrated how the trauma of these early years of colonisation, displacement, brutality, dispossession and isolation, these frightening aspects of life consigned to the shadows, clamoured for expression through the symbolism of ghosting.

Ghosts were proving to be an uncomfortable anachronism in public discourse through the press and in the views of the Ballarat city council, the latter being eager to move past the perception of Ballarat as a lawless and uneducated site of gold fever. The problem was not just the embarrassment caused by enthusiastic working-class superstition. Despite the best efforts of educators and clergymen, the ghosts stubbornly refused to be exorcised. Ghosts are not just representative reminders of the past, or even of the place from which they originate; ghosts demand that something be addressed. They also serve as a place to preserve local ethnic identity via heritage, and in the goldfields they formed a site of resistance against British rule, especially for the Irish population, and thus proved difficult to simply educate away.[43]

George Ewart Evans argued that there was inherently a contradiction where people were born into a rich legacy of folklore as an important and deeply emotive part of their cultural heritage, yet also felt extremely awkward and dismissive of their own beliefs and customs as superstitious and irrational. This became exacerbated amongst those who aspired to join the middle class and intelligentsia of polite society, especially in the goldfields of Australia with its disconnect from Europe. Evans saw this pattern as characterising people who have been raised with a modern Enlightenment-based education system while also inheriting a culture with deeply entrenched beliefs in superstitions, ghost stories and legends. The experience of living in a culturally and intellectually contradictory world of science and supernaturalism fed a sense of cultural anxiety.[44] This was exacerbated in the immigrant population of colonial Ballarat, with its rich mix of rural working-class peoples from across Europe, Asia and the Americas who brought their rituals, folklore and beliefs with them. Given their huge awareness of distance from their homelands, these traditions also became a vehicle to maintain a connection with ancestry: a means of cultural preservation in the face of rapid industrialisation, geographical displacement, emergence from an impoverished rural background and British rule. The class struggle inherent to emergence from impoverished rural backgrounds across

---

[42]   *The Age*, 14 July 1871, p. 3.
[43]   See Blee, 'Banshees'.
[44]   Evans, *Pattern Under the Plough*, pp. 21–5.

the globe further sharpened this population's experience of these same processes and conditions.[45]

Similar issues, arising from dispossession through invasion and colonisation, affected indigenous Australians. The Aboriginal people formed a significant part of the goldfields population, and their own experiences, beliefs and folklore also played a role in the proliferation of belief in ghosts. This is particularly pertinent as regards stories which began to emerge in the 1870s of indigenous ghosts tied to stories of massacres and conflicts with the colonists. As Fred Cahir argues,

> The gold rushes were the precursor for 'a world turned upside down', not just for the immigrant colonists but for Aboriginal people as well. The gold rushes were not uniform or ordered events that can be categorized easily. Non-Indigenous commentators at the time of the rushes testify to the higgledy-piggledy nature of people's movements. Streams of people from socially and racially diverse backgrounds sojourned from one goldfield or gully to another'.[46]

Perhaps one of the most intriguing of these ghost stories was the 1870s' 'Harton Hills ghost', west of Ballarat, who, purporting to be an Aboriginal ghost from massacres of the past, haunted sites of conflict between the Gundjitmara people and settlers. The sightings of this ghost and its ties to the traumatic experiences of the Eumerella wars of western Victoria between colonists and the indigenous population quite terrified people, and led to claims in the local paper that it was, in fact, an example of Ngamadidj, or white spirits, rising from the bodies of slain Aboriginals. A local woodcutter by the name of Robert Downey was eventually discovered to be the perpetrator of the 'ghost' and severely beaten by vigilantes after he confessed. He claimed it was simply meant to be a harmless prank, yet the choice of sites and the enormous anxiety the story brought to local law enforcement and the public implied a far deeper significance to the Harton Hills ghost. Similarly, the region around Portland, west of Ballarat, was the site of a large number of ghost stories tied to events from the Eumerella wars. Reported in the local papers, they included the story of a haunted redgum tree where it was claimed settlers were murdered for their kidney fat, to be used in magical rituals by the Gundjitmara.[47]

---

[45] For more on this, see Ian Evans, 'The Wider Picture: Parallel Evidence in America and Australia', in *Physical Evidence for Ritual Acts, Sorcery and Witchcraft in Christian Britain: A Feeling for Magic*, ed. Ronald Hutton (Oxford, 2015), pp. 232–54.
[46] Fred Cahir, *Black Gold* (Canberra, 2012), p. 5.
[47] See *Australasian*, 17 September 1932, p. 1.

Making sense of ghosts

Public intellectual debate surrounding ghosts, hoaxes and hauntings proved to be extremely popular in the print media, Mechanics Institutes and public gatherings of nineteenth-century Victoria. The proliferation of the 'ghost nuisance', as it came to be called by the press, began increasingly to attract intellectual attention. In a public lecture held on 9 June 1860, Sir. Archibald Michie, later the agent general for the colony of Victoria, addressed a capacity crowd on the subjects of ghosts and the current rash of haunting and hoaxing that plagued central Victoria. He argued that a man

> may be wiser, he may have read physiology, he may have studied insanity and the various forms of delusion springing from morbid action of the brain, but he has lost forever the supernatural shudder, the terrifically delicious creeping of the hair, and the heart coming up into the mouth, attendant on his listening to, or reading of, for the first time, a good authentic, and by justices of peace attested, ghost story.[48]

From Michie's perspective, while the Enlightenment had disproved the existence of ghosts, the proliferation of the 'ghost nuisance' resulted from something still endemic to the human condition. He claimed that the experiences of 'ghost seeing' and 'ghost feeling' were 'uniquely the preserve of humanity', and that their return to prominence was an inevitable concomitant of the loss of connection to heritage and folklore, especially in a remote colony such as Victoria.[49] His lecture apparently struck a nerve, as it initiated a flurry of letters and editorials in the local papers and led to a series of regular seminars and public discussions on the subject. It also reflected a sense in which the populace of Ballarat and its surrounds were creating their own unique ghostly folklore synergistically out of the rapidly industrialising cultural melting pot of the goldfields.

The high public profile of these lectures and debates was both fuelled by and supported the rash of ghost sightings, hoaxes and séances in Ballarat (and indeed throughout central Victoria).[50] Underlying this intellectual discussion, however, was the proliferation and intermingling of beliefs and customs of

---

[48]   *The Argus*, 5 June 1860, p. 5.

[49]   Ibid.; and *Ballarat Star*, 23 November 1861, p. 2.

[50]   A cursory search through newspapers reveals many articles about ghosts, hauntings and exorcisms, as well as many lectures and discussions pertaining to spiritualism, séances and attempts to contact the dead. In Ballarat's case, much of this is chronicled in James Curtis, *Rustlings of a Golden City: Being a Record of Spiritualistic Experiences in Ballarat and Melbourne* (London, 1902). See also R. Lorimer, *Report of the Ballarat Psychological Association; Referring to a series of séances held*

immigrants who flooded to the goldfields in the 1850s, creating a uniquely vibrant cultural synthesis of beliefs, religious traditions and ideas. In this way, local folklore and superstition took on an additional function of reaffirming community identity in the face of substantial social change and threats to community cohesion wrought by immigration, industrialism and exposure to new cultures and traditions.

It is important to note that culturally specific beliefs in the spirit world form a profound link to homeland, community identity and connection to heritage.[51] Similarly, it is worth noting that folklore, heritage and tradition become a focal point of concern for a community precisely when extant traditions come under threat through social, cultural and economic transformation.[52] At the same time, those beliefs, traditions and symbols that were popularly associated with the past by these communities were romantically and nostalgically reconstructed through the veil of the anxieties of the present. Although in his approach to the 'ghost nuisance' Michie rejected the actual existence of ghosts, in accordance with the framework of scientific progress, his nostalgic longing for the folklore of haunting and ghost stories as part of the sublime experience of life and heritage particularly reflected these romantic themes. As a result, the rationalisation of supernatural belief into folklore appropriated the heritage of ghostly hauntings, yet also relegated them to the realm of safe and controlled nostalgic spaces, thus stripping them of their connection to trauma and injustice within a community. As the Ballarat community became more homogenised in the late nineteenth century through the establishment of mass education and industrialism, this pattern became more pronounced.

Bell has argued that

> [s]uch experience arises in part from the social relations of memory, and the memory of social relations. But the ghosts of place should not be reduced to mere memories, collective or individual. To do so would be to overlook the spirited and live quality of their presence, and their stubborn rootedness in particular places. Moreover, the ghosts of place are not only ghosts of the past; they can as well be of the present, and even the future. However we locate them temporally, the ghosts of place are always presences and as such

---

with *Mr Jesse Shepard, the celebrated musical and physical medium* (Ballarat, 1879), p. 2; *The Argus*, 23 July 1871, p. 2.

[51] For more on this, see Evans, *Pattern Under the Plough*; David Waldron and Christopher Reeve, *Shock! The Black Dog of Bungay: A Case Study in Local Folklore* (Hertfordshire, 2010); Diarmuid O'Giollan, *Locating Irish Folklore: Tradition, Modernity, Identity* (Cork, 2000).

[52] O'Giollan, *Locating Irish Folklore*, pp. 8–9.

appear to us as spirits of temporal transcendence, of connection between past and future.[53]

As suggested by this chapter, perhaps the key role of these haunting experiences is that they invest place with a sense of presence expressive of identity, values and emotional impact. Furthermore, these emotive dark stories of the past bypassed the nationalist and triumphalist stories of national identity tied to progress, economic growth and civilisation, but drew attention to the hidden and concealed traumatic experiences, events and tragedies that had occurred in the path of colonisation. Their emotive and subaltern presence challenges both the dominance of scientific rationality and the positive narrative of colonisation as the march of progress and civilisation. Importantly, they also invest the urban landscape with a sense of place, creating landmarks which bear a sense of connection and presence, forging powerful emotional links to these sites via storytelling and symbolic, supernatural representations.

Bibliography

Primary sources

Curtis, James, *Rustlings of a Golden City: Being a Record of Spiritualistic Experiences in Ballarat and Melbourne* (London, 1902)

Lorimer, R., *Report of the Ballarat Psychological Association; Referring to a series of séances held with Mr Jesse Shepard, the celebrated musical and physical medium* (Ballarat, 1879)

National Library of Australia, 'Botany Bay' (song), https://catalogue.nla.gov.au/Record/1399842

Withers, William Bramwell, *The History of Ballarat: From the First Pastoral Settlement to the Present Time* (Ballarat, 1887)

Newspapers

The Age
The Argus
The Australasian
The Avoca Mail
The Ballarat Courier
The Ballarat Star
The Bendigo Advertiser
The Clarence and Richmond Examiner and New England Advertiser
The Kilmore Free Press
The Land

---

[53] Bell, 'Ghost of Place', p. 816.

The Queanbeyan Age
Sydney Evening News
Telegraph and St Kilda, Prahran and South Yarra Guardian

Secondary sources

Bath, Jo and John Newton, 'Sensible Proof of Spirits: Ghost Belief during the Later 17th Century', *Folklore* 117 (2006), 1–14

Bell, Michael, 'The Ghosts of Place', *Theory and Society* 26 (1997), 813–36

Bennett, George, 'Prostitution in Victoria: The Role of Local Government: An Inner City Persepctive', in *Sex Industry and Public Policy*, conference proceedings, May 1991, https://aic.gov.au/publications/proceedings/14

Blee, Jill, 'Banshees', in *Goldfields and the Gothic*, ed. Waldron, pp. 43–54

Cahir, Fred, *Black Gold* (Canberra, 2012)

Carroll, Diana, 'Talking to the Dead: An Ethnographic Study of Contemporary Spiritualism in Australia' (PhD thesis, University of South Australia, 2013)

Clark, Ian, 'Indigenous Folklore of the Northern Wathawurrung peoples', in *Goldfields and the Gothic*, ed. Waldron, pp. 151–64

Clarke, Philip A., 'Indigenous Spirit and the Folklore of Settled Australia', *Folklore* 118 (2007), 141–61

Evans, George Ewart, *The Pattern Under the Plough* (London, 1966)

Evans, Ian, 'The Wider Picture: Parallel Evidence in America and Australia', in *Physical Evidence for Ritual Acts, Sorcery and Witchcraft in Christian Britain: A Feeling for Magic*, ed. Ronald Hutton (Oxford, 2015), pp. 232–54

Freud, Sigmund, 'The Uncanny', in *The Penguin Freud Library*, vol.14: *Art and Literature*, ed. Richard Wollheim (Harmondsworth, 1990), pp. 339–76

Gordon, Avery, *Ghostly Matters: Haunting and the Sociological Imagination* (Minneapolis, 2008)

Hollis, James, *Hauntings: Dispelling the Ghosts Who Run Our Lives* (Asheville, NC, 2013)

Jung, Carl, 'Analytical Psychology and Weltanschauung', in *The Collected Works of C. G. Jung* 2nd edn, vol. 8, ed. Herbert Read, Michael Fordham and Gerhard Adler (London, 1991), pp. 358–81

——, 'Archetypes and the Collective Unconscious', in *The Collected Works of C. G. Jung*, Bollingen series 20, vol. 9, part 1, ed. Herbert Read, Michael Fordham and Gerhard Adler (Princeton, NJ, 1980), pp. 3–41

——, 'The Shadow', in *The Collected Works of C. G. Jung*, Bollingen series 20, vol. 9, part 2, ed. Herbert Read, Michael Fordham and Gerhard Adler (Princeton, NJ, 1979), pp. 8–10

Lynch, John, *The Story of the Eureka Stockade* (Ballarat, 1999)

O'Giollain, Diarmuid, *Locating Irish Folklore: Tradition, Modernity, Identity* (Cork, 2000)

Reid, Richard, and Cheryl Morgan, *'A Decent Set of Girls': The Irish Famine Orphans of the Thomas Arbuthnot, 1849–1850* (Yass, 1996)

Rolls, Eric C., *They All Ran Wild: The Story of Pests on the Land in Australia* (Melbourne, 1969)

Sabol, John, *Haunting Presences, Ruins, and Ghostly Entanglements: Excavations at the Edge of Performance* (Charleston, SC, 2015)

Twomey, Christina, ' "Without natural protectors": Responses to Wife Desertion in Gold-Rush Victoria', *Australian Historical Studies* 27 (1997), 22–46

Waldron, David, *Goldfields and the Gothic: A Hidden Tradition of Heritage and Folklore* (Melbourne, 2016)

—— and Christopher Reeve, *Shock! The Black Dog of Bungay: A Case Study in Local Folklore* (Hertfordshire, 2010)

—— and Sharn Waldron, 'Playing the Ghost: Ghost Hoaxing and Supernaturalism in Late Nineteenth-Century Victoria, Australia', *Folklore* 127 (2016): 71–90

Williams, Leonard Murton, and the New Australasian Commemoration Committee, *Diary of Disaster: The New Australasian Mine Tragedy, Creswick, 1882* (Creswick, 1982)

Wright, Clare, *The Forgotten Rebels of Eureka* (Melbourne, 2013)

Young, Greg, 'Spiritualism in Nineteenth-Century Ballarat', in *Goldfields and the Gothic*, ed. Waldron, pp. 3–18

12

Spectral Mexico City

————◆◆◆————

MARÍA DEL PILAR BLANCO

A photograph haunts Mexico City across the nineteenth and twentieth centuries – a sepia image showing the corpse of Emperor Maximilian I of Mexico inside a semi-standing casket. By orders of Benito Juárez, the Habsburg emperor was executed by firing squad in the Cerro de las Campanas in Querétaro on 19 June 1867. The story of Maximilian and Juárez, of empire and republic, shapes the politics and culture of the mid-nineteenth century and, as I will argue in this chapter, gives a spectral edge to historical imaginings of the country's capital city in the twentieth century and beyond. The image of Maximilian's corpse, taken after the body had been embalmed a first time, shows him wearing false porcelain eyes, which as Arturo Aguilar Ochoa explains, were taken from a religious icon.[1] The photograph is jarring for a number of reasons. Pictures of the dead have been commonplace since the birth of photography, and yet they never cease to shock us. In the case of this particular photograph, a viewer might be taken aback by the uncanny and empty way in which Maximilian stares directly at us (a look, of course, that is rendered the more horrific by the knowledge that these are artificial, exogenous eyes), the way that he is standing up straight, or even, as Aguilar Ochoa intimates, how the deceased emperor, who was once photographed amongst opulent furnishings, is captured here in such bare surroundings. This image emerged and was circulated alongside other equally striking photos of Maximilian's bullet-torn shirt, waistcoat, and frock coat.

---

[1] Arturo Aguilar Ochoa, *La fotografía durante el imperio de Maximiliano* (Mexico City, 1995), p. 45.

Fig. 6. Photograph of Emperor Maximilian, by François Aubert (1867)

Images of the dead demand comparisons with visions of the pictured subject in life; they are, in this sense, intensely dialectical. This particular picture
is starkly opposed to other images of Maximilian surrounded by his court,
his family, and particularly his wife Charlotte. Aguilar Ochoa and others have
argued that the Second Empire in Mexico marks an especially auspicious
moment for photography in the country, as it was during this time that the
medium became commercialised and widespread. In an effort to make the

emperor and empress more palatable to the Mexican population, images of Maximilian and Charlotte and their court were reproduced and made available in a variety of formats, particularly in *cartes de visite*. The photograph of Maximilian's corpse makes a chilling counterpoint to such representations of the privileged and charmed life of monarchs. As Roland Barthes reflects in *Camera Lucida*, a corpse photograph 'certifies, so to speak, that the corpse is alive, as *corpse*: it is the living image of a dead thing'.[2] To this conundrum of our observation of a corpse photograph, he adds the following and now well-known argument:

> [B]y attesting that the object has been real, the photograph surreptitiously induces belief that it is alive, because of that delusion which makes us attribute to Reality an absolutely superior, somehow eternal value; but by shifting this reality to the past ('this-has-been'), the photograph suggests that it is already dead.[3]

As a final pose for the emperor whose life is represented in poses, the medium of the photograph lends the dead subject a rare form of life. The photographs of Maximilian's brief existence are all, in Barthes's conception, announcements of a 'this-has-been', all of which lead inevitably to that striking representation of the Habsburg's death that opens this chapter. While the photograph acts as a certification of the end of his life, and therefore can be taken to symbolise a resounding death of empire, its very existence continues to act as a reminder of the ongoing presence of things past. At a point in time in which the photographic image was fast becoming the most powerful conveyor of life as it happened in different points across the globe, the image of Maximilian's dead body has, of course, geopolitical implications. The image of the dead emperor standing in his casket serves as a modern-age allegory of the volatility of fortune in the context of a violent clash of cultures. More specifically, it is a visual marker of the constant and problematic contact, often violent, between local and foreign interests in Mexico's history since the beginning of the country's republican age.

From the nineteenth century into the present, photography works with writing – and eventually surpasses writing – as a most powerful medium through which to depict the urban, everyday dimensions of this history. As photography entered a stage of accelerated development during Maximilian's reign, its uses became diversified: according to Aguilar Ochoa, these ranged from images of the impressive list of people who worked in the imperial court, to a

---

[2]   Roland Barthes, *Camera Lucida: Reflections on Photography*, trans. Richard Howard (New York, 1999), pp. 78–9.

[3]   Ibid., p. 79.

photographic register of Mexico City's prostitutes.[4] Maximilian and Charlotte effectively cemented a cult of the image in the capital, which in turn reflected practices detailing the complex interaction of urbanism with foreign and local politics. As an empire of the image, Maximilian's time in Mexico inaugurates a particularly modern tension between efforts at preservation (monuments, photographs) and absence in the context of Mexico's urban environment. We can call this moment the entry of a new form of spectrality into Mexico City's everyday life. This chapter traces a cartography of sorts of Maximilian's spectral dimensions, in photographic and literary texts from his reign into the mid-twentieth century. How does Maximilian move across time and into the twentieth century, and why does he persist in this collective memory? How is the cartography of the city that he inaugurated remembered and dismembered across time?

Beginning with an exploration of the photographic legacy of Mexico's Second Empire, this chapter explores the literary afterlife of that period, in particular the novels *Las vueltas del tiempo* (written between 1945 and 1951, published in 1973) by Agustín Yáñez, and *Aura* (1962) by Carlos Fuentes. While critics have tended to overlook the first of these novels, the second stands as a paragon of the Latin American Gothic. The two novels were written at a moment in the twentieth century that saw a kind of boom in explorations of Mexico's national character, as well as of the legacies of the Revolution of 1910. One salient example of this is Octavio Paz's *El laberinto de la soledad* (1950). Books like *El laberinto* not only sought to make sense of what transpired during the revolution, but also explored the history leading up to an event that, as Paz notes, is a 'verdadera revelación de nuestro ser' ('a true revelation of our being').[5] In *El laberinto*, Paz traces the intellectual, political, and economic intimacy between Mexico and Europe. As novels that reflect on the urban in incisive though extremely different ways, Yáñez's and Fuentes's novels turn to the moment of Maximilian's Second Empire to contemplate the private and public dimensions of this difficult transnational relationship; they also write a Mexico City that is haunted by this history, even after the revolution's supposed opening of new beginnings.

Yáñez's and Fuentes's novels portray the capital city at mid-century by very different means: the first is a polyphonic novel set in a single day in October 1945 – the day of the funeral of the ex-president Plutarco Elías Calles (in power between 1924 and 1928), who led some of the biggest reforms in the country after the revolution. Yáñez stated in 1961 that his plan for this novel was to

---

produce 'una síntesis de nuestra historia. Más aún: la idea de la Historia como eterno retorno' ('a synthesis of our history. Furthermore, the idea of History as an eternal return').[6] Fuentes's novel is, by contrast, a claustrophobic one; using only second-person narration, it is the story of a young historian hired by an ancient woman to organise the papers of her deceased husband, a general in Maximilian's imperial army. While Yáñez's novel listens in on the thoughts and conversations of ten characters who, hailing from different social extractions, participate in Calles's funeral procession, Fuentes's is a tale of obsession, indelible memory and the loss of youth. Yáñez's novel belongs to the tradition of mid-twentieth century experimental realism, while Fuentes's is a fantastic narrative that freely uses supernatural elements. Despite these differences, and as I go on to show in this chapter, *Las vueltas del tiempo* and *Aura* are both haunted narratives that reveal a modern capital city where time is out of joint. Read together, the two novels reveal a cartography that tracks the persistence of the past in Mexico City's exteriors and interiors; they also outline the morbid erotics of the spectacle inaugurated in the Second Empire. The persistence of this network of political, erotic, and intellectual dynamics that emerges during Maximilian's reign are explored, one century on, in these fictions from the mid-twentieth century. The spectacle of death that the emperor's final photograph puts into place is reflected, in fascinating ways, in these narratives.

Maximilian's city

Maximilian's arrival in Mexico needs to be understood in terms of the political landscape of the country in the mid-nineteenth century. In the late 1850s, Mexico underwent a tense battle between liberals and conservatives. The Constitution of 1857 marked an important victory for liberalism, guaranteeing freedom of conscience and of speech, and a separation between church and state. The conservative government of Miguel Miramón (1859–60), opposed to the Constitution, then left the country immersed in debt. When Benito Juárez restored the Republic in 1860, he was forced to cancel debt payments to Mexico's most powerful foreign debtors: Spain, Britain, and France. On 31 October 1861, these three European countries signed a treaty in London forcing Mexico to pay back its debts as well as damages to French, British, and Spanish citizens who had lived and fought in the Central American country. 'The British', Alfred and Kathryn Hanna explain, 'were determined not to involve themselves in the internal affairs of Mexico.'; Spain, on the other

---

[6]   Emmanuel Carballo, *Diecinueve protagonistas de la literatura mexicana del siglo XX* (Mexico City, 1965), p. 298.

hand, plotted a 'resurgence of monarchy',[7] though it soon became apparent that Napoleon III had much more ambitious designs: to appoint Maximilian of Habsburg as emperor of Mexico, whilst maintaining a significant military presence in the country. Spain and Britain removed their troops from Mexico in April 1862; the French remained, and on 10 June 1863, Napoleon III's army marched into Mexico City. Meanwhile, Juárez departed from the city to create a government in exile, taking the republic's archive with him. Maximilian was named Emperor of Mexico in April 1864.

Whilst Juárez plotted the ousting of the Habsburg from the country, Maximilian and his wife Charlotte made their home in the palace at the top of Chapultepec Hill, built by the Spanish viceroy in 1785. The castle and its immediate surroundings constitute a first point in the spectral cartography of Mexico City that I want to trace. Chapultepec Hill is surrounded by a large forest that has been of political and military importance since pre-Columbian times. It was also a luxurious playground for the powerful. During the reign of Emperor Moctezuma II, for example, the ruler is said to have built a reservoir for exotic fish and plants in the forest. During its colonial history and in the days of independence, the building went from being abandoned to becoming the site of the Colegio Militar, or military college. At the time of the Second Empire, Chapultepec stood outside of the western limits of the capital city; its location was pleasing to Maximilian, who did not like the climate in the city centre. According to Jasper Ridley,

> Maximilian had the palace rebuilt and enlarged, and Charlotte herself planned part of the garden. Maximilian drove every day from Chapultepec to the government palace in Mexico City along a road, built at his orders, that ran down from the castle through the park and the countryside to the Carlos IV Square in the city.[8]

This avenue, designed by Ferdinand von Rosensweig in imitation of the Parisian boulevards built by Haussmann during Napoleon III's reign, is what has been known since Juárez's return to power as the Paseo de la Reforma. It represents a second important point in the spectral cartography plotted in this chapter. Chapultepec Hill became a kind of nature reserve for Maximilian, who was deeply influenced by ideas of the Enlightenment. On this subject, Octavio Paz explains that Maximilian represents a 'nueva ambigüedad histórica' ('new historical ambiguity') for Mexico, as he was a liberal who 'soñaba con crear un Imperio latino que se opusiese al poderío yanqui' ('dreamed of creating a Latin

---

[7]   Alfred Jackson Hanna and Kathryn Abbey Hanna, *Napoleon III and Mexico: American Triumph over Monarchy* (Chapel Hill, NC, 1971), p. 39.

[8]   Jasper Ridley, *Maximilian and Juárez* (London, 1993), p. 167.

empire to stand against US power').[9] The press of the republican period that directly followed Maximilian's demise reported on how he revived the features once fostered by Moctezuma II. Santiago Sierra wrote in the popular-science magazine *El Mundo Científico* (1877–78) that Maximilian was a great 'artista y naturalista', and during his ephemeral reign great attention was paid to Chapultepec Forest: 'el agua de las albercas circuló con profusion; comenzaron a cultivarse plantas raras y exóticas, y se establieció una pequeña y bonita *menagerie*' ('the water from the reservoir flowed abundantly; rare and exotic plants were planted, and a small and pretty menagerie was set up').[10] While praising Maximilian, Sierra underlines how the emperor's efforts at naturalism were rather more recreational than useful, adding to the general perception of Maximilian's penchant for the spectacular.

As mentioned above, Maximilian's progressive agenda for Mexico extended beyond his forays into naturalism. Another of his initiatives entailed bringing to Mexico the practice, employed in France, of keeping a photographic register of Mexico City's prostitute population. Instituted in 1865, this collection of images, which document the erotic past of the city – of gendered, inter-class transactions that move from open spaces into interiors – is a haunted trace of Maximilian's empire of the image. While the register represents an archive of how a society operated its flexible morality at a given point in time, to the present-day observer it revivifies a mobile erotic economy of the city. The *mujeres públicas* ('public women'), for whom there was a caste system that divided them between those who worked for wealthy customers, in brothels, and on the street, were asked each to bring a picture of herself to be included in the register; this was then accompanied in the books by personal details, including any illnesses suffered.[11] (The register is currently kept in the public health institute in the city of Cuernavaca.) Maximilian's register is completely in line with his efforts to bring modern European practices to Mexico, as Aguilar Ochoa argues: during the Second Empire 'se reconoció la necesidad higiénica de tolerar la prostitución como se toleran las alcantarillas; aislarla y circunscribirla, ocultarla, vigilarla y clausurarla' ('the sanitary need to tolerate prostitution as one tolerates sewers was recognised; it had to be isolated, circumscribed, hidden, watched and kept enclosed').[12] The register was useful to Maximilian's government as a way to maintain an operational link with the

---

[9] Paz, *El laberinto*, p. 268.
[10] Santiago Sierra, 'Un museo de historia natural', *El Mundo Científico* (7 July 1877), p. 86.
[11] Aguilar Ochoa, *La fotografía*, p. 79.
[12] Ibid., p. 80.

metropolis; it also helped to ensure that the members of the French army who were stationed in Mexico could steer clear of possible contagion.

In his alignment of prostitution and sewage, Aguilar Ochoa is echoing the language of the urban reformers of the period: the prostitute was a necessary ailment of public life in the Mexican capital. To photograph her was to fix her in the eyes of the law. The photographs, many of which appear in Aguilar Ochoa's volume, are nevertheless far from being the 'mugshots' employed in current policing. Instead, they show the prostitutes assuming for the camera different poses, from pensive to coquettish, set against the florid backgrounds common to photographic studios of the period. In this way, the register of 'public women' is another facet of Maximilian's attempt to modernise Mexico through the importation of new visual practices. Bringing the prostitutes inside the photographer's studio represents, moreover, an ambiguous act, involving both the domestication of what was considered a public ill, and the use of the lens to document the erotic everyday of a capital. The images stand as spectral reminders of how the city harbours movements from the streets and into spaces of intimacy and pleasure.

Aguilar Ochoa stresses that the photographic memory of the Second Empire is one that primarily focuses on interiors.[13] This said, the photographs by Maximilian's court photographer François Aubert are a visual record of many of Mexico's sights during the Second Empire. One of his images shows Chapultepec Castle – a photograph that, according to Aguilar Ochoa, was undoubtedly popular at the time, given its significance to the emperor and his wife. If the castle's exterior manifests the grandeur of a military citadel turned suburban idyll, Maximilian's desire to move to the west of the historic city centre augurs the migration trend of the upper classes in Mexico City in the second half of the nineteenth century. The old centre of Mexico City around the mid-century, as John Lear explains, retained 'its Hispanic organization', and was concentrated around the Zócalo, the Cathedral, and the Palacio Nacional.[14] This is the third and final point in this chapter's cartography of Mexico City. At the time of the Second Empire, the residences of the wealthy started shifting from the east of this traditional centre to the west. According to Lear, this had more to do with economic changes than 'demographic pressures'.[15] The avenue built by and for Maximilian, the Paseo de la Emperatriz (later renamed Paseo de la Reforma), would become during Porfirio Díaz's presidency (1876–1910) 'a major impetus to the direction of growth, articulating centers of transport,

[13] Ibid., p. 135.
[14] John Lear, 'Mexico City: Space and Class in the Porfirian Capital, 1884–1910', *Journal of Urban History* 22 (1996), 454–92 at 459.
[15] Ibid.

commerce, and residence'.[16] On this last point, Lear also explains that 'in the late 1880s, there began a steady flight of wealthy Mexicans and foreigners to build their houses near the Paseo'.[17] Maximilian's highway represents within the map of Mexico City that I have been tracing thus far a cipher for a number of the Second Empire's waves of modernisation. Its institution by the Habsburg emperor demonstrates how Mexico City's movements in time and space are affected, and transformed, by foreign influences at this tumultuous point in the country's history, and beyond. The highway was, as we have seen, a conduit connecting the intimacies of privileged domestic life to the seat of political and financial power – a movement of humans and capital that, as noted above, extended into the next decades and centuries.

Maximilian worked to deliver a European capital to the Mexican population – an environment in which, as Marshall Berman described Haussmann's Paris, the city would become 'a visual and sensual feast'.[18] Avenues opened to broad vistas for the promenading subject; meanwhile, the inhabitants of Mexico City experienced the spectacularisation of public and private life, increasingly commemorated and fixed as they were through the photographic image. Within and across such structural and technological forms of heightened visuality in the Second Empire, a new ghostly dimension came into being.

Reignited erotics of the imperial city

Carlos Fuentes has explained how Henry James's *The Aspern Papers* (1888) is one of the main inspirations behind his own *Aura* (1962).[19] James's novella is set in Venice during the final decades of the nineteenth century. Venice is, for James's narrator, a 'city of exhibition'.[20] This narrator is a researcher who has dedicated the bulk of his life to the study of Jeffrey Aspern – a (fictitious) North American Lord Byron. He travels to Venice in search of never-before-seen letters by Aspern, which are in the possession of Miss Bordereau, an old woman with the reputation of being a witch, who had been one of Aspern's love interests. She is so intensely old that the narrator describes her as a 'terrible … relic'.[21] In James's novel, Venice is a constant exhibition of a beautiful and glorious dilapidation (making it quite distinct from Haussmann's Paris). The character of Miss Bordereau represents the human version of this ageing

---

[16]   Ibid., p. 466.
[17]   Ibid., p. 469.
[18]   Marshall Berman, *All that Is Solid Melts into Air* (New York, 1988), p. 151.
[19]   Carlos Fuentes, 'On Reading and Writing Myself: How I Wrote *Aura*', *World Literature Today* 57 (1983), 531–9.
[20]   Henry James, *The Aspern Papers and The Turn of the Screw* (London, 1988), p. 48.
[21]   Ibid., p. 60.

process, though the organic result is what lends *The Aspern Papers* one of its Gothic edges (Miss Bordereau, like Charles Dickens's Miss Havisham, is an example of the grotesque representation of female ageing). For James's narrator-researcher, what remains most surprising is how Miss Bordereau and her niece have managed to remain invisible in a museum-city, living as they did in an 'undiscoverable hole' during the second half of the nineteenth century, 'the age of newspapers and telegrams and photographs and interviewers'.[22]

In *Aura*, Miss Bordereau's counterpart is an equally ancient woman named Consuelo (whose romantic-obsessive character bears an interesting comparison with Empress Charlotte).[23] She lives in the historic centre of Mexico City – a space that by the mid-twentieth century also lends itself to touristic exhibition – at Donceles (Street), number 815, an address that constitutes the first moment of disorientation for the narrator, Felipe Montero, who, in Fuentes's second-person narration in which this character continuously addresses himself, notes 'siempre has creído que en el viejo centro de la ciudad no vive nadie' ('you've always thought that no one lives in the old city centre').[24] In the first pages of the novella, we see how Montero is unable to find the address listed in the advert he found in a newspaper – one that offers work to a 'joven historiador' ('young historian'):

> Caminas con lentitud, tratando de distinguir el número 815 en este conglomerado de viejos palacios coloniales convertidos en talleres de reparación, relojerías, tiendas de zapatos y expendios de aguas frescas. Las nomenclaturas han sido revisadas, superpuestas, confundidas. El 13 junto al 200, el antiguo azulejo numerado – 47 – encima de la nueva advertencia pintada con tiza: *ahora 924*.

> ('You walk slowly, trying to find number 815 within this amalgam of old colonial palaces turned into repair shops, watch shops, shoe stores and refreshment shops. The names had been revised, superimposed, confused.

---

[22] Ibid., p. 48.

[23] There were several cinematic and theatrical representations of Maximilian and Charlotte from the 1930s onwards, which are expressive of the public fascination with the ill-fated couple. These include Miguel Contreras Torres's *Juárez y Maximiliano* (1933), *La paloma* (1937), *Caballería del imperio* (1942), and *The Mad Empress* (1939), a Mexico-US co-production. In 1939, Warner Brothers released *Juarez* (directed by William Dieterle), starring Bette Davis as the fragile Charlotte. In the theatre, a notable example of the dramatisation of Maximilian and Charlotte's life is Mexican playwright Rodolfo Usigli's *Corona de sombra* (1942).

[24] Carlos Fuentes, *Aura* (Mexico City, 1962), p. 13.

Number 13 next to number 200, the old plate with the number 47 above which was a new sign that read "*now* number 924"?)[25]

Montero's comment about the desertion of the city centre reflects the conjecture on the narrator's part that the individual who authored the advertisement for the historian is a wealthy person (an assumption that is not unjustified given the generous remuneration offered). The more affluent families in the city began to move out of the centre and towards the west in the final decades of the nineteenth century, while the centre itself turned into an administrative and financial hub. A different feature of this residential shift from the centre remains hidden in this passage: the trajectories of indigent citizens who try to remain in the centre throughout the fin-de-siècle and the twentieth century. Indeed, as Lear explains, throughout the nineteenth century, the centre, while harbouring the homes of the rich, was also the site of a marked social diversity. This variety began to change under Porfirio Díaz. Lear cites Gonzalo de Murga, from the Mexican Society of Geography and Statistics, who in 1913 wrote with dismay that it was possible in the capital to see 'a half-dressed Indian' living in an urban tenement (*corral de indios*) passing by a '*demimondaine*' clothed in Parisian fashion.[26] This diversity was common throughout most of the nineteenth century but became more intolerable to individuals like Murga after municipalities attempted to segregate the city's poor. In her insistence on remaining in Donceles 815, Consuelo is – in the fin-de-siècle as in 1960 – an exception within the history of urban migrations in Mexico City. This detail only strengthens the perception the reader shares with Montero: that she exists not only outside time, but also within a dislocated temporality. Doggedly hanging on to a place and mode of existence that have faded to the point of being unrecognisable in mid-twentieth century Mexico City, Consuelo occupies a place in time that is simultaneously frozen and eerily protracted. Much like Barthes's corpse photograph, she amounts to a 'living' trace 'of a dead thing'.[27]

If, in James's novella, Venice makes a spectacle of its constant decay, in the mid-twentieth century Mexico illustrated in *Aura* we encounter a reality of a 'revised, superimposed, confused' form of urban planning that, little by little and also incompletely, creates a palimpsest of addresses and orientations. It constitutes a kind of psychogeography that simultaneously reflects the

---

[25] Ibid., p. 13.
[26] Lear, 'Mexico City', p. 476.
[27] For an extended reflection on Fuentes's use of the photographic motif, see Adriana Gordillo, '*Aura*, "Constancia," and "Sleeping Beauty": Carlos Fuentes's Little History on Photography', in *Latin American Gothic in Literature and Culture*, ed. Sandra Casanova-Vizcaíno and Inés Ordiz (New York, 2018), pp. 172–88.

directions in which capitalism travels within the capital as well as the generations of municipal administrations that have distinct ideas and methods for
dealing with social problems affecting the urban centre. In *Aura*, we therefore
find another palimpsest that reveals itself in the exterior of Consuelo's house
on Donceles in the old city centre, one which represents a locus for the spectrality that runs through the novel: the spectres of distinct social and historical
realities that uncomfortably become superimposed, one over another. This
spectrality reveals the historical, social, racial, and even ontological realities
that Montero calls, from his readings of the papers of General Llorente (Consuelo's husband), papers, a 'siglo en agonía' ('an agonising century').[28]

The magical-erotic fantasy central to this novel revolves around the galvan-
isation of the past: Consuelo wants Montero to revise and organise the papers
of her late husband, a general in Maximilian's time. Montero, meanwhile, tries
to decipher the identities of the old woman and her young and beautiful companion, Aura. The two women are inseparable. When Moreno and Aura (who
ages on a daily basis) inevitably come together in scenes of eerily beautiful
bliss, the historian sees Consuelo at the foot of the bed, 'la señora Consuelo
que te sonríe, cabeceando, que te sonríe junto con Aura que mueve la cabeza al
mismo tiempo que la vieja: las dos te sonríen, te agradecen' ('Consuelo smiling
at you, nodding, smiling at you with Aura, who moves her head at the same
time as the old lady: the two smile at you, thanking you').[29] Consuelo and Aura
are here bound in a scene of grotesque ventriloquy, as the older woman appears
to control, and indeed galvanise (in the original sense of the term), the movements of Aura's body. Indeed, as it turns out, Aura is precisely what her name
announces: the magical product of the witch-like Consuelo's desire to return
to her youth. While the exterior of Donceles 815 represents an architectural
preamble that begins to announce the out-of-jointness of time experienced on
a quotidian level, the bulk of the narrative transpires in Consuelo's mausoleum-house. Of the changes that have happened to the city outside, she explains
to Montero, 'Es que nos amurallaron, señor Montero. Han construido alrede-
dor de nosotras, nos han quitado la luz.' ('They have walled us in, Mr. Montero.
They've built all around us, they've taken away the light.').[30] (It is interesting
to compare Consuelo's assertion to a line from James, in which the narrator
congratulates himself for 'opening lights into [Aspern's] life.'[31] To a great extent,
the also over-confident Montero shares these aspirations with his counterpart,
before becoming entombed himself in Consuelo's home.)

---

[28] Fuentes, *Aura*, p. 56.
[29] Ibid. p. 50.
[30] Ibid., p. 29.
[31] James, *Aspern Papers*, p. 47.

The present that Consuelo tries to make eternal in the darkness of her mausoleum-house reveals itself slowly in the 'papeles amarillos' ('yellowed papers') that belonged to Llorente, written in inelegant French, and where the imperial general reveals his

> amistad con el Duque de Morny, con el círculo íntimo de Napoleón III, el regreso a México en el estado mayor de Maximiliano, las ceremonias y veladas del Imperio, las batallas, el derrumbe, el Cerro de las Campanas, el exilio en París.

> ('friendship with the Duke of Morny, with Napoleon III's intimate circle, the return to Mexico at the height of Maximilian's power, the ceremonies and evening parties during the time of empire, the battles, the fall, the Cerro de las Campanas, the exile in Paris').[32]

That 'siglo en agonía' mentioned above – which could be read as the nineteenth, covering the span of Llorente's life, or the one that begins in the 1860s and continues into the present of the novel – is, of course, one in which visual representation is of great importance. To add to this, it is a century that becomes fixated by the documentation of agony and death. Within the space of Donceles 815, Consuelo collects her private history in photographs, simultaneously projecting her dream of youth and immortality, the product of which is Aura. Consuelo's witchcraft, which can only survive within the mausoleum that is that house, is a fervid attempt to battle the mortality that, according to Barthes, is prophesied in every photograph. The fantasy reaches its climax and conclusion when Montero finally recognises himself in the photographs of Llorente:

> Pegas esas fotografías a tus ojos, las levantas hacia el tragaluz: tapas con una mano la barba blanca del general Llorente, lo imaginas con el pelo negro y siempre te encuentras, borrado, perdido, olvidado, pero tú, tú, tú.

> ('You bring those photographs close to your eyes, you lift them toward the skylight: with one hand, you cover General Llorente's white beard, you imagine him with black hair and you always find yourself, blurry, lost, forgotten, but it's you, you, you.')[33]

In Fuentes's novel, the Second Empire and its demise appear as a very particular incongruence of history reanimated through its material, visual remnants. The incongruence is multifaceted: from Llorente and Consuelo's love letters in French, to Consuelo's precarious survival in the city centre while it changes

---

[32] Fuentes, *Aura*, p. 30.
[33] Ibid., p. 58.

irrevocably. *Aura* presents the reader with a fantasy that transpires indefinitely in obscured interiors hidden by the city's facades, where the past obstinately clings on to the present. Fuentes's decision to make that period central to his erotic tale of eternal youth heightens the sense of fantasy's foreignness in everyday urban life, as much as it also energises the fantasies of idyll in a period of unrest such as Maximilian's imperial reign.

Death's processions

In the world outside Donceles 815, during the century of photographs, telegrams, and newspapers (to paraphrase James's narrator in *The Aspern Papers*), the streets bore witness to the end of an empire; the luxuriousness of the Porfirian age, and the social divisions it drew; the political tensions that launched the country into a revolution. These 'vueltas del tiempo' (the literal translation of this phrase would be 'cycles', but also the 'paths' or 'turns' of time) that continue to have an effect on Mexico's mid-twentieth century present are represented in Agustín Yáñez's novel.[34] As noted at the opening of this chapter, the plot focuses on the long funeral procession carrying the body of ex-president Calles. The novel's narrative combines a physical journey through the city's many landmarks – among them Chapultepec forest and castle, which was Calles's residence during his presidency – with a flow of conversations and discussions among characters who take the death of this important political figure as an opportunity to think and engage in debates about unresolved conundrums of the nation's past, present, and future. The characters come from all social backgrounds; all of them are connected by a deep historical perception of modern Mexico, with the revolution as a central point of this history. Yáñez's choice of polyphonic structure, which is separated into vignettes showing different characters connected by a single event, has led Mark D. Anderson to describe *Las vueltas del tiempo* as a 'total' novel, that is, one that – in its formal and thematic structure – attempts to offer a synoptic view of a society at a given time.[35]

The private realm inside Donceles 815, where the erotics of imperial Mexico revolve indefinitely, finds a public counterpoint in Chapultepec castle, Maximilian's residence, and later the residence of a number of presidents of the

---

[34] John A. Skirius argues that Henri Bergson's concept of duration (*durée*) and the 'intuitive understanding of memory and time' is palpable in *Las vueltas del tiempo*. See Skirius, 'The Cycles of History and Memory: *Las vueltas del tiempo*, a Novel by Agustín Yáñez', *Mester* 12 (1983), 78–100 at 86.

[35] Mark D. Anderson, 'Agustín Yáñez's Total Mexico and the Embodiment of the National Subject', *Bulletin of Spanish Studies* 84 (2007), 79–99.

Mexican Republic. (It became a history museum in 1944.) Yáñez sets a number of the novel's scenes within Chapultepec forest (the first point in my spectral cartography), the ecosystem at the centre of modern Mexico City; through these journeys we gain a kaleidoscopic, multiple vision of Mexican history. One of the characters connected to the body of Plutarco Elías Calles in *Las vueltas del tiempo* is Heliodoro Camacho, originally from Sonora, who is an employee for the funeral company in charge of the ceremony and procession. For him, Calles is not a hero of the nation, but the man responsible for his father's death (Calles was leader of the Constitutional Army in Sonora from 1915), an event that pushed the family into a prolonged state of exile:

> Pudo ver todo: la desesperación del condenado para desasirse de los gen-darmes, los golpes que le daban, la soga que le echaban al cuello, el forcejeo supremo. Pudo escuchar los gritos que daba como bramidos, rugidos, aulli-dos, gruñidos de bestia perseguida, en que reconocía la voz paterna.

> ('He saw everything: the condemned man's desperate attempts to free himself from the guards, the way they hit him, the noose they put around his neck, the incredible struggle. He could hear the screams that were like howls, roars, bellows, the growls of a hounded beast, in which he could rec-ognise his father's voice.')[36]

Heliodoro Camacho is indelibly marked by the country's revolutionary history – a series of traumas that spells out his migratory history from Sonora to the capital, and his perception of the spaces that he inhabits in the present. In his reluctant participation in the procession (the promise of a bonus keeps him going), Heliodoro and the rest of the attendees go into Chapultepec forest. He is at first taken with the serene beauty of the park, where he has taken his family a few days earlier. The forest, however, is also a repository of spectres of the revolution:

> Bonito ver los animales. León. Tigre. Aquí: el muerto. ¡Cómo van saliendo historias olvidadas! No yendo lejos, allí, en la fuente que llaman de las ranas, estuvieron tirados los cadáveres de un general y de los que mataron esa vez. Él no quiso verlos. Pero le dijeron que los habían traído en camión amonto-nados, como reses, amarradas las manos con alambres.

> ('So lovely to see the animals. Lion. Tiger. Here: the dead man. How forgot-ten stories start to emerge! Without going far, there, next to what they call the frog fountain, lay the bodies of a general and the men they killed that

---

[36] Agustín Yáñez, *Las vueltas del tiempo* (Mexico City, 1973), p. 41.

time. He didn't want to see them. But they told him that they had been piled up in a truck, like cattle, their hands tied up with wire.')[37]

In this passage, Chapultepec is shown as a palimpsest of historic temporalities: the present state of the city forest, where Maximilian's bucolic designs continue to live on, is shaken and disturbed by such appearances of subjective and national trauma. Simultaneously with Heliodoro's visions of disjointed times, other more powerful figures in the procession (journalists, officials, a US businessman, and filmmaker called Max Goldwyn who has rubbed shoulders with generations of Mexican presidents) engage in prolonged conversations about the flows of power in Mexico. Unlike Heliodoro, whose memories of past events are visceral and deeply transformative on a personal level, other characters in Yáñez's novel show their privilege in their informed recollections of major events across centuries, from the conquest to the present: 'Sereno, el aire acompasaba los vuelos de la enseña nacional, despidiendo al antiguo señor de la mansión … Cargada de significaciones, la contemplación del espectáculo absorbió a los acompañantes' ('The air, serene, kept in step with the flows of the national flag, waving goodbye to the former man of the house … The members of the party were absorbed in the contemplation of this spectacle, so charged with meaning').[38]

The castle on the hill is itself a public spectacle that comes to symbolise a variety of social anxieties and the perennial flows of power. In Heliodoro Camacho's narration, we see how the forest and castle become spaces in which the spectres of the nation shock those citizens who exist outside of tight-knit circles of the powerful. Chapultepec, according to Pablo Juárez (one of the other voices in the novel, who expresses his discontent with the current state of institutionalised revolution) 'es lugar profanado, ultrajado por los extranjeros y los malos mexicanos' ('is a profaned place, violated by foreigners and bad Mexicans alike'). It is, according to Juárez, 'una casa de recreo para políticos enriquecidos, hechura de virreyes y capricho del Habsburgo' ('a pleasure palace for the rich, the handiwork of viceroys and the whim of a Habsburg').[39] The funeral procession that arranges the events of Yáñez's novel itself traces a map of the history of power in Mexico. Different sites and place names galvanise a series of unresolved questions and traumas for the novel's characters; this is represented in terms of dead ends along the streets and walkways of the city, which in turn echo the impasses among subjects who search for meaning and redemption in Mexico's history.

[37] Ibid., p. 46.
[38] Ibid., p. 173.
[39] Ibid., p. 294.

Near the end of the novel, the state funeral concluded, two characters –
Goldwyn, the American, and Santos Munguía, a Catholic activist – stroll into
the historic centre of the city, towards the Zócalo (in the historic centre, the
third point in this chapter's spectral cartography).[40] Santos Munguía recalls his
first sight of this main square, 'en una peregrinación guadalupana, el año de
1922' ('as part of a pilgrimage in honour of the Virgin of Guadalupe, in 1922').[41]
To this, the US director replies, in broken Spanish,

> Yo querer hacer película que comienza aquí, muy a mañana, y termina
> aquí, muy pasadas las doce de noche, y sale todo que aquí pasó en siglos,
> como sueño y mareada: indios y españoles, virreyes y obispos, presidentes
> y emperadores, revoluciones, fiestas … Arrancar secretos a plaza y piedras.
> Estas piedras vivir.

> ('I want to make a film that starts here, very early in the morning, and ends
> here, way past midnight, where everything that has happened here comes
> out, as a dream or a tide: Indians and Spaniards, viceroys and bishops, pres-
> idents and emperors, revolutions, feasts … To tear away the secrets of the
> plaza and the stones. These stones are alive.')[42]

According to Skirius, Yáñez's choice of name for his US businessman, Max
Goldwyn, is not a subtle one. Aside from sharing a surname with an iconic Hollywood film mogul, Skirius explains, the Mexican novelist identifies a modern
version of the Habsburg emperor, for he is 'the Yankee who has adjusted to the
Mexican milieu, has settled down there, has learned a grammatically atrocious
Spanish, and has taken a liking to Mexican culture and people – much like
Maximilian'.[43] The Santos Munguía-Goldwyn episode in the Zócalo brings the
reader to a historic and symbolic centre of Mexico City – arguably the main
protagonist of a novel without human subjects as protagonists. Santos Munguía recalls the importance of the Zócalo as a place of religious processions,
while Goldwyn, the foreigner (like his historical predecessor Maximilian, if
we follow Skirius's argument) admires it for its spectacular possibilities – as
an open theatre in which to turn the spectres of the nation into a monumental
phantasmagoria show.

In *Death and the Idea of Mexico*, Claudio Lomnitz recounts the evolution of
Day of the Dead celebrations in the country during the nineteenth century and

---

[40] Plutarco Elías Calles was president of Mexico during the conflict known as the
    Cristero war, when priests took up arms against the revolutionary government. In
    Yáñez's novel, we learn that Santos Munguía fought against Calles's army.

[41] Yáñez, *Las vueltas*, p. 318.

[42] Ibid., p. 319.

[43] Skirius, 'Cycles of History', p. 89.

beyond. In his discussion, he focuses on the evolution of the Paseo de Todos los Santos, the promenade/procession and festival around the Zócalo that, at its apogee at the end of the 1860s, came to interpreted by the bourgeois class in terms of the 'complementarity and compatibility between mourning and vanity'.[44] Throughout the first half of the nineteenth century, this tradition had been a source of consternation for municipal and Church authorities alike, as the religious feast day was treated with what they believed to be a lack of decorum. As Lomnitz explains, however, things changed when Maximilian became emperor. Looking for public approval, another of his reforms was to reinstate the *paseo* for the Day of the Dead. Thanks to him, the celebrations became more sophisticated and splendid.[45] His seal of approval for the *paseo* fed the practice of promenading – of seeing others and being seen. The Zócalo, with Maximilian's blessing, is a meeting point between the fervours of religion and the desire for exhibition. In Yáñez's novel, the episode in the Zócalo with Santos Munguía and Goldwyn is a twentieth-century rendition of that negotiation, cast on to the broader problems of cyclical Mexican history.

The figure of Maximilian represents, in the context of modern Mexican history, the incongruity of an empire in the time of republics, as well as the farcical necessity to fight anew for an independence already obtained. Maximilian is, as Max Goldwyn observes, a reminder of the problematic permeability of national borders. With his death, writes Lomnitz, Benito Juárez 'present[ed] Europe with the spectacle of its own death, just as Mexico had been forced to ponder its mortality'.[46] Between spectacle and vanity, the death of imperial Europe in Mexico and the birth of a recognition of mortality in the young Latin American republic transpired during a period that perfected the cult of images; it also, inadvertently perhaps, opened the door to new spectres for the nation.

Maximilian's death is among the most spectacular in the nineteenth century. This has little to do with his qualities as an emperor; naïve as he was till his last breath, he unfailingly thought himself a friend of the country he ruled that was, meanwhile, undergoing the deepest upheaval. Rather, Maximilian has been remembered in terms of his magnificently tragic ingenuousness. As Kristine Ibsen explains, the events that transpired during his final days are notable for their theatricality: his final words ('Muero por una causa justa, la de la independencia y la libertad de México' ['I die in the name of a just

---

[44]   Claudio Lomnitz, *Death and the Idea of Mexico* (New York, 2005), p. 309.

[45]   Ibid., pp. 316–19.

[46]   Ibid., p. 32.

cause – that of Mexico's independence and liberty']) are 'his final and most important performance'.[47]

This portrait of power leads us back to the question of how, as contemporary observers, we should read the image of Maximilian standing inside his open casket, and how we insert it into a broader understanding of the space of the Mexican nation and its capital city. Yáñez's and Fuentes's novels galvanise a *paseo* through city streets and avenues in which the living and the spectres of the past pass by on a daily basis. *Las vueltas del tiempo* follows a singular commemoration of death, Calles's state funeral, along these spaces to rouse a vaster gathering of national ghosts. Fuentes's narrative, meanwhile, guides us into the interiors inhabited by subjects for whom the flows of time, the passing of events both major and minor, do not constitute a progressive chronology. Both writers represent a period in which the increasingly pervasive photographic medium, more than representing forward-moving modernisation, describes a Mexican modernity full of markers detailing time's loops and returns. In its perennial play between the *there* and *not-there*, presence and absence, the image fixes spectrality into historical understanding, allowing for the resurgence of not-quite-buried pasts. In their novels, Yáñez and Fuentes open figurative caskets that contain the private and public lives of a moment – a fold in national time – from which new anxieties and new disquietudes continue to emerge.

Bibliography

Aguilar Ochoa, Arturo, *La fotografía durante el imperio de Maximiliano* (Mexico City, 1995)

Anderson, Mark D., 'Agustín Yáñez's Total Mexico and the Embodiment of the National Subject', *Bulletin of Spanish Studies* 84 (2007): 79–99

Barthes, Roland, *Camera Lucida: Reflections on Photography*, trans. Richard Howard (New York, 1999)

Berman, Marshall, *All that Is Solid Melts into Air* (New York, 1988)

Carballo, Emmanuel, *Diecinueve protagonistas de la literatura mexicana del siglo XX* (Mexico City, 1965)

Gordillo, Adriana, '*Aura*, "Constancia," and "Sleeping Beauty"': Carlos Fuentes's Little History on Photography', in *Latin American Gothic in Literature and Culture*, ed. Sandra Casanova-Vizcaíno and Inés Ordiz (New York, 2018), pp. 172–88

Fuentes, Carlos, *Aura* (Mexico City, 1962)

——, 'On Reading and Writing Myself: How I Wrote *Aura*', *World Literature Today* 57 (1983), 531–9

---

[47] Kristine Ibsen, *Maximilian, Mexico, and the Invention of Empire* (Nashville, TN, 2010), p. 7.

Hanna, Alfred Jackson and Kathryn Abbey Hanna, *Napoleon III and Mexico: American Triumph over Monarchy* (Chapel Hill, NC, 1971)

Ibsen, Kristine, *Maximilian, Mexico, and the Invention of Empire* (Nashville, TN, 2010)

James, Henry, *The Aspern Papers and The Turn of the Screw* (London, 1988)

Lear, John, 'Mexico City: Space and Class in the Porfirian Capital, 1884–1910', *Journal of Urban History* 22 (1996), 454–92

Lomnitz, Claudio, *Death and the Idea of Mexico* (New York, 2005)

Paz, Octavio, *El laberinto de la soledad* (Madrid, 2002 [1950])

Ridley, Jasper, *Maximilian and Juárez* (London, 1993)

Sierra, Santiago, 'Un museo de historia natural', *El Mundo Científico* (7 July 1877), 85–6

Skirius, John A., 'The Cycles of History and Memory: *Las vueltas del tiempo*, a Novel by Agustín Yáñez', *Mester* 12 (1983), 78–100

Yáñez, Agustín, *Las vueltas del tiempo* (Mexico City, 1973)

13

Ghostlore of Contemporary Beijing

—◄◆►—

ALEVTINA SOLOVYOVA

This chapter explores supernatural beliefs in the urban space of contemporary Beijing. It examines representations of traditional demonic characters and plots in modern urban culture, the ways in which they survive and adapt in new social and cultural contexts, forms of interaction between traditional and contemporary mass culture, and some specific features of Asian traditions of ghostlore and ghost storytelling. It also discusses demonology as a special realm of Chinese culture, and its main features and new functions in urban conditions, as well as various authorities which influence the content of the supernatural in the spaces of the capital.

Drawing upon a range of interpretative concepts that have been proposed and contested in folklore studies and anthropology since the second half of the twentieth century, the chapter considers ghost storytelling in Beijing in terms of folk memory, the pragmatic and regulative functions of folk narratives, and folk narrative traditions as a part of local group identities.[1] It examines how events, beliefs, supernatural entities, and narratives from different periods of the past have been transmitted to and now circulate within younger generations. Beyond Beijing's haunted historical places such as Gugong (the Forbidden City), the ghosts of schools, university dormitories, and hospitals are initiating the city's twenty-first century urban dwellers into contemporary

---

[1] For urban cultures see, for example, Linda Dégh and Andrew Vázsonyi, 'Does the Word "Dog" Bite? Ostensive Action: A Means of Legend Telling', *Journal of Folklore Research* 20 (1983), 5–34. See also Diane E. Goldstein, *Haunting Experiences: Ghosts in Contemporary Folklore* (Logan, UT, 2007).

folk communities. In turn, those ghosts and their narratives are being used to articulate the specific concerns, tensions, and worries of individuals and the wider communities to which they belong.

This research is based on data collected during my field work in Beijing, interviews conducted with some of the capital's residents in China and abroad, and materials devoted to the supernatural on the Chinese internet. The research started in 2012, when with my colleague Julia Ershova, lecturer at the Russian State University for the Humanities, I conducted our first field-work in Beijing. The main aims of our research were to find out about the content of the capital's supernatural world, what kinds of folkloric characters were accommodated in its urban spaces, and how their images and functions, as well as the motifs and ritual practices connected to them, were adapted and transformed in Beijing's modern urban culture. During the preliminary planning for this research, it was not certain what could be attained through this venture, or even if it could be carried through. We were confronted by two major issues: firstly how, and secondly whom, to ask about demons and ghosts on the streets of a megalopolis in the ideological environment of a socialist state, especially one that had undergone the painful experience of a cultural revolution.

Our first interviewees were the owners of our small guesthouse in an old district or *hutong*, where everyday life and the common activities of local people are more open and accessible to an 'outsider'.[2] Day by day, our neigh-bours grew more used to our presence and became friendly, curious, and talkative. This group then expanded to include the service workers at the same and other hotels, cafes, and small stores, their family members, students, and their friends. Thus our data were gathered from a fairly organic and infor-mal network that developed as trust grew. As researchers, we also became better at overcoming ethnic and cultural barriers and discussing less welcome topics. This first experience produced unexpectedly encouraging results, and I conducted further expeditions subsequent years (2014–16), together with a number of personal and digital interviews with people who have lived in Bei-jing and who kindly talked to me about the urban supernatural.

Supernatural beliefs cannot be demolished by education, technological progress, official ideology, television, mainstream culture, or even by cul-tural revolution and campaigns against 'superstition', although socio-political

---

[2]   The *hutong* are a type of old urban district (situated within the city and often close to the centre) with narrow streets and traditional courtyard residences, commonly associated with northern Chinese cities, especially Beijing. Since the middle of the twentieth century a large number of Beijing hutongs have been demolished to make space for new roads and buildings.

contexts have a strong influence on the conditions and ways in which these traditions exist and develop.[3] Given this, the supernatural in contemporary Chinese society has a very complicated and contradictory status, caught as it is between differing authorities and influences. This complexity might be regarded as a conflict of statuses and attitudes within the urban community. The first influence in contemporary China is the state, for the supernatural is still under some pressure from the socialist regime and its atheistic ideology. Beliefs, narratives, and rites concerning such topics are dismissed as 'superstitions', worthless knowledge, and a useless part of tradition.

Yet the supernatural in Chinese culture has a special status, supported by centuries of written tradition. This forms a second source of influence and authority. Narrative plots concerning the unusual and the supernatural, ghosts, spirits, and demons were adapted by and embodied in discrete literary genres known as *zhiguai xiao shuo* ('tales of the miraculous', or 'tales of the strange') in the Han dynasty (206 BC– AD 220).[4] The topic was also very popular in Chinese novels and urban legends (*huaben*). Some examples of this literary tradition, such as the famous novels written by Pu Songling, are even included in Chinese school syllabuses.[5] This written tradition serves as a bridge between what official authorities regard as 'high' and 'low', 'respectable' and 'unworthy of attention'. In the context of everyday life, it means more: it legitimises personal supernatural experience, and provides models for interpreting it, for individuals, families, and communities.[6] It also allows for discussion of forbidden 'superstitions'. This situation was reflected in the narratives collected during our interviews (and found in written form at forums and websites specialising in supernatural topics). Interviewees' personal experiences of encounters with the supernatural were frequently recounted following references to the famous authors of the written tradition. In this situation, common interactions between written and oral folkloric traditions took on additional

---

[3]   For more on this see Alan Dundes, 'Folkloristics in the Twenty-First Century', *The Journal of American Folklore* 118 (2005), 385–408.

[4]   See, for example, Karl S. Y. Kao (Gao, Xinyong), 'Classical Chinese Tales of the Supernatural and the Fantastic: Selections from the Third to the Tenth Century' (Bloomington, IN, 1985). One of the earliest and most popular editions is '*In Search of the Supernatural*', believed to be written by Gan Bao. See Gan Bao, *The Written Record*, trans. Kenneth J. DeWoskin and James Irving Crump (Stanford, CA, 1996).

[5]   Pu Songling was a famous writer from the Qing dynasty. See Pu Songling, *Strange Stories from a Chinese Studio* (*Liaozhai zhiyi*), trans. and annotated by Herbert A. Giles, 2nd edn (Taipei, 1965).

[6]   Thus current misfortunes and bad luck in one's life are commonly interpreted as a sign of the malevolent influence of a supernatural agent (demon, ghost, disappointed spirit of a relative, etc).

meanings and functions; written tradition not only provided motifs and narrative patterns, but also helped to legitimise private supernatural experiences.[7]

The third powerful influence which shapes contemporary conditions for the supernatural in Beijing is modern mainstream culture. In China, mass culture has its own specific regional features and inflections, but shares in general, and with Western culture, a popular interest in the demonic, mystical, and infernal. In contemporary culture, the supernatural and the frightening have been exploited in the production of successful brands, attractive especially to young people. Examples are to be found in clothing fashion, decor, literature, art, films, and tourism. Ghosts, demons, the living dead, and sacred animals able to turn into humans: all have become popular themes in contemporary mass culture.

These three agents – the state, written tradition, and contemporary mass culture – together shape the specific framework for the expression of supernatural beliefs in China's modern urban spaces. Within this context, the examples discussed below illustrate different features of contemporary Beijing's demonology, its images, functions, and meanings. In particular, they emphasise the role of ghostlore and ghost storytelling in the city and highlight *gui* (demon, ghost, homeless spirit) as a key urban supernatural entity. They also enable us to consider the types of urban locality that accumulate ghost stories, and various examples of plots connected to them.

As one of the most common expressions of demonological belief, ghost stories are closely connected to everyday life. Sensitive to its changes and challenges, they tend to reflect actual situations, processes, problematic questions, and conflicts, both individual and collective. In doing so, they also articulate the social, political, economic, and cultural concerns of certain communities. As Avery F. Gordon has noted, a ghost 'is not simply a dead or a missing person, but a social figure, and investigating it can lead us to that dense site where history and subjectivity make social life'.[8] A number of researchers exploring different contemporary societies (including post-socialist spaces) have noted that the popularity of ghost stories and ghost storytelling is often connected to radical changes in the community. For example, ghost stories can express

---

[7] For instance, Chinese literature offers many examples of communication between people and sacred animals (most famously foxes) which are able to change their appearance into human form. Meetings with such animals in real life, and their potentially harmful influence, is a popular subject for discussions on internet forums. These discussions often reference well-known literary examples and personal experiences. For more on this, see below.

[8] Avery F. Gordon, *Ghostly Matters: Haunting and the Sociological Imagination*, new edn (Minneapolis, 2008 [1997]), p. 8.

'the tension between cultural conservatism and rapid change'.[9] They might also relate to conflicts between ideological, social, and economic interests. Thus, one of my recent fieldwork cases (from Outer Mongolia, in 2018) revealed that a certain old temple building is regarded as haunted. The temple's keeper and manager confirmed this, regarding it as one of a number of reasons to apply for funding for a new building with 'a positive karma'.[10]

In contemporary Beijing, many traditional beliefs have successfully migrated into urban culture, maintaining their customary meanings and cultural functions whilst adapting to the new conditions of urban life. The list of the demonological creatures represented in the folk life of Beijing is long. The main types mentioned here are spirits of ancestors, house and patron spirits, sacred animals and creatures able to change their appearance, and ghosts. These characters and groups of beliefs connected to them are common and might be found in various regions of China. In Beijing, expressions of these beliefs have some regional and social specifics, especially given that the capital's spaces are more directly under the control of the official culture.

The worship of ancestors still has a very important place in contemporary culture, including urban centres. In the capital, it is still forbidden to keep ritual plates at home.[11] However, after the 1990s, when religious life started to become less restricted, many Buddhist and Taoist temples were revived and the ritual part of their worship was moved to the temples.[12] In some of them might be found special rooms full of plates with names and photographs of dead relatives. These rituals are still to an extent performed at home, albeit behind closed doors. The production of goods associated with the cult of the ancestors has developed very rapidly, involving new forms convenient or desirable for urban people. Nowadays, besides traditional items like special

---

[9] Keping Wu, ' "Ghost City": Religion, Urbanization and Spatial Anxieties in Contemporary China', *Geoforum* 65 (2015), 243–5 at 245. See also Mayfair Mei-Hui Yang, 'Spatial Struggles: Postcolonial Complex, State Disenchantment, and Popular Reappropriation of Space in Rural Southeast China', *The Journal of Asian Studies*, 63 (2004), 719–55.

[10] For research regarding ghostlore and its relations to economic questions and changing property rights, see Ülo Valk, 'Ghostly Possession and Real Estate: The Dead in Contemporary Estonian Folklore', *Journal of Folklore Research* 43 (2006), 31–51.

[11] These ritual plates, often wooden, have the names of dead relatives written on them and, nowadays, include their photos. According to the ritual tradition, people are supposed to make offerings to ancestors, leaving food, drinks, and incense in front of these plates at home or in temples. If this is not possible, offerings may be left at a crossroads, as it is believed that all gods and demons pass there.

[12] See A. D. Safronova, *Vozrozhdenie prihramovoj obchini na severe Kitaja* ['The Revival of the Temple Communities in North China'] (Moscow, 2006).

paper money (which is supposed to be burnt as a means of transferring it to another world for deceased relatives), specialist shops sell paper versions of everything, including branded clothing, jewellery, iPhones and other popular devices, houses, furnishings, and expensive cars, all of which are burnt for the sake of ancestors. Old rituals have also been successfully adapted to twenty-first century technologies. Instead of offerings to spirits actually being burnt, they might be transferred by virtual burning via specific smartphone applications.[13]

House and patron spirits are also popular in urban life. Images of Zao Wang (the deity of the hearth) and *menshen* (door spirits/deities), together with other deities, protect the domestic space and family. According to widespread belief in various Asian traditions, everything has its own patron spirit. Usually this concerns landscape and nature spirits (*tudishen*). Through these countless patrons, the local community ritually establishes a proper relationship with the environment and nature. In Chinese culture, this principle is extended to all kinds of objects, including the non-natural: a bridge, a car, household items, and even the tip of a needle might have a patron spirit. Their images are represented in a special type of icon (*zhima*), and rituals are performed occasionally. In Beijing, nature spirits still receive offerings on special occasions, such as the beginning of building works.[14] This ritual seeks to obtain permission from the spirits, and furnishes some compensation for disturbing them.[15]

Another group of traditional characters that have successfully moved to the city is that of sacred animals and creatures able to change their appearance.[16] Among the most popular in the capital are foxes, hedgehogs and weasels. These are believed to be able to turn into humans and communicate with people. These interactions might have a malevolent influence on human beings, causing serious illness and even death. This problem is one of the popular topics on the Internet, where users share their experiences of meeting these animals,

---

[13]   Generally this involves 'burning' special ritual money – joss bank notes, also called 'hell money' or 'ghost money'. See 清明网上祭祀平台, 清明节网上祭奠 (纪念), 祈恩网, or http://www.qew666.com/ (accessed 9 June 2019).

[14]   In the case I saw in Beijing, people constructed a simple altar (even without an image of *tudishen*) and left their offerings to the patron spirits – flowers, fruits, and incense.

[15]   See Adam Yuet Chau, *Miraculous Response: Doing Popular Religion in Contemporary China* (Stanford, CA, 2005); Catherine Bell, 'Religion and Chinese Culture: Towards an Assessment of "Popular Religion" ', *History of Religion* 29 (1989), 35–57.

[16]   See Li Wei-Tsu, *On the Cult of the Four Sacred Animals in the Neighbourhood of Peking* (Nanzan, 2013). The difference between the two types of animal is complicated by the fact that there are different interpretations concerning the same characters, their powers, and the narrative plots concerning them.

in order to discuss consequences and worries, and to ask for advice from the online community. According to beliefs, for example,

> When a weasel is nearby, people feel bad, get sick, and often argue with each other. A weasel makes noise at night, cries like a baby … It also steals small things. When a weasel comes into a family house, the members of the family should go out and shout ribaldries, very loud so as it can hear them. I remember that one day my grandfather ran out, cursed it, and it never came again. [T.B., 1952, 2012][17]

The following information was given by the owner of one hotel where we stayed, when we asked him about a real weasel we saw running across the yard. The man readily talked about the animal, but refused to admit that there was one in the hotel:

> It is forbidden to kill a weasel, because it is believed that in its body lives the soul of a beautiful girl. It can beguile people, can turn into a beauty. If some-one meets a rat he will kill it, but he will not kill a weasel. There are three other animals people do not kill – a snake, a fox and a tiger, because they have souls and can change their shape, turning into humans sometimes. [J.G., 1956, 2012]

Alongside the notion of shapeshifting animals, many folkloric beliefs persist connected to old household objects (clothes, books, furniture, or a broom, for example) which, over time, can gain the ability to act independently and even change shape, turning into humans. These beliefs are especially common in the second-hand shops to be found in big cities. Interpretative models preserved in Chinese tradition might explain these powers in several different ways: according to one of these, the age of the object and time spent near people allow it to accumulate the necessary amounts of human energy (*yang* energy or *ci* energy) [E.Z., 1946, 2014]; according to another, objects must have a soul, for only then are they able to practise self-improvement and to accumulate merit, and in this way they derive their special powers [Ch.T., 1987, 2015]. The first version would seem to refer to Daoist and the second to Buddhist ideas.[18] The general belief can extend beyond individual objects to

---

[17]   Here and below, initial letters represent the interviewee's name, the first date gives their year of birth, and the second date the year in which the interview was conducted.

[18]   As traditional components of Chinese vernacular religion, Buddhist and Daoist ideas remain popular, despite the period of religious persecutions. They are still features of everyday life, aided by the government's recent softening in religious policy.

particular urban sites too, for among Beijing's supernatural entities are the spirits of night alleys:

> When walking at night in the city, in some dark places, it seems that some-body is walking by your side or a bit behind. You can hear steps or sounds of breathing. But when you turn around – there is nothing ... Here you can meet the spirit [C.J., 1985, 2012]

As the above examples suggest, a large number of characters and traditional beliefs have successfully migrated and adapted to the modern urban life of Beijing. The diversity of characters also indicates some important features of the city's urban culture. The number and variety of folk characters involved in everyday urban life correlates with the age and historical development of that culture. In this sense, Chinese urbanism obviously represents an old-estab-lished city culture, as is particularly evident when it is compared with younger urban traditions, such as those in Outer Mongolia, where the urban supernat-ural is represented mostly by a single character (*chötgör*, a character similar to *gui*, explored below).[19] Other Mongolian supernatural characters are still only in the process of moving to the cities. Many rituals are devoted to the deity of the hearth or to nature spirits, for example, but most of these are still supposed to be performed in a rural space; as yet, there are no narrative traditions con-cerning these characters in urban spaces.

As an urban space, contemporary Beijing represents a melting pot of dif-ferent local traditions, beliefs, rites, characters, and narratives brought in by people from various parts of China. These regional and local versions inter-act, aligning or becoming fused into the tradition of Beijing. This informs the shaping of a new urban identity – that of the citizens of Beijing, people who share the same space and similar fears. This is mostly reflected in another spe-cies of character, *gui*, an entity which deserves to be recognised as Beijing's most ubiquitous supernatural citizen. *Gui* literally means spirit, demon, soul of the deceased, or ghost; it is a very popular type of character in Chinese folklore, and in the written tradition many types of *gui* were specified and classified.[20] In Chinese folklore, *gui* are regarded as restless souls which, for a variety of reasons (a tragic or early death, strong attachments to a past life, the

---

[19]   For more on Mongolian urban ghostlore, see Alevtina Solovyova, 'Chötgöriin Yaria in the Twenty-First Century: Mongolian Demonological Beliefs and Mass Culture in the Age of Globalisation', in *Mongolian Responses to Globalization Processes, Bon-ner Asienstudien*, vol. 13, ed. Ines Stolpe, Judith Nordby and Ulrike Gonzales (Ber-lin, 2017), pp. 129–48.

[20]   Among many Chinese encyclopedias and dictionaries devoted to the supernatural, see *Zhong guo guihua cidian* (Beijing, 1996); *Zhongguo gui hua* (Shanghai, 1991); *Nü gui cidian* (Ningxia, 1991); *Zhonghua gudai gui shen wenhua da cidian* (Jiaxi, 1992); Xu

Fig. 7. A t-shirt print of a demonic character from Japanese folklore, popular in contemporary Chinese mass culture and associated with the Chinese *gui*. Photograph by Alevtina Solovyova.

absence of relatives who might care about the soul and give it offerings) have stayed in the human world. As one interviewee put it,

> *Gui* appear only at night, after midnight, because they are afraid of the sun, they do not like sun light. They are like wild animals; people are afraid of them, they are scared of people. They always groan because they are unfairly offended. They do not help people, they are scared and scare. [T.B., 1952, 2013]

The ubiquity of this character in urban space derives from its uncertainty. In comparison with other characters, it does not haunt any fixed location. It might be anywhere, rural or urban – in abandoned places, on roads, in rivers; it might come to somebody's home, settle down in different objects (cloth, furniture, clocks, books). In Chinese folklore, common places to encounter *gui* in rural locations are rivers and lakes, forests, cemeteries and their surrounding area, roads, and especially crossroads.[21] In urban spaces, *gui* usually inhabit abandoned houses, old buildings, urban cemeteries, schools, hospitals,

---

Hua Long, *Gui xue quan shu* (Beijing, 1998); idem, *Zhongguo gui gushi* (Beijing, 2001).

[21] See for example *Xu Hua Long. ZHongguo gui gushi*. According to traditional beliefs, one might encounter *shoui gui* near rivers and lakes – ghosts of drown people, looking for a replacement.

and student dormitories. Nor do they have any particular, fixed appearance. *Gui* might be invisible and act as poltergeists, or be partially visible (just eyes, hands, legs), have an uncertain shape (something black, shadowy, something fuzzy but human shaped), or be very definite and realistic in terms of human form. As one interviewee reported,

> There are many stories about that room. Those who know do not live there, only new students live in that room. They usually stay for a semester and move out. Many strange things go on there: sounds as if somebody is walking around at night, whispering something unclear. Guys who lived there say that if you switch off the light at night and look at the window, you might see in the glass two big sad eyes looking at you. People say that one girl lived at that dormitory and one day she committed suicide, something bad happened to her and made her unhappy. It was many years ago. Her soul turned into *gui*, stayed at the dormitory and keeps coming to that room. [P.H., 1989, 2015]

Unlike patron spirits, *gui* do not have any special functions. This ambiguity allows this character to fit easily into different contexts, conditions, and situations, to take on different appearances and carry out different roles according to the needs of a certain narrative, enabling it to adapt rapidly to new features and plots. A *gui* in contemporary Beijing might be a soul from the past, dressed in the old-fashioned clothes of a court eunuch or concubine, someone who died during the revolution, or a modern girl who committed suicide because of an unhappy relationship. Yet equally, it could be a random homeless spirit wandering about looking for offerings, or a demonic hitchhiker, similar to the one to be found in modern mass culture and international folklore.[22] *Gui* in Beijing might be very Chinese, accumulating native ethnic, cultural, and historical characteristics, images, and meanings; yet they might equally be very international, behaving like the widely familiar poltergeist, or the denizens of haunted houses.

Ghostlore, as a part of folklore, enables us to analyse important and problematic issues in the life of urban communities. In folklore studies, considerable attention has been paid to the question of the pragmatics of ghostlore.[23] Two concepts in particular might be identified with regard to ghost stories and ghost storytelling: they serve as statements about community processes,

---

[22] See Jan Harold Brunvand, *The Vanishing Hitchiker: American Urban Legends and their Meaning* (New York, 1981).

[23] See Ülo Valk, 'Ontological Liminality of Ghosts in Vernacular Interpretations: The Case of a Haunted Hospital in Tartu', lecture, November 2015, https://isthmus.com/events/ontological-liminality-of-ghosts/; Gillian Bennett, *Alas, Poor Ghost! Traditions of Belief in Story and Discourse* (Logan, UT, 1999); Gordon, *Ghostly Matters*;

situations, and conflicts in different realms, including the economic and political; and they serve a cultural function, in terms of educating or helping people to overcome and adapt. Together these perspectives allow us fruitfully to regard ghosts as 'social figures', and discuss their pragmatics and functions.[24]

The functions and meanings of ghostlore might be interpreted in a variety of ways, depending on context. In the personal sphere, an encounter with *gui* is regarded as cause to worry about the current state of one's mental or physical health.[25] Ghost storytelling in this context is often an aspect of (self-)reflection and explanation of a person's current circumstances. For example, one interviewee made the following observation: 'After this [encounter with a ghost] happened I got problems at work and my girlfriend broke up with me.' [J.Y., 1974, 2014]. Another noted that 'during that period, I was not quite myself, I was acting as in a dream, and all misfortunes were mine, from the coffee spilled on a white blouse to the car accident' [X.F., 1982, 2016]. A third interviewee observed, 'When that strange creature was finally gone, everything became normal again. My sister stopped getting sick so often, my business problems got fixed, everything worked out well.' [N.M., 1980, 2015]

In this context, ghostlore and ghost storytelling are also features communication. The sharing of a personal supernatural experience often figures in consultations (about what the experience might mean, how dangerous it is, what can be done to prevent or stop its malevolent influence and consequences) with religious specialists, relatives, friends, and internet communities. Both traditional and modified motifs connected to ghosts are used as interpretative models for individual and collective self-reflection in the context of modern urban lives. Often an encounter with a ghost is regarded as a cause of negative conditions, be it poor health, a lack of energy, bad luck, or problems with work and relationships. One interviewee provided us with the following example:

Once I walked in Bei Hai and saw one strange creature near the water.[26] It was doing something on the bank, moving very slowly and weirdly. It

---

David Hufford, *The Terror That Comes in the Night* (Philadelphia, 1982); Katherine Ramsland, *Ghost: Investigating the Other Side* (New York, 2002); Judith Richardson, *Possessions: The History and Uses of Haunting in the Hudson Valley* (Cambridge, MA, 2003).

[24] Gordon, *Ghostly Matters*, p. 8.

[25] According to traditional beliefs, when someone can see the ghost it means that his/her vital *yang* energy is weak, and such a person might be seriously ill or close to death. The ghost's predominantly *yin* energy represents opposite and dangerous influences for living beings.

[26] Bei Hai Park is a public park and former imperial garden located in the north-western part of the Imperial City in Beijing.

looked a bit like a human, but I could not understand whether it was male or female, an adult or a kid. I tried to come closer. It was staring at me for a while. I stopped, then it jumped into the water and disappeared. It was probably a water ghost, *shui gui*, the soul of somebody who has drown[ed] there. In former times, many people died there during the building works in this garden. I was very scared and started to call friends. They said they would come to meet me. I told them everything I saw. One of them said that I [was] crazy and should go to see a doctor, but others said that it might be dangerous and I should go to a temple and ask people there what it might mean and what is [best] to do. [H.G., 1990, 2016]

Beyond the personal, ghostlore and ghost storytelling can also be regarded as a feature of group folklore: a means towards defining the boundaries and identities of certain groups of people such as students, hospitals, schools, or the local community. In this context, ghostlore represents one of the markers of the group, their shared beliefs and narratives, and can be used to express worries and problematic issues specific to that group. For example, a significant part of student ghostlore is devoted to the ghosts of unhappy lovers (generally females) who committed suicide. In his article concerning students' ghost storytelling in Hong Kong, Joseph Bosco suggests we analyse and interpret such narratives through their problem-related aspects: for example, the tensions and conflicts between 'loving' and 'studying', cultural norms and social expectations (including, in Chinese society, the dependence of students on their families, their immature status, traditional stereotypes of gendered behaviour, and the setting-up of their own families), and interest in romantic and sexual relationships.[27] The image of this type of Chinese female ghost is so widespread that it extends beyond China's borders: similar student dormitory ghostlore stories might be found, for example, in Russian and Mongolian cities.[28] On the other hand, the image is deeply rooted in traditional Chinese (*zhiguai xiao shuo*) and Japanese (*kwaidan*) literature about the supernatural, which provides models of characters and plots for contemporary folklore and its mass-cultural expressions.

Ghosts with broken hearts are very popular, but they are not the only supernatural inhabitants of student dormitories. There are also souls of former

[27] Joseph Bosco, 'The Supernatural in Hong Kong Young People's Ghost Stories', *Anthropological Forum* 13 (2003), 141–9. Such issues surface in the story related above, about the haunted dormitory room.

[28] While in Chinese ghost stories female ghosts chase male students, in foreign ghostlore (Russian or Mongolian examples) Chinese ghost girls usually chase and scare the new female inhabitants of their former rooms. See Solovyova, 'Chötgöriin Yaria in the Twenty-First Century'.

owners of the land, founders of the university, builders, lecturers, and random restless spirits. Nor are the tensions of social pressure and the conflicts of interests the only issue of student ghostlore. For example, very popular among student narratives is that of a demonic ride in a bus. According to the main plot, a student going home late in the evening catches the last bus, with very peculiar passengers (a pale girl with flowing hair, or a strange gang of people in old- fashioned clothes), who by the end turn out to be *gui*. Some unknown passenger or helper, often an old man with a white beard, pulls the young man out of the bus, thus saving his life. The bus then disappears, or is found wrecked and bloodstained outside the city. [M.J., 1994, 2016].

This plot is very popular in various Chinese cities, although it is given local inflections. In Beijing, it is given the peculiarity of referencing the imperial court, through the clothing of the ghosts.[29] Although representing a variant of the famous demonic hitchhiker, popular in contemporary mass culture, the story is framed in a specifically Chinese social and cultural context.[30] For example, students and young people in China tend to use public transport rather than having the private cars that usually appear in Western narratives. The ghost's old-fashioned clothing references the courtiers of former imperial times, and the absence of feet is a special feature of many Chinese ghosts. The configuration of characters is also recognisable from traditional Chinese literary tales of the supernatural – a student (traditionally the main hero and/or victim of the supernatural in such tales), a mysterious helper (often an old person, monk, or Daoist saint), and demonic characters pretending to be humans.

The idea of the haunted dormitory is echoed in hospital ghostlore, where among the most popular types of *gui* are the souls of former patients. As noted in a Chinese folk tale,

> When his favourite daughter falls ill, Yanwang, the ruler of the underworld, sends his servants to look for a doctor who has as few ghosts as possible following him. This means that he is a better doctor than others, because when a patient dies, its ghost follows and haunts the doctor.[31]

---

[29] I have examples of these narratives from Beijing, Shanghai, Uhan, and Hong Kong. These appear as examples of local ecotypes. For more on ecotypes, see, for example, Lauri Honko, 'Types of Comparison and Forms of Variation', *Journal of Folklore Research* 23, 2/3 (special double issue: 'The Comparative Method in Folklore') (1986), 105–24.

[30] See Brunvand, *The Vanishing Hitchhiker*; Janet L. Langlois, '*The Vanishing Hitchhiker: American Urban Legends and Their Meanings*, by Jan Harold Brunvand' (review article), *The Journal of American Folklore* 96 (1983), 356–7.

[31] Li Qunying and Louis Han, *The Doctor who was Followed by Ghosts – The Family Saga of a Chinese* (Toronto, 2007), p. vii.

As in student dormitories, ghosts of former patients come to visit new room-mates, chasing, scaring, complaining, and emphasising the fragility and vagueness of the boundaries between the human and supernatural worlds. Of course, these motifs are common to many different cultures, where notions of the 'wrong' type of death – too early, tragic, or far from home – might cause the spirits of the deceased to return.

Collected examples of Beijing's school ghostlore usually refer to the (pseudo-)history of the buildings and the land upon which the school is situated. For example, one narrative tells of a lavatory situated in the school yard where pupils heard sounds of a wheelchair coming from outside the closed door, and sometimes even saw the ghost of an old lady in a wheelchair moving through the air to hover half a metre from the ground. Later, a student's parent found out that twenty years earlier the building had served as a hospital for old people [Y.X., 1991, 2014]. These motifs often represent expressions of folk memories, with past episodes from the history of specific locations and buildings being embodied in the ghosts and stories of former occupants.

While the informative potential of ghost stories and ghost storytelling is valuable to researchers, and while we should not underestimate the entertainment function of ghostlore, it also has practical functions, especially inside groups. It can often serve as part of a process of initiation, a way to adapt to and be incorporated into the community. Ghost stories also have regulating functions, establishing certain rules of behaviour. Some hint of this function is visible in the night-bus story outlined above, the narrative serving as a warning against travelling late at night on the last bus. In a similar context, one interviewee warned, 'Do not go to the shower at night! Something can jump upon you, something black, in a human shape, like shadows. They will take away your soul. Because of this, no one goes to get washed at night.' [D.X., 1989, 2011]

Besides personal supernatural experiences and the ghostlore of particular groups, we can also identify examples of contemporary ghostlore concerning a wider population – Beijing's urban community as a whole. Part of this repertoire is represented by topics and narratives coming from certain groups (students, for example), but in some cases these cross the boundaries of specific groups and become popular with and shared by people who do not belong to them. Certain tales are shared among residents of an entire district, or, even more widely, between Beijing's citizens in general. Often, as in the accounts below, such narratives contain additional statements about broader problematic issues. For example, they might articulate a view on the use of traditional ritual attributes, reflecting concerns about the interruption to religious life and the loss of traditional knowledge:

I shall tell you a story, then you will understand ... I read it in a newspaper. It is an example of why it is important to know and to understand rules and rituals, and should not do something if you do not know what it means. Otherwise, it may be dangerous and can lead to harm. There is a school, I do not remember which one, in the south of the city. One day they decided to do a holiday or something like this. Preparations started. They wanted to decorate the area in traditional style, took everything they could and hung it everywhere. The holiday was nice. But very soon after, strange things started there. Pupils became scared and [said] they heard something, they saw something, and so on. One day, there was a water pool, pupils were swimming and a boy suddenly began to drown. He was very near to death! When they pulled him out there were traces on his leg as if somebody had ... tried to pull him to the bottom. After this, many parents did not want ... their children to go to the school. And they had to call someone to clear the space there. And some people thought that it happened because they used traditional decorations and ritual things in a wrong way and dead souls, *gui*, they were attracted by the decorations, they thought that it was something for them, that there are offerings and they came. I do not know how they managed to send them away, but later everything became calm again. [T.Ch., 1966, 2014]

This topic probably originated from the school's ghostlore, but as it reflected wider problematic issues it became quite popular among a broader audience. The main issue here might be interpreted as a tension between old ritual traditions and contemporary life. This tension was exacerbated by the interruption to religious life and ritual practices for almost half a century. This concern is often implicit, and sometimes discussed explicitly, during interviews and comments on narratives.

The urban community's current tensions between the traditional and modern are also suggested by the way in which Beijing's modern streets are haunted by crowds of ghosts from pre-revolutionary times.[32] Narratives with topics that are widely shared by different groups of citizens also suggest concerns about dealing with the shadows of past events. Among the characters most commonly involved in such narratives are victims of violent rulers or revolutions, ghosts of the Kuomintang army, and ghosts of foreigners who lived in Beijing (the most popular being those of Dutch and British people, especially diplomats, traders, and missionaries). Often these topics are inserted

---

[32]   The historical features of ghosts, as well as their social functions and interactions with contemporary mass culture, are very fruitfully discussed in Grant Evans, 'Ghosts and the New Governor: The Anthropology of a Hong Kong Rumour', in

in narratives connected to historical places. For example, in a popular story it is believed that the old walls preserve the spirits devoted to house No. 81 on the prospectus Chaonei. According to different versions, this house was built in the nineteenth century by the order of the emperor as a temple for European people, as a hospital built by an English married couple living in Beijing, or as the residence of a Dutch military official.[33] Similarly, different reasons are given for why the building was not completed. Depending on the version told, different tragic incidents happened there, leaving restless ghosts as a form of folk memory. In one version it is said that during the revolution, the English couple had to leave very urgently. Their female servant had to stay in the house, where she met a dramatic death. In another, a Kuomintang army officer who lived in the house with his concubine had to travel with his army from Beijing to Taiwan. Left alone, the concubine committed suicide. After this, the house started to be haunted. The first part of the narrative, in which the storyteller sets the context of the story, is full of historical and cultural details linked to Beijing. In some narratives, much attention is also paid to the building itself: it is said that it contains old hidden tunnels, secret rooms, and locked doors. The second part, describing the haunting manifestations, is familiar to international ghostlore and includes such elements as human voices, female crying, sounds of steps and movement and lights inside the house, shadows visible from the broken windows, people vanishing, and 'people getting sick after a visit to this house'. And the most convincing reason why this house is haunted is that it 'is situated almost in the very centre of the city, the land there is so expensive! But no one, no one can stay there, no one can live there or demolish this house ... because it belongs to ghosts.'[34] [L.H., 1983, 2015]

As the above accounts suggest, many of the locations which accumulate ghost stories in Beijing are typical of hauntings internationally: public places such as schools, dormitories, and hospitals, and also cemeteries and abandoned houses. Like other old cities, Beijing's historical buildings, places, and spaces are a popular loci for ghostlore. My collection includes narratives linked to a number of historical sites, including Bei Hai, The Forbidden City, house 33 at Hutong Xia Shihu, the old Hotel Huguan, the old market Panjiayuan (also called 'Ghost market'), the Lang family mansion, and Caishikou, the old

---

Hong Kong: The Anthropology of a Chinese Metropolis, ed. idem and Maria Tam Siu-mi (Richmond, 1997), pp. 267–96.

[33]   I have five narratives collected by interview. This plot is also popular on the internet.

[34]   For an examination of the connection between ghostlore and changes in economic and judicial spheres concerning property (in Estonia), see Ülo Valk, *The Black Gentleman: Manifestations of the Devil in Estonian Folk Religion* (Helsinki, 2001).

place of executions at the crossroads, among others. Together with the public places noted above, these haunted loci compose a rich map of contemporary Beijing's ghostlore. A special 'demonic' topography of the city has its social and spatial characteristics reflected in its own way by citizens, as one informant notes: 'The south of the city is very poor, there are many poor people from all over China and many hungry ghosts from the old cemeteries. Most of the ghosts come from there.' [N.Y., 1987, 2014]. Although this appears to demonise (in a literal sense) local poverty, the motif derives too from practical issues, connected to the ritual of funerals and post-funeral ceremonies that involve offerings to ancestors' spirits. According to traditional Chinese beliefs, spirits of deceased people who do not receive sufficient or proper offerings (which costs money in the real world), turn into hungry *gui* and disturb the living.

One of the city's most famously haunted locations is Gugong, the Forbidden City. Located in the centre of Beijing, the Forbidden City was the Chinese imperial palace from the Ming dynasty to the end of the Qing dynasty, and now houses the Palace Museum. For almost five hundred years, it served as the home of emperors and their households, as well as the ceremonial and political centre of the Chinese government. According to collected narratives and stories available from Chinese internet communities, there are crowds of ghosts remaining in the old palace from former times, so it is not particularly safe to visit or stay there:

> One of the security guards said that sometimes in pavilions of the palace sounds, music, and human shadows in clothes of old times move from one room to another. They are spirits, *gui* of service people, imperial concubines, and eunuchs. Later the child of that man was born very sick. Many people thought that the cause was too much energy (*yin*) … at his working place, at the palace. Everybody knows that a lot of pavilions are closed and forbidden to enter. And it is not because there is something very valuable there. It is because strange things are happening there, things which cannot be explained by science. Before the revolution of 1949 many people died there. Some of them just disappeared and nobody could find them; some died without known reasons. But there was one strange specific; in cases where the body was found there was no skin on their faces.' [S.W., 1972, 2014]

This narrative draws upon traditional beliefs and folk images, linked, in this case, to certain historical details. Ghostly inhabitants in the story are from different periods of the past, sharing the space of the palace. Here again is the traditional belief in the *yin* energy of ghosts, and that overexposure to it has a malevolent influence upon humans. The account also includes some interesting demonic details. The face, its absence or hiding (partly or entirely), is a significant feature in demonology and a very common motif in a variety of traditions. In Chinese, Japanese, and Mongolian traditions, malevolent demonesses coquettishly cover their faces with sleeves or fans, to hide zoomorphic features such as a beak, fangs, or a bloody mouth. In Chinese and Japanese literary traditions, ghosts do not have faces (instead, they look 'like the palm of a hand'), or have a second braid instead of a face.[35] Bosco, analysing students' ghost stories from Hong Kong, interprets this detail as a folk metaphor for the loss of virginity.[36] In the context of these narratives, losing the faces of victims might be connected with another common demonic characteristic and motif: if the ghost is missing something from its own body (most famously its head), it tries to substitute it from a human victim.

Another narrative connected to the haunted palace tells of a certain place there, the old well:

> There is one very famous place in the palace. It is a well that still scares people. During the armed revolt of Yihetuan, when the Empress Ci Xi was leaving Beijing, she ordered Zhen, the concubine of Emperor Guan Xui, thrown into the well. If someone looks inside the well at day time, they will not see anything, only stones and grass. But if you look there at night time, especially [in] moonlight, you find out that there are no stones or grass any more, the well is full of water again, and the reflection on the water you can see is not yours at all ... [G.D., 1976, 2014]

Narratives of this kind are very popular in oral form and can be easily found on the internet. They contain lots of historical and pseudo-historical details linked to some of Bejing's most famous old buildings and places, including the Forbidden City and Bei Hai Park. The models for these encounters with the demonic and their consequences are rooted in traditional beliefs, about the soul and its existence after death, the supernatural, the demonic, and traditional categories such as *yin*, *yang*, and *ci*. The details of the plots and figures of the narratives are partly derived from real life, but also draw upon traditional literature and modern historical observations included in contemporary education programs. In modern Beijing, these example of ghostlore obtain additional functions and become part of advertising and tourist enterprises, being found in booklets and specialised websites, or told by guides who turn old pavilions into sites of amusement or horror. This interaction between traditional and tourist culture transforms the perception of the demonic and

---

[35]   See Bosco, 'The Supernatural'.
[36]   Ibid. In Chinese '*diu mianzi*', a common expression for loss of reputation, literally means 'losing face'.

supernatural. In the context of traditional culture, ghosts were to be feared and avoided, while in contemporary mass culture they have become objects of attraction and consumption. This is common to modern mainstream cultures in general, and despite certain officially-imposed limits on technological communication in China, these similarities are nurtured via literature, film and video production, and the internet.

Demonological beliefs and images successfully survive and adapt in the urban space of a modern megalopolis such as contemporary Beijing. They are woven into everyday life and remain very popular in modern urban culture. The contemporary demonology of Beijing includes plots and actors drawn from both traditional and contemporary mass culture; house and patron gods and spirits, ancestors and sacred animals, ghosts of imperial eunuchs and concubines share the space of old apartments with ghosts of soldiers of the Kuomintang, souls of bankrupt traders, foreigners, students, and poltergeists. Ghostlore is the central component of urban demonology, reflecting personal and collective views, problematic issues, changes, worries, and memories. Ghost storytelling has a variety of functions in everyday urban life, providing means through which to interpret personal and collective situations, reinforcing social mores and cultural rules, and helping to regulate behaviour inside communities. Ghostlore shapes a special, supernatural image of contemporary Beijing, one which both scares and attracts, one in which traditional beliefs and narrative motifs are actively involved in navigating the challenges and concerns of China's twenty-first century urban modernity.

Bibliography

Bell, Catherine, 'Religion and Chinese Culture: Towards an Assessment of "Popular Religion" ', *History of Religion* 29 (1989), 35–57

Bennett, Gillian, *Alas, Poor Ghost! Traditions of Belief in Story and Discourse* (Logan, UT, 1999)

Bosco, Joseph, 'The Supernatural in Hong Kong Young People's Ghost Stories', *Anthropological Forum* 13 (2003), 141–9

Brunvand, Jan Harold, *The Vanishing Hitchhiker: American Urban Legends and Their Meanings* (New York, 1981)

Chau, Adam Yuet, *Miraculous Response: Doing Popular Religion in Contemporary China* (Stanford, CA, 2005)

Dégh, Linda, and Andrew Vázsonyi, 'Does the Word "Dog" Bite? Ostensive Action: A Means of Legend Telling', *Journal of Folklore Research* (1983), 5–34

Dundes, Alan, 'Folkloristics in the Twenty-First Century', *The Journal of American Folklore* 118 (2005), 385–408

Evans, Grant, 'Ghosts and the New Governor: The Anthropology of a Hong Kong Rumour', in *Hong Kong: The Anthropology of a Chinese Metropolis*, ed. idem and Maria Tam Siu-mi (Richmond, 1997), pp. 267–96

Gan Bao, *The Written Record*, trans. Kenneth J. DeWoskin and James Irving Crump (Stanford, CA, 1996)

Goldstein, Diane E, *Haunting Experiences: Ghosts in Contemporary Folklore* (Logan, UT, 2007)

Gordon, Avery F., *Ghostly Matters: Haunting and the Sociological Imagination*, new edn (Minneapolis, 2004 [1997])

Honko, Lauri, 'Types of Comparison and Forms of Variation', *Journal of Folklore Research*. 23, 2/3 (special double issue: The Comparative Method in Folklore) (1986), 105–24

Hufford, David, *The Terror That Comes in the Night* (Philadelphia, 1982)

Kao, Karl S. Y. (Gao, Xinyong), *Classical Chinese Tales of the Supernatural and the Fantastic: Selections from the Third to the Tenth Century* (Bloomington, IN, 1985)

Langlois, Janet L., ' *The Vanishing Hitchhiker: American Urban Legends and Their Meanings*, by Jan Harold Brunvand' (review article), *The Journal of American Folklore* 96 (1983), 356–7.

Li, Qunying and Louis Han, *The Doctor who was Followed by Ghosts – The Family Saga of a Chinese* (Toronto, 2007)

Li, Wei-Tsu, *On the Cult of the Four Sacred Animals in the Neighbourhood of Peking* (Nanzan, 2013)

Nü gui cidian ['*The Dictionary of Female Gui-Ghosts*'] (Ningxia, 1991)

Pu, Songling, *Strange Stories from a Chinese Studio* (*Liaozhai zhiyi*), 2nd edn, trans. and annotated by Herbert A. Giles (Taipei, 1965)

Ramsland, Katherine, *Ghost: Investigating the Other Side* (New York, 2002)

Richardson, Judith, *Possessions: The History and Uses of Haunting in the Hudson Valley* (Cambridge, MA, 2003)

Safronova, A. D. *Vozrozhdenie prihramovoj obchini na severe Kitaja* ['*The Revival of the Temple Communities in North China*'] (Moscow, 2006)

Solovyova, Alevtina, 'Chötgöriin Yaria in the Twenty-First Century: Mongolian Demonological Beliefs and Mass Culture in the Age of Globalisation', in *Mongolian Responses to Globalization Processes*, Bonner Asienstudien, vol. 13, ed. Ines Stolpe, Judith Nordby and Ulrike Gonzales (Berlin, 2017), pp. 129–48.

Valk, Ülo, *The Black Gentleman: Manifestations of the Devil in Estonian Folk Religion* (Helsinki, 2001)

——, 'Ghostly Possession and Real Estate: The Dead in Contemporary Estonian Folklore', *Journal of Folklore Research* 43 (2006), 31–51

——, 'Ontological Liminality of Ghosts in Vernacular Interpretations: The Case of a Haunted Hospital in Tartu', lecture, November 2015, https://isthmus.com/events/ontological-liminality-of-ghosts/

Wu, Keping, ' "Ghost City": Religion, Urbanization and Spatial Anxieties in Contemporary China', *Geoforum* 65 (2015), 243–5

Xu, Hua Long, *Gui xue quan shu* ['*Ghostlore Studies*'] (Beijing, 1998)

——, *Zhongguo gui gushi* ['*Chinese Folk Tales about Gui-Ghosts*'] (Beijing, 2001)

Yang, Mayfair Mei-Hui, 'Spatial Struggles: Postcolonial Complex, State Disenchantment, and Popular Reappropriation of Space in Rural Southeast China', *The Journal of Asian Studies*, 63 (2004), 719–55

Zhong guo guihua cidian ['*The Dictionary of Chinese Gui-Ghost Stories*'] (Beijing, 1996)

Zhongguo gui hua (Shanghai, 1991)

Zhonghua gudai gui shen wenhua da cidian ['*The Dictionary of Literature about Shen-Spirits and Gui-Ghosts*'] (Jiaxi, 1992)

清明网上祭祀平台, 清明节网上祭奠（纪念）, 祈恩网, or http://www.qew666.com/

14

'There's Something in the Water!' A Psychogeographical Exploration of What Lurks Beneath the Surface of Manchester

⸺◈⸻

MORAG ROSE

A splash, a scream, a sigh, a glimpse of something terrible reflected in the water …

This chapter explores myths, legends and stories clustered around water in Manchester. Taking its inspiration from contemporary psychogeography, it uses creative walking as a method to explore, interrogate and understand urban space. Beginning with a brief introduction to the historical and cultural context of Manchester, it then discusses how psychogeographical methods can offer affective and creative insights into the symbiotic relationship between storying and the city. The focus will then turn to the monsters which lurk in the waterways, encountering ice maidens, serial killers, boggarts and crypto-zoological creatures. The chapter argues that these are representative of the dreamwork of supernatural Manchester as it struggles to reconcile the ruptures caused by its industrial past, giving rise to what I term 'hipcholia'. The work is interspersed with field notes taken on pedestrian expeditions along the rivers and canals that cross Manchester.

Manchester, in north-west England, is one of ten metropolitan boroughs which comprise Greater Manchester, the second largest conurbation in the United Kingdom after London. It bills itself as the 'original modern city', and in the popular imagination conjures a range of visions from clichés of the grim, rainy north to Madchester swagger, celebrity footballers and Coronation Street's cobbles.[1] Kevin Hetherington identifies three distinct phases of Manchester's development. During the first of these, it earned the name Cottonopolis, as an epoch-making crucible when it became '*the* city of Britain's industrial revolution (1840s–1920s): a mythic time of city prosperity, change and growth.' Hetherington views Manchester subsequently, between the 1930s and the 1980s, as 'a city of grim: a city of urban decline and de-industrialisation'. Since the late 1980s, however, 'Manchester, more than London or any other British city, has been represented as 'cool' and benefited from a range of urban regeneration policies'.[2]

Water has always played an important role in the city. The rivers Medlock, Irwell and Irk are represented on its coat of arms and the development of the canal network was pivotal to its gaining international status and prosperity. However, Manchester's wealth has never extended to all its inhabitants. During the boom times of the industrial revolution, Friedrich Engels dwelt in the city and documented its horrific slums and exploitation in *The Condition of the Working-Class in England in 1844.*[3] Today, the apparent affluence and hedonism of the city centre is belied by persistent inequality and growing levels of homelessness.[4] Concerns are voiced about gentrification as a process of social cleansing and an erasure of working-class heritage.

The landscape is a repository for a complex web of individual emotions, collective memories and historical relics. Psychogeography seeks to channel these hidden stories and uncover invisible power structures, using creative walking methods to reveal what lies beneath. It was first defined by avant-garde neo-Marxist Guy Debord as 'the study of the precise laws and specific effects of the geographical environment, consciously organised or not, on the emotions and behaviours of individuals'.[5] Psychogeography is a theory best understood through practice. It reconfigures walking as a revolutionary tool, using the dérive, or drift, to affectively re-imagine and re-map space. It is a critical,

---

[1] 'Original Modern' was the branding Peter Saville devised for Marketing Manchester in 2009.

[2] Kevin Hetherington, 'Manchester's Urbis: Urban Regeneration, Museums and Symbolic Economies', *Cultural Studies* 21 (2007), 630–49 at 632.

[3] Friedrich Engels, *The Condition of The Working Class in England in 1844*, trans. Florence Kelley Wischnewetzky (Cambridge, 2010).

[4] See, for example, the work of Greater Manchester Poverty Action, http://www.gm-povertyaction.org/about-us/

[5] Guy Debord, 'Introduction to a Critique of Urban Geography', in *Situationist International Anthology*, ed. K. Knabb, rev. and expanded edn (Berkeley, CA, 2006), pp. 8–12

political act but (re-)enchantment and playfulness are core elements too. The cultural theorist Greil Marcus attests that '[t]he point was to encounter the unknown as a facet of the known, astonishment on the terrain of boredom … The physical town replaced by an imaginary'.[6] Since its inception, psychogeography has mutated and evolved in various directions, most prominently in the work of celebrity flâneurs such as Iain Sinclair and Will Self. Beyond this is a plethora of walking artists, wanderers and collectives.[7]

Manchester Area Psychogeographic (MAP) were a key part of a strand of psychogeography that mischievously blends collective wandering, political satire, samizdat print and magical ritual.[8] They stated,

> Our aim is to bring to light the truth about Manchester that remains hidden by time, buried under layer upon layer of concrete, shovelled aside by banal culture. Our interests lie in the hidden history, the ulterior motive, and the suppressed geography that the consumerised city centre masks. To detect that geography we are prone to the use of disorientating and de-normalising methods in language and testimony.[9]

MAP's most spectacular act was an attempt to levitate Manchester Corn Exchange, thus revealing the home of Elizabethan alchemist John Dee. This action, both absurd and sublime, drew attention to an occult past which, MAP felt, still resonated. Although much contemporary walking art may ostensibly lack revolutionary or magical zeal, there remain elements of a desire to rupture surface illusions and to understand what lies beneath.

This chapter draws on my explorations with the LRM (Loiterers Resistance Movement), broadly placed within Richardson's 'new psychogeography', which

---

[6]   Cited in Rebecca Solnit, *Wanderlust: A History of Walking* (London 2001), p. 213.

[7]   For an overview of contemporary British psychogeography, see Tina Richardson (ed.), *Walking Inside Out: Contemporary British Psychogeography* (London, 2015); Phil Smith, *Mythogeography: A Guide to Walking Sideways* (Charmouth, 2010). The Walking Artists Network also has many excellent examples at www.walkingartists-network.org (accessed 26 July 2018).

[8]   For an overview see Alastair Bonnett, 'The Enchanted Path: Magic and Modernism in Psychogeographical Walking', *Transactions of the Institute of British Geographers* 42 (2017), 472–84.

[9]   Manchester Area Psychogeographic published a series of pamphlets (1995–98) which are held now in private collections. My thanks to Ian Trowell for trusting me with his copies. The MAP online archive contains extracts, including accounts of several of the expeditions: see http://www.twentythree.plus.com/MAP/index.html. Pertinently, they also walked the Nico Ditch, an ancient fortification, which they linked to the eponymous chanteuse who lived in north Manchester for several years. The quotation is from MAP1, Autumn 1995.

she identifies as being, amongst other things, heterogeneous, critical, strategic and somatic.[10] The LRM manifesto says it is a

> Manchester based collective of artists, activists and wanderers interested in psychogeography, public space, creative mischief and the hidden stories of the city … Gentrification, advertising and blandness make us sad. We believe there is magic in the mancunian rain. Our city is wonderful and made for more than shopping. The streets belong to everyone and we want to reclaim them for play and revolutionary fun.[11]

Attentive walking enables points of interest to emerge from a seemingly banal landscape. Observing the presences and absences in space, experiencing material environments and collectively channelling the atmospheres evoked enables an affective, haptic re-mapping. In common with many psychogeographers, the LRM is often drawn to liminal spaces, places of threshold, refuge and blurred boundaries. Accessing these habitually overlooked, dismissed or denigrated places frequently requires moving beyond the pedestrian. Edgelands, as conceived by Marion Shoard, contrast with and betray the logic of capitalism which transforms land into money.[12] Unproscribed wasteland resists and provides a glimpse of an alternative reality, perhaps even the supernatural. It may not always be conventionally attractive, and frequently repels, but an edgeland can also be a space for imaginaries and possibilities. It is a buffer between the planned city and the – usually equally managed and commodified – countryside. Edgelands are perhaps the last true commons, unclaimed and unloved by officialdom (although their creation may be deliberate), and therefore open to appropriation, enchantments, transgressions and personal attachment.

However, access to these commons is not equally distributed. Psychogeography has long been haunted by the figure of the flâneur, a lone urban wanderer of immense privilege who wanders space untouched and untouching. A voyeur, he is (of course) an able bodied, wealthy, heterosexual white man. The truth of the flâneur is, as Rebecca Solnit insists, that 'he did not exist, except as a type, an ideal, and a character in literature'.[13] Many are not afforded the luxury of unfettered roaming toward their desires, and a complex web of

---

[10] Tina Richardson, 'The New Psychogeography' (2014), retrieved from http://particulations.blogspot.co.uk/2014/10/the-new-psychogeography.html (accessed 1 April 2018).

[11] The LRM Manifesto can be found on various postcards, flyers, pamphlets and other ephemera. It is also available online at www.thelrm.org (accessed 1 April 2018).

[12] Marion Shoard, 'Edgelands', in *Remaking the Landscape: The Changing Face of Britain*, ed. Jennifer Jenkins (London, 2002), pp. 117–46.

[13] Solnit, *Wanderlust*, p. 200.

barriers, material and invisible, act to exclude people from space. For example, the present chapter also draws on research specifically centring the experience of women who walk in Manchester.[14] Many wished to explore the waterways but were inhibited in doing so by a hostile environment, everyday sexism and warnings from a variety of sources.

A central aim of the communal dérive practiced by the LRM is to democratise and open up psychogeography, offering a more inclusive starting point for the curious. A dérive along waterways offers a conduit to explore wider issues within a landscape that is a repository of cultural memory, industrial relics and deep topography. In addition to those observed today, Manchester has a subterranean network of lost rivers. These continue to intrigue and entrance, and have been mapped comprehensively by Geoffrey Ashworth.[15] The river Tib was culverted in the mid-1700s, but its name still resonates. Using Ashworth as a guide, in 2008 the LRM traced its course above ground.

The illustration opposite is a map, drawn by Caroline Turner, showing the images representing the tales told by the LRM, transposed on to the route depicted by Ashworth. The aim of this walk was to explore the role water has played in the city, not just in its days as the crucible of industrialisation, but more recently in terms of commodification, flooding and suchlike. Channelling both the spirit of MAP and a ghost river, we constructed a performance which incorporated the use of dowsing rods and a team of storytellers interjecting at various points on the route. The rods were conceived primarily as a ludic theatrical device; we were following a non-existent river in a rainy city. However, they became an object of fascination and great debate amongst participants. Some attendees were angry at dabbling with what they considered occult mumbo-jumbo, but others offered large amounts of money to take the implements home. The LRM had hit a rich wellspring of passion, and an unreconciled tension between the converging streams of psychogeography.

Field Notes

I need to stand on tiptoes to see the Irk as it flows under a bridge near Victoria Station. It's just by the side of an area called Scotland, and very near Angel Meadow. The soil round here remembers when water was a killer and a curse; King Cholera ravaged the slums and made lives hell. The poor were buried

---

[14]   I conducted a series of walking interviews with women who live, work or study in Manchester as part of my PhD research. See Morag Rose, 'Women Walking Manchester: Desire Lines through the Original Modern City' (PhD thesis, University of Sheffield, 2017).

[15]   See Geoffrey Ashworth, *The Lost Rivers of Manchester* (Altrincham, 1987).

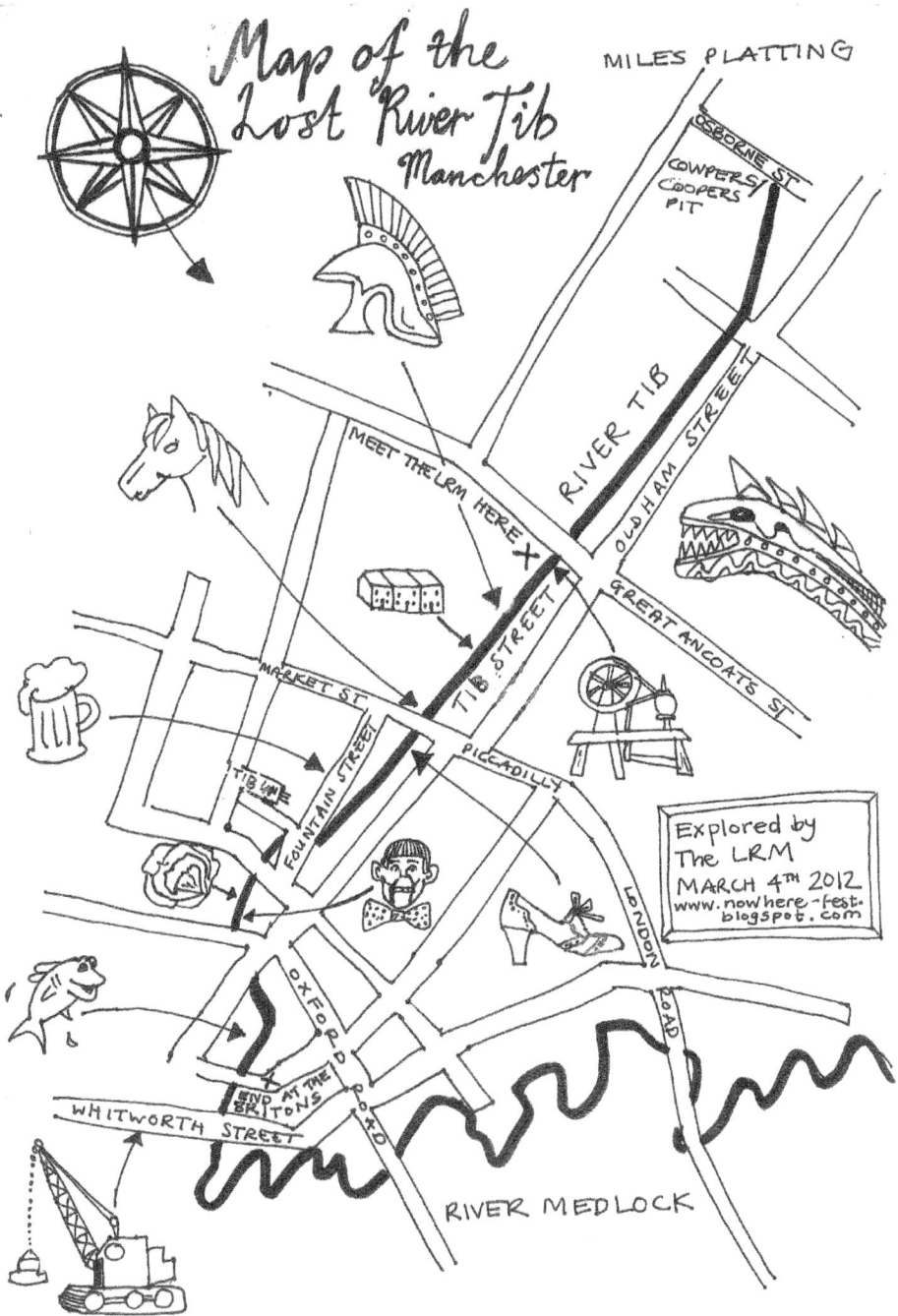

Fig. 8. Map of the lost river Tib, Manchester. Image courtesy of Caroline Turner.

together in pits; they put the Angels into the Meadow. Flagstones stopped bodies floating away but that's not the only time rivers carried bodies. Kankey's Ginnel in Middleton is named after the graverobber and body snatcher who used it as a shortcut from churchyard to river. Ambling up the canal through Ancoats I forage blackberries and admire spectacular graffiti to a snatched soundtrack of bands rehearsing in seemingly derelict warehouses. You can follow lines of regeneration with your feet as the music is pushed further and further out; eventually you reach the Etihad Stadium, football on the site of what was once a coal mine. The canal goes on, further into Ashton-Under-Lyne and linking into the country's canal network. Leaks in the palimpsest are almost palpable as the city unravels along the towpath.

I meet some older ladies on their perambulations. They talk to me about work, proper work, the weather and how their community was destroyed by the unrealised vision of 'New Islington'. I turn and head back towards Manchester city centre, under and over bridges and past the Paradise Wharf apartments. A cluster of people are playing Pokémon; a water monster has been sighted in the area and they are striving to transform a magicarp. From where I stand their quest appears bizarre, an invisible avatar placed by random algorithms but I have no doubt the same could be said of the phantasmagorias I am seeking.

At Piccadilly Basin I descend into darkness at The Undercroft where I'm greeting by pungent smells and a fading mural commemorating the Commonwealth Games. Police signs warn of penalties for lewd behaviour in the tunnels. Friends who have worked and played here talk of community, resistance, friendship and creativity. As I emerge near the court I pass under a stencilled Andy Warhol watching over the scene. Some things will always find a way to blossom in harsh environments, like the audacious buddleia, the pride of broken buildings.

A Treasury of Water Monsters

It was whilst tracing the Tib that a woman shared her encounter with the Boggart of Boggart Hole Clough, in Blackley, North Manchester. She claimed it was a slender, stealthy and fast moving apparition, shadowy and just out of reach, which ran past her in the woods. Despite being startled, she did not really think it was going to harm her. Her companion also reported a sighting, but her boggart was short, fat and squat, rather more like a traditional troll. She believed he lived under a rock which she played near as a child. The pair swapped stories and saw no contradiction in the differences because the Boggart, after all, it is an arch trickster.[16] The most common tale attached locally is

---

[16] For the Boggart's many linguistic occurrences, see Simon Young, 'Joseph Wright meets the Boggart', *Folk Life* 56 (2018), 1–13.

that of a farming family tormented by the Boggart's malevolence. They plan to flit, but the creature hides in a milk churn and calls out from the back of their cart that he is coming too. Realising there is no escape, they stay and an uneasy truce is declared.

Blackley is not the only place where boggarts thrive. They were a real and terrifying enough phenomenon for Droyslden (now part of Greater Manchester) to employ a boggart watcher up until the 1850s.[17] Ceri Houlbrook has conducted extensive research on the Boggart Hole Clough myth and its resilience and evolution over the years.[18] Popular culture and canny marketing have meant boggarts have remained in the local consciousness, and she documents some of their spectacular manifestations. This includes transforming boggarts into cartoon characters and their use as an advertising device to sell beer from the Boggart Brewery. Houlbrook's work demonstrates the mutability of myth, and how it becomes transformed into a commodity. There are parallel processes at work in other cases explored in this chapter, and this highlights a paradox. Such processes can make the supernatural banal, but simultaneously promote a sense of urban enchantment. The existence of magical creatures becomes entwined with the hidden workings of capitalism, as revealed by psychogeographers.

Today, Boggart Hole Clough is a nature reserve incorporating ancient woodland. The waterways are a respite from the commerce and bustle of the city, in contrast to their past life at the centre of industry. Fish thrive in the once polluted waters, and an attentive eye can spot herons, kingfishers and otters amongst the urban wildlife. The flora and fauna provide contact for curious visitors with natural wildness and moments of ostensibly unmediated pleasure. The Canal and River Trust promote the joys of a stroll, and holidaymakers are a precious cargo, but this is not a natural landscape, and much work has gone into this reinvention.[19] Not every riverbank or towpath in Manchester is perceived as welcoming. There remain sections that appear wild and unloved, where you can wander, wonder and not see another living soul, and where the illusion of human control is shattered. This duality is key to understanding the subconscious role of water in Manchester.

---

[17] See Karl Bell, *The Magical Imagination: Magic and Modernity in Urban England, 1780–1914*, (Cambridge, 2012), p. 62.

[18] See Ceri Houlbrook, 'The Suburban Boggart: Folklore of an Inner-City Park', *Gramarye: The Journal of the Sussex Centre for Folklore, Fairy Tales and Fantasy* 11 (2017), 19–32.

[19] See The Canal and River Trust, https://canalrivertrust.org.uk/ (accessed 20 July 2018).

The waterways are betwixt and between, absolutely central and integral to the topography of the city, but also apart, separating and separate, and frequently hard to traverse. Nature thrives where development has yet to intrude and the abruptly terminated cantilevered walkways on the Irwell illustrate how Manchester has been uncharacteristically slow in capitalising large swathes of its post-industrial waterways. Unlike many cities, where waterfronts immediately became stylish and desirable, Manchester has sometimes seemed to turn its back upon its watery heritage. For example, the regenerated Castlefield contrasts with Middlewood Locks, which was an abandoned brownfield site for many years. Perhaps this is because the water is a repository of stories, many shameful, of the exploitation and horror the city was built upon. Steve Pile writes persuasively about how the dreamscape of cities is vital to understanding them, and the psychogeographer who wishes to explore Manchester needs to engage with and think about water.[20]

The Ashton and Rochdale canals both pass through Ancoats, once the burning heart of Cottonopolis. It has been dubbed the hippest neighbourhood in the United Kingdom, an idea doubtless unthinkable both to nineteenth-century mill workers and to twentieth-century residents displaced by the demolition of the Cardroom Estate.[21] Before the current renaissance, the LRM encountered two retired ladies who were revisiting childhood memories. They began reminiscing about how as children the canal often turned fantastical colours or bubbled as a result of industrial effluents. They were always warned to stay away and keep safe lest, if they went to close to the edge, Jinny Green Teeth got them and dragged them to her watery lair. She was a terrible hag, green-skinned and disgusting, living under the water and devouring naughty children. She served the function of many such tales, namely to warn and guide young people.[22] Some call her Jenny or Grintooth, and Jinny has kindred all over the world fulfilling the same function, to protect through fear. In Ireland, manifestations share her name, but similar entities include the Australian bunyip and Japanese kappa. Jinny is an archetype and almost universally recognised despite her chameleonic tendencies.[23]

---

[20] See Steve Pile, *Real Cities: Modernity, Space and the Phantasmagorias of City Life* (London, 2005).

[21] See https://www.manchestereveningnews.co.uk/whats-on/ancoats-northern-quarter-best-manchester-12465732. For a more critical view, see Owen Hatherley, *A Guide to the New Ruins of Great Britain* (London, 2010).

[22] Bell, *Magical Imagination*, p. 188.

[23] See Alanna More, *A Geomantic Guidebook to Water Spirits of the World – From Nymphs to Nixies, Serpents to Sirens* (Castlemaine, 2012).

The Demon Dog, or Black Shuck, is another classic supernatural tale manifested in or near Manchester waterways. The dog scared many people, including a workman near the cathedral in 1825, and so it was hunted and killed. It was buried under the Blackfriars bridge which traverses the river Irwell, the traditional boundary line between Manchester and Salford.[24] The two cities have a symbiotic and sometimes acrimonious relationship, and today are both part of a municipal Greater Manchester. The burial of the dog on the ground between them underlines the defensive nature of water and the need to keep the supernatural 'other' contained in the liminal watery space between the two cities. Some versions of the story claim that Manchester is only protected from the devilish hound for 999 years, and so there is a tantalising sense of threatened return too.

The Irwell was also the last resting place for 'Manchester's Ophelia', a tragic heroine with supernatural beauty and a power to entrance. She has an orange-selling kinswoman in Virginia Woolf's *Orlando*, and others in tales of ice-maidens trapped in another world. Broadsheets were sung and folktales evolved about a beautiful young girl preserved perfectly under ice, a magnet for tourists, thrill seekers and lovers of spectacle. Investigation of the provenance of oral history reveals she was not a myth, however: she was Lavinia Robinson, who lived on Bridge Street, had five sisters and was engaged to John Holroyd, a male midwife. Allegedly she had been unfaithful, and they argued fiercely. She vanished on the night of 12 December 1813 and was never seen alive again. Her body was discovered, frozen and missing a shoe, in the Irwell on 7 February 1814, after a particularly harsh winter. Autopsies revealed she had died a virgin and her fiancé later committed suicide through shame and heartbreak.[25] Lavinia Robinson represents the familiar trope of a beautiful, doomed young women whose sacrifice offers salacious entertainment. Many interpretations of her story emphasise the dangers of unbridled female sexuality and the importance of modesty. Lavinia's tragic fate was determined by a combination of physical, social and cultural positionality, her memory distorted, transmogrified by mediated retellings. Her sisters include victims in murder ballads such as the Oxford/Wexford/Knoxville girl; and, as even a casual glance at the TV listings shows, dead girls still sell. The fear generated can have an oppressive and all too real impact on women's perception of safety in public space.

---

[24] The Black Dog is documented in many collections of local folklore, including P. Portland, *Around Haunted Manchester* (Purley, 2002).

[25] Naomi Clifford has drawn together the scant historical information about Lavinia Robinson. See her article at https://www.naomiclifford.com/lavinia-robinson/ (accessed 11 June 2019).

Sex and water are intertwined locally in many other ways. Canal Street itself is at the heart of Manchester's LGBTQ village and the association between the towpath and illicit sex is borne largely of barbaric laws criminalising homosexuality until 1968. The Undercroft offers a hiding place, and has long been associated with cottaging, procurement and illicit rendezvous of all kinds. Today this stretch of towpath is closed at night, ostensibly for public safety. However, a whiff of hypocrisy and homophobia can be detected, as it was the sensibilities of guests in the newly built hotels which appeared to be most salient in much public discourse focused on regeneration.[26] The decision to close the Undercroft faced very little opposition, partly because fears about the canal-side linger; there is a suspicion that to roam freely at night is to be dangerous and deviant.[27] This is reflected in the lurid and sensational claims about Manchester's latest canal monster.

'The Pusher' is the nickname given to an alleged serial killer, held responsible for a large number of deaths in the canal. At the time of writing, there have been seventy-six deaths in Manchester waterways since 2007, and the majority of the victims have been young men. Rumours that there was more to these deaths than a series of personal tragedies, and the suggestion that something foul was afoot, arose from speculation posted on several internet forums. The web is both a generator and disseminator of new urban folklore, circulating rumours, often masquerading as fact, and escalating cyber-gossip into something with a tangible impact. 'The Pusher' is allegedly and variously a lone hooded figure, a criminal gang, somebody living or working on the canals, an occult ritualist, or a peripatetic American psychopath.[28] Greater Manchester Police have repeatedly asserted that there is no evidence to link the deaths but, as is the manner of conspiracy theories, denial is no proof of innocence. Mainstream media attention has recently been focused on the allegations, with a range of lurid tabloid headings and a Channel Four documentary examining the evidence. Although (unsurprisingly) no conclusion is reached, all cast

---

[26] This was a walk undertaken with members of The Open Spaces Society and Pedestrian Association as well as community police. I had been contacted by various people who asked me to voice their concerns about the closure.

[27] Suspicion of those who walk at night is not, of course, restricted to canals. For another view of wandering nocturnal Manchester, see Nick Dunn, *Dark Matters: A Manifesto for the Nocturnal City* (Alresford, 2016).

[28] See, for example, https://forums.bluemoon-mcfc.co.uk/threads/serial-killer-at-large-in-manchester.261695/; https://forum.davidicke.com/showthread.php?t=234897. For the 'smiley face killer', a conspiracy theory with equally scant evidence, see https://en.wikipedia.org/wiki/Smiley_face_murder_theory.

doubt on official denials.[29] The Pusher's alternative alias of 'Jack the Dipper' hints at his genealogy. He is the most recent manifestation of primal fears: cold, dark water, stranger danger, drowning and, of course, the urge to spin yarns and make connections between disparate events. He (all theories have assumed his gender) has proved singularly elusive and successful, with no survivors or witnesses as yet. The water has claimed many victims, each a tragedy, but slippery cobbles, intoxication and dark nights are a dangerous mix, and a cipher is not necessary to make the waters treacherous.

The Pusher is a ghoul who frequents the towpaths and riverbanks, not an aquatic phantom. However, there have also been rumoured sightings of something unnamed and unknown actually lurking in the water. News first reached the LRM via someone who had seen something from the bridge near the Mark Addy pub, and there was an assumption that alcohol may have influenced their vision.[30] The witness recalled something moving strangely in the water, joking that it was the Loch Ness monster on holiday. No regard was given until the LRM was exploring Pomona one day, and several people confided that they had spied something lurking ominously in the water. Each had glimpsed a vague but monstrous shape, shiny and elusive, gliding past. Various fanciful suggestions were given, all of which used historical events to catapult their explanations into fantastical realms. These included the idea of Masonic rituals during the construction of the canal, an animal escaped from Buffalo Bill's circus, a spell cast by a vengeful mariner's ghost and a theory that something foul travelled in crates of cotton, 'like a spider in a banana but bigger and much, much worse'.[31] These theories all allude to hidden horrors and the legacy of colonialism, always lurking beneath the veneer of the modern city. Since those initial conversations, an informal and ad hoc collection of these accounts has accrued in the LRM archives. No claims to academic rigour are made, and I have not seen anything personally; our 'Messie' remains a word-of-mouth

---

[29] See *First Cut: Manchester's Serial Killer?*, dir. Darren Lovell, Brightspark Films, first broadcast on Channel 4 on 19 January 2016.

[30] Incidentally, the Mark Addy has closed due to irreparable damage sustained during the floods of 2015; a reminder of water out of place and out of control. The pub's eponymous hero rescued many people from drowning until he himself perished. The bridge nearby also carries a plaque to heroism, although it is not dedicated to Addy. *The Emma* crashed during its maiden voyage at Christmas 1828, and forty-seven people perished. Curiously, the memorial commemorates a rescuer who died of hypothermia because his clothes were stolen.

[31] This history is a source of major local pride. A brief account can be found at https://www.independent.co.uk/news/uk/this-britain/from-the-wild-west-to-the-north-west-how-buffalo-bills-travelling-show-left-a-sioux-legacy-in-6108690.html (accessed 1 April 2018).

phenomenon. However, the tales that surface do share key characteristics and deserve further exploration beyond these tentative thoughts.

Curious about the possibility of an actual cryptoid to substantiate claims, we consulted Richard Freeman, zoological director at the Centre for Fortean Zoology.[32] Distinctly less dismissive of our questions than we had expected him to be, he said,

> In the early 1990s there were a series of reports from the Birmingham Ship Canal of giant eels, twenty to twenty-five feet long. The European eel lives in freshwater but when it reaches sexual maturity it swims out to the Sargasso Sea and spawns. The eels then die and the young (leptocephalus) follow scent trails back to the freshwater homes of their ancestors. Sometimes a freak occurs, an individual that does not mature sexually. These sterile eels are said to stay in fresh water getting older and larger. No work has been done on them and no one knows how big they can get or how long they live for ... At Loch Mora I was told of two Yorkshire lads who encountered a serpentine monster, grey/brown in colour and looking like a swimming tree trunk. Sounds like a giant eel. Giant eels make more sense as lake monsters than prehistoric reptiles extinct for 65 million years. Eels can live in dirty water with low oxygen content.[33]

Freeman offers a tantalising but unsubstantiated theory. Returning to the psychogeographical realm, the corporeal reality of the monster is less vital than what it represents. Perhaps Messie should be considered as a manifestation of the city's subconscious, the past made flesh and returned to haunt a landscape that seeks to bury history under layers of regeneration. This emergent water monster offers us clues beyond the masquerade of progress and prosperity in the original modern city.

Field Notes

Oxford Road is bustling with traffic but descend the steps opposite the Palace Theatre and you enter a parallel world. The tarmac is transformed into water and crowds vanish; you are alone save for the geese and an occasional jogger or hurried commuter on a phone. This part of the canal is saturated with stories for me; so many times I've walked here with friends, colleagues, lovers or just wandered off on my own. Turn left and skirt the remains of the Hacienda; the

---

[32] The Centre for Fortean Zoology (CFZ) claims to be the largest professional, scientific and full-time organisation in the world dedicated to cryptozoology, the study of unknown animals. See www.cfz.org.uk.

[33] Personal correspondence, December 2017.

nightclub synonymous with Madchester cool and named after the Situationist text, 'Formulary for a New Urbanism'.[34] *In popular memory it casts a spell over the city, suggesting one kind of culture above all others, and indeed its transformation into apartments continues that legacy.*

In Castlefield I keep an admiring but respectful distance from geese protecting their young families. There's a community of narrow boats and the oldest railway in the world, severed from the mainline it's a mobile museum, and then soon the red brick and bustle fades away again. On the opposite bank are a group of tents pitched by homeless people, forced to survive in the margins.

A little further on and I'm at Pomona, once the site of pleasure gardens named after the Goddess of abundance. When the attraction opened one of its specialities was 'monster demonstrations'.[35] *These usually involved a vile and exploitative exhibition of Black people from colonised lands or people with visible disabilities. (This dark history deserves more attention and atonement than this chapter allows but it is another kind of shame that has seeped into the landscape here). In 1887 The Royal Pomona Palace, larger than the Royal Albert Hall, burnt down and the Manchester Ship Canal cut the island in two. Its birth and construction were controversial, requiring financial bailouts and escalating rivalries with Liverpool. Promenading gave way to hard graft as docks were built, until railways, containerisation and new global trade practices meant this too passed. There were plans in the 1980s to build a Dan Dare Theme Park but instead the space was reclaimed by nature, transmogrifying wasteland into an unofficial oasis. Long neglected by authority, it subsequently became an ad hoc haven for all kinds of transgressions. As property speculation becomes rife again it is now, suddenly, springing into mechanical life and apartment blocks replace apple trees, despite community battles to save the greenspace.*

Out towards Salford Quays the Manchester Ship Canal finds itself in the middle of media city, surrounded by TV studios, theatres and the Imperial War Museum. 'Wake Up With The Stars!' proclaims the billboard selling luxury apartments sparkling under electric lights. What you can't see from the river or the tram stop, is two minutes away: behind the television studios lies Dallas Court deportation centre. The Canal is oblivious, the wonder of the industrial

---

[34] See Ivan Chtcheglov, 'Formulary for a New Urbanism', in *Situationist International Anthology*, ed. Knabb, pp. 1–7.

[35] The history of Pomona has been explored by many local historians and several events at Manchester Histories Festival have discussed its past. Terry Wyke of Manchester Metropolitan University is a particular expert and a summary of the site by Dominic Smithers can be found at https://www.manchestereveningnews.co.uk/news/nostalgia/fascinating-history-behind-pomona-greater-13340688 (accessed 18 June 2019).

age meandering to the sea, facilitating global links and continuing to influence the fluid contours of the city.

Uncovering the hipcholic city

The canal's link to the identity of the city is key to unravelling the enduring popularity of water-based spectres. There has been a denial of the horrors perpetrated during the industrial revolution, but also, conversely, a mourning for a lost sense of collective identity, purpose and future. Over years of walking their towpaths, the complicated relationships many people in Manchester have with their canals and rivers is revealed. They speak of them with love and pride, yet also revulsion and fear. Many feel intimidated and unsafe there on their own, unable to relax and enjoy the surroundings. Instead, they adopt a defensive stance, looking straight ahead, moving quickly, perhaps carrying keys or suchlike in their hand, if they dare to venture there at all. If one asks people what they think of the canal, many draw upon body metaphors. The canal is occasionally imagined as the heart of the city, but more frequently its guts or bowels. They are vital but somehow disgusting, carrying effluents and shame.[36] The visceral description embodies a complex relationship with the past, felt and expressed in many different ways. There is an implicit understanding that the waterways were both a blessing and a curse for all but the richest, even whilst under construction, although there are no memorials to anonymous labourers. During the building of Manchester Ship Canal alone 130 men were killed, 165 permanently injured and 997 slightly injured, those losing limbs retaining employment as watchmen and joining the ranks of 'fragments'.[37]

On the ground today there is no perception of a utopian golden age, but an embodied sense that the city and its wealth were built on the back of suffering and slavery. The price paid for our prosperity was an international network of unspeakable horrors, and although historical in origin, their resonances linger still. When I walked with Kathleen, she described visions of blood pouring out of buildings that she loved and felt an intense attachment to, despite the horrors she knew were buried in the red brick.[38] Pile suggests a psychogeographical analysis can be useful when seeking to understand space because it goes

[36] The exercise referred to was one of three sensory walks I was commissioned to undertake by The Cornerhouse Arts Centre in 2013.

[37] See Nick Robins, *The Ships That Came to Manchester. From the Mersey and Weaver Sailing Flat to the Mighty Container Ship* (Amberley, 2015), p. 33. The particularly difficult relationship the Left has with nostalgia is explored in Alastair Bonnett's *Left in the Past: Radicalism and the Politics of Nostalgia* (London, 2010).

[38] 'Kathleen' and 'Arlene' are pseudonyms given to two of the women interviewed during my PhD research.

beyond the surface appearance of things ... perhaps we can also make out other (hi)stories of the city. It is the porosity of these urban spaces that evokes *both* the multiplicity of stories *and also* the many time-spaces of the city, only some of which are allowed to become real. Others become ghosts; some remain dreams.[39]

This may be unsettling and destabilising, but it is necessary to even begin to understand a space like the waterways of Manchester. Pile's text considers the emotional, mental and dream work of cities to be as important as other forms of producing space.[40] These sensed, felt and imagined phantasmagorias are central to psychogeographical investigation. For example, in *Savage Messiah* Laura Oldfield Ford documents the ghosts of punks, ravers and squatter communities in a landscape of tower blocks ripped apart and left to decay by Thatcherite and subsequent neo-liberal economic policies.[41] The artist Jane Samuels has also produced a body of work, based on urban exploration of abandoned buildings, which brings these ideas to startling and unsettling life. Her work transgresses boundaries on foot and in print, as she trespasses into derelict schools, asylums and warehouses. She takes a cast of pookas, demons and animal-human hybrid creatures with her to stage enigmatic tableaux. On occasion, she has returned to leave copies of her images, a double haunting resonating through the empty rooms.[42] The city remains enchanted, and anxious, and although it materialises in new ways, Bell's description of a persistent magical imagination still resonates.[43]

When seeking to understand the prolonged enchantment of Manchester, and the prevalence of legends and monsters linked to the city's waterways, Mark Fisher's 'hauntology' is clearly useful. Fisher links the concept to a society ravaged by free market capitalism and nostalgic for a time when there were collective visions of a brighter future. Half-remembered dreams are similar to those moments of desire glimpsed through gaps in Debord's spectacle, when the mediated illusion is ruptured and 'authenticity' is felt. Fisher illustrates

---

[39] Pile, *Real Cities*, p. 15.

[40] Ibid. Although not explicitly referenced in this text, Doreen Massey's conception of space is vital to the ontology of this work, especially her view of place as a simultaneity of stories-so-far and a constellation of trajectories. See Doreen Massey, *For Space* (London, 2005).

[41] Laura Oldfield Ford does not appreciate being termed a psychogeographer. However, her work explores many themes similar to those examined in psychogeography. See Laura Oldfield Ford, *Savage Messiah* (London, 2011).

[42] Samuels's 'The Abandoned Buildings Project' is an astonishing portrayal of haunted space. Images can be viewed at http://www.milliondollaryack.com/GhostStations/ (accessed April 1 2018).

[43] See Bell, *Magical Imagination*, pp.1–5.

his concept using examples from popular culture where time is experienced as fragmented and non-linear, and art has a deep affective resonance in the consumer.[44] These spectral forces are kin to the phantasmagoria that Walter Benjamin, Pile, Oldfield Ford and Samuels conjure, and which psychogeographers have long claimed to attend to. A combination of memory, imagination, folklore and material remains, they can have a tangible affective impact. A hauntological state encompasses presence, absence and never-was; an uncanny, dynamic mélange of spectral visions. Describing his walking art, Roy Bayfield says that he has been

> making real walks, to, in and around unreal places. The places I moved through were of course physically, prosaically real, as was the body doing the walking. However, the more I walked, the more I experienced landscapes as being undercut with unreal elements: stuff that isn't there but nevertheless has an effect.[45]

For Bayfield, these elements include the phantom smell of a remembered but long-gone bakery, or the warnings of a folktale. For women I have walked with, like Kathleen, they include an empathetic understanding of the suffering of those whose labour contributed to her cherished everyday environment. Walking with Arlene, she described feeling 'foreign' along the canal, outside her familiar landscape. Despite her being in the middle of her actual home city, her surroundings were rendered supernatural. She took pleasure in noting traces of demolished buildings and layers of development, and revelled in the sensation that she was in a maelstrom. Feeling like a tourist in familiar territory is one of the functions of a dérive, but one does not have to be a psychogeographer to experience being transported to an imaginative or enchanted city whilst simultaneously existing, unlost and visible, in the material world. This is to sense and channel both the here and not-here, the uncanny dynamics of hauntology.

In Manchester, the waterways facilitate a fluid, shimmering vision of its founding myths. Flotsam and jetsam are tangled up with past lives and folk memories to give shape to the city's emotional life. Manchester is particular, but not special, and there is no one true essence of the place. Its soul is constantly rewritten and reinterpreted by all those who travel through it and, like the boggart, our *genius loci* is a shapeshifting multitude. The uneasy affects articulated via Manchester's water monsters are highly specific – clearly related to one's sense of belonging – but also a widespread and dispersed result of

---

[44] Mark Fisher, *Ghosts of My Life: Writings on Depression, Hauntology and Lost Futures* (Winchester, 2014).

[45] Roy Bayfield, *Desire Paths: Real Walks to Nonreal Places* (Charmouth, 2016), p. 115.

global processes. This is the feeling of horror, aching and longing, an ambivalent nostalgia and haunted sense of place. I term this complicated assemblage of feelings 'hipcholia'.[46]

I use 'hipcholia' to describe an impossible search for the soul of a city which has no *genius loci*. This quest for an elusive, enigmatic 'authenticity' is another consequence of the all-pervasive spectacle. Hipcholia is a yearning for something that never quite was, a hauntological future perished before it was even a shimmer. Hipcholia is a dynamic, affective force that paradoxically embraces both attraction and repulsion. It is an amorphous nostalgia, a luxurious ennui, a conscience pricked by sensing that your comfort is built on historical wrongs but that your complicity is so complex, and the spoils so tempting, that atonement feels impossible. It is a deep and painful concern for the erasure of working-class narratives, and a desire to commemorate a tormented past, the truth of which is barely conceivable. 'Sur le pavés, la plage', the Situationists claimed; but beneath the pavements are the ruins of older human constructions alongside geological phenomena, waterways culverted and drained, courses corrupted by the flow of Capital.[47] Hipcholia gives shape to myths, monsters and magick that dwell in our rivers and canals, continuing to haunt our contemporary everyday landscapes.

We need water to live, and yet we fear it too. In Manchester, the water has been a conduit of death and despair in so many ways: cholera, pollution, class, poverty, crime, exploitation. These are not natural or supernatural forces, but their ghostly, ghastly presence and the terrible impact they have had flow through the city. The rivers and canals carry the echoes of their cries, stories of freedom curtailed and life-force denied, drifting away on the tide of progress.

---

[46]   Etymolgically speaking, I have derived the word 'hipcholia' from a number of sources. The closest term I could find was 'solastalgia', which relates to extreme distress precipitated by environmental loss and damage. This devastation is generally caused by climate chaos or natural disaster. See Glenn Albrecht, ' "Solastalgia." A New Concept in Health and Identity', *PAN: Philosophy Activism Nature* 3 (2005), 41–55. The neologism is inspiring, but not appropriate to the present context. Capitalism and neo-liberalism are not natural forces, and their impact is diffuse and complex; critics are entwined with the system and often benefit from it. Melancholia is a sadness, a suffering, but also has romantic associations and intersects somewhat with nostalgia, another term that does not quite fit the ambivalent, amorphous loss of an imagined past and future. 'Hip' indicates a knowingness, a complicity in the change. It also relates to concepts such as hipsterfication, the aesthetic and cultural impact of gentrification. Furthermore I enjoy the double meaning of 'hip', as it links to bodily sensations and movement through space. The development of this concept is explored further in Rose, *Women Walking Manchester*.

[47]   'Underneath the pavement, the beach': the slogan was scrawled on walls during the 1968 Paris riots and is typical of the Situationists.

Phantasmagoria swirl through the canal network alongside lost visions of prosperity and the poisonous legacies of colonialism. The rivers remind us that we are not truly in control; they may be tamed or culverted, but could burst their banks and invade our world at any time. The waterways haunt and hypnotise the rainy city, saturating the material world with a torrent of stories, whispers, promises and nightmares. They rupture our everyday landscape; an interruption, a portal, a memory, a sigil, a spell, a scar etched by memory on to the fabric of the city that still bleeds from its self-inflicted wounds.

Acknowledgements

Heartfelt thanks to everyone who has walked Manchester's waterways with me and shared their stories as part of the LRM (Loiterers Resistance Movement). Early versions of this paper or various aspects of it were presented to the RGS-IGB, Gothic Manchester and Supernatural Cities conferences, and in Stepz zine; collegiate discussions which ensued were invaluable. Particular thanks to Craig Almond, who named Messie, Helen Darby, Richard Freeman, Julian Holloway, Steve Millington, Bren O'Callaghan, Jane Samuels, Alan Smith, Maureen Ward and Natalie Zacek, all experts in different aspects of monstrous Manchester and urban enchantment, to Caroline Turner for permission to share her magical map, and to the wonderful John Hawes who beguiles a monster better than anyone else I know.

Bibliography

Albrecht, Glenn, ' "Solastalgia." A New Concept in Health and Identity', *PAN: Philosophy Activism Nature* 3 (2005), 41–55.

Ashworth, Geoffrey, *The Lost Rivers of Manchester* (Altrincham, 1987)

Bayfield, Roy, *Desire Paths: Real Walks to Nonreal Places* (Charmouth, 2016)

Bell, Karl, *The Magical Imagination: Magic and Modernity in Urban England, 1780–1914* (Cambridge, 2012)

Bonnett, Alistair, 'The Enchanted Path: Magic and Modernism in Psychogeographical Walking', *Transactions of the Institute of British Geographers* 42 (2017), 472–84

——, *Left in the Past: Radicalism and the Politics of Nostalgia* (London, 2010)

Chtcheglov, Ivan, 'Formulary for a New Urbanism', in *Situationist International Anthology*, ed. K. Knabb, rev. and expanded edn (Berkeley, CA, 2006), pp. 1–7

Clifford, Naomi, '1814: The death of Lavinia Robinson, the Manchester Ophelia', https://www.naomiclifford.com/lavinia-robinson/

Debord, Guy, 'Introduction to a Critique of Urban Geography', in *Situationist International Anthology*, ed. K. Knabb, rev. and expanded edn (Berkeley, CA, 2006), pp. 8–12

Dunn, Nick, *Dark Matters: A Manifesto for the Nocturnal City* (Alresford, 2016)

Engels, Friedrich, *The Condition of the Working Class in England in 1844*, trans. Florence Kelley Wischnewetzky (Cambridge, 2010)

Fisher, Mark, *Ghosts of My Life: Writings on Depression, Hauntology and Lost Futures* (Winchester, 2014)

Hatherley, Owen, *A Guide to the New Ruins of Great Britain* (London, 2010

Hetherington, Kevin. 'Manchester's Urbis: Urban Regeneration, Museums and Symbolic Economies', *Cultural Studies* 21 (2007), 630–49

Houlbrook, Ceri, 'The Suburban Boggart: Folklore of an Inner-City Park', *Gramarye: The Journal of the Sussex Centre for Folklore, Fairy Tales and Fantasy* 11 (2017), 19–32

Massey, Doreen, *For Space* (London, 2005)

More, Alanna, *A Geomantic Guidebook to Water Spirits of the World – From Nymphs to Nixies, Serpents to Sirens* (Castlemaine, 2012)

Oldfield Ford, Laura, *Savage Messiah* (London, 2011)

Portland, P., *Around Haunted Manchester* (Purley, 2002)

Pile, Steve, *Real Cities: Modernity, Space and the Phantasmagorias of City Life* (London, 2005)

Richardson, Tina, 'The New Psychogeography' (2014), http://particulations.blogspot.co.uk/2014/10/the-new-psychogeography.html

——, (ed.), *Walking Inside Out: Contemporary British Psychogeography* (London, 2015)

Robins, Nick, *The Ships That Came to Manchester. From the Mersey and Weaver Sailing Flat to the Mighty Container Ship* (Amberley, 2015)

Rose, Morag, 'Women Walking Manchester: Desire Lines through the Original Modern City' (PhD thesis, University of Sheffield, 2017)

Samuels, Jane, 'The Abandoned Buildings Project', http://www.milliondollaryack.com/GhostStations/

Shoard, Marion, 'Edgelands', in *Remaking the Landscape: The Changing Face of Britain*, ed. Jennifer Jenkins (London, 2002), pp. 117–46

Solnit, Rebecca, *Wanderlust: A History of Walking* (London 2001)

Smith, Phil, *Mythogeography: A Guide to Walking Sideways* (Charmouth, 2010)

Smithers, Dominic, 'The fascincating history behind Pomona – Greater Manchester's "forgotten island" ', https://www.manchestereveningnews.co.uk/news/nostalgia/fascinating-history-behind-pomona-greater-13340688

Young, Simon, 'Joseph Wright meets the Boggart', *Folk Life* 56 (2018), 1–13

Index